P9-BXZ-292

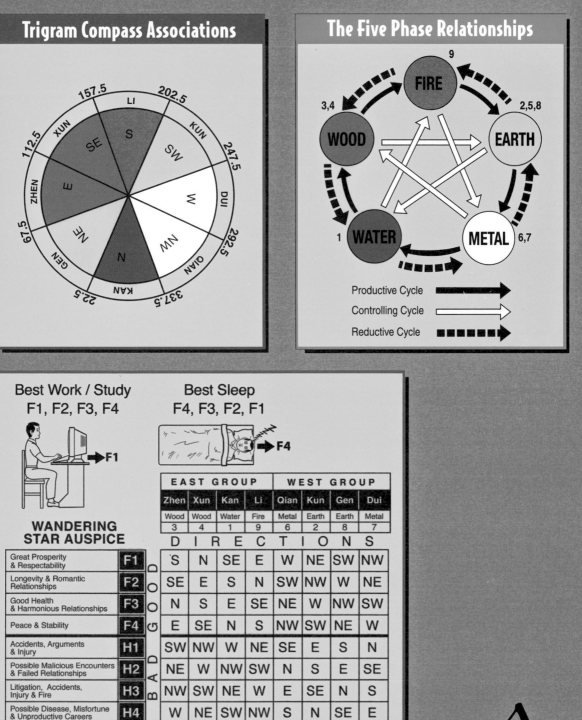

Trigram Compass Associations

157.5 — LI
202.5 — KUN
112.5 — XUN
247.5 — DUI
ZHEN
292.5
67.5 — GEN
22.5 — KAN
337.5 — QIAN

SE, S, SW, E, W, NE, NW, N

The Five Phase Relationships

FIRE — 9
WOOD — 3,4
EARTH — 2,5,8
WATER — 1
METAL — 6,7

Productive Cycle →
Controlling Cycle ⇒
Reductive Cycle ▪▪▪▶

Best Work / Study
F1, F2, F3, F4

→ F1

Best Sleep
F4, F3, F2, F1

→ F4

WANDERING STAR AUSPICE

	EAST GROUP				WEST GROUP			
	Zhen	Xun	Kan	Li	Qian	Kun	Gen	Dui
	Wood	Wood	Water	Fire	Metal	Earth	Earth	Metal
	3	4	1	9	6	2	8	7
	D	I	R	E	C	T	I	O	N	S

Auspice			DIRECTIONS							
Great Prosperity & Respectability	F1	G	S	N	SE	E	W	NE	SW	NW
Longevity & Romantic Relationships	F2	O	SE	E	S	N	SW	NW	W	NE
Good Health & Harmonious Relationships	F3	O	N	S	E	SE	NE	W	NW	SW
Peace & Stability	F4	D	E	SE	N	S	NW	SW	NE	W
Accidents, Arguments & Injury	H1	B	SW	NW	W	NE	SE	E	S	N
Possible Malicious Encounters & Failed Relationships	H2	A	NE	W	NW	SW	N	S	E	SE
Litigation, Accidents, Injury & Fire	H3	D	NW	SW	NE	W	E	SE	N	S
Possible Disease, Misfortune & Unproductive Careers	H4		W	NE	SW	NW	S	N	SE	E

ALPHA

Personal Trigram Chart

Year	Male	Gua	Phase	Female	Gua	Phase	Year	Male	Gua	Phase	Female	Gua	Phase
1924	Xun	4	Wood	Kun	2	Earth	1964	Li	9	Fire	Qian	6	Metal
1925	Zhen	3	Wood	Zhen	3	Wood	1965	Gen	8	Earth	Dui	7	Metal
1926	Kun	2	Earth	Xun	4	Wood	1966	Dui	7	Metal	Gen	8	Earth
1927	Kan	1	Water	Gen	8	Earth	1967	Qian	6	Metal	Li	9	Fire
1928	Li	9	Fire	Qian	6	Metal	1968	Kun	2	Earth	Kan	1	Water
1929	Gen	8	Earth	Dui	7	Metal	1969	Xun	4	Wood	Kun	2	Earth
1930	Dui	7	Metal	Gen	8	Earth	1970	Zhen	3	Wood	Zhen	3	Wood
1931	Qian	6	Metal	Li	9	Fire	1971	Kun	2	Earth	Xun	4	Wood
1932	Kun	2	Earth	Kan	1	Water	1972	Kan	1	Water	Gen	8	Earth
1933	Xun	4	Wood	Kun	2	Earth	1973	Li	9	Fire	Qian	6	Metal
1934	Zhen	3	Wood	Zhen	3	Wood	1974	Gen	8	Earth	Dui	7	Metal
1935	Kun	2	Earth	Xun	4	Wood	1975	Dui	7	Metal	Gen	8	Earth
1936	Kan	1	Water	Gen	8	Earth	1976	Qian	6	Metal	Li	9	Fire
1937	Li	9	Fire	Qian	6	Metal	1977	Kun	2	Earth	Kan	1	Water
1938	Gen	8	Earth	Dui	7	Metal	1978	Xun	4	Wood	Kun	2	Earth
1939	Dui	7	Metal	Gen	8	Earth	1979	Zhen	3	Wood	Zhen	3	Wood
1940	Qian	6	Metal	Li	9	Fire	1980	Kun	2	Earth	Xun	4	Wood
1941	Kun	2	Earth	Kan	1	Water	1981	Kan	1	Water	Gen	8	Earth
1942	Xun	4	Wood	Kun	2	Earth	1982	Li	9	Fire	Qian	6	Metal
1943	Zhen	3	Wood	Zhen	3	Wood	1983	Gen	8	Earth	Dui	7	Metal
1944	Kun	2	Earth	Xun	4	Wood	1984	Dui	7	Metal	Gen	8	Earth
1945	Kan	1	Water	Gen	8	Earth	1985	Qian	6	Metal	Li	9	Fire
1946	Li	9	Fire	Qian	6	Metal	1986	Kun	2	Earth	Kan	1	Water
1947	Gen	8	Earth	Dui	7	Metal	1987	Xun	4	Wood	Kun	2	Earth
1948	Dui	7	Metal	Gen	8	Earth	1988	Zhen	3	Wood	Zhen	3	Wood
1949	Qian	6	Metal	Li	9	Fire	1989	Kun	2	Earth	Xun	4	Wood
1950	Kun	2	Earth	Kan	1	Water	1990	Kan	1	Water	Gen	8	Earth
1951	Xun	4	Wood	Kun	2	Earth	1991	Li	9	Fire	Qian	6	Metal
1952	Zhen	3	Wood	Zhen	3	Wood	1992	Gen	8	Earth	Dui	7	Metal
1953	Kun	2	Earth	Xun	4	Wood	1993	Dui	7	Metal	Gen	8	Earth
1954	Kan	1	Water	Gen	8	Earth	1994	Qian	6	Metal	Li	9	Fire
1955	Li	9	Fire	Qian	6	Metal	1995	Kun	2	Earth	Kan	1	Water
1956	Gen	8	Earth	Dui	7	Metal	1996	Xun	4	Wood	Kun	2	Earth
1957	Dui	7	Metal	Gen	8	Earth	1997	Zhen	3	Wood	Zhen	3	Wood
1958	Qian	6	Metal	Li	9	Fire	1998	Kun	2	Earth	Xun	4	Wood
1959	Kun	2	Earth	Kan	1	Water	1999	Kan	1	Water	Gen	8	Earth
1960	Xun	4	Wood	Kun	2	Earth	2000	Li	9	Fire	Qian	6	Metal
1961	Zhen	3	Wood	Zhen	3	Wood	2001	Gen	8	Earth	Dui	7	Metal
1962	Kun	2	Earth	Xun	4	Wood	2002	Dui	7	Metal	Gen	8	Earth
1963	Kan	1	Water	Gen	8	Earth	2003	Qian	6	Metal	Li	9	Fire

If you were born between January 1 and February 2, use the year prior to your actual birth year. If you were born on February 3, 4, or 5, consult Chapter 21 to determine your Chinese solar birth year. For extended dates, see Chapter 10.

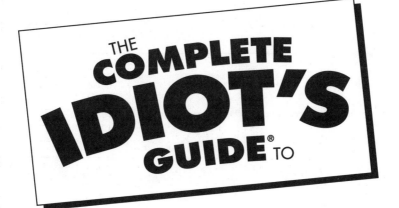

Feng Shui

Second Edition

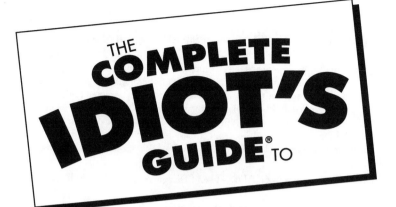

THE COMPLETE IDIOT'S GUIDE® TO

Feng Shui

Second Edition

*Elizabeth Moran, Master Joseph Yu,
and Master Val Biktashev*

ALPHA

A member of Penguin Group (USA) Inc.

International Standard Book Number: 0-02-864339-9
Library of Congress Catalog Card Number: 2002101641

06   05   04   8   7   6   5   4

Interpretation of the printing code: The rightmost number of the first series of numbers is the year of the book's printing; the rightmost number of the second series of numbers is the number of the book's printing. For example, a printing code of 02-1 shows that the first printing occurred in 2002.

Printed in the United States of America

Publisher: *Marie Butler-Knight*
Product Manager: *Phil Kitchel*
Managing Editor: *Jennifer Chisholm*
Acquisitions Editor: *Mike Sanders*
Development Editor: *Amy Gordon*
Production Editor: *Katherin Bidwell*
Copy Editor: *Cari Luna*
Illustrator: *Tim Neil*
Cartoonist: *Jody Schaeffer*
Cover/Book Designer: *Trina Wurst*
Indexer: *Julie Bess*
Layout/Proofreading: *Mark Walchle*

Contents at a Glance

Part 1:   **Let's Get Into Feng Shui**   1

   1   What Is Feng Shui?   3
*Understand the difference between authentic and faux
schools of feng shui. Learn how this ancient art and science
can help you improve your health, wealth, and relationships.*

   2   Western Intellectual Heritage and the Holy Grail   17
*How we have become a culture of separatist thinkers and
how we are becoming a culture of unified reformers.*

   3   The Great Wall of Knowledge and the Rise of
Feng Shui   29
China's reverence for nature gives rise to feng shui.

   4   Qi Wiz! It's Life's Force!   41
*Identifying and understanding the underlying essence of all
things.*

Part 2:   **The Fundamental Principles of Feng Shui**   53

   5   The Principle of Yin and Yang   55
*Separate, but together, yin and yang express the movement
and transformation of all things.*

   6   The Principle of the Five Phases   63
*The qi expressions of fire, earth, metal, water, and wood
enhance favorable qi and remedy unfavorable qi.*

   7   The Principle of the Eight Trigrams   75
*The yin and yang lines combine to produce eight trigrams
associated with the eight directions of the compass, the five
phases, familial relations, and parts of the body.*

Part 3:   **Understanding Your Environment**   85

   8   Turtles, Tigers, and Dragons, Oh My: Evaluating
Your Environment   87
*How celestial deities became terrestrial landforms that
influence your health and livelihood. Roadways and river
courses are evaluated.*

9 Home Sweet Home: Evaluating Your House and
   Its Surroundings   97
   Recognize internal and external factors that may influence
   how you sleep, think, and feel. Bed and desk positions are
   evaluated.

Part 4:   Feng Shui Mechanics 101   111

10 The Eight Houses, Part 1   113
   Determining your ming gua—your personal trigram.

11 The Eight Houses, Part 2   129
   Determining your home's trigram by taking a compass
   reading.

12 The Eight Houses, Part 3   141
   Understanding the qi distribution of your dwelling. Learn
   to remedy bad qi and enhance good qi.

Part 5:   Feng Shui Mechanics 201   151

13 The Flying Stars, Part 1   153
   The history behind the number-based system: The Hetu
   (Before Heaven) and Luoshu (After Heaven) maps and
   their significance to feng shui.

14 The Flying Stars, Part 2   165
   Learn about the Chinese concept of time. Determine to
   which of the 24 mountains (directions) your dwelling
   corresponds.

15 The Flying Stars, Part 3   177
   Create a numeric qi map of your dwelling by flying the
   stars (numbers).

16 The Flying Stars, Part 4   215
   The numeric qi distribution determines if your house may
   belong to four special types.

17 The Flying Stars, Part 5   223
   Analyze a Flying Star chart. Learn how the position of the
   stars (numbers), their inherent nature, timeliness, and the
   number it's combined with influences your well-being.

18 The Flying Stars, Part 6   235
   Fly the annual star. Learn how the yearly influence affects
   your health and financial outlook.

Part 6:   **Practical Application**   **243**

19 A House Hunting We Will Go   245
Follow a couple as they select an auspicious home.

20 Does Your Office Measure Up?   257
Will harmony replace discord?

Part 7:   **Fate or Free Will: What's Your Destiny?**   **265**

21 Introducing the Twelve Animals of the Chinese Zodiac   267
*Learn your animal sign! Learn how to determine who's
your friend and who's your foe.*

22 The Four Pillars of Destiny, Part 1   281
*Construct your life chart comprising the year, month, day,
and hour pillars.*

23 The Four Pillars of Destiny, Part 2   307
*Discover the strength of your chart. What are your lucky
colors or suitable careers and environments?*

24 The Four Pillars of Destiny, Part 3   319
Calculate your 10-year luck period.

25 The Four Pillars of Destiny, Part 4   331
Determine your most favorable months and days.

Appendixes

A Glossary   345

B Common Questions and Practical Answers   353

C Learn More About Feng Shui   357

D Chinese Periods and Dynasties   363

E Learn More About Taking a Proper Compass
Reading Using the 24 Mountains   367

Index   371

Contents

Part 1: Let's Get Into Feng Shui   **1**

1 What Is Feng Shui?   **3**

The Feng Shui IQ Test 4
What Feng Shui Is Not..5
What Feng Shui Is..7
Who Practices Feng Shui? 9
Feng Shui's Beginnings in the East...*10*
Feng Shui Moves West *10*
Feng Shui and You..11
What Do I Need to Practice Feng Shui? 11
Twenty Ways to Benefit from Feng Shui 13
Pinyin and Wade-Giles: Chinese Romanization 14

2 Western Intellectual Heritage and the Holy Grail   **17**

Mind Power 101 18
Twelve Percent of the Whole..*18*
Faux Feng Shui and the Western Mind *20*
In Search of the Holy Grail 20
United We Stand 22
Scientific Holistic Theories *23*
Holistic Theories...*23*
Nature Speaks Mathematics, Too 24
Fascinating Fibonacci and the Golden Ratio *25*
Other Profound Patterns *26*
A New World Vision for the Millennium 27

3 The Great Wall of Knowledge and the Rise of Feng Shui   **29**

Made in China 30
China's Greater Nature 30
Skywatcher for Hire 31
The Art of Astrology...*31*
The Science of Astronomy *32*
Confucianism and Daoism: 33
Experience vs. Experiment *34*
Reversal Is the Movement of the Dao *34*

Change Is in the Wind 35
   The Masked Origin of the Yijing 35
   Changing Patterns 36
How Does Feng Shui Fit In? 36
   Neolithic Feng Shui 37
   The Form School of Feng Shui 37
   The Compass School of Feng Shui 38
Feng Shui Today 39

4 Qi Wiz! It's Life's Force!   41

What Is Qi? 42
Qi Around the World 43
Qi on the Move 43
The Three Forces of Qi Energy 43
   Heaven Qi 44
   Earth Qi 45
   Human Qi 46
Feeling Qi's Power 47
   Sheng Qi 49
   Sha Qi 49
   Poison Arrow Qi 50
The Holy Trinity, Chinese Style 50

Part 2: The Fundamental Principles of Feng Shui   53

5 The Principle of Yin and Yang   55

The Big Bang, Chinese Style 56
   The Nothing of Everything 56
   Yin: The Feminine Side 57
   Yang: The Masculine Side 58
   The Symbol of Taiji—Opposites Do Attract 59
Which Way Is Up? 60
Yin and Yang Culture Clash 61
   Western Yang 61
   Eastern Yin 62
Yin and Yang and Feng Shui 62

6 The Principle of the Five Phases   63

What Are the Five Phases? 64
If It's Fire, It Must Be Summer...................................64

The Productive Cycle 66
The Controlling Cycle 67
The Weakening Cycle 67
A Spoonful of Sugar 69
The Five Phases of Buildings 71
The Five Phases Quiz 72

7 The Principle of the Eight Trigrams   75

Motion over Matter—Qi's Pattern of Movement 75
Eight Is Enough..76
Meet the Bagua Family 77
The Cyclic Pattern of the Bagua 80
Patterns of Numbers 82

Part 3:   Understanding Your Environment   85

8 Turtles, Tigers, and Dragons, Oh My: Evaluating Your Environment   87

Here a Totem, There a Totem 88
Circus of the Stars 88
Read All About It: Heaven Falls to Earth! 89
In Search of the Dragon's Lair 90
Climb Every Mountain 90
Have a Seat...92
City Slickers...92
Rolling on the River; Ease on Down the Road 93

9 Home Sweet Home: Evaluating Your House and Its Surroundings   97

Church Bells and Power Poles 98
Land Sakes Alive!..98
Over Hill, Over Dale..99
Lots of Plots 101
House of Shapes 102
A Grand Entrance 104
Room for Improvement...106
Now I Lay Me Down to Sleep 106
Working Nine to Five 107
Moving Day 109

Part 4: Feng Shui Mechanics 101   **111**

10 The Eight Houses, Part 1   **113**

About Face: The Eight House System 114
What's Your Trigram? 115
Personal Trigram Formula: Male...*116*
Personal Trigram Formula: Female *117*
The Personal Trigram Quick Reference Chart *117*
The Eight Wandering Stars 119
Changing Your Fortune..120
East Meets West 123
Are You Compatible?..125

11 The Eight Houses, Part 2   **129**

Your House Has a Trigram, Too..130
Comparing Your Personal Trigram to a Home's Trigram........132
Determine Your Home's Sitting and Facing Directions 133
Using a Compass to Determine Your Home's Trigram............134
What's Your House Trigram? 136
Assembling a Simple Floor Plan 136
Great Grids! 138

12 The Eight Houses, Part 3   **141**

Do You Know Where Your Palace Is? 142
Do You Know Where Your Wandering Star Is? 142
Qi-ing In on Qi 145
The Good, the Bad, and the Possibilities 145
The Rules of the Eight House Game 147
The Analysis..148

Part 5: Feng Shui Mechanics 201   **151**

13 The Flying Stars, Part 1   **153**

What Is the Flying Star System? 154
Ancient Beginnings 154
The Hetu River Map *155*
The Luoshu Writing *156*
The Magic Square of Three *157*

The Nine Imperial Palaces 160
Here's to the Nines *161*
Feng Shui and Nine *162*

14 The Flying Stars, Part 2 **165**

Space: The 24 Mountains 165
Do You Know Where Your House Is? *167*
The Luopan Charted *167*
Time: Three Cycles and Nine Periods..169
It's All in the Numbers 170
In Sync with Greater Nature *171*
The Attack on America *171*
A Number Is Worth a Thousand Words 172
The Ruler Principle *173*
Wheel of Fortune *174*
In Sickness and in Health: The Timeliness of the Stars *175*

15 The Flying Stars, Part 3 **177**

Do Stars Fly? 177
Flying Stars! *178*
Flying the Stars *179*
Constructing a Flying Star Chart 180
Flying Forward, Flying Backward *181*
More Flying Forward, More Flying Backward *183*
Charted Floor Plan 184
Great Charts! 185

16 The Flying Stars, Part 4 **215**

Yin and Yang, Mountain and Water 215
Fortunate Mountain Fortunate Water 217
Reversed Mountain and Water 218
The Double Facing Star Chart...220
The Double Sitting Star Chart 221

17 The Flying Stars, Part 5 **223**

The Mountain, Water, and Time Stars 223
The Central Palace 225
It's All in the Stars: The Star Combination Chart 226
A Simple Analysis...232

18   The Flying Stars, Part 6   **235**

The Annual Star 235
The Annual Star Chart 236
Flying the Annual Star..237
The Annual Star for 2002 237
The Annual Star for 2003 240

Part 6:   Practical Application   **243**

19   A House Hunting We Will Go   **245**

Doing Your Homework..245
Putting Your Best Direction Forward 246
Homeward Bound 247
There's No Place Like Home 248
Side-by-Side, Qi-by-Qi 251
The Analysis..253

20   Does Your Office Measure Up?   **257**

Labor Pains 257
First Things First...258
Let's Get Compatible 259
Dui Have a Match? 259
Won't You Please Come In? 260
Sitting Pretty 262
A Means to an End 263

Part 7:   Fate or Free Will: What's Your Destiny?   **265**

21   Introducing the Twelve Animals of the Chinese Zodiac   **267**

What Is the Chinese Zodiac? 268
Twelve Animals, Twelve Earthly Branches 268
What's Your Animal Sign?..270
Who Are Your Friends?..272
Who Are Your Foes? 273
Good Year/Bad Year 274
Personality Profiles 274
The Industrious Rat 274
The Methodical Ox 275
The Unpredictable Tiger 275

The Lucky Rabbit...275
The Dynamic Dragon 276
The Wise Snake...276
The Independent Horse...276
The Sensitive Sheep 277
The Mischievous Monkey 277
The Meticulous Rooster...278
The Devoted Dog 278
The Nurturing Pig 278

22 The Four Pillars of Destiny, Part 1   281

How Free Is Free Will?...282
What Is the Four Pillars of Destiny? 282
Time, Chinese Style 283
The Ten Heavenly Stems 283
The Twelve Earthly Branches 284
The Cycle of Sixty 285
Calculating Your Four Pillars 287
The Year Pillar 287
The Month Pillar..289
The Day Pillar..300
The Hour Pillar...304

23 The Four Pillars of Destiny, Part 2   307

The All-Important Day-Master 307
The Timeliness of Your Day-Master 308
Day-Master Relations 310
Strong or Weak? 311
The Strong Day-Master..311
The Weak Day-Master 312
What Are Your Favorable and Unfavorable Phases? 313
A Strong Day-Master's Favorable and Unfavorable Phases........314
A Weak Day-Master's Favorable and Unfavorable Phases 315
The Phases of Our Lives..315
The Fate of Princess Diana...317

24 The Four Pillars of Destiny, Part 3   319

The Axiom of Luck 320
Lucky Me 320
Yang Male or Yin Female, Please Step Forward 321
Yin Male or Yang Female, Please Step Forward 323

Wheel of Fortune 325
It Was a Very Good Year 326
Your Sixty Cycle's Destiny 326
The Fate of Princess Diana, Part 2............................328

25   The Four Pillars of Destiny, Part 4   331

What's in a Horoscope?...332
That Was Then, This Is Now......................................332
Oh, What a Month!...336
Around and Around We Go: Determining a New
   Sixty-Day Cycle..338
Day by Day 338

Appendixes

A   Glossary   345

B   Common Questions and Practical Answers   353

C   Learn More About Feng Shui   357

D   Chinese Dynasties and Periods   363

**E   Learn More About Taking a Proper Compass Reading
      Using the 24 Mountains   367**

   Index   371

Foreword

Much has been written about feng shui in English: At the time of this writing there are over 300 separate titles in English and many thousands of websites on the subject. Yet 25 years ago the subject was virtually unheard of in the United States and very difficult to discover amongst Western-educated Chinese. Before that there were only books written by missionaries and colonial administrators living in the nineteenth century. Western interest was probably sparked by my first book, *The Living Earth Manual of Feng Shui*, which was written in 1976 when most material on feng shui was still available only in Chinese. Feng shui did not however become "dinner party conversation" until the late 1980s, and Lillian Too did much to popularize it in the 1990s.

However, when interest in feng shui did finally gather speed, because of the lack of source material, many well-meaning teachers and writers seemed to forget that it is a really precise and exacting subject, and extended it in ways not originally part of its traditional Chinese roots. Now, although any science can be extended by new research and testing, this has got to be done with a full knowledge of all that has gone before. It is sometimes forgotten that feng shui is *not* a branch of interior decorating, but a practical science in its own right.

To put not too fine a point on it, a lot of later-day Western feng shui has been simplified beyond the point where it works, or has been invented or "intuited." Often intuition has provided a key or a direction in which to look, but it is never sufficient in itself to declare "it must be so" because I feel it to be so.

It therefore came as a delight and a breath of fresh air when I laid my hands on *The Complete Idiot's Guide to Feng Shui*. It was even more of a surprise to find that what at first glance (from its cover) was just another popularization of the subject, was in fact a very detailed text going a lot further than many of the apparently more ponderous texts, but starting with the real basics.

Elizabeth Moran and Masters Joseph Yu and Val Biktashev have among them produced an excellent and detailed book, explaining precisely the detailed calculations undertaken to this day by professional Chinese feng shui practitioners. As complex as these calculations are, the authors have presented them in a way that is easy to grasp. Even if you fail to absorb all the detail, many excellent tables make it easy to read the type of house, the Four Pillar horoscope of its owner, and the subtle interaction between these two, which modifies the luck, health, wealth, and happiness of its occupants.

Even now people question the effectiveness of such feng shui "luck manipulation." Let me assure you that, properly done, it is every bit as effective as the curative properties of acupuncture, and if wrongly applied, every bit as devastating as a karate blow. Feng shui, acupuncture, and karate are the product of thousands of years of refinement by one of the most practical races on earth. Their recent arrival does not diminish their effectiveness.

The fact that these three traditional Chinese sciences have only recently made their presence felt in the West is a tribute to the canniness of the Chinese, who kept the knowledge of gunpowder (among other things) from the West for hundreds of years.

To transplant from one culture to another a science that is based on a completely different worldview is a very difficult thing to do. To counter some of the myths that have sprung up around modern feng shui is even more so, but to do this in bite size chunks and with considerable humor is truly a *tour de force*. Tying in Isaac Newton, Albert Einstein, and David Bohm sets feng shui in the context of science, and using the latest scholarly approaches to Chinese civilization and science keeps the material up to date.

Feng shui is such a huge subject, that with any book on it, the main problem is what to leave out. The authors have handled this dilemma, by touching briefly upon most of those schools/methods of feng shui currently represented in the West (like Form School and Eight House feng shui), whilst choosing to focus on two main areas. These are Flying Star feng shui and its interrelation with that branch of Chinese astrology that deals with your personal Four Pillars of Destiny. Both of these aspects make up a large portion of the feng shui currently practiced in Hong Kong today.

I heartily recommend this book.

—Stephen Skinner
Bali, 2001

Stephen Skinner, originally an academic and lecturer in geography, first came across feng shui in the 1970s in Hong Kong and Singapore, where he observed the work of feng shui practitioners firsthand. As a result of what he saw, he wrote the first English book on the subject in the twentieth century, *The Living Earth Manual of Feng Shui*, in 1976. He is the founder of *Feng Shui for Modern Living* magazine, the world's largest selling feng shui magazine, which even publishes a regular monthly edition in Chinese. Therefore, Stephen is uniquely placed to comment upon the rise of feng shui in the West. He is author of five books on feng shui, including the *KISS Guide to Feng Shui*, and is presently engaged in researching the Chinese classics of feng shui back as far as the Tang dynasty.

Introduction

So, you want to try feng shui? You've heard it discussed at parties, you've read about it in magazines, and now you're willing to give it a try. Why not? But what is feng shui, exactly? Something to do with moving furniture around and hanging mirrors? Something to do with the flow of qi, (don't worry, we'll tell you all about qi in Chapter 4, "Qi Wiz! It's Life's Force!")? How do you even pronounce feng shui, anyway? (We'll tell you that, too.)

Well, all of your questions about this ancient Chinese tradition will be answered in a way that you, the Western reader, can understand. No boring treatise—just the need-to-know basics presented in a fun, interesting, and enlightening manner.

Okay, but what *is* feng shui? Feng shui is the art and science of living in harmony with your living space. Specifically, feng shui seeks to harness nature's positive forces and correct the negative ones with the intention of promoting better health, wealth, and relationships. You see, beginning 6,000 years ago, the Chinese monitored the cyclic movement of nature and recorded how its changes affected us. This may sound goofy, but science is coming to agree with the ancient Chinese notion that we're all bundles of one interconnected energy.

Out of the ancients' reverence for nature, three fundamental principles developed: yin and yang, the five phases, and the eight trigrams. Shared by other Chinese traditions such as acupuncture, acupressure, and herbs, these principles form the basis of two classical methods of feng shui: Eight House and Flying Star, both of which you'll learn about. These systems will help you find a house compatible with your qi. You'll discover how external and internal factors influence your health and livelihood. You'll learn the most auspicious position to place your bed and desk.

But, hey, we also offer a short study of Chinese astrology. Besides identifying your animal sign, we'll show you how to calculate your life chart using a method called The Four Pillars of Destiny. You'll learn how to determine your favorable colors, careers, and environments. Also, you'll learn how to calculate your 10-year, annual, monthly, and daily luck.

Feng shui will not only help you to improve many aspects of your life, but it will also help *you* to understand *you!* By making simple adjustments, you'll gain harmony in your home and workplace. With harmony comes the likelihood of better health, wealth, and relationships.

How to Use This Book

This book is divided into seven parts, each advancing you further along the feng shui path:

Part 1, "Let's Get Into Feng Shui," eases you into the concept of feng shui. We explain what feng shui is and what it isn't. We explain why this ancient Eastern tradition is relevant to modern Westerners.

Part 2, "The Fundamental Principles of Feng Shui," teaches you the fundamental principles of feng shui. You will learn how these age-old concepts apply to the here and now—and you!

Part 3, "Understanding Your Environment," helps you recognize, avoid, and alter external and internal factors that may influence your well-being.

Part 4, "Feng Shui Mechanics 101," introduces you to one method of classical feng shui called Eight House.

Part 5, "Feng Shui Mechanics 201," introduces you to another method of classical feng shui called Flying Star.

Part 6, "Practical Application," gives you practical experience evaluating and remedying a house and a business.

Part 7, "Fate or Free Will: What's Your Destiny?" teaches you about the Chinese zodiac and a system of astrology called The Four Pillars of Destiny.

We've also included five neat appendixes designed to assist your expanding knowledge of feng shui.

Feng Shui Features

In addition to all the information you'll find in the parts, you'll find five types of boxes throughout the text. These boxes will explain unfamiliar terms, further explore certain topics, give you helpful information or interesting quotes about feng shui, or alert you to any pitfalls.

Feng Facts

In these boxes, you'll find interesting tidbits and helpful information that are related to feng shui principles.

Wise Words

These boxes define new words so that you can speak the lingo.

Master Class

These boxes offer tips to make the most of your feng shui journey, as well as quick and interesting facts about feng shui.

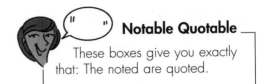

Notable Quotable

These boxes give you exactly that: The noted are quoted.

Feng Alert

In these boxes, you'll find warnings that will keep you on the right path.

Acknowledgments

Compiling material on a subject as esoteric as feng shui is not easy. We sincerely wish to thank our students, clients, and friends for urging us to present a deeper level of understanding of classical feng shui. Also, we wish to acknowledge …

Andree Abecassis: Our agent, advisor, mediator, cheerleader, and friend. We appreciate your professionalism more than you can ever know. Mike Sanders: Thanks for allowing us to compile new information for this second edition. Amy Gordon, Kathy Bidwell, and Cari Luna: Thanks for your attention to detail. Tim Neil: The most fabulous art slave in the world! Thanks. Scott Ransom: Thanks for the best sitting/facing explanation around! Viktoriy Yudkin: Val's best friend.

The author would like to thank the following for permission to use their original work:

Chapter 1

Photograph of Silva Explorer Model 203 used with permission of Johnson Outdoors Inc.

Chapter 2

Quotation from *The World Order of Bahá'u'lláh* by Shoghi Effendi used with permission of the publisher, the Bahá'í Publishing Trust, Wilmette, IL. Copyright © 1938, 1955, 1974, 1991 by the National Spiritual Assembly of the Bahá'ís of the United States.

Definitions of the terms conscious and subconscious mind, the critical area of the mind, knowns and unknowns are used with permission of the Hypnosis Motivation Institute.

Quotation by Albert Einstein taken from *The Quotable Einstein*, collected and edited by Alice Calaprice, is used with permission of Princeton University Press. © 1996.

Information about Fibonacci numbers is taken from *Fascinating Fibonacci: Mystery and Magic in Numbers*, by Trudi Hammel Garland. © Dale Seymour Publications, an imprint of Pearson Learning, a division of Pearson Education, Inc. Used with permission.

The idea of "McFengshui" is used with permission of Cate Bramble.

The nine aspirations for a New World Vision for the Millennium are identified with the Bahá'í Faith. For more information, go to www.bahai.org/.

Chapter 3

Quotation from *Tao Te Ching* (St. John's University Press, 1961) by Lao Tzu, translated by John C.H. Wu. Reprinted by arrangement with Shambhala Publications, Inc., Boston, www.shambhala.com.

Chapter 4

Quotation from *The Tao of Physics*, by Fritjof Capra. © 1975, 1983, 1991, 1999, by Fritjof Capra. Reprinted by arrangement with Shambhala Publications, Inc., Boston, www. shambhala.com.

Chapter 5

Quotation from *The Hidden Words*, by Bahá'u'lláh used with permission of the publisher, the Bahá'í Publishing Trust, Wilmette, IL. Copyright © 1932, 1975, by the National Spiritual Assembly of the Bahá'ís of the United States.

Chapter 9

Definition of fight or flight taken from the *Professional Hypnotism Manual*, by John G. Kappas, is used with permission of George Kappas, Vice President of Panorama Publishing. © 1999.

Chapter 13

The quotation by Richard Wilhelm in *The I Ching Book of Changes* is used with permission of Princeton University Press. © 1950.

The quotation by Joseph Needham in *Science and Civilisation in China* is used with permission of Cambridge University Press. © 1956.

Chapter 14

The quotation by Annemarie Schimmel in *The Mystery of Numbers* is used with permission of Oxford University Press. © 1993.

Chapter 24

The Four Pillars of Destiny charts were created, in part, by the American Feng Shui Institute in Monterey Park, California. They are used with permission of Master Larry Sang.

Every effort has been made to secure permissions for use of any original work appearing in this book. Please contact the author with any oversight at GlobalFengShui@aol.com. Thank you.

Trademarks

All terms mentioned in this book that are known to be or are suspected of being trademarks or service marks have been appropriately capitalized. Alpha Books and Penguin Group (USA) Inc. cannot attest to the accuracy of this information. Use of a term in this book should not be regarded as affecting the validity of any trademark or service mark.

Part 1

Let's Get Into Feng Shui

Part 1 is an introduction and more. You'll learn what feng shui is and what it isn't. You'll learn who uses this ancient Chinese art and science and how it can benefit you. What do I need to begin my study, you ask? Well, besides your brain and integrity, the most important thing you'll need is a compass. Details about this and other things you'll need are explained in Chapter 1.

Part 1 also introduces you to, well, you. Let's face it, we Westerners think in a way that's different from our Eastern neighbors. We're a logical lot, preferring rational knowledge over intuitive wisdom. So, before you can embark on a journey into an age-old Eastern tradition—one that requires you to push aside your rational mind-set—you must first understand how you, the Westerner, think. You'll also learn how the Chinese think and discover how both thought processes have come to the same conclusion—that everything and everyone is one interconnected dance of energy.

What Is Feng Shui?

In This Chapter

♦ Taking the feng shui IQ test

♦ Understanding faux and authentic schools of feng shui

♦ Discovering what you need to practice feng shui

♦ Learning 20 ways feng shui can improve your life

You're not an idiot if you're confused about feng shui (pronounced fung schway). This ancient Chinese tradition has bulldozed its way into the West, becoming the craze du jour. It seems everyone is either doing it or dissing it. Feng shui articles, books, entire magazines, complete schools, and comprehensive websites have crowded the market. Some of these offer advice and varied techniques far removed from the real thing. They all seek to cash in while misleading the unsuspecting, taking full advantage before the uninformed consumer wises up and begins to question the myriad inconsistencies.

Actually, this dilution of the classic tradition can be likened to playing "telephone." Remember that childhood game? One kid whispers a sentence into the next kid's ear. Something like, "My 50-foot alligator lives in a black lagoon." By the time the sentence reaches the end of the line of kids, it may have become, "My pin-striped crocodile swims in a pink polka-dot pool." Get the idea? This book will avoid such silliness and present to you a clear, concise explanation of feng shui. Let's get started by taking a little quiz.

The Feng Shui IQ Test

Before you learn what feng shui actually is (and what it isn't), let's test your feng shui IQ. For each of these questions, pick the answer you believe is correct. (Hint: Some questions may have more than one correct answer.) Don't worry, your grades won't be sent home to Mom!

1. What is feng shui?
    a. A specialty of Chinese cuisine
    b. The study of time and space
    c. A belief system of warding off evil spirits using mirrors

2. You should always sleep with your head pointed north.
    a. True
    b. False

3. Which instruments are used by a feng shui practitioner?
    a. A smudge stick
    b. Crystals
    c. A compass

4. You're practicing good feng shui when you:
    a. Open the window to let fresh air in
    b. Hang a mirror in a small room
    c. Hang a wind chime in your entrance

5. Which sort of house promotes a more healthful well-being?
    a. A house made of bricks
    b. A house built on a level lot
    c. A house built on a hilltop

6. You and your significant other have submitted an offer on a new house. At the last minute, you discover the previous two sets of owners divorced while living in the dwelling. Do you withdraw your offer?
    a. Yes
    b. No

7. You should always keep toilet lids down so your money *qi* (pronounced chee) won't flush away.

    a. True

    b. False

8. Feng shui can help you:

    a. Find love and romance

    b. Increase your earning potential

    c. Gain fame and respect

9. The object of feng shui is to activate your fame, marriage, children, helpful people, career, knowledge, family, and wealth qi sectors within your home.

    a. True

    b. False

10. Feng shui is practiced by:

    a. Individuals like yourself

    b. Major corporations

    c. The Asian population

Wise Words

Qi (also spelled ch'i) is the life force underlying everyone and everything. It is a field of information connecting us with each other and with our environment. The goal of feng shui is to balance qi in your living and/or working space to promote the likelihood of better health, wealth, and relationships. Qi is the subject of Chapter 4, "Qi Wiz! It's Life's Force!"

Feng shui IQ answers:

1. b, 2. b, 3. c, 4. a, 5. b, 6. b, 7. b, 8. all of the above, 9. b, 10. all of the above.

So, how did you do? Did the correct answers surprise you? Or maybe you feel more confused than ever. Don't worry—we'll tell you everything you need to know to understand feng shui. It's time to embark on a unique journey that will change the way you view the world. Let's start by discussing what feng shui *isn't*.

What Feng Shui Is Not

From the many questions we receive from readers, clients, and students, there is great confusion about the different schools of feng shui: "They all conflict." "Which one is right?" "How do I activate my wealth corner?" "Where is my wealth corner?" To address these concerns, we have added information to this chapter—information that will help you separate fact from falsehood; information that will help set you on the proper feng shui path.

Unfortunately, feng shui is plagued with many misconceptions. Largely steeped in myth and superstition, a discriminating feng shui enthusiast can easily learn to distinguish faux from authentic schools of feng shui by a number of telltale factors. Here are some attributes associated with faux schools of feng shui:

- They are often linked with Life Aspirations or Black Sect (also known as Black Hat Sect Tantric Buddhist feng shui) theory. Developed during the 1970s and 1980s respectively, these commercialized schools are referred to as "modern" or "Western" schools of feng shui.

- They divide a home into eight "life aspirations" or eight "life stations" of career, knowledge, family, wealth, fame, marriage, children, and helpful people.

- They use the location of the front door to determine the orientation of the eight life aspirations/stations. See the following figures (Life Aspirations theory and Black Sect theory).

- They match each of the five phases of qi (fire, earth, metal, water, and wood) with its affiliated direction. Stated another way, fire "activates" the southern fame aspiration/station; earth activates the northeastern knowledge and southwestern marriage sectors; metal activates the western children and northwestern helpful people sectors; water activates the northern career sector; and wood activates the eastern family and southeastern wealth sectors. The five phases is the subject of Chapter 6, "The Principle of the Five Phases."

- They also use "cures" such as mirrors, crystals, bamboo flutes, red ribbons, and statues or sculptures of fu dogs, frogs, and cats, among other things, to "activate" the eight life aspirations/stations. Statements like "A mirror will help to ward off evil spirits," "A fish tank placed in the north will bring prosperity," or "Hanging bells inside your door will ring in joy and happiness" are commonplace among these schools.

It's a pity these inaccuracies have clouded the nature of feng shui. In fact, these widespread assumptions have made the practice seem like a fad reserved for the gullible and eccentric. As you get further along into this book, you'll understand how these misrepresentations have never been part of classical feng shui. For example, 2 + 2 = 4, correct? Could you be convinced otherwise?

Surely not.

Just to set the record straight, feng shui is not a charming Eastern philosophy grounded in superstition. It is not a religion, nor does it derive from any religion. Feng shui does not provide elixirs or cure-alls for your problems. It is not magic. It is not a New Age discovery. Feng shui will not reduce your wrinkles, zap your fat, or help you win the lottery.

Life Aspirations Theory

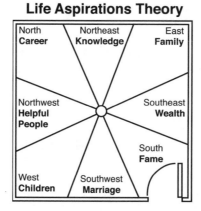

North Career	Northeast Knowledge	East Family
Northwest Helpful People		Southeast Wealth
		South Fame
West Children	Southwest Marriage	

The eight life aspirations are correlated with a direction. The magnetic orientation of the main entrance determines the placement of the life aspirations map. In this example, the front door faces south.

Black Sect Theory

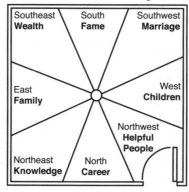

Southeast Wealth	South Fame	Southwest Marriage
East Family		West Children
		Northwest Helpful People
Northeast Knowledge	North Career	

The eight life stations are correlated with a direction. The northern stations always correspond to the wall containing the main entrance even if the door does not face a northerly direction. Whether the doorway is on the left, center, or right side of the wall (if you face the dwelling) will determine if you enter the knowledge, career, or helpful people sectors respectively.

What Feng Shui Is

Authentic *feng shui*, which we will hereafter refer to as "traditional" or "classical" feng shui, is an ancient practice first developed some 6,000 years ago by the Neolithic Chinese. The early findings blossomed into a sophisticated, well-honed tradition by the Tang dynasty (618–907 C.E.). Essentially, classical feng shui is a system based on keen observation of heavenly (time) and earthly (interior and exterior space) forces and how the qi of each interact. It is a practice of balancing these forces. With balance comes the likelihood of better health, wealth, and relationships. With balance, feng shui gives you the impetus, and the drive, to succeed!

Wise Words

Feng shui literally translates to "wind water," the two natural elements that direct qi to a settlement, dwelling, or burial site. Figuratively, the term represents the art and science of living in harmony with your environment.

Here are a few distinguishing factors about classical feng shui:

- The principle tool of the practitioner is a compass. While a Chinese *luopan* compass contains many concentric rings of information, for our purposes a basic protractor compass will suffice. You'll learn more about the type of compass you'll need later in this chapter.

- The magnetic (space) sitting or backside of the dwelling (as opposed to the location of the front door) and the year (time) the building was built are used to draw up an intricate numeric qi map of your dwelling (see the following figure). This technique is called Flying Star, the most sophisticated method of feng shui and the subject of Part 5, "Feng Shui Mechanics 201." For reasons that will be explained in successive chapters, there are 216 types of houses. In other words, a pre-fabricated, one-size-fits-all qi map composed of eight life aspirations/stations does not exist in classical feng shui. Like a snowflake or a fingerprint, each home is unique and individual.

- The year the occupant(s) was born is an important factor in determining his or her innate compatibility with the house.

- *Only* the five phases of qi (fire, earth, metal, water, and wood) are used to transform the home's qi into a productive cycle, fostering the probability of increased prosperity, better health, and beneficial relationships. Where each phase is placed depends on the number combination in the area in question.

The year the building was built and its magnetic sitting direction yield a numeric qi map. The classically trained feng shui practitioner studies the individual numbers, combination of numbers, and location of the numbers, among other things, to determine the likelihood of specific events occurring within the home. The practitioner balances the dwelling's qi to enhance its positive aspects and discourage its negative ones.

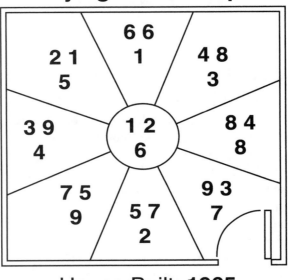

Classical Feng Shui Flying Star Qi Map

	6 6	
2 1	1	4 8
5		3
3 9	1 2	8 4
4	6	8
7 5	5 7	9 3
9	2	7

House Built: **1965**
Facing: **10° N**

Compasses and number schemes? Yikes! This sounds complex. It seems hard! Will I be able to grasp and implement classical feng shui's fundamentals and techniques? Of course! Don't fear. Forge ahead. While classical feng shui certainly cannot be fully learned in a weekend seminar or even in this book, you *can* learn the basics of two methods (Eight House and Flying Star) that you *will* employ and benefit from.

Master Class

The time your house was constructed or "born" and the time you were born are important considerations in a classical feng shui analysis. What does this mean, you ask? Well, many Chinese believe the first breath you take at birth marks your innate destiny. In the same way, when the foundation is set, the walls are secured, and the roof is affixed, your house is born. It, too, has a core personality. The central premise of feng shui is to correct and/or enhance your dwelling's personality so that its qi forces nourish your well-being, inspiring you to maximize your potential.

As you will learn in later chapters, classical feng shui is based, in part, on modern scientific reasoning. For example, acclaimed physicist Albert Einstein (1879–1955) proved that matter is an illusion, a masked form of energy. In other words, we, and our living space, are actually bundles of intertwining, connecting energy. All in flux, all confluent, pervading our very being. If not properly or effectively harnessed, human possibility is wasted. Doesn't it make sense to enhance our environment positively and productively?

Who Practices Feng Shui?

You need not be Asian or of Asian descent to practice feng shui. You don't have to be an interior designer, architect, or landscaper. Nor a philosopher, scientist, or celebrity. In fact, there are no prerequisites to practicing feng shui. Yet, this is not to say that feng shui practitioners don't share common traits. They do.

Generally feng shui practitioners …

- ◆ Have an open mind.
- ◆ Are willing to try alternative forms of therapy.
- ◆ Believe that the world and its peoples are interconnected.
- ◆ Believe in God or a Higher Power.
- ◆ Believe harmony and balance are essential to our well-being.
- ◆ Believe in a sense of fate or destiny.

Feng shui practitioners are global. They transcend cultural, racial, economic, and political barriers.

Feng Shui's Beginnings in the East

In medieval China, feng shui was a closely guarded secret. Its masters were restricted to the ruling class of emperors, aristocrats, and the privileged elite. By deliberately excluding commoners from feng shui's power, they ensured their stately positions. Feng shui masters were greatly rewarded for their expertise, and severely punished, or even killed, if they were known to aid the masses.

Feng Facts

One notable master, Yang Yunsong, managed to escape the Forbidden City (the famous complex of buildings in Beijing so called because at one time, only the emperor, his female entourage, and eunuchs lived there) during the Yellow Bandits Rebellion of 907 C.E. Yang sought refuge in the mountainous area of northwest China. There, he helped the poor by using his skills in feng shui. Nicknamed "Save the Poor," Yang Yunsong is still revered today for being among the first to explain and share some of the shrouded secrets of the tradition.

Today, feng shui is a way of life in many parts of Asia. In Hong Kong, Singapore, Taiwan, and Malaysia, feng shui masters are regularly called upon to bring prosperity, good health, and beneficial relationships to individuals and businesses alike. Meanwhile, feng shui is enjoying a resurgence on mainland China. After being long suppressed by the Communist regime, feng shui—along with many of China's other traditions—is once again being embraced.

Feng Shui Moves West

As Asians move west, so do their traditions. Oriental medicine (such as acupuncture and herbal remedies), Far Eastern cuisine, and the martial arts have all been accepted in our multicultural societies. Following their influences, feng shui is on the verge of being accepted by mainstream America. As we mentioned, feng shui is cropping up everywhere. Adult education courses, magazines, and websites are helping it to become a household word. Indeed, this cultural exchange of ideas will help facilitate communication and better understanding between two divergent peoples. Perhaps a time will come when feng shui will lose its distinctly cultural identity and become a worldwide tradition.

Would you be surprised to learn that some of the Western world's largest corporations use feng shui? Here are a few examples of progressive Western feng shui partisans:

- Trump Towers in New York City
- Creative Artists Agency in Beverly Hills, California
- MGM Grand Hotel and Mirage Resorts in Las Vegas, Nevada

- The Deepak Chopra Center in California
- Sydney Harbour Casino and Hotel in Australia

While there are myriad Eastern companies that adhere to feng shui principles, you might be interested to learn that Hong Kong Disneyland, scheduled to open in 2005, is being constructed according to feng shui principles.

Feng Shui and You

You don't have to be a mover or shaker to partake in feng shui's power. Feng shui is meant for everyone. We have two kinds of clients: those who are seeking desperate measures for desperate times, and those who are looking for a winning edge. They share a desire to improve their living and/or working conditions. Do you see yourself in any of the following situations?

- Helen is a nurse practitioner. She's smart, attractive, funny, and single. She has grown tired of blind dates, bad dates, and no dates. She wants to settle down and have a family. How can she attract Mr. Right?

- Alex and Anna want to buy a house. Three years of scrimping and saving has rewarded them with $50,000 for a down payment. It's a big investment. How can they find a home best suited to them?

- Mr. Smith owns a small insurance agency. Despite competitive salaries, bonuses, and other incentives not offered by many employers, his staff can't get along. Will the bickering ever end?

The fact that these people will consider feng shui to improve their situations is testimony to their open minds. They will take a leap of faith and extend their common senses to the realm of the invisible, the realm that extends beyond our five senses of sight, touch, hearing, taste, and smell.

But, you may ask, exactly how will these people be helped? Patience, our friends! Later on, after you've learned feng shui's fundamental principles, we'll review two of these case studies, and see how they remedied their situations. Patience, perseverance, and reading to the end will enable you to solve these mysteries.

What Do I Need to Practice Feng Shui?

The most important thing you need is a positive attitude—a willingness to want to improve your life and that of your loved ones. While feng shui is used to balance your home's space, the onus is on you to balance your own space, your own mind and body. By living the Golden Rule, by refraining from gossip, maliciousness, and hate, you will

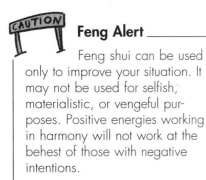

Feng Alert_____

Feng shui can be used only to improve your situation. It may not be used for selfish, materialistic, or vengeful purposes. Positive energies working in harmony will not work at the behest of those with negative intentions.

become a more centered being. You will be working with feng shui's power. It's a two-way street, friends! How can you expect feng shui to fully work if you're arguing incessantly, spending beyond your means, or living in a cluttered and disorderly environment? Take charge! Seize the day. Become proactive and not reactive to your own wants and needs and life's situations. Help to create a positive destiny by performing good deeds, uttering good words, and eating healthful food. Balance and harmony begins with you!

Here's a short list of things you'll need to begin your study of classical feng shui:

♦ Your brain.

♦ Integrity.

♦ A clear plastic, 6-inch, 360-degree protractor with half-inch gradations. This can be found in any office supply store. We recommend the Mars College protractor.

♦ A straight edge ruler.

♦ A basic protractor compass. This can be found in any outdoor equipment and camping store. A model that graduates in two-degree steps where directions are clearly marked is best. Also, a compass featuring a line of sight is beneficial. We recommend the Silva Explorer Model 203 compass. It costs about $25 and is shown in the following photo.

Example of a basic protractor compass.

(Photograph courtesy of Johnson Outdoors Inc.)

The final thing you'll need is patience. To the newcomer, feng shui's principles may seem abstract and difficult to comprehend. Our advice is to take your time. Read each chapter thoroughly. Digest it. Review it again. If you become frustrated, confused, or just plain fed up, relax and take a break. The Great Wall of China wasn't built in a day. Neither was feng shui!

Twenty Ways to Benefit from Feng Shui

Here are 20 ways feng shui can potentially help you. We'll be covering many of these topics in later chapters:

1. Getting a job, raise, or promotion
2. Improving health
3. Getting married
4. Getting pregnant or preventing miscarriages
5. Guarding against separations or divorce
6. Increasing motivation
7. Creating more harmonious family/work relationships
8. Developing better study habits
9. Increasing creativity
10. Feeling more in control
11. Feeling more comfortable in your home/office
12. Eliminating depression
13. Stimulating social life
14. Spurring better business
15. Preventing lawsuits or malicious influences
16. Preventing accidents
17. Finding an apartment, home, or business
18. Warding off addictions
19. Promoting better sleep
20. Bringing respect and fame

Even if you feel your life is on track, practicing feng shui is fun. Get involved. Enlist your friends and family.

Pinyin and Wade-Giles: Chinese Romanization

In this book, we use the *Pinyin* system of romanization that uses the Roman or Latin alphabet to spell Chinese words. Developed by the Chinese in the mid-twentieth century Pinyin was accepted as the international standard in 1979. Nevertheless, many Western authors still use the older Wade-Giles system of transliteration, which was developed by two British sinologists (a person who studies Chinese culture, customs, language, and the like): Sir Francis Wade (1818–1895) and Herbert Allen Giles (1845–1935). For our readers who have books about feng shui that use Wade-Giles, here's the Pinyin equivalent of some of the words you'll encounter in this book:

Wade-Giles	PinYin	Meaning
Ch'i	Qi	Life's breath
Lo p'an	Luopan	Chinese compass
Pa-k'ua	Bagua	Eight Trigrams
Kua	Gua	Natal trigram number
Ch'ien	Qian	Northwestern trigram
Tui	Dui	Western trigram
Li	Li	Southern trigram
Chen	Zhen	Eastern trigram
Sun	Xun	Southeastern trigram
K'an	Kan	Northern trigram
Ken	Gen	Northeastern trigram
K'un	Kun	Southwestern trigram
I Ching	*Yijing*	*Book of Changes*

Don't worry if you're not familiar with these words. In coming chapters, you'll understand all of them!

Wise Words

Hanyu Pinyin Wenzi (the alphabet of Chinese phonetic combinations) is a system of romanization that uses the Roman or Latin alphabet to spell Chinese words. Based on the Peking dialect of Mandarin Chinese, Pinyin was developed by the Chinese after the advent of Communism in 1949. In 1979, it became the international standard and is used in all forms of printed material, television, Braille for the blind, and finger spelling for the deaf. Wade-Giles is an older system of transliteration first developed by a Cambridge University sinologist, Sir Thomas Francis Wade (1818–1895) and improved upon and popularized by another British sinologist, Herbert Allen Giles (1845–1935).

So, where do we go from here? Before you depart on this journey, you must first understand how you think as a Westerner. Understanding how you are a product of a culture of rational thinkers will enable you to set aside your preconceptions. Only then can you investigate and accept alternative ways of thinking based on intuitive knowledge—a method primarily used by our Eastern counterparts. Yet, regardless of how anyone thinks, we'll all arrive at the same conclusions about the world we live in. What's that? Keep reading!

The Least You Need to Know

- Feng shui is not a superstition, philosophy, or religion.
- Feng shui is the study of time and space. The practice seeks to harmonize nature's forces within your living/working space and surrounding environment.
- The use of mirrors, crystals, bamboo flutes, and red ribbons, along with the concept of dividing a home into sections of career, knowledge, family, wealth, fame, marriage, children, and helpful people belong to faux schools of feng shui.
- Feng shui can potentially improve your health, wealth, and relationships.
- A positive attitude, integrity, patience, and a basic protractor compass are all that you need to begin practicing classical feng shui.

Chapter 2

Western Intellectual Heritage and the Holy Grail

In This Chapter

- ◆ How our minds work
- ◆ Our scientific legacy
- ◆ A holistic universe
- ◆ The relationship between nature and mathematics
- ◆ A New World Vision for the Millennium: suggestions to implement global harmony

Pretend the universe is a car. We all know that a car is an intricate mechanism comprised of thousands of pieces, all functioning as parts of the whole. We know that it would be impossible to discern how the car operates by studying, say, a tire. Ironically, this is how most Western scientists study the universe. They focus on one spot or element, disregarding the interconnectedness of that which surrounds and/or encompasses it.

Yet, the Big Picture is now beginning to emerge. As modern scientists delve deeper into the celestial heavens and probe deeper into the infinitesimal, many are becoming aware of the unity of all things. The acceptance of universal wholeness will guide and enable us to define a new world vision—a vision that will change our fundamental moral, social, political, and religious order.

This chapter is about understanding how our minds work and how we have tuned in to nature's truths. This chapter is about our intellectual heritage—how the Western world has become a culture of rational thinkers and how we are becoming a people of united reformers. What does this have to do with feng shui? Our Eastern neighbors have always favored the Big Picture, the unity of all things. As you will come to learn, feng shui is about harnessing nature's forces, which connect us all. Understanding and accepting this concept will lead you to better health, wealth, and relationships.

Mind Power 101

The human mind is a powerful tool. Using our minds we have progressed from being a tribe of hunters and gatherers to a society overly dependent on our inventions and discoveries. Without such conveniences as telephones, computers, automobiles, or microwave ovens, we'd feel lost, frustrated, and frazzled. The last 150 years alone have yielded mind-boggling advances in the fields of science, medicine, genetics, and technology, unequaled during any other time in the history of humankind. The endless stream of wonders continues still, each new development vastly increasing our knowledge and capabilities.

Using our minds we have ushered in the Information Age: An age where communication devices like the telephone, cellular phone, fax machine, and especially the computer, have connected people all over the world. An age where ideas can flow freely, where walls of judgment are breaking down. Using our minds we have collectively taken a step toward global integration and unity of all peoples.

> **Feng Facts**
>
> Believing that everything of value and usefulness had already been invented, the U.S. Patent Office sought to disband its establishment in 1844. But from that year forward, an outpouring of important discoveries and inventions caused the office to remain open. Such things as the telegraph (1844), elevator (1854), telephone (1876), automobile (1885), Kodak camera (1888), and airplane (1903) became realities, changing the world forever.

> **Notable Quotable**
>
> "A mechanism of world intercommunication will be devised, embracing the whole planet, freed from national hindrances and restrictions, and functioning with marvelous swiftness and perfect regularity."
>
> —Shoghi Effendi, *The World Order of Bahá'u'lláh,* 1938

Twelve Percent of the Whole

Logic and reason are the bulwarks of Western thinking. But did you know that these abilities compose only 12 percent of our mind's power? Considering the level of intellect, sophistication, and complexity needed to generate such far-reaching advances as satellites and space stations, this is truly remarkable. Yet it is a physiological fact.

The adult mind comprises two contingent but distinctly different components: the *conscious* mind (12 percent) and the *subconscious* mind (88 percent). Separating the realms is the critical area of the mind. Part conscious, part subconscious, the critical area accepts and rejects information based on *knowns*, units of communication that have been learned before.

Wise Words

The **conscious**, or waking, state of mind gives us logic, reason, and willpower. The **subconscious** realm is the area of the mind that receives and stores information. A **known** is a unit of communication that has been learned before. It can be positive or negative and will be accepted into the subconscious mind. An **unknown** is a unit that is rejected by the critical area of the mind and will not enter the subconscious.

Imagine your mind is a computer. The input of information is tremendous. Files are constantly being made: Belief files, feeling files, habit files, and everything else that is a known are filed in your subconscious memory. If a computer encounters an instruction or data that are totally foreign to its known programs, it is rejected. Likewise, if your mind receives information unknown to your frame of reference, it is immediately dismissed. For example, if we said you could derive nature's truths by meditating, you would probably reject this idea, if you had an analytical, scientific way of thinking.

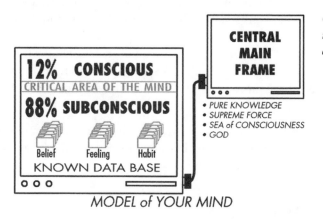

Our mind accepts and rejects information similar to how a computer processes data.

As a culture, we have learned to isolate, compartmentalize, and fragmentize information. Only in the West do we tend to separate such things as mind from body and faith from reason. Our separatist notion and the way we view the world stems from our linear scientific heritage. We are comfortable with taking a step-by-step, logical approach to problem solving. Everyday phrases like "Let's be reasonable," and "This is not logical" are testament to our deeply ingrained thought process.

Faux Feng Shui and the Western Mind

The Western mindset helped, in part, to create faux feng shui! The keen masterminds behind Black Sect and Life Aspirations feng shui (see Chapter 1, "What Is Feng Shui?" for a reminder of faux feng shui) understood that Westerners like things neat and orderly. Westerners need to break things down. Westerners need to label things. Hence the creation of distinct components or life aspirations/stations of wealth, career, knowledge, and the like.

Remember the television commercial: "Two all-beef patties, special sauce, lettuce, cheese, pickles, onions, on a sesame seed bun"? Quick, was it McDonald's or Burger King? Chances are, you had to think about it. The point is, the savvy production team hired by the owners of McDonald's capitalized on the Western obsession with parts. Little emphasis was placed on the whole burger.

Continuing with our fast-food analogy, Westerners want things bigger-better-faster. We want things now-now-now. Borrowing a term from our friend and feng shui teacher and practitioner Cate Bramble, feng shui has become "McDonaldized." Simply, most Westerners do not have the patience to fully understand a complicated concept. We want the *Reader's Digest* version—only part of the story.

Friends, understand that classical feng shui is the study of qi, the holistic, pervasive, and uniting force underlying everyone and everything. While you'll learn about qi in Chapter 4, "Qi Wiz! It's Life's Force!" understand that qi is not like a pet dog. Qi cannot be commanded and taught to separate into different sociological factions. Wealth qi, over here. Sit and stay. Career qi, over here. Sit and stay. Remember, feng shui is the study of time (heaven qi) and space (earth qi). Each dwelling's space is different, born into different times. Actually, you may have more than one area within your home or office that promotes prosperity and promotion!

The study of classical feng shui will not only free us, allowing for alterations in the way of seeing and thinking, but also help us grow, develop, progress, and succeed. It will help us become more holistic, shedding our separatist ways.

In Search of the Holy Grail

Before we move on to presenting scientific evidence and theories about a holistic universe, it's worth understanding from where our rational and separatist mindset derives.

Since ancient times, philosophers and scientists have searched for the Holy Grail of Knowledge: the origin, structure, and order of the universe. With each new discovery, myths were dispelled and replaced by new "truths," which often carried over into successive centuries, becoming firmly rooted in our collective consciousness. Over the past 2,500 years, there has been an impressive roster of individuals whose scientific discoveries or philosophical ideas changed the way we view the world. Here is a brief overview of those who have helped to form our rational, separatist mindset:

◆ **The Greek Age:** The ancient Greeks considered the study of science a noble pursuit. It was not inspired by religion, which at the time was polytheistic—a belief in or worship of more than one god. Science that presents a rational and orderly view of the cosmos developed in ancient Greece around the sixth century B.C.E. with Thales of Miletus. A seafaring and trading people, the Greeks developed an acute sense of time and space, their observations giving

Wise Words _____

The method of reaching a conclusion by deducing laws through observation is **deductive reasoning**. The method of reaching a conclusion by developing specific cases based on general laws is **inductive reasoning**.

birth to the fields of astronomy and geometry. We can credit Pythagoras (560–500 B.C.E.) and Aristotle (384–322 B.C.E.) with instituting scientific methods based on logic and reason. These methods of *deductive* and *inductive reasoning* still play a role today in scientific thinking.

◆ **The Newtonian Age:** English physicist Sir Isaac Newton's (1642–1727) universe was black and white, void of gray. Now called "classical" or "mechanical" physics, Newton's belief was that simple and permanent mechanical laws that could be understood by careful observation and experimentation governed the universe. Based on the Greeks' deductive and inductive methodology, Newton explained his theories using mathematics. He maintained that we are separate from nature and thus are able to observe the world objectively. Although Newton sought to reconcile his deep religious convictions with science, his ideas set the stage for a break between science and religion, or physics and metaphysics (philosophy).

◆ **The Enlightenment Age:** Coined by German philosopher Immanuel Kant (1724–1804), the term "enlightenment" took God out of the scientific equation, viewing natural phenomena entirely as a mechanical scheme. Kant sought to bring together two divergent philosophical ideas developed during the seventeenth century—the notion that knowledge is derived from observation and experience and not theory (empiricism) and the notion that knowledge is derived from reasoning (rationalism). According to Kant, the concepts of time and space cannot be fully understood using sensory perception. Because of these limitations, the physical world must be studied using a rational system like mathematics. Other enlightened philosophers include Denis Diderot (1713–1784), Julien Offra de la Mettrie (1709–1751), and David Hume (1711–1761).

♦ **The Darwinian Age:** The split between science and religion was fully realized with British naturalist Charles Darwin (1809–1882). Postulated in his book, *On the Origin of the Species by Means of Natural Selection, or the Preservation of Favoured Races in the Struggle for Life* (1859), Darwin's groundbreaking and controversial theory of evolution and natural selection caused much discord between the scientific and religious factions. The schism deeply impacted the Western mindset.

The preceding examples demonstrate how we have learned to rationalize, separate, and isolate information as a means of understanding the totality of the universe and its inhabitants. As a result, we have effectively disengaged, separating science, religion, mind, and body into distinct and fortified camps—a mindset that would be shattered with twentieth-century science.

United We Stand

The discoveries made by twentieth-century physicists have rocked the scientific world, crushing long-held traditional views spearheaded by Newtonian mechanics. A unified world picture is emerging that no longer reduces nature (and human nature) to a series of isolated parts. Modern scientists now view the cosmos as a web of interconnected and interrelated events. As you'll soon learn, many modern scientists believe in the existence of God or a Higher Power to which we are connected. The new scientific paradigm—the whole is the sum of its parts—is replacing the common ideology—the parts are the means to the whole.

While these two ideologies may sound alike, they really are not. The distinction may be subtle but, nonetheless, significant. We are speaking of ways of thinking, considering, and perceiving the world. Remember the car at the beginning of this chapter? Today, when we look at it, we see more than just a set of tires, a carburetor, or a fuel tank. We see all these things and more: a means of transportation, a status symbol, a product of a powerful worldwide industry. When we drive this car on a highway, we are involved in more than going from point A to point B; we are utilizing a vast and vital, well-connected national and interstate road system upon which the economic health of our nation depends. When we consider our nation, we do not stop at borders. We belong to a community of nations, diverse peoples all sharing the same planet.

In feng shui, the totality is what is stressed—a rich totality comprising of a harmonious unity of parts. This is opposed to a collection of distinct and singular parts (the eight life aspirations/stations) joining together to form a loose federation. So, as scientists continue to search for "pure truth," feng shui helps to provide an alternate path, if you will, new frames of reference to our collective consciousness.

Scientific Holistic Theories

Two influential and revolutionary scientific theories surfaced during the twentieth century that played a leading role in changing how scientists understand the world. On a larger scale, the discoveries enabled us to see the Big Picture, a holistic reality.

♦ **Theories of relativity:** Postulated by German physicist Albert Einstein (1879–1955), his theories state that mass is nothing more than a different manifestation of energy. It means that the book you're now reading and the chair you are sitting in are forms of energy at rest. Also, Einstein understood that space and time were not separate entities, but are connected to form a fourth dimension called space-time.

♦ **Quantum physics:** Formulated in the 1920s by Niels Bohr (1885–1962), Max Planck (1858–1947), and Werner Heisenberg (1901–1976), among others, quantum physics is the study of subatomic particles such as electrons and atoms. In a nutshell, quantum theory reveals the unity of all things. It shows that we cannot use isolation as a method to gain knowledge of the whole.

> **Notable Quotable**
>
> "Everything is determined … by forces over which we have no control. It is determined for the insect as well as for the star. Human beings, vegetables, or cosmic dust—we all dance to the mysterious tune, intoned in the distance by an invisible piper."
>
> —Albert Einstein, in *The Saturday Evening Post*, October 26, 1929

If these theories seem like old hat to you, ideas that have lost their power and passion, consider the following theories that many people are not yet aware of.

Holistic Theories

Perhaps the most exciting theories cannot be fully scientifically proven. Nevertheless, they cause us to broaden our minds, raising us to new levels of understanding, wisdom, and insight. Here is a short description of the work generated by three innovative and progressive Western scientists.

♦ **David Bohm** (1917–1992): Based in part on his work concerning the behavior of electrons, Bohm believed the universe can be likened to a hologram in which each part of the image contains the entire picture. He believed the universe is "an undivided and unbroken whole" and that there exists a hidden primary reality (the quantum potential) that provides information to the totality of humankind and its environment. Bohm's beliefs give a scientific explanation to the phenomenon of synchronicity—a pattern of correlated coincidences (thoughts, objects, numbers, and/or events) linked together to form a theme of meaning to the observer.

♦ **Rupert Sheldrake** (modern-day biologist): Sheldrake claims that the development and evolution of an organism and human consciousness is guided by a holistic force that he calls the morphic field. Specifically, the morphic field is a phenomenon of nature whereby if a form or thought occurs in nature, it is likely to repeat again in another species; and if a thought occurs, it is likely to be thought again by another person. In nature, the spiral shape of conch shells, hurricanes and galaxies are examples. In human nature, the independent and almost simultaneous "discovery" of calculus in 1675 by English mathematician and philosopher Sir Isaac Newton (1642–1727) and German mathematician and philosopher Gottfried Leibniz (1646–1716) is an example of humankind tapping into the morphic field.

♦ **Andrew Newberg** (1967–): Neuroscientist Andrew Newberg believes he can prove that a Higher Power exists by the way the brain functions during states of deep concentration, meditation, and prayer. In these states the "line" that separates the self from the world disappears, producing the effect of a mystical union with God (or the Sea of Consciousness, a Higher Power). The question remains: Is God an illusion produced by the brain's activity or has God wired our brain to experience a holistic reality? These mysteries and many other studies about the convergence of science and religion are being funded by the John Templeton Foundation.

Indeed the notion of a holistic world order is quite profound and worthy of more study. Please see Appendix C, "Learn More About Feng Shui," for a list of Bohm's, Sheldrake's, and Newberg's thought-provoking works. Also, see Chapter 11, "Science, Synchronicity, and the *Yijing*," in *The Complete Idiot's Guide to the I Ching* (Alpha Books, 2001). Here, we give a detailed account of David Bohm's ideas as they relate to the *Yijing*, a book of divination developed at the end of the second millennium B.C.E.

In the meantime, if we can accept their ideas, it means we are able to draw from an infinite well of potential and possibilities. This is the hallmark of feng shui—to harness nature's well (qi) to better our existence.

Nature Speaks Mathematics, Too

Scientists use mathematics to help explain what we cannot understand using sensory perception. Somehow, this man-made abstraction magically conforms to nature's truths. Put another way, somehow we conform to mathematical principles in the universe. Whether we do it on a conscious or subconscious level is not known, but we've stumbled on mathematical patterns in nature that continue to perplex and inspire, propelling us to new levels of understanding about ourselves and the world in which we live.

While modern scientists understand that mathematics is the language of the universe, the ancient Chinese understood that mathematics was the language of the gods—that the pantheon of ancestors in heaven "spoke" to their descendants using numbers. The Chinese used the numeric information made apparent in the celestial heavens to improve their well-being. Eventually, their astute knowledge of the cosmos evolved into a system of feng shui called Flying Star, the subject of Part 5, "Feng Shui Mechanics 201."

Fascinating Fibonacci and the Golden Ratio

1,1,2,3,5,8,13,21,34,55,89,144,233,377,610 …

This is a sequence of numbers called the *Fibonacci Sequence*, named after thirteenth-century mathematician Leonardo of Pisa, also known as Fibonacci. By charting a population of rabbits, Fibonacci stumbled upon a certain numeric pattern as a solution to a story problem: Each number in the series is the sum of the two previous numbers. For example, 3+5=8; 5+8=13; 8+13=21, and so on to infinity.

Pretty neat, but it gets even better. Dividing each number in the series by the one preceding it yields a ratio that stabilizes at 1.618034. For example, 2 ÷ 1 = 2, 3 ÷ 2 = 1.5, 1597 ÷ 987 = 1.618034, 4181 ÷ 2584 = 1.618034, and so on to infinity. This figure has come to be known as the *Golden Ratio*. Big deal, you say.

Wise Words _____

The **Fibonacci Sequence** is a series of numbers where each number in the series is the sum of the two previous numbers. A **Golden Ratio** is a special number approximately equal to 1.6180339887498948482. The digits of the Golden Ratio go on to infinity without any pattern repeating. It's related to the Fibonacci Sequence and is obtained by dividing each number in the series by the one that precedes it.

Okay, here's the cool stuff. Fibonacci numbers and the Golden Ratio can be found in nature and our bodies, and has influenced art, architecture, and music. Fibonacci proportions can even be found in everyday items like playing cards, notepads, mirrors, windows, and credit cards. Simply, we are drawn to certain number proportions. Put another way, we, and our surroundings, conform to mathematical principles made manifest in universe.

Here is a short list of things in which you can find Fibonacci numbers and the Golden Ratio:

◆ On pinecones, artichokes, pineapples, and sunflowers, the bracts, petals, scales, and seeds respectively exemplify Fibonacci ratios. There are 5 steep and 8 gradual spirals on pinecones and artichokes. There are 8 and 13 gradual and 21 steep spirals on a pineapple. The head of a sunflower shows 55 rows of seeds revolving counterclockwise and 89 rows of seeds revolving clockwise.

◆ We have Fibonacci fingers: 2 hands, each of which has 5 fingers broken into 3 parts of 2 knuckles. Our body and face conform to Fibonacci proportions.

◆ On a piano keyboard, 13 keys comprise an octave (chromatic scale). These are broken down into 8 white keys and 5 black keys, which are divided into groups of 2 and 3 keys. Moreover, the pentatonic scale is made up of 5 keys, and the diatonic scale with 8 keys.

Fibonacci numbers and the Golden Ratio are manifestations of the innate harmony, symmetry, and balance in the universe. As we stated at the beginning of this section, whether consciously or subconsciously, we have tapped into and benefited by nature's truth. Indeed, we are all part of a cosmic dance in which we affect and are affected by everyone and everything.

For more information about the Fibonacci Sequence, please see Trudi Hammel Garland's inspiring book, *Fascinating Fibonaccis: Mystery and Magic in Numbers* (Dale Seymour Publications, 1987).

Feng Facts

Add up any 10 consecutive numbers in the Fibonacci Sequence and divide the sum by 11. You'll find that not only is the sum always evenly divisible, the sum is a Fibonacci number! For example, $2 + 3 + 5 + 8 + 13 + 21 + 34 + 55 + 89 + 144 = 374 \div 11 = 34$; $8 + 13 + 21 + 34 + 55 + 89 + 144 + 233 + 377 + 610 = 1584 \div 11 = 144$. See Chapter 13, "The Flying Stars, Part 1," for more interesting information about how the number 11 is mysteriously linked with the catastrophic events surrounding the September 11, 2001, World Trade Center attack.

Other Profound Patterns

The Fibonacci Sequence and the Golden Ratio aren't the only number series found in nature. There are many other transcendental mathematical examples, but space restricts us from presenting them.

As we have mentioned, feng shui is a system of mathematical patterns in nature discovered by the ancient Chinese. In fact, four of feng shui's fundamental principles correspond to numbers in the Fibonacci Sequence: taiji (1), yin and yang (2); heaven, earth, and human qi (3), five phases (5), and eight trigrams (8). Part 3, "Understanding Your Environment," is devoted to learning the principles of these patterns.

A New World Vision for the Millennium

If we do discover a single unifying force or scientifically prove the existence of God or a Higher Power, how will that affect our everyday life? Will we lay down our warheads and use this knowledge constructively? Will we become united as citizens of planet Earth? Perhaps we earthlings should establish a New Vision for the Millennium, a set of principles that will unite us on a fundamental human level. These principles will heal cultural and racial tensions resulting from dogmas and superstitions of the past, as well as elevate our awareness so that we can create a harmonious and peaceful world.

If for no other reason, our common purpose of survival will force us to adopt a New World Vision for the Millennium. Our goals could include, but not be limited to …

- Independent search for truth.
- The harmony of science and religion.
- The oneness of all belief systems.
- Equality of men and women.
- The elimination of extremes of wealth and poverty.
- The abolition of prejudices.
- Universal compulsory education.
- A universal language.
- The establishment of a world government.

The implementation of world harmony begins with you. Before we can hope to change our global frame of reference we must each foster unity and harmony in our own home. We hope that you'll set aside your rational mindset and opt for a more holistic way of thinking. Feng shui is a powerful tool that can help do this.

In the next chapter, you'll learn how the Chinese have always viewed the world as a holistic reality. Also, you'll learn how feng shui developed.

The Least You Need to Know

- Logic and reasoning constitute just 12 percent of our mind power; the other 88 percent is our subconscious.
- Our logical, rational mindset stems from the ancient Greeks.
- With the advent of Einstein's theories of relativity and quantum physics, modern science has begun to accept the "oneness" of all things.

◆ Theoretical scientists like David Bohm, Rupert Sheldrake, and Andrew Newberg propose that the world is a holistic entity from which we can draw information.

◆ Mathematics is the language of nature.

◆ A set of principles must be developed to secure harmony on a human level.

Chapter 3

The Great Wall of Knowledge and the Rise of Feng Shui

In This Chapter

- ◆ Chinese inventions
- ◆ How nature has influenced science and philosophy
- ◆ The development of feng shui
- ◆ Form School and Compass School: the two classic schools of feng shui

Dim sum, the Great Wall, kung fu, the Cultural Revolution, scroll painting, mah jongg, the Forbidden City, rice fields, rickshaws, Chairman Mao, the Silk Road, Beijing, terra-cotta warriors, Confucius, acupuncture, Daoism …. What comes to mind when *you* think of China?

No doubt China is an ancient culture whose enduring traditions, colorful symbolism, and systems of government captivate us. Yet, did you know that for 2,000 years, beginning around 500 B.C.E. to 1500 C.E., this Eastern nation's scientific and technological advances exceeded anything found in the West?

The Chinese have always believed in the oneness of all things. The practice of feng shui was born out of China's reverence for nature. The Chinese believed if they could reflect the balance of nature's forces in their daily lives, they could achieve a more harmonious living condition. That assumption was correct. In this chapter, you'll learn how the Chinese developed a thought process based, in part, on intuitive wisdom, and how they derived mathematical truths from nature.

Made in China

A common misunderstanding among Westerners is that the Chinese lack scientific and technological know-how. The ubiquitous "Made in China" label, stuck to the bottom of practically every inexpensive trinket, probably contributes to this stereotype. But the fact is we have the Chinese to thank for inventing many things that have improved our lives and made them more pleasurable. The wheelbarrow, umbrella, animal harness, stirrups, the game of chess, paper money, fishing reels, matches, and kites are all products of Chinese ingenuity. Also, the Chinese developed the first seismograph and planetarium. They created movable sails, the rudder, and bulkhead. Iron casting and silk harvesting originated in China.

But, surely, China's four most important inventions are the developments of papermaking, printing, gunpowder, and the compass. The compass is the tool of the feng shui practitioner. You'll be learning more about this later on.

China's Greater Nature

The ancient Chinese took what they called "Greater Nature" (Da Zi Ran) very seriously. Its forces inspired, awed, and humbled. It was a favorite subject of artisans. Greater Nature even gave rise to earth sciences like geology, cartography, and chemistry. The Chinese believed they were a product of nature's forces. They believed these forces determined their fate. To the farmer, gentle winds meant abundant crops, prosperity, and good health. Conversely, harsh winds, floods, and drought meant devastation, misfortune, and illness.

Natural phenomena were important to the emperor, too. Since the Shang dynasty (c. 1600–1045 B.C.E.) these semi-divine leaders petitioned Shangdi (their high god who ruled over lesser gods and spirits of the departed) on behalf of their kingdom. If Shangdi approved of his leadership, he blessed the kingdom with favorable weather, thus securing the king's position. If Shangdi disapproved of the king's leadership, the lord above punished him by sending bad weather and illness. Considered an evil omen, such harsh conditions were a direct communication from above that the king should rectify his poor behavior.

Skywatcher for Hire

When Marco Polo visited China in 1275 C.E., purportedly he described Beijing as a city of 5,000 skywatchers. He was probably right. Some of those skywatchers were astrologers, some were astronomers. Both ran flourishing businesses in interpreting and divulging nature's secrets.

Feng Facts

In her recent book, *Did Marco Polo Go to China?* (Secker & Warburg, 1995), British librarian Frances Wood claims he didn't. This comes as quite a shock to Western minds who believe Polo discovered China; so entrenched are his fantastic adventures and importation of things like spaghetti, salt, pepper, jade, and silk. While Wood makes a compelling case, she can't emphatically prove her claim. If Polo did visit China in 1275 C.E., why is there no court documentation of his governorship of Yangshou or his 17-year relationship with Mongol leader Kublai Kan? In Polo's 1299 epic travelogue, *Divisament dou Monde* (*Description of the World*), why doesn't he mention such Chinese peculiarities as chopsticks, tea drinking, and the Great Wall? Wood theorizes that Polo may have taken details from Persian and Arabic guidebooks on China acquired by the Polo family and that Polo never ventured beyond the family's trading posts on the Black Sea and in Constantinople.

The Art of Astrology

Astrologers analyze cycles of time. They study the position and movements of the sun, moon, stars, and planets in association with the consistency of human characteristics and the occurrence of human events on earth. Based on the position of the heavenly bodies at any given point in time, astrologers can then "map" your fate. In China, the imperial court relied on a stable of learned astrologers to map out the most auspicious and inauspicious time to do just about everything, including the signing of documents, the construction of buildings, travel, military excursions, and marriage.

Astrology is considered an art because its predictions are based on supposition. While an astrologer can forecast your fate, the conclusions cannot be scientifically proven. Astrology requires you to believe in a force of destiny predetermined by the cosmos. This is not to say that destiny replaces free will. Astrological calculations can foretell only *possibilities*. The astrologer who foretold accurate possibilities was held in high esteem and paid handsomely. The astrologer who was proven wrong was not so lucky. He was either exiled or executed.

Feng shui derives, in part, from astrological observations. While feng shui studies a building's fate, a synthesis of heaven (time) and earth (space) luck, methods of Chinese astrology like The Four Pillars of Destiny (Ziping Bazi), and Purple Constellation Fate Computation (Ziwei Doushu) focus on man luck; a person's natal character. You'll learn about The Four Pillars of Destiny in Part 7, "Fate or Free Will: What's Your Destiny?"

> ### Master Class
>
> A wide range of divinatory methods was used in China. Besides astrology, the Chinese practiced chronomancy (an astro-calendrical system of determining favorable and unfavorable days), oneiromancy (divination based on dreams), physiognomy (divination based on facial features), scapulimancy and plastromancy (divination based on heating and interpreting the cracks formed on the scapula or shoulder bones of animals and the plastron or bottom shell of turtles), and sortilege (divination by drawing lots). The last method is especially significant to the formulation of the *Yijing* (*The Book of Changes*), a book of divination written by King Wen and his son, the Duke of Zhou, about 3,000 years ago.

The Science of Astronomy

Astronomy is based on factual information derived from studying the cosmos. Chinese astronomers dealt with the practical needs of society. They developed almanacs and calendars. Because China's farmers produced food for every stratum of civilization, it was important for them to know the best times to plant and harvest their crops. According to markings found on a bone fragment some 3,500 years ago, Chinese astronomers understood the year is 365¼ days long, a statistic strikingly similar to today's precise measurement of 365.24219.

Aided by astronomical instruments, the Chinese also observed and recorded a number of celestial events:

- They began noting eclipses of the moon in 1361 B.C.E. and eclipses of the sun in 1217 B.C.E.

- They recorded a nova (an exploding star) in the area now known as Antares in 1300 B.C.E.

- They witnessed Haley's comet in 467 B.C.E.

- They documented a supernova (a really big exploding star) in 1054 C.E. Their accurate observation allowed modern astronomers to establish that the supernova was the origin of the Crab Nebula.

By 400 B.C.E., Chinese skywatchers had recorded 1,464 stars, dividing many of them into the 28 constellations of the zodiac.

Confucianism and Daoism:

Beginning in the sixth and fourth centuries B.C.E. respectively, two main schools of philosophy flourished in China: Confucianism and Daoism.

Confucianism, based on the teachings of Confucius (551–479 B.C.E.), was a system of ethics designed to cultivate moral virtues and social values in humankind. It dealt with practical and earthly affairs. Confucius's primary interest lay in proper behavior and social harmony. He emphasized rational knowledge and education. Later on, obedience to one's parents became one of the most important virtues of Confucianism. The philosophy became so influential that it was taught in Chinese schools from the advent of the Han reign in 206 B.C.E. to the founding of the People's Republic of China in 1949.

Daoism (also spelled Taoism), on the other hand, was concerned with intuitive insight and heavenly affairs. One could attain intuitive or true knowledge by communing with nature and being at one with it, the Dao (or what Westerns variously call God, the Sea of Consciousness, the Higher Power). To understand the Dao (also spelled Tao) meant to recognize the inherent unity of all things and live your life accordingly. This meant trusting your intuition, your gut instinct, your sixth sense. The person who could cultivate his or her spirituality and develop this kind of character is following the Dao.

Wise Words

Confucianism, based on the sixth-century B.C.E. teachings of Confucius, is a system of ethics designed to cultivate moral perfection. **Daoism** is concerned with intuitive knowledge acquired by communicating with nature and being at one with it, the Dao. The founding fathers of Daoism emerged as a group of like-minded persons who lived and taught from the fourth to the second centuries B.C.E.

There is great debate about who founded the school of Daoism. While many steadfastly hold the opinion that Laozi (also spelled Lao Tzu) founded the school, many contemporary scholars disagree. In fact, they maintain that Laozi, whom revered scholar Richard Wilhelm describes as a "shadowy figure," is not an individual, but a committee of like-minded people, who lived and taught from the fourth to the second centuries B.C.E.

Huh? This is perplexing. But, what of Laozi's famous work, the *Daode jing* (also spelled *Tao Teh Ching*)? Well, how this legendary figure is connected to the text is a mystery (and not our concern here). However, we do know that the *Daode jing* was actually written in the Warring States Period (403–221 B.C.E.), at least 200 years after its purported authorship. We know this because the text is commented on and criticized by various people of that era. Furthermore, the *Daode jing* and another great Daoist work called the *Zhuangzi* (also spelled *Chuang Tzu*) was written by an actual person of the same name before the school of Daoism emerged in the Han dynasty (206 B.C.E.–220 C.E.).

Experience vs. Experiment

To the Daoists, rational thinking and experimentation (hallmarks of the Western mindset) are totally inadequate methods of understanding nature's truths. True knowledge extends beyond sensory perception; it can be experienced only in a meditative state of consciousness. The Daoists quiet their minds to let nature's truths flow into their beings from a supreme force.

 Notable Quotable

Without going out of the door
You can know the ways of the world.
Without peeping through the window,
You can see the Way of Heaven.
The farther you go,
The less you know.
Thus, the sage knows without traveling,
Sees without looking,
And achieves without ado.

—*Daode jing*

The Daoists believe you can't comprehend the Dao, the unnamed and unknowable, by describing it with words. Words were limited, nature was limitless. Words restricted, they barricaded the self from the universe of truth. This is why the Daoists and other Eastern mystics express their teachings in the form of aphorisms (concise statements of a principle or truth), huatou (paradoxical statements meant to be meditated upon to gain sudden intuitive enlightenment), or illustrations. These short verses showed the inconsistencies with rational communication.

Reversal Is the Movement of the Dao

When anything comes to its extreme, be it on the natural or human plane, a reversal to the other extreme takes place. This idea is central to both the Daoists and the Confucianists. But what does it mean, you ask?

It means that everything is cyclical, moving through ceaseless cycles of birth, growth, decay, and death. Everything is in a constant state of flux and change. Everything is interrelated and interconnected. With the extreme of winter comes the beginning of spring and renewal. With the extreme of night comes day. With the extreme of war comes peace. With the extreme of despair comes hope, and so forth.

To achieve anything, the general rule of thumb is to acknowledge its opposite. You need not experience it literally. Noting and respecting its possibility will help to keep you aware of sudden shifts of fortune. For example, being content and humble safeguards the possibility that the opposite nature won't be reached. If you have wealth, recognize the possibility that you may lose it. This concept has greatly impacted the Chinese to this day. It's all about balance and harmony.

This polarity of opposites is known as the theory of yin and yang. It is a fundamental principle of feng shui. You'll learn all about yin and yang in Chapter 5, "The Principle of Yin and Yang," but we'll touch on it in the following sections.

Change Is in the Wind

Generally speaking, the philosophy of the *Yijing*, or *Book of Changes*, is the first known attempt by the Chinese to formulate a system of knowledge around the interplay of opposites (yin and yang). The *Yijing* is a deceptively simple yet complex system of understanding the patterns of change in our universe. The *Yijing* can foretell your present and future prospects made manifest by changes you make in your attitude, actions, and activity. In other words, the *Yijing* suggests the appropriate change to achieve the desired result.

These patterns of change were recorded symbolically in the form of solid (yang) and broken (yin) lines called trigrams and hexagrams. While we won't concern ourselves with the 64 hexagrams (six-tiered configurations of solid and broken lines) comprising the *Yijing*, the eight fundamental trigrams (three-tiered configurations of solid and broken lines) are central to practicing classical feng shui. Simply, the eight trigrams represent transitional stages of all possible natural and human situations.

The eight fundamental trigrams.

You'll be learning all about the meaning of these trigrams in Chapter 7, "The Principle of the Eight Trigrams."

The Masked Origin of the Yijing

A lot of misinformation has been written about the origin of the *Yijing*. For the record, here is a short chronology of its origins (part mythical, part historical). For more detailed information, please see *The Complete Idiot's Guide to the I Ching* (Alpha Books, 2001) by Elizabeth Moran and Master Joseph Yu.

Initially, the *Yijing* was called the *Zhouyi*, or *The Changes of Zhou*. Initiated by King Wen and completed by his son, the Duke of Zhou of the Zhou dynasty (1045–221 B.C.E.), the *Zhouyi* draws on information gained by some of China's legendary figures. Specifically, the 8 trigrams and 64 hexagrams (composed of 2 trigrams each) are thought to have been devised by Fuxi.

As the story goes, the mythical sage-king Fuxi invented the eight trigrams after observing celestial and terrestrial activity. The idea was to create heaven on earth, to emulate nature's perfection. Perhaps to reward his efforts, Fuxi received a gift from heaven, a diagram of the perfect world. A world that was motionless, void of change. Sometime later, heaven bestowed a gift on another sage-king, Yu the Great. He also received a diagram, but this one represented the world in motion. Called the Luoshu, this diagram (its parts correlated to the eight trigrams) provides the foundation for a classical method of feng shui called Flying Star, the subject of Part 5, "Feng Shui Mechanics 201."

Returning to the development of the *Yijing*, sometime during the Han dynasty (206 B.C.E.–220 C.E.), scholars set about collecting the great texts of their culture. At this time, commentaries, known as the *Ten Wings*, were attached to *Zhouyi*. Basically, the seven essays "philosophized" the oracle by attempting to give meaning to the arrangement of yin and yang lines composing each hexagram and the archaic text. The new compilation was called the *Yijing*.

Changing Patterns

You might be interested to learn that trigram and hexagram symbols were not part of the *Zhouyi* text. In the 1970s, Zheng Zhenglang, a Chinese scholar of the Chinese Academy of Social Sciences in Beijing, discovered that the symbols were recorded in numeric form, a finding made after examining markings on oracle bones and bronze sacrificial containers dating from 1500–1000 B.C.E. (the late Shang and early Zhou dynastic periods). Zheng's discovery proved that from the beginning, the *Yijing* was based on numerological divination. Looking back to the previous chapter, you'll remember that the Chinese believed their ancestors spoke to them using numbers. In other words, they believed the deceased manipulated the stalks of yarrow (the instruments used in a casting procedure that yields a hexagram, the answer to a question). Over time, the collection and examination of the divinatory records produced a text that matched a question with a numeric answer, and an answer with a likely result.

But, while the Chinese believe their forebears were responsible for imparting wisdom and clarity, you may believe the answer is derived from the holistic realm of pure knowledge, a totality that can be analyzed mathematically.

How Does Feng Shui Fit In?

Classical feng shui combines elements of astrology and astronomy, geology, physics, mathematics, philosophy, and intuition—all the stuff you've just read about.

Now that you understand feng shui's components, you can better appreciate what the whole of feng shui means. Feng shui is the art and science of analyzing nature's forces with the intent of influencing its positive manifestations in you. A balanced environment leads to better health, increased prosperity, and beneficial relationships. And who doesn't want that?

> **Feng Facts**
>
> The term "feng shui" was first used in Guo Pu's (276–324 C.E.) *Zangshu* (*Book of Burial*), a short text describing the disposition of qi (life's breath) on the earth's plane. Yet, earlier, during the Warring States Period (403–221 B.C.E.), feng shui was known as an art of divination called kanyu. "Kan" means "way of heaven" and "yu," "way of the earth." Together, kanyu translates: "The way of heaven and earth."

Neolithic Feng Shui

Feng shui is a lot older than you might think. It predates Daoism, and even the *Yijing*. So how old do you think feng shui is—2,000, 4,000, or 6,000 years old? If you guessed the latter, you're right—for the time being, anyway.

In 1988, a Neolithic gravesite was excavated in Henan province in central China. It revealed that the ancient Chinese were practicing some form of primitive feng shui some 6,000 years ago.

The head of the gravesite is rounded and points toward the south. The grave is squared at the body's feet, facing north. This arrangement conforms to the Chinese view of the cosmos. Symbolically, the sky is represented as round or domed, and the earth as square or flat. On each side of the remains, and outlined with shells, is a representation of two Chinese constellations—the azure dragon and the white tiger. A representation of the Big Dipper (Beidou) lies in the center. These artifacts testify to the fact that the Neolithic Chinese were already orienting their graves with the revolution of the Big Dipper around the North Star, the polestar (in Ursa Minor) in the northern hemisphere toward which the axis of the earth points.

The Form School of Feng Shui

The *Form School* (*Xingfa*) is the first and oldest school of feng shui officially dating to Qing Wuzi's (whom many believe is a fictitious figure) late Han (190–220 C.E.) text, the *Zangjing* or *Classic of Burial*. Some 100 years later, Guo Pu clarified and expanded upon the *Zangjing* in his book, the *Zangshu* or the *Book of Burial*, the same text from where the term feng shui derives.

Even before Daoism and Confucianism, ancestor worship was an intrinsic and important part of the Chinese belief system. They believed the spirits of the deceased directly affected the well-being of the living. Fortunes could be made or lost depending, in some measure, on the favorable location and orientation of their ancestors' tombs. If you think this is an outdated custom, think again. Today, feng shui masters run a brisk business selecting the most auspicious gravesites for their clientele.

The orientation of homes is also a part of Form School feng shui. Landforms and waterways were intensely scrutinized to determine the location of the dragon's lair (long xue), the place on the terrain where qi converges. The place that qi can be carried by the wind (feng) and settle in water (shui). In today's urbanized world, buildings, fences, and hedges represent terrestrial features and roadways represent watercourses. You'll learn more about this in Chapter 8, " Turtles, Tigers, and Dragons, Oh My: Evaluating Your Environment," and Chapter 9, "Home Sweet Home: Evaluating Your House and Its Surroundings."

The intuitive approach characterized Form School feng shui.

The Compass School of Feng Shui

The term *Compass School* is a Western invention. In Chinese, the school that uses a compass and analyzes heavenly (time) and earthly (space) forces is called *Liqi Pai, Patterns of Qi School*. Because the English translation is a mouthful, we'll conform to the Western vernacular.

Formally dating to the Spring and Autumn Period (722–481 B.C.E.) with a simplistic method called Diagramatic Houses for the Five Families (Tuzhai Wuxing), which is no longer used, the Compass School is an umbrella term encompassing a host of more sophisticated techniques that are still widely used today. Flying Star (Xuankong Feixing), Three Harmonies (Sanhe), Mystical Doors (Qi Men), and Changing Trigrams/Eight House/Eight Mansions/The East West System (Yigua) are examples of Compass School methods.

The Compass School is based on the concept that each of the eight cardinal directions holds a different type of qi. Around this central premise, other factors are added, including astrology and numerology. The Compass School method is very computational, relying on intellect, observation, and experimentation rather than intuitive insights.

The tool of the trade is, you guessed it, the compass. An early version dating to about 83 C.E. was a two-part, south-pointing instrument—a metal spoon made of magnetic lodestone and a square baseplate (see the color insert) called a sinan. This developed into what is now called a luopan compass (see the cover photo) used by practitioners today. The luopan has anywhere from 4 to 40 concentric rings of information featuring things like the 8 fundamental trigrams, the 28 constellations, the 5 phases of qi, and the 9 "stars" or numbers of the Luoshu.

But, for your purposes, all you need is a basic protractor compass with clear markings (refer to Chapter 1, "What Is Feng Shui?" for specific guidelines in choosing a compass).

Master Class

The ancient Chinese choose to think of a compass needle pointing south because it is the region from which warmth, light, and goodness come; whereas cold, darkness, and barbarian attacks come from the north.

Feng Shui Today

Today, both Form School and Compass School methods are used to perform an accurate feng shui reading. For the most part, today's practitioners have combined both schools into one system commonly referred to as "classical" or "traditional" feng shui.

In the next chapter, you'll learn about qi, the physical and metaphysical life force underlying all things.

The Least You Need to Know

- For 2,000 years, beginning in 500 B.C.E., the Chinese led the West in scientific and technological advances.

- Feng shui was born out of China's reverence for nature. The practice stems from the Neolithic Chinese.

- Form School is a classical method that studies landforms and waterways with the intention of locating the place on the terrain where qi converges.

- Compass School, a term invented by Westerners, is called the Patterns of Qi School in China. It studies how time and space impact the livelihood and health of an individual.

- Form School and Compass School have merged into one school of thought called "classical" or "traditional" feng shui.

Chapter 4

Qi Wiz! It's Life's Force!

In This Chapter

◆ Qi: the life force at the heart of it all

◆ How other cultures define qi

◆ The three primal forces of qi: heaven qi, earth qi, and human qi

◆ Good vibes and bad vibes: types of qi

What we've been describing as nature's "forces" is what the Chinese call *qi* (also spelled ch'i). Qi has many meanings. It's described as the air we breathe. It's the earth's magnetic field, cosmic radiation, and the sun's light. Qi is our spirit. Qi is luck. As you shall soon see, qi underlies all these things and more. While this may seem somewhat abstract to us Westerners, Eastern cultures believe this holistic force governs our health, wealth, and happiness. Feng shui seeks to harness qi's positive aspects to better our well-being.

Now, to be perfectly clear, the existence of qi can't be fully scientifically proven. In fact, some of qi's more mystical aspects can never be proven using quantitative measurement. For example, can you prove the existence of your "sixth sense"? Can you prove luck or fate? Can you prove intuition? Surely not. Yet, most us believe these things exist. Simply, qi's metaphysical or supernatural features defy measurement.

Wise Words

Qi is the underlying and unifying "substance" and "soul" of all things. Both physical and metaphysical, qi is the nourishing force at the heart, growth, and development of the heavens, earth, and humanity. It is also called "life's breath."

But, we shouldn't be too hasty and dismiss this notion of a partly nonmeasurable force. After all, it wasn't so long ago that Benjamin Franklin "discovered" electricity—considered a mysterious force of nature at the time. We certainly have harnessed this energy, making our lives more pleasurable in the process. And what about the discovery of x-rays, radioactivity, and subatomic particles? All have led to a profound revolution in how we view the world.

This chapter is all about understanding qi, the foundation upon which many Eastern practices are based. So, keep your mind open and let's take a journey into the force unifying us all.

What Is Qi?

Simply, qi (pronounced chee) is the underlying quintessence, "soul," and "substance" of all things. It is the all-encompassing, all-permeating, unifying force at the heart of the heavenly, earthly, and human realms. Both physical and metaphysical, qi is the fundamental, vital, nourishing force that drives life forward. It is the field of information connecting us all. Although there is no direct English translation for qi, it can best be called "life's breath."

This definition may seem rather vague and even abstract. But actually, the idea of qi bears a striking resemblance to the quantum field in modern physics. Fritjof Capra in his best-selling book, *The Tao of Physics* (Shambhala Publications, 1991), makes the correlation: "Like the quantum field, qi is conceived as a tenuous and nonperceptible form of matter which is present throughout space and can condense into solid material objects. The field, or qi, is not only the underlying essence of all material objects, but also carries their mutual interactions in the form of waves."

Feng Facts

The Chinese concept of qi was first recorded in the *Ten Wings*, a Warring States Period (403–221 B.C.E.) text appended to the *Zhouyi* (*The Changes of Zhou*), which was later renamed the *Yijing* (*The Book of Changes*). For a detailed discussion about the historical development of qi, please consult Chapter 8 of *The Complete Idiot's Guide to the I Ching* (Alpha Books, 2001).

Still need clarification? Qi is the "stuff" of and behind it all. It's the stuff that breathes life into plants, animals, the mountains, oceans, and us. It's the stuff of dreams, intuition, fate, and luck. It's the stuff at the core of non-living matter such as airplanes, buildings, and the chair on which you sit. It's the stuff acupuncturists stimulate with their needles. It's the stuff martial artists conjure up to split solid objects. And, it's the stuff feng shui practitioners harness to improve the health, wealth, and relationships of their clients.

Qi Around the World

The concept of qi is not unique to the Chinese. It's also known to other cultures:

- Ki to the Japanese
- Prana to the Hindus
- Pneuma to the Greeks
- Ankh to the Egyptians
- Ruah to the Hebrews
- Tane to the Hawaiians
- Arunquiltha to the Australian Aborigine
- Orenda to the Iroquois

Whatever you choose to call it, identifying, controlling, and directing this invisible life force for the benefit of your well-being is what feng shui's all about.

Qi on the Move

Qi moves. It is in a perpetual process of change. Qi accumulates, disperses, expands, and condenses. It moves fast, slow, in, out, up, and down. Qi meanders and spirals. It flows along straight, angular, and curved pathways. It rides the wind (feng) and is retained in water (shui). There's no escaping qi's influence. We are all products of, and subject to, qi's enormous power.

The Three Forces of Qi Energy

The Chinese believe three primal forces of qi sustain all that exists: heaven qi, earth qi, and human qi. To ignore their effects on your body is like ignoring a virus that weakens and depletes your strength. Viruses and other setbacks (like financial loss, unemployment, and illness) can be directly challenged through a harnessing of qi's beneficial qualities, leading to a strengthened body, an alert mind, and a full and contented spirit.

What does this mean exactly? As you will come to learn in later chapters, the ancient Chinese have determined how to manipulate qi such that it promotes harmony in your living/working space. When there is balance and harmony in your environment, there's a good chance your being will be in balance, too. Of course, you must also maintain a proper diet and exercise regime. You must get a good night's rest. You must live by the Golden Rule. All of these components foster a healthful whole. Only when we are at our optimum capacity can we be inspired to succeed.

Within these forces, there exists an abundance of other lines of qi that impact every aspect of our lives—as you'll see a little later in this chapter.

We are the balance of heavenly and earthly forces.

Heaven Qi

What comes from above is known as heaven qi. It's the first force of nature. It's the qi that spirals down from the celestial heavens—the sun, moon, planets, and stars. If you have difficulty accepting the idea that heavenly qi can affect us, consider the sun, the central star of our solar system. Without its force, life would cease to exist. Disregard its force, and you may be prone to sunburn, heatstroke, skin cancer, and even death.

And the moon? Well, if the moon can deform the shape of the solid earth and the oceans roughly every 12 hours, doesn't it stand to reason that its forces will, in some measure, affect you? After all, the earth's main component is water—and so is ours. In fact, when the moon is full, we tend to retain water. Also, the migration and reproductive patterns of animals, fish, and birds conform to or are in harmony with the moon's phases. The same applies to vegetation. Studies have shown that planting seeds two days before to seven days after a new moon yields a better crop.

Weather qi is also a component of heaven qi. There's no question that weather phenomena affect our well-being. Extremes of cold "chill us to the bone," while extremes of heat create "dog-day afternoons" and heighten passions. For some people, lack of daylight and long periods of rain cause depression—even suicide. Although this is more common in northern countries, any variant in weather can influence a person's health and mood.

Finally, heaven qi is associated with time, a factor indubitably associated with change and transformation. The time of day and season changes as a result of celestial activity. The time your home was constructed is essential information, for it determines, in part, the inherent personality of your dwelling.

> **CAUTION**
>
> **Feng Alert**
>
> If you feel different during a full moon, it's not just your imagination! A condition called "Full-Moon Madness" can occur when an excess of fluid accumulates in the skull, causing some of us to feel increased levels of passion, anxiety, and tension. In fact, the word lunatic ("luna" means moon in Latin) derives from the notion that the moon's phases produce lunacy, insanity.

Earth Qi

The forces of mountains, waterways, deserts, valleys, and plains all carry earth qi currents that can affect our physical health, temperament, and compatibility with others. While mountain ranges protect us from harsh elements, they also provide psychological support. We tend to feel more stable and grounded if there is a mountain to our backs.

In classical feng shui, the mountain force is synonymous with the yin or female force of nature. Like a mother guarding her children from illness caused by gusting winds and torrential rain, the mountain force governs our health and relationships. A feng shui practitioner's goal is to study and direct qi associated with the external mountains (or man-made mountains such as buildings and tall hedges) surrounding the dwelling, and internal mountains made manifest as walls and large furniture so that they bolster good health and relations with other people.

Conversely, watercourses correspond to the yang or male force. Traditionally, the man is responsible for generating wealth. Like water's flow, wealth qi is retained in lakes and oceans. It's carried down rivers, streets, and hallways. It flows through windows and doorways. All of these things must be considered when assessing a person's living and/or working space.

Finding a balance among natural elements is the fundamental premise of classical feng shui. You'll learn more about this in Chapter 8, " Turtles, Tigers, and Dragons, Oh My: Evaluating Your Environment," and Chapter 9, "Home Sweet Home: Evaluating Your House and Its Surroundings," as well as in Part 5, "Feng Shui Mechanics 201," where mountain (health and relationship) and water (wealth) qi manifest as number schemes on a qi map.

The earth's magnetic field is also a component of earth qi. Coupled with the time your house was constructed, the magnetic orientation characterizes your home's qi, its innate essence. It's important also to understand that the electromagnetic field influences the quality of qi flowing into and inhabiting your house. There's no question that fields generated by high-voltage power lines and modern-day electrical conveniences affect our health in some way. We must be mindful of such potential and exercise caution when we use electrical appliances and live in close proximity to power plants, electrical transformers, and the like.

Human Qi

You have qi, too. Your own qi is marked at birth, the time when you inhaled your first breath. Like a fingerprint, your qi is singular and unique. In feng shui, the year of your birth is a vital source of information. The energy you were born into (your birth year) determines how your life force is compatible to that of other people and to your home's qi. This notion will become clearer when you learn a method of feng shui called Eight House—the sole subject of Part 4, "Feng Shui Mechanics 101."

For now, understand that many Western scientists and medical experts are accepting and embracing the idea that some kind of vital and holistic force exists within the body that regulates the totality of our mental and physical well-being. Moreover, this bio-network connects us with the whole of our environment, and on a broader scale, the collective consciousness, the source of pure knowledge. In fact, the force field emanating from your body (what many call an aura) can actually be captured on film. Known as Kirlian photography, the technique was developed by two Russian scientists, Semyon and Valentina Kirlian.

While the connective force within the human body is known by many names in the West (the odic force, life fields, entelechy, animal electricity, subtle spirit, pneuma, for example), generally the progressive Western pioneers who have adopted the idea believe the field is electrical in nature. Well, human qi may very well be partly electrical, but let's not lose sight of the fact that aspects of this unifying force cannot be measured or fully understood with our five senses of sight, taste, smell, touch, and hearing. Harkening back to the beginning of this chapter, remember that qi is physical *and* metaphysical (beyond physical or supernatural), the latter including fate, luck, and intuition.

Nevertheless, it seems that experts in divergent fields (physics, biology, psychology, religion, anthropology, neurology, and linguistics, for example) are coming together, realizing that the question about our existence and purpose in life cannot be answered by any one part. Using an analogy, a cake is created by the fusion of distinct and different ingredients. Similarly, the auspiciousness or inauspiciousness of a house is a result of layers of merging information. Get the idea?

Feng Facts

Besides feng shui (which seeks to balance your home's qi), the Chinese also use acupuncture to restore balance to your body's qi. They believe 14 interconnected main qi highways (meridians) exist on each side of the body that surface at some 360 acupuncture points. The meridians correspond to one or more specific areas or organs. When an imbalance or illness occurs, an acupuncturist stimulates the appropriate points with needles. Also, there's The Four Pillars of Destiny. This is a method of Chinese astrology that studies your birth qi. Here, you can learn to calculate your luck. You can determine the colors, environment, and career best suited to you. We offer the beginning level of Four Pillars in Part 7, "Fate or Free Will: What's Your Destiny?"

Feeling Qi's Power

How qi directly or indirectly affects you is vital to your state of being. To illustrate this point, let's do a simple exercise. But first, turn off the television and radio, and find a quiet place free of distractions. It's important that you actually participate in this exercise to fully understand how qi's flow impacts you.

Ready?

Now, look at the following photo. Imagine you are sitting on the bench facing the waterfall. If we told you that suddenly the falls rushed at you in violent gushes of water, wind, and noise, buffeting and overwhelming your being, how would you feel? Scared, confused, disoriented, or tired perhaps? But what if we told you the water gently sprays in a cool cascade of mist and soft, gentle breezes, soothing and refreshing your body? Does this sensation promote feelings of relaxation, balance, comfort, and security? The feeling is quite different, isn't it?

*Cascade Park, Monterey
Park, California.*

(Photograph by Val Biktashev)

What we've demonstrated is how the flow of qi can affect your mood—and ultimately your health—over a period of time. Nourishing qi circulates. It gently revolves and curves. It creates a healthful, balanced environment. Strong qi (or what is actually called *sha qi*—a term you'll soon learn) disturbs, especially if you're in its powerful path. Strong qi can cause mental and physical illness. Qi can also be weak. Weak qi is stagnant and sickly. A stuffy, airless room is an example of weak qi.

So, can we control weak or negative qi? Absolutely! If the waterfall featured in the preceding photograph was a flood of gushing water, wouldn't you move? If your house is stuffy, wouldn't you instinctively open a window to let fresh air circulate? While much of feng shui relies on plain old common sense, there are factors that are not obvious. Like determining the quality of qi your home innately carries. And, the change in qi ushered in with each new year. You'll learn how to determine these numerological aspects in upcoming chapters.

Sheng Qi

Sheng qi is positive qi. It carries auspicious currents that nourish your well-being. We can detect some of sheng qi's aspects with our five senses:

1. **Sight sheng.** Manicured gardens and lawns, neatly painted exteriors, tidy, clean, and organized interiors, and happy and cooperative people. Basically, sight sheng is anything you find pleasing to the eye.

Wise Words

Sheng qi is positive qi carrying auspicious currents that can influence your well-being.

2. **Sound sheng.** Babbling brooks/fountains, chirping birds, wind chimes, cooing babies, certain types of music. It's important to understand, however, that what you may consider soothing to the ear, may be an auditory disturbance to someone else. For example, many people prefer quiet solitude or the peace of rural areas or suburbs. Others thrive on the high-intensity atmosphere of cities. While you may find classical music soothing, your friend may disagree, changing the station to rock-and-roll.

3. **Touch sheng.** Smooth surfaces, pets, a warm bath, a kiss, a massage, silk, satin, and velvet are examples of touch sheng.

4. **Smell sheng.** Flowers, perfume, scented candles, and food inspire smell sheng. Again, what you find a pleasing, fragrant odor, another person may find sickening. Cigarette smoke is an example of subjective smell sheng.

5. **Taste sheng.** Home-cooked meals, comfort food, chocolate, a fine wine or liqueur are all associated with taste sheng. It is anything you find satisfying. If this includes tobacco products, then, for you, these items are taste sheng.

There also exists a sixth sheng qi. Somewhat esoteric and metaphysical, it can be compared to your "sixth sense." It is the "vibe" you feel when you're about to get a raise or a promotion. It's how you feel when you "click" with someone. It's the feeling of being "in love." Sheng qi is the "look" of confidence and contentment. It's the resonance of helpful and kind people.

Sha Qi

Sha qi is negative qi. It carries inauspicious currents that create negative influences on your body. Sha qi is anything antagonistic to your five senses:

1. **Sight sha.** Glaring lights; dark places; offensive, disturbing art; clutter; trash; dead or dying things; and anything you find threatening or looming. We believe a good example of the latter is the interior of the pyramid-theme Luxor Hotel in Las Vegas.

Upon entering the inverted interior, you are at the mercy of overhanging tiers of floors, which can cause vertigo. It looks and feels as if the upper levels can and will come crashing down on you like a house of cards. (We left with a headache, feeling disoriented and quite off balance!) Sight sha also includes acts of violence, prejudice, or intolerance.

2. **Sound sha.** Noise pollution like traffic, sirens, construction work, loud arguments, screaming babies, and certain types of music are examples of sound sha.

3. **Touch sha.** Grime, filth, dust, and mold; splinters, cracks, and tears. Maneuvering a rickety staircase or bridge, skating on thin ice, and scaling unsteady terrain are examples of touch sha, as are unwanted sexual advances and physical aggression.

4. **Smell sha.** Pollution, exhaust fumes, mildew, rot, pollen, and toxins are examples of smell sha.

5. **Taste sha.** Bitter, sour, rotten, food. Unfamiliar foodstuffs might prove distasteful and unpleasant experiences. Yet, we must remember that raw fish, insects, and seaweed are considered normal foods by many cultures. Vegetarians find animal products unpalatable.

Just like there exists an extrasensory sheng qi, so, too, is there a sixth sha qi. It is the "vibe" you feel when "Something's in the air," or when "You can cut the tension with a knife." It's the queasy feeling you get when "Something's wrong," or when you feel you are being watched or followed. This sixth sha also takes the form of anger, hate, and jealousy. It can be the resonance of "evil spirits."

Poison Arrow Qi

Also called, "killing breath," poison arrow qi hits you like a bullet. The offending culprit can be straight roads, opposing doorways or windows; sharp, pointed edges of objects and buildings; and anything else directed at you in a straight line.

Poison arrow qi is extremely inauspicious and carries misfortune, illness, and even disaster. You will be learning more about poison arrow qi and how to avoid and remedy it in Chapters 8 and 9.

The Holy Trinity, Chinese Style

As you're learning, feng shui is the art and science of living in harmony with your environment and gaining the maximum benefit by being in the right place at the right time. The key phrase being, living in the "right place" (or space), built in the "right time."

Simply, with humankind acting as matchmaker, heaven and earth qi marry. While the changing forces of heaven qi correspond to the time in which your house was constructed, the stable force of earth qi corresponds to the magnetic space it sits on. Viewing it this way, wouldn't it make sense to produce a good marriage, one generating prosperity, compatibility, and good health? Its influence affecting your well-being positively and productively?

In the next chapter, you'll learn about yin and yang, the two dynamic qi forces of nature.

The Least You Need to Know

◆ Qi is the underlying "substance" and "soul" of all things.

◆ Heaven, earth, and human qi compose all that is.

◆ Sheng qi is positive qi that can influence your well-being.

◆ Sha qi is negative qi that can impact your health and livelihood.

Part 2

The Fundamental Principles of Feng Shui

Before you walk you must crawl. Before you read and write you must learn the alphabet. Before you practice feng shui you must learn its fundamental principles—the same principles that form the basis of Chinese medicine, acupuncture, martial arts, and military strategy.

First, you'll learn about yin and yang, the eternal interplay of opposites governing all that exists. Next, you'll learn about the five phases, the backbone of feng shui and other Chinese disciplines. (The five phases are particularly important because their principles hold the key to remedying and enhancing qi.) Finally, you'll learn about the eight trigrams. These relate to a host of things such as the magnetic directions, familial relations, and parts of the body.

The Principle of Yin and Yang

In This Chapter

◆ The source of everything
◆ Yin: The passive principle
◆ Yang: The active principle

Can there be male and no female? Can there be left and no right? Can there be hot and no cold? How about day and no night, or anger and no happiness? Of course not. Although each is a counterpart of the other, each is dependent on the other's existence. Separate but together, yin and yang illustrate the evolution of all things.

The concept of yin and yang is the first principle of feng shui. Initially yin and yang meant the shady (yin) and sunny (yang) sides of a hill, an idea ascribed to Zhou ancestor Gong Liu when he set about selecting an auspicious site for his people. However, some five centuries later during the mid to late Zhou dynasty (c. 770–481 B.C.E.), yin and yang came to symbolize the two primal forces of qi. Yin was classified as the female principle of nature, and thus, was regarded as passive and weak. Yang was classified as the male principle of nature and was regarded as active and strong.

The yin-yang and wuxing (the five phases of qi which you'll learn about in the next chapter) models were used to explain the structure, order, and change within the universe. Perhaps the primary champion of correlating the cosmological theories was the Naturalist philosopher, Zou Yan (305–240 B.C.E.). A follower of Confucian and Mencian teachings, Zou Yan was given considerable space as a leading intellectual thinker in the *Shiji* (*Records of the Grand Historian*), a Western Han (206–24 B.C.E.) text assembled by Sima Tan and his son, Sima Qian.

The concept of yin and yang is firmly embedded in Chinese philosophy, science, and medicine. In fact, the terms yin and yang originate in the *Dazhuan* or *Great Commentary* of the *Yijing*. The *Dazhuan*, along with six other essays (collectively called the *Ten Wings* or *Shi Yi*, in Chinese), were philosophical theories about the meaning of the divinatory text written some 600 years earlier by King Wen and his son, the Duke of Zhou.

Needless to say, the principle of yin and yang is fundamental to understanding and practicing feng shui. Master the principle and you will forever change the way you interact with people, your living/working environment, and the outside natural world.

The Big Bang, Chinese Style

Ever since the dawn of humankind we've wondered where we come from. Where did it all begin? Why are we here? What happens when we die? Indeed, the mystery of life intrigues us all, spawning all sorts of theories attempting to answer these age-old questions. Many of us believe an all-knowing, all-seeing presence created everything. In the West, this presence is variously called God, the Supreme Force, or the Sea of Consciousness. Some believe we're a product of pure happenstance. Others even maintain extraterrestrial creatures planted us on planet earth as colonists. (Of course, there's also the strictly scientific approach, but we won't get into that here.)

No one really knows for sure the true source of existence. Yet, our curiosity and determination drive us forward to investigate and understand the unknown.

The Nothing of Everything

The Chinese Daoists have their own idea. By observing nature's forces and monitoring their effect on our bodies, they've concluded we are a microcosm of the macrocosmic natural world. This means the microcosmic ("small") universe within our bodies is a reflection of the macrocosmic ("big") universe outside of our bodies. Therefore, a comparison can be drawn between our own birth and the birth of the universe.

The Daoists believe that we come from a great void out of which everything emerges. They call this great void *Wuji*. Wuji is believed to be the fountainhead of creation, the source of pure knowledge. It is expressed as a circle, an unbroken whole.

Symbolizing eternal motion and wholeness, the circle may appear empty, containing nothing. Yet, actually, it's full of possibility. Similar to the womb, it is both empty *and* full. When an egg (yin) is fertilized by a sperm (yang), the unified state is broken. The tranquil nucleus containing ceaseless possibilities is set in motion, ready to give life. Change occurs. The single primordial entity divides, forming the two fundamental qi forces of the universe—yin and yang. They are represented as tadpole-like symbols, with a bulge at the top for the head and a pointed end for the tail. Since fish swim head first, this shape accounts for taiji's (the composite of yin and yang) "movement," or balancing motion.

Yin: The Feminine Side

Yin is expressed as the stable matter of earth. It contracts and condenses. Yin represents the passive principle in nature exhibited as darkness, cold, and wetness. On a human level, yin symbolizes femininity and inertia. Other traits of yin are shown in the following figure.

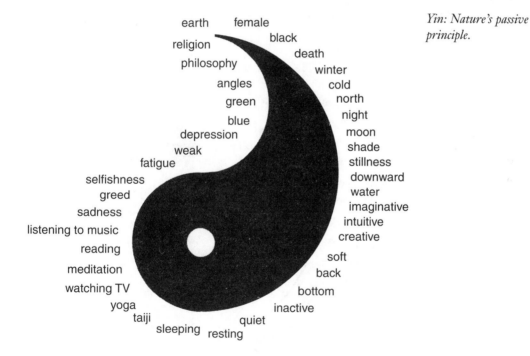

Yin: Nature's passive principle.

You may be wondering (especially if you're female) if yin's dark qualities express the Chinese view of women. No! Even though yin's associated traits may seem offensive, they are not meant to be taken personally. Think about it—yin is quiet and inward. Traditionally, women stayed at home inside their dwelling. Women receive sperm (inward) and protect the fetus inside. As you shall soon see, yang is associated with the male, activity, and outwardness. Traditionally, men are more active outside of the home. Men send sperm outward.

Wise Words

Yin represents the passive principle in nature exhibited as darkness, cold, and wetness. On a human level, yin symbolizes femininity and inertia. Also, yin represents the realm of the dead.

But what does the dot mean, you ask? Well, it's not a dot at all; rather, a knowing awareness. The white eye amid yin's blackness symbolizes the potential for change. Nothing can be wholly yin, just as nothing can be wholly yang. For example, night inevitably changes into day; death and decay always give rise to new life. Even the most heinous criminal and stingiest tightwad have a hint of goodness in them. Just think of Ebenezer Scrooge or the Grinch who stole Christmas!

Yang: The Masculine Side

Yang is expressed as heaven force. Yang expands. It represents the active principle in nature exhibited as light, heat, and dryness. On a human level, yang represents masculinity and the positive side of our emotions. Yang represents the land of the living; yin the realm of the dead. Other traits of yang are shown in the following figure.

Yang: Nature's active principle.

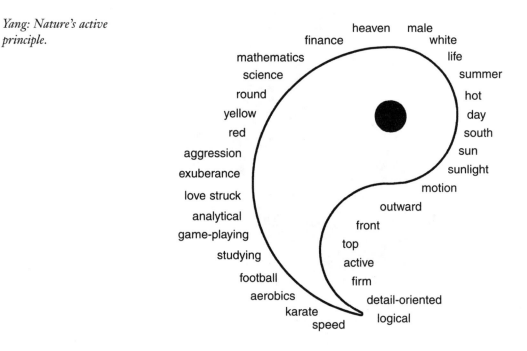

Yang also contains an aspect of its counterpart, giving credence to the phrase, "What goes up, must come down." If the sun didn't rise, we'd all die. If you don't give your body a rest after a strenuous workout, you might drop dead from exhaustion. Get the idea?

The Symbol of Taiji—Opposites Do Attract

The taiji symbol illustrates the eternal inter-action between yin and yang. Like two sides of a coin, yin can never separate from yang. Together, yin and yang represent the law of nature: perpetual and unceasing change. Time changes, seasons change, qi changes, your environment changes, and *you* change. Indeed, the universe, and everything in it, oscillates from birth to death in a beautiful dance of intertwining and interconnected energy.

Wise Words

Yang represents the active principle in nature exhibited by light, heat, and dryness. On a human level, yang represents masculinity and the positive side of our emotions. Also, yang represents the realm of living.

The "S"-like curve separating/connecting yin and yang illustrates that nothing is complete, fixed, or absolute. In other words, life isn't defined by rigid black and white thinking, but rather varying shades of gray. In yin there is the seed of yang, a white tone. In yang there is a seed of yin, a black tone. In the clearest sky you'll find a cloud; in the darkest night you'll find a star. On your happiest day, there is a hint of sadness; on your saddest day, there is hope.

The taiji represents the eternal interplay between yin and yang.

Despite how complicated the universe may seem, everything is subject to the laws of yin and yang. Finding a balance between the two is primary to feng shui.

Which Way Is Up?

No doubt you've seen various illustrations of the taiji. But have you ever wondered if there is a correct orientation? While an argument can be made that a model in motion cannot possibly have a defined point of reference, we say that if you had to capture the taiji on a two-dimension plane, a certain configuration embodies the inherent meaning of the symbol. Let's take another look at the symbol in the following figure.

The traditional orientation of the taiji.

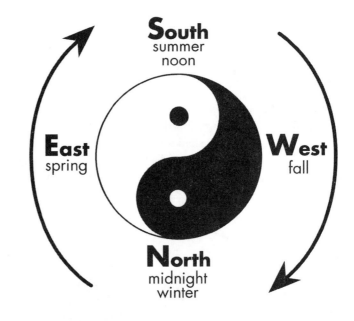

In Chinese cosmology, the south is always situated at the top. This is because it's the direction from which warmth and soft winds come, factors that favorably influence crop yield and good health. As you've just learned, summer and noon are symbolic of yang. Because heat rises, it follows logically that yang's "head" of energy orients at the top-left side of the taiji. The fact that the sun rises in the east further illustrates yang's orientation.

Master Class _____

How a feng shui practitioner orients the taiji is a strong indication of his or her knowledge of basic feng shui principles. The traditional and correct way to orient the taiji is with the yang white head at the top-left side.

Conversely, north is associated with cold, harsh winds, barbaric attacks, and possible illness. The north is symbolic of yin qi. The "weight" of cold "falls." Summer slides into autumn. The sun sets in the west. Daylight descends to midnight. Get the idea? Logically, then, the black head of yin should rest at the bottom-right side of the taiji.

Yin and Yang Culture Clash

The imbalance of the world's ideas, values, and attitudes can be explained using yin-yang terminology. Perhaps if Eastern and Western cultures recognize that each contains an element of the other, factions and frictions can heal. Only then can we unite in harmony. Only then can we say the earth is but one country, one people.

Western Yang

Let's face it, we Westerners are yang-oriented. We consistently favor the masculine over feminine; reason over faith; separation over integration; and spending over saving. Our impatience has given rise to fast-food restaurants, microwave ovens, automatic teller machines, self-service gas stations, credit cards, and the ubiquitous remote control. We are besieged with advertisements for all kinds of things, each claiming to be "the best." Such thinking filters down to national and individual levels, causing division. When will we realize that we as a culture, and we as individuals, aren't better than our neighbors?

Yet, as the principle of yin and yang teaches, our "yangness" will eventually revolve to yin. Remember, balance must be achieved. As the seasons give way to one another, the day to night, so too do yin and yang. In fact, we can witness this evolution now. Holistic health care, strengthening faith, and movements for social equality all embody the yin in our culture. Can we build, construct, and evolve further? Feng shui provides an answer.

Notable Quotable

"Know ye not why We created you all from the same dust? That no one should exalt himself over the other. Ponder at all times in your hearts how ye were created. Since We have created you all from one same substance it is incumbent on you to be even as one soul, to walk with the same feet, eat with the same mouth and dwell in the same land, that from your inmost being, by your deeds and actions, the signs of oneness and the essence of detachment may be manifest."

—Bahá'u'lláh (1817–92), the prophet founder of the Bahá'í faith, *The Hidden Words*, 1932

Eastern Yin

Our Eastern counterparts have traditionally been more yin-oriented. They favor philosophy and religion over science; intuitive wisdom over rational knowledge; traditions over progress; family over the individual. Developing the inner spirit has always taken precedence over materialism, technology, and the outer world. Respecting nature's beauty has been far more important than extracting something from it.

However, the seed of yang is growing. Now more than ever, the Chinese are embracing Western ideas. Elevating their national status, economically and progressively, has become paramount. The spirit of yangness that produced the many scientific and technological advances discussed in Chapter 3, "The Great Wall of Knowledge and the Rise of Feng Shui," is returning. The balance is shifting as yin revolves into yang.

Yin and Yang and Feng Shui

So what do yin and yang have to do with feng shui? A lot. If yin and yang aren't balanced in your environment, their imbalance can produce unwanted emotional and physical effects. We have many clients who complain of fatigue, depression, and lack of motivation. Generally, these people spend much time in dark places. Conversely, we have clients who live in bright, sun-filled homes, offering no relief from the sun's intensity. Is it any surprise these clients complain of headaches?

Much of feng shui relies on plain old common sense. If a room is dark, add more light. If a room is overly bright, add window blinds or curtains. If a room is stuffy, open the window. If it's too warm or too cool, adjust the thermostat. This is the easy stuff. Yet, life is not always easy. Feng shui is here to help us confront and overcome the difficulties.

The Least You Need to Know

◆ Yin and yang represent eternal change.

◆ Everything seeks a state of harmony and balance.

◆ Nothing can be wholly yin or wholly yang.

◆ The taiji is oriented with its white yang head at the top-left side.

Chapter 6

The Principle of the Five Phases

In This Chapter

- ◆ Understanding the five phases of fire, earth, metal, water, and wood
- ◆ Learning the cycles of the five phases
- ◆ Balancing qi using the five phases

With keen interest the ancients watched, monitored, compared, and contrasted that which occurred in nature to that which was made manifest in our bodies and in our lives. Over time, an accumulation of knowledge and experience produced the principle of the five phases. Based on an acceptance of how the world operated, the principle offered a predictable and systematic solution to how qi moves through the cyclic changes of yin and yang.

In feng shui, the interaction of the five phases is used extensively to enhance positive qi and correct negative qi. Understanding its cycles is what this chapter's all about. The principle of the five phases is the backbone of feng shui. Also, you'll need a solid understanding of the phase relationships in order to make sense of the two methods of feng shui we present in this book—Eight

House and Flying Star, as well as a method of Chinese astrology called The Four Pillars of Destiny—something you'll learn about in Parts 4, 5, and 7, respectively.

What Are the Five Phases?

Like yin and yang, the five phases are five characteristics or types of qi that change over time. For example, ice, snow, steam, and fog represent types of water that transform over time. Similarly, the five phases are five physical elements in nature—*fire, earth, metal, water,* and *wood*—that represent different manifestations of qi. The operative word here is *phases*. The movement, transformation, and interaction of each phase are what is studied, not the particular element itself. Remember, a tree, a rock, and a human being are actually bundles of intertwining energy—phases interacting. From creation and birth to maturity and decay, everything revolves around the changes of yin and yang.

Wise Words

The five phases of **fire**, **earth**, **metal**, **water**, and **wood** represent characteristics of qi that change over time.

The ancient Chinese believed that the interaction of the five phases creates all that exists on the heaven, earth, and human planes. Each phase has its own qi character, and thus interacts with other phases in different ways. Fire qi radiates, earth qi compacts, metal qi contracts, water qi falls, and wood qi grows upward. How the five phases interact with one another determines the balance of qi in nature, in our living/working space, and in our beings.

If It's Fire, It Must Be Summer

Each phase element is associated with a season, direction(s), weather condition, color(s), number(s), and a trigram (the subject of the next chapter). Referring to the following table, you may question why earth can have three direction values, or how numbers correspond to each element. This is because the five phases, the eight trigrams, and the Luoshu, or magic square (which we'll tell you about in the coming Chapter 13, "The Flying Stars, Part 1"), have been correlated into a nice, neat package.

What does this mean? In the early Warring States period (475–221 B.C.E.), the principles of the five phases, the eight trigrams, and the nine numbers of the Luoshu magic square all existed separately. By the time of the Han dynasty (206 B.C.E.–220 C.E.), the principles combined, correlating into an integrated whole.

First, the five phases were correlated to the four cardinal directions. With the phase earth placed in the center, fire-metal-water-wood readily connected to south-west-north-east. Then, this diagram was correlated to the eight directions, eight trigrams, and nine numbers of the Luoshu. Of course, correlating four- and five-term systems to eight- and nine-term systems posed problems. To solve the matter, the Chinese arbitrarily assigned phases to the four corner directions/Luoshu numbers. All of this may seem confusing. To better grasp what we've described, find the illustration of the nine-celled grid (called the bagua) in Chapter 7, "The Principle of the Eight Trigrams."

Master Class _____

In Chinese, the five phases are known as *wuxing* or technically, *wu zhong liu xing zhi qi,* meaning "the five kinds of qi prevailing at different times." With earth positioned in the center, fire qi (south) dominates in summer, metal qi (west) in autumn, water qi (north) in winter, and wood qi (east) in spring.

The Five Phase Associations of Each Element

Element	Season	Direction	Condition	Color	Number
Fire	Summer	South	Heat	Red, Purple, Dark Orange, Pink	9
Earth	Late summer	Northeast, Southwest, Center	Wet	Brown, Yellow	2, 5, 8
Metal	Autumn	West, Northwest	Dry	White, Silver, Gold	6, 7
Water	Winter	North	Cold	Black, Blue	1
Wood	Spring	East, Southeast	Wind	Green	3, 4

But wait! The preceding table shows five seasons. This is to accommodate the phase earth (remember, initially, earth was placed in the center of the four cardinal directions and corresponding phases). Among other associations, earth now corresponds to late summer, the northeast, southwest, and the center cell of the bagua (a term you'll become familiar with in the next chapter).

Feng Facts

In humans, the five phases correspond to our vital organs, senses, body characteristics, and emotions. For example, fire is associated with the heart/small intestines and joy; earth with the spleen/stomach and intense concentration; metal with the lungs/large intestines and grief; water with the kidney/urinary/bladder and fear; wood with the liver/gallbladder and anger. Considering these relationships, it's not surprising that an overly sad person taxes his lungs to cry and sigh. That intense fear may cause a release of the bladder. That excessive joy could produce heart ailments. Recently, a friend of ours was playing the slot machines. She won the $5,000 jackpot, but her jubilation triggered a heart attack. Practitioners of acupuncture, acupressure, and herbs use the five phases concept to correct imbalances of qi in our bodies.

The Productive Cycle

The productive cycle, shown in the following figure, is one of balance and creation. Each phase produces, or enhances, the succeeding phase. This progressively producing relationship of the five phases is known as the "mother-son" relationship. Each phase is the "son" of the phase that produces it, and the "mother" of the one it produces.

Fire produces earth. Like the heat of full summer, fire qi radiates burning the accumulation of wood to produce ash.

Wood produces fire. Wood's expansion and fullness, and eventual drying decay, give life to fire.

Earth produces metal. Earth qi compacts, giving birth to the contractive, inward pulling qi of metal.

Water produces wood. Water's flow nourishes and stimulates the growth of wood.

Metal produces water. Out of metal's contracting force, water qi condenses and liquefies.

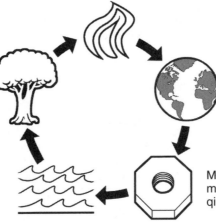

The Productive Cycle

As you can see, each phase follows a natural progression, the sequence of change creating harmony and balance. On paper, this seems logical. It makes sense. Yet, we react much differently when confronted with, say, an out-of-control brush fire threatening to consume our home. We must understand that actually, things are in control. Rainfall produces lush greenery that dries, causing raging fires. End of story. Think about this next time you're tempted to buy that mountain retreat or beachfront cottage!

The Controlling Cycle

The controlling cycle, shown in the following figure, is just that. Each phase controls its counterpart. It's a cycle of imbalance. The controlling cycle sets into motion weakened and depleted qi, which stagnates the environment and causes illness and other unwanted effects in us.

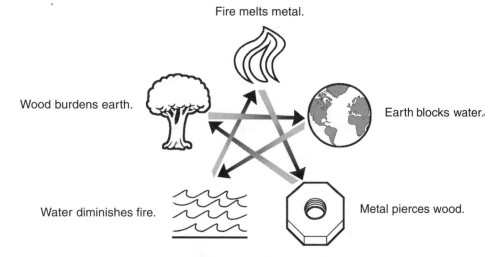

Fire melts metal.

Wood burdens earth.

Earth blocks water.

Water diminishes fire.

Metal pierces wood.

The Controlling Cycle

In the controlling cycle, the phases control or dominate each other. Harmony and order give way to discord and chaos.

The Weakening Cycle

The weakening cycle, shown in the following figure, reduces the power of the controlling phase and restores the sequential balance (the productive cycle) of the phases in question. In feng shui,

Master Class

The controlling cycle describes a battle between confronting qi. On the positive side, qi's counterpart keeps it under control, in check. On the negative side, qi's counterpart suggests unceasing conflict.

more often than not, the weakening cycle is used to remedy negative, or controlling, qi. The weakening cycle combines the productive and controlling cycles and is represented by the dotted lines revolving in a counterclockwise motion.

Master Class

Many have mistakenly called the controlling cycle "the destruction cycle." Remember, energy cannot be destroyed, it can only change form.

But, you may ask, how does a reductive phase remedy controlling qi? Good question. Let's look at a few examples. If water controls fire, how would you propose to lessen water's power? Would you add earth, metal, or wood? If you answered earth, guess again. Earth would certainly dominate (controlling cycle) water's power, but it will also reduce (reductive cycle) fire. Earth would then become too dominant over water and fire. If you believe metal will reduce water's control, this, too, is an incorrect assumption. Metal produces (productive cycle) water. You would be adding to water's power. The correct answer is wood. Wood both absorbs (reductive cycle) water's power and fuels (productive cycle) the weakened fire. By adding wood, the natural sequence of qi is restored.

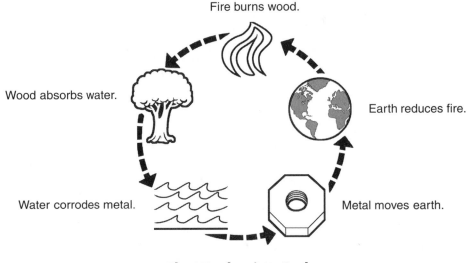

The Weakening Cycle

Here's another example. In this situation, let's make earth the controlling agent over water. How would you propose lessening earth's power? Would you add wood or metal? If you answered wood, guess again. Wood diminishes earth and reduces water. It would dominate over two weakened agents—earth and water. If you answered metal, you're getting it! Metal both reduces earth and produces water. For example, if a mudslide dams the little creek in your backyard, you'd use a shovel (metal) to clear the earth, allowing the water to flow. Right? If this mudslide blocked a river, you'd use a bulldozer (a really big piece of metal). Get the idea?

The following table shows the relationship between any two phases and their corresponding remedy. If the relationship is productive, a remedy is not needed (there are exceptions to this rule, which you'll find out about in Chapter 17, "The Flying Stars, Part 5"). If one phase controls another phase, the reductive phase is used to revert the cycle to a productive one.

Master Class

The weakening cycle provides a means to remedy controlling qi.

Remember, the weakening cycle creates balance, restoring the productive sequence of qi without creating any side effects. Metal's contractive qi force and wood's expansive qi are balanced with water's downward pull. Fire's rising qi and metal's contractive qi are balanced with earth's compacting force. And so forth.

The Relationship Between Phase Elements

Phase	Relationship	Weakening Agent
Fire and Earth	Productive	None
Fire and Metal	Controlling	Earth
Earth and Metal	Productive	None
Earth and Water	Controlling	Metal
Metal and Water	Productive	None
Metal and Wood	Controlling	Water
Water and Wood	Productive	None
Water and Fire	Controlling	Wood
Wood and Fire	Productive	None
Wood and Earth	Controlling	Fire

A Spoonful of Sugar

In feng shui, recognizing the correct remedy and selecting the proper remedying agent are key to promoting balance in your home. With balance comes better health, wealth, and relationships. But, you ask, how can I recognize what's out of balance? How can you remedy invisible forces? Should a room include a representative of all five phases? Stay tuned—we'll answer all these questions in the coming chapters!

Master Class _____

The vibration of the remedy's qi must be strong enough to balance the controlling agent. Therefore, the size of the remedy must be proportional to the size of the room. You must feel its essence.

When correcting a controlling interaction you can use either the weakening phase itself or its corresponding color(s). Although using the actual phase is preferred, sometimes this isn't always possible. For example, leaving a candle burning or a fire blazing in the fireplace is negligent if left unattended. When using color, it's important that items such as walls, upholstery, carpets, bedspreads, and drapes *be of the same color* for maximum benefit to your well-being. Following are suggested remedies for each of the five phases.

Fire remedies a wood-earth domination. Fire remedies include …

- A burning candle or working fireplace.
- Lamps with red shades or red light bulbs burning 24 hours.
- The colors red, purple, dark orange, and pink.

Feng Alert _____

You cannot mix phase elements. In other words, if the water phase is needed in a particular area, make sure other phase elements don't conflict with the remedy. In this case, the room mustn't be a red tone (fire). Avoid placing plants (wood) here. An abundance of earthenware may also upset the balance. While metal produces water, make sure metal objects don't overwhelm water's essence.

Earth remedies a fire-metal domination. Earth remedies include …

- Rocks.
- Ceramic, clay, or cement figurines, sculptures, table bases, or lamps.
- The colors brown and yellow.

Metal remedies an earth-water domination. Metal remedies include …

- Brass, steel, silver, gold, copper, or bronze figurines, picture frames, bed frames, planters, exercise equipment, pendulum clocks, filing cabinets, lamps, or fixtures.
- The colors white, gold, and silver.
- The metallic sound of wind chimes, a chiming clock, or piano playing.

Water remedies a metal-wood domination. Water remedies include …

- Aquariums*, table fountains**, a container of clean moving water, or humidifiers.
- The colors black and blue.

A water bed is not a water remedy because the water is concealed.

Wood remedies a water-fire domination. Wood remedies include …

- A living plant or tree.
- The color green.

Dead wood such as hardwood floors and furniture cannot be used as a remedy.

* Although fish are aesthetically pleasing, they aren't necessary.

** The best types of fountains are made of glass, plastic, or metal. Those made from earth elements will eliminate water's power. Why? Because earth dominates water. Water must be clean and exposed.

The Five Phases of Buildings

Building shapes correspond to the five phases, too. Triangular buildings are associated with fire qi. Many churches conform to this shape. So does your local International House of Pancakes! Square and rectangular buildings represent earth qi. Most of our homes are square, allowing qi to meander and spiral from room to room. Round or domed-shaped buildings represent metal qi. Sports arenas, coliseums, and observatories conform to this shape. New York's Guggenheim Museum is an excellent example. Round on the outside, its inner art galleries are spirally arrayed, inviting onlookers to be swallowed along a circular path. Wavy shapes correspond to water qi. Structures with variegated roof/ceiling lines conform to this shape. Finally, tall buildings, like skyscrapers, correspond to wood qi's growth and expansion.

Is one shape better than the other? Do certain shapes promote a healthy well-being while others inspire illness and misfortune? These questions and more will be addressed in Chapter 9, "Home Sweet Home: Evaluating Your House and Its Surroundings."

Feng Facts

Mirrors have never been used as a remedy in classical feng shui. The belief that mirrors can ward off evil omens, absorb, deflect, or stimulate qi's movement is wishful thinking. Mirrors only reflect light hitting its glass surface. So, where does the misconception about mirrors come from? The precursor to the modern loupan compass was called a *shi pan*. Made of a round "heaven" disc that swivels on a square "earth" base plate, the shi pan was inscribed with various images of the cosmos, including an image of the Big Dipper (Beidou). Interestingly, the inscribed Dipper is a mirror opposite from its true configuration in the heavens. This is because the shi pan "mirrors" the perfect and ideal world. In the Han dynasty (206 B.C.E.– 220 C.E.), mirrors were made of polished bronze, also illustrating the model world. Both the bronze mirrors and shi pan were considered magical because they reflected an absolute balance between heaven and earth. They were even buried in tombs to help the deceased into the next world.

The Five Phases Quiz

You know this stuff must be important if there's a pop quiz! If you're going to practice feng shui, understanding the five phases is just as important as learning how to tie your shoelaces and drive a car. Give it a try.

1. Stated in this order, fire, wood, water, metal, earth represent what cycle?

   a) The productive cycle

   b) The controlling cycle

   c) The weakening cycle

2. Fire controls _____.

   Earth controls _____.

   Metal controls _____.

   Water controls _____.

   Wood controls _____.

3. The color white, autumn, and west are associated with which phase?

   a) Fire

   b) Earth

   c) Metal

   d) Water

   e) Wood

4. Which phase acts as the weakening agent for metal's control over fire?

   a) Fire

   b) Earth

   c) Metal

   d) Water

   e) Wood

5. Fire produces _____.

   Earth produces _____.

   Metal produces _____.

   Water produces _____.

   Wood produces _____.

6. Wooden furniture can be used as a wood remedy.

   a) True

   b) False

7. Wood acts as a weakening agent for which controlling relationship?

   a) Fire-metal

   b) Metal-wood

   c) Water-fire

8. The color black, north, and winter are associated with which phase?

   a) Fire

   b) Earth

   c) Metal

   d) Water

   e) Wood

9. You must have fish in your aquarium for the water remedy to work.

   a) True

   b) False

10. The five phases provide the only remedies to correct negative qi.

    a) True

    b) False

Answers: 1. c; 2. Fire controls metal; earth controls water; metal controls wood; water controls fire; wood controls earth; 3. c; 4. b; 5. Fire produces earth; earth produces metal; metal produces water; water produces wood; wood produces fire; 6. b; 7. c; 8. d; 9. b; 10. a.

So, how did you do? Are you ready to move on to some heavier stuff? Bravo! Keep your thinking cap on and let's proceed to succeed!

The Least You Need to Know

◆ The five phases are five physical elements in nature that characterize different types of qi that change over time.

◆ The five phases are fire, earth, metal, water, and wood.

◆ The five phases combine to form a productive or controlling cycle.

◆ The five phases are used to balance negative qi and enhance positive qi.

The Principle of the Eight Trigrams

In This Chapter

◆ What are the eight trigrams?

◆ The symbols of the eight trigrams

◆ The meaning of the eight trigrams

◆ The Before Heaven and After Heaven sequence of trigrams

The eight trigrams are the fundamental building blocks that form the 64 hexagrams of the *Yijing* (*The Book of Changes*). Each trigram expresses patterns of movement and change. Each has been used extensively in the fields of philosophy, astrology, Chinese traditional medicine, numerology, the martial arts, mathematics, and, of course, feng shui.

Understanding the eight trigrams will give you greater insight into the patterns of change inherent in nature and in you.

Motion over Matter—Qi's Pattern of Movement

As you learned in Chapter 4, "Qi Wiz! It's Life's Force!" feng shui is wrapped around the concept of qi—the mysterious underlying force whose existence has yet to be proven scientifically. To the Chinese, whether or not this age-old notion is bolstered by scientific data is irrelevant. In the East, intuitive wisdom has always reigned over rational knowledge. Qi is a fact of life. They know it's here, there, and everywhere. So, how can you study that which cannot be seen?

Simply, the ancient Chinese followed how qi navigates through the cycles of yin and yang. Studying its patterns of movement, transformation, and evolution through nature's elements was considered far more important than studying the isolated element itself. In fact, the whole of nature was seen as a network of interconnected and interdependent events. These events, phases, or patterns were correlated into a symmetrical model representing all possible natural and human situations. This model is called the principle of the *eight trigrams*.

Interestingly, Fritjof Capra, in his thought-provoking book, *The Tao of Physics* (Shambhala, 1991), points out that this Eastern concept bears a striking resemblance to German physicist Werner Heisenberg's (1901–76) S-Matrix theory. In the theory developed in 1943, Heisenberg described the realm of hadrons (a class of subatomic particles) as a network of inseparable reactions. Reactions connect particles to other reactions. The particle is secondary to its chain of movement and transformation. Like the principle of the eight trigrams, Heisenberg's S-Matrix theory explains all possible reactions relating to hadrons.

Wise Words

The **eight trigrams** are symbols representing transitional phases of all possible natural and human situations.

In feng shui, the movement, change, and interactions of qi, together with the elements of time and space, determine your state of being. Understanding the eight trigrams and their associations will help you to enhance good qi and correct bad qi.

Eight Is Enough

Out of the dynamic interplay of yin and yang, a family of eight trigrams is born. Take a look at the following illustration. As indicated, yang (male) is represented by a solid line, and yin (female) by a broken line. Individually, yang and yin each produce two offspring. How so? Upon closer examination of respective offspring, you'll notice that the bottom line corresponds to the "parent" yang or yin line in question. The addition of the top yang or yin line results in the production of four unique pairs or bigrams (sixiang, in Chinese). Next, each of the four bigrams produces two trigrams each, the bottom two lines identical to the parent pair. Again only the addition of the top yang or yin line distinguishes the trigram from its "sibling."

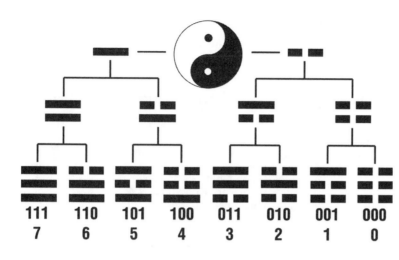

The evolution of the eight trigrams. The three-term numbers on the bottom of each trigram represent its binary correlation.

Together, the eight trigrams, or what is known as the *bagua*, represent the maximum number of yang or yin combinations in sets of three. If you continue multiplying the eight trigrams by themselves, you'll end up with the 64 hexagrams of the *Yijing*, but we won't concern ourselves with that here.

How do you interpret the trigram symbols? What do they mean? And what do they have to do with feng shui? You'll soon find out!

Wise Words

The **bagua** are the eight trigrams of the *Yijing*. "Ba" means "eight" and "gua," "the result of divination." Figuratively, the bagua suggests creating heaven on earth.

Meet the Bagua Family

As you have just learned, the eight fundamental trigrams (and hexagrams) are built from the bottom line up. The bottom line represents earth. The middle line represents humankind, and the top line, heaven. The line that is different determines the trigram's gender (a fuller explanation of this is coming up).

Aside from their gender identity, the trigrams are associated with a host of natural and human phenomena: the seasons, the time of day, magnetic directions, the five phases and their corresponding colors, animals, human personality types (merchants, teachers, thieves, and so on), body parts, related illnesses, and numbers. The trigrams are even given a name appropriate to their qi energy ("the arousing," "the gentle," "the clinging"). Although each association is significant, we've listed only those attributes that will be the most useful to your study and practice of feng shui.

So, let's meet the men in the bagua family. Remember, a male is represented by the solid yang line. Referring to each illustration, watch how line 1 (the bottom line) moves up the trigram creating each new male family member.

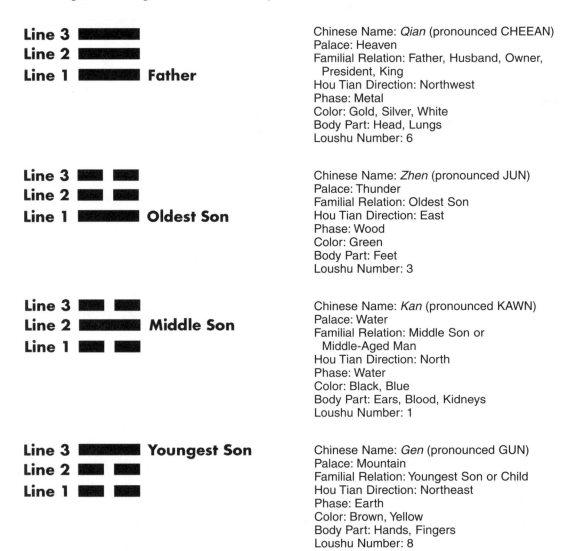

Line 3 ▬▬▬
Line 2 ▬▬▬
Line 1 ▬▬▬ **Father**

Chinese Name: *Qian* (pronounced CHEEAN)
Palace: Heaven
Familial Relation: Father, Husband, Owner, President, King
Hou Tian Direction: Northwest
Phase: Metal
Color: Gold, Silver, White
Body Part: Head, Lungs
Loushu Number: 6

Line 3 ▬ ▬
Line 2 ▬ ▬
Line 1 ▬▬▬ **Oldest Son**

Chinese Name: *Zhen* (pronounced JUN)
Palace: Thunder
Familial Relation: Oldest Son
Hou Tian Direction: East
Phase: Wood
Color: Green
Body Part: Feet
Loushu Number: 3

Line 3 ▬ ▬
Line 2 ▬▬▬ **Middle Son**
Line 1 ▬ ▬

Chinese Name: *Kan* (pronounced KAWN)
Palace: Water
Familial Relation: Middle Son or Middle-Aged Man
Hou Tian Direction: North
Phase: Water
Color: Black, Blue
Body Part: Ears, Blood, Kidneys
Loushu Number: 1

Line 3 ▬▬▬ **Youngest Son**
Line 2 ▬ ▬
Line 1 ▬ ▬

Chinese Name: *Gen* (pronounced GUN)
Palace: Mountain
Familial Relation: Youngest Son or Child
Hou Tian Direction: Northeast
Phase: Earth
Color: Brown, Yellow
Body Part: Hands, Fingers
Loushu Number: 8

Do you see how each family member is created? Now, let's meet the women of the bagua family. Again, watch how the bottom yin line moves up the trigram creating each new female family member.

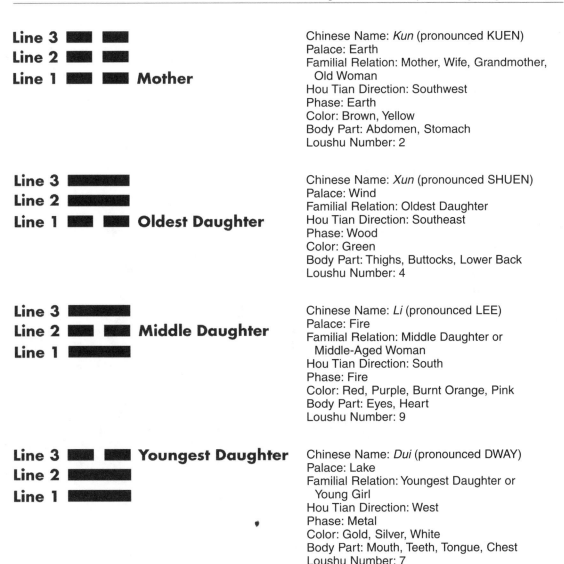

Line 3

Line 2

Line 1   **Mother**

Chinese Name: *Kun* (pronounced KUEN)
Palace: Earth
Familial Relation: Mother, Wife, Grandmother,
   Old Woman
Hou Tian Direction: Southwest
Phase: Earth
Color: Brown, Yellow
Body Part: Abdomen, Stomach
Loushu Number: 2

Line 3

Line 2

Line 1   **Oldest Daughter**

Chinese Name: *Xun* (pronounced SHUEN)
Palace: Wind
Familial Relation: Oldest Daughter
Hou Tian Direction: Southeast
Phase: Wood
Color: Green
Body Part: Thighs, Buttocks, Lower Back
Loushu Number: 4

Line 3

Line 2   **Middle Daughter**

Line 1

Chinese Name: *Li* (pronounced LEE)
Palace: Fire
Familial Relation: Middle Daughter or
   Middle-Aged Woman
Hou Tian Direction: South
Phase: Fire
Color: Red, Purple, Burnt Orange, Pink
Body Part: Eyes, Heart
Loushu Number: 9

Line 3   **Youngest Daughter**

Line 2

Line 1

Chinese Name: *Dui* (pronounced DWAY)
Palace: Lake
Familial Relation: Youngest Daughter or
   Young Girl
Hou Tian Direction: West
Phase: Metal
Color: Gold, Silver, White
Body Part: Mouth, Teeth, Tongue, Chest
Loushu Number: 7

These are the eight members of the bagua, or trigram, family. Although the symbols may seem abstract and their configurations daunting, don't worry. In time you'll come to recognize each trigram and its corresponding associations. It's similar to learning to understand road signs. After a while, the abstract symbols for Yield, No Entry, and No Passing become absorbed into your subconscious realm of knowns. So will the trigrams, if you give them a chance.

The Cyclic Pattern of the Bagua

Although the eight trigrams can be arranged in many different ways, there are really only two configurations that make sense. The first arrangement, shown in the following illustration, is called the *Before Heaven* sequence. "Before Heaven" is an interpretive translation of the Chinese term *Xian Tian*, which means "prior to the appearance of the phenomenal world." The Before Heaven sequence denotes perfect balance and harmony.

The Before Heaven sequence of the eight trigrams.

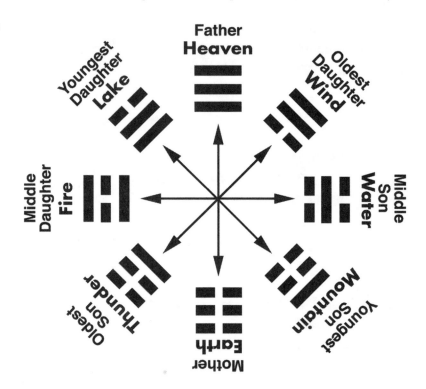

All eight qi forces are balanced by their counterparts: Heaven is balanced by earth, water by fire. Or, father is balanced by mother, and middle son by middle daughter. In essence, this arrangement represents the ideal world, the underlying reality. The problem with the Before Heaven sequence is that it's motionless, a study of still life. It doesn't move, transform, or interact. Let's move on.

The second arrangement, shown in the following illustration, is called the *After Heaven* sequence. Translated from the Chinese term *Hou Tian*, it means "after the appearance of the phenomenal world." The After Heaven sequence follows the cyclic changes of yin and yang. Each trigram evolves in a natural sequence of events in a lifelike world. In feng shui, we use the After Heaven sequence to analyze how the movement of qi's forces affects you.

The After Heaven sequence of the eight trigrams.

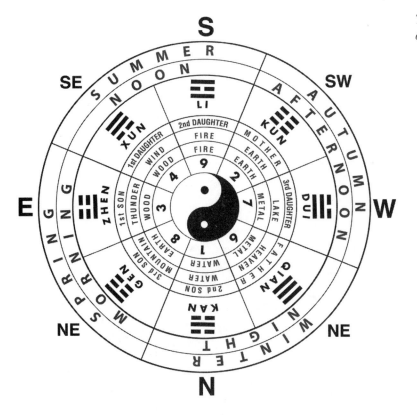

Beginning with the Zhen trigram to the east and moving in a clockwise motion, spring arrives with a clap of thunder. Next, the Xun trigram's gentle winds nourish the growth and development of summer's expansion. Li follows. The intensity of Li's brightness gives rise to early autumn's soft light. In human consciousness, Li is a time of love and curiosity. You are the middle daughter exploring new concepts.

Next comes Kun, early autumn. You are maturing and receptive to new ideas. But it is in Dui that you turn inward, harvesting what you've learned. It's a time of reflection and self-assessment. With Qian's emergence comes the beginning of winter. Intuitive wisdom takes over as you develop your inner spirit. In Kan, you submerge yourself even further into the profundities of life, deep meditation. You are still and quiet as midnight. Your

Wise Words

The **Before Heaven** sequence of trigrams, called the *Xian Tian* in Chinese, represents an ideal reality where natural and human qi forces are in perfect balance. The **After Heaven** sequence of trigrams, called the *Hou Tian* in Chinese, denotes motion, transformation, and interaction of natural and human qi forces.

inward journey is now completed. In Gen, clouds form over winter's repose and thunder heralds a new cycle of growth and development.

As shown in the next illustration, the eight trigram circle is squared off to form a grid of eight place values (with the center representing earth). This allows the principle of the eight trigrams (along with the yin and yang and five phase theories) to correlate to the Luoshu, also known as the magic square, which you'll learn about in Chapter 13, "The Flying Stars, Part 1."

The bagua grid.

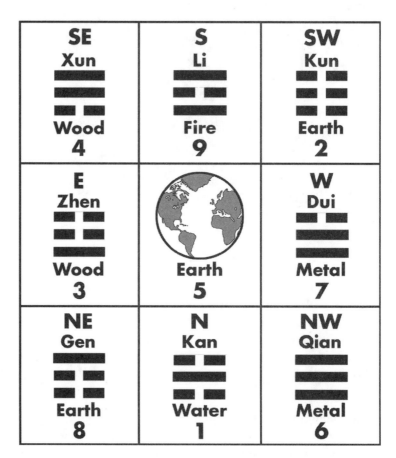

Patterns of Numbers

The combination of solid and broken lines forming the trigrams and hexagrams corresponds to the binary system of mathematics—the same system used today in computer programming. Every function your computer performs—calculations, graphics, and word processing—uses binary numeration. The system uses 01 for the number 1 and 10 for the number 2. The succeeding numbers compute as shown in the following table.

1	=	01	6	=	110	11	=	1011
2	=	10	7	=	111	12	=	1100
3	=	11	8	=	1000	13	=	1101
4	=	100	9	=	1001	14	=	1110
5	=	101	10	=	1010	15	=	1111

In the same way, if you let yang (solid line) represent the number one, and yin (broken line) represent zero, you can see that the combinations follow the rules of binary numeration. For example, reading the trigrams from the bottom line up, trigram ☳, or 001, represents binary number 1.

Trigram ☵, or 010, represents binary number 2.

Trigram ☲, or 011, represents binary number 3, and so forth.

Get the idea? Flip back a couple of pages to the illustration of the bagua family tree. We've included the binary code for all eight trigrams.

How this mathematical interpretation of the trigrams and hexagrams was discovered is an interesting story. It began with German philosopher and mathematician Gottfried Wilhelm von Leibnitz (1646–1716), who believed the mathematical system proved God's creation of the world: Everything was created by God (1) from nothing (0).

As the story goes, Leibnitz was corresponding with a Jesuit missionary in China, Father Joachim Bouvet, at the time. In 1701, hoping to persuade the Chinese to accept the Christian doctrine with his mystical calculations, Leibnitz sent Bouvet a copy of his published work on binary numeration. Bouvet recognized a connection between the binary system and the *Yijing*'s symbols and sent him a circular arrangement of the hexagrams composed by Song dynasty philosopher Shao Yong. Remarkably, Yong's arrangement was a mirror image of the base-two system from 0 to 63.

Can the fact that the East and West independently invented binary mathematics serve as an example for our ability to subconsciously tap into the Sea of Consciousness? Well, in this case, no. As we mentioned in Chapter 3, "The Great Wall of Knowledge and the Rise of Feng Shui," the original *Yijing*, the *Zhouyi*, was strictly a system of numerological divination in which sequences of odd and even numbers had significance. A Chinese scholar named Zhang Zhenglang made this discovery in the 1970s, theorizing that over time the odd numbers became the solid yang lines and the even numbers, the

Notable Quotable

"The nature of the Ultimate Supreme [Taiji] is total balance. When motion is initiated, it generates spirituality. Spirituality generates numbers. Numbers generate emblems. Emblems generate vision. Vision generates transformation, everything returning to spirituality."

—Cosmological philosopher Shao Yong (1011–77 C.E.)

broken yin lines as we know them. Moreover, at the time the *Yijing* was assembled at the end of the second millennium B.C.E. by King Wen and the Duke of Zhou, the concept of zero was not yet known. (For a detailed account of Leibnitz, binary numeration, and the *Yijing*, see Chapter 10 of *The Complete Idiot's Guide to the I Ching*.)

So the real question is, what is the meaning of the patterns of numbers underlying the trigrams and hexagrams? Although we may never learn their meaning, clearly the ancient Chinese recognized correlative mathematical patterns made manifest in nature and human nature/events. They recorded how these macrocosmic events affected our microcosmic beings. You'll study one such number-based system in Part 5, "Feng Shui Mechanics 201." Until then, you must first learn how your home's external and internal environments play a significant role in how you think, feel, and relate.

The Least You Need to Know

◆ The eight trigrams represent transitional phases in nature and in humans.

◆ The eight trigrams are associated with things such as magnetic directions, colors, body parts, illness, and numbers.

◆ The eight trigram symbols are read from the bottom line up. The bottom line represents earth; the middle line, humankind; and the top line, heaven.

Part 3

Understanding Your Environment

Did you know that landforms, building shapes, rivers, and roads influence your well-being? That living near places of worship, hospitals, and schools governs how you think, feel, and relate? That your front yard, backyard, window and door alignment, ceiling beams, and furniture placement affect your prosperity? Indeed, there's much to consider when analyzing your external and internal environment.

Part 3 is all about recognizing these natural and man-made factors. You'll learn how to distinguish that which brings favorable qi from that which brings unfavorable qi. Moreover, you'll learn how to remedy inauspicious situations. The simplest modifications can turn a bullfrog into a prince and your home into a comfortable, prosperous, and healthful haven.

Chapter 8

Turtles, Tigers, and Dragons, Oh My: Evaluating Your Environment

In This Chapter

- The Four Celestial Palaces: totems worshipped by the ancient Chinese
- The four terrestrial animals: landform and building shapes that affect our well-being
- River and road patterns

Feng shui's all about living in harmony with your environment. It's about harnessing sheng, or positive qi, to promote better health, wealth, and relations with others. It's about avoiding or correcting sha, or negative qi, a detriment to your well-being. In this chapter, you'll learn about ancient Chinese cosmology—how four celestial deities (the crimson bird, azure dragon, white tiger, and black turtle) worshipped by the Chinese transformed into terrestrial landforms. You'll discover how to recognize these landforms and how they offer protection and security. Also, we'll show you how neighboring buildings, river courses, and roadways play a role in your life and livelihood.

We guarantee you'll see your neighborhood, city—heck, even the world—with new vision. Can a film editor watch a film without critiquing its edits and pace? Can a fitness professional look at a body without assessing the person's physique? Certainly not.

Here a Totem, There a Totem

All ancient societies worshipped the heavens, envisioning their gods, guardians, and clan ancestors as configurations of celestial bodies. For the most part, these star-patterned deities were represented in animal form. Called *totems*, the animals were worshipped in exchange for protection. Originating from the Algonquin tribe of North America, the word "totem" describes a clan's emblem—an animal or natural object with which a group feels a special affection or attachment.

Wise Words _____

Totem is an Algonquin word describing an animal or natural object with which a clan feels a special attachment. Symbolizing group membership, the totem is worshipped by the members of the clan bearing its name.

Why the affinity with a particular animal? This is a mystery. Although we'll probably never know why a tribe chose a particular animal as its emblem, the geographic region of the culture in question may provide important clues. Also, it's reasonable to assume the animal embodied positive attributes (like courage, strength, or loyalty) with which the tribe wished to associate itself. But, before we get into these aspects, let's first define the totems worshipped by the ancient Chinese. Then we can learn how these totems relate to the art and science of feng shui.

Circus of the Stars

In China, four celestial deities revered by ancient tribes combined to help form the culture we know today. What would come to be known as the *Four Celestial Palaces*—the *crimson bird*, *azure dragon*, *mysterious black turtle*, and *white tiger*—are actually macroconstellations, or an enormous stellar division, composed of seven independent constellations each. Together, the 4 macroconstellations make up the 28 constellations of the Chinese zodiac.

Wise Words _____

Called the **Four Celestial Palaces**, the **crimson bird**, **azure dragon**, **mysterious black turtle**, and **white tiger** are macroconstellations. Composed of 7 constellations each, they comprise the 28 constellations of the Chinese zodiac.

Signaling the arrival of the solstices and equinoxes, each macroconstellation represents a quarter of the night sky, each visible in its entirety only in the season with which it's associated (you'll learn more about this later). As an aside, it's important to understand the Chinese use the *celestial equator* to track stellar positions. In China's mountainous regions, it makes more sense to base observations on the times when the heavenly bodies come into view overhead. In the Western world, emphasis is placed on the rising and setting of celestial bodies on the terrestrial horizon. Called the *ecliptic* system, it originated in subtropic regions where the land is flat and the view unobstructed.

Read All About It: Heaven Falls to Earth!

You may be wondering how ancient cosmology relates to feng shui, how celestial deities are associated with harnessing positive qi. Unfortunately, like many ancient traditions, the answers are swathed in myth. Sometime between the 6000 B.C.E. Neolithic tomb (described in Chapter 3, "The Great Wall of Knowledge and the Rise of Feng Shui") and the writing of the 4th century C.E. *Book of Burial*, the bird, dragon, turtle, and tiger deities came down to earth to represent four unique types of landforms associated with Form School feng shui—the practice of locating the most auspicious sites on which to construct a building or bury the dead.

Wise Words

The **celestial equator** is the circular path the constellations traverse perpendicular to an imaginary line joining the celestial north pole to the earth's North Pole. The ancient Chinese called the celestial equator the Red Path. Westerners developed an **ecliptic** system. It traces the path of the sun through the sky. The ancient Chinese called this system the Yellow Path.

As the story goes, the circular (or domed) heaven and square (or flat) earth were once perfectly balanced, eight majestic mountains (corresponding to each of the eight directions) separating the two realms. However, this ideal and perfect world came to an end when the water demon Gong Gong battled the fire god Zhu Rong. During the battle, Mount Buzhou, the northwest "pillar," collapsed. As a consequence, heaven came crashing down, causing the earth plane to rise in the southeast and fall in the northwest. Somehow, the four macroconstellations transformed into terrestrial shapes, each associated with one of the four cardinal directions: the crimson bird to the south, the white tiger to the west, the black turtle to the north, and the azure dragon to the east.

Although an exciting tale, we all know this primeval battle didn't really occur. How the star-patterned deities entered the earth plane is anyone's guess. Nevertheless, their shape and proximity to one another help to describe the disposition of qi, ultimately providing the foundation of Form School (Xingfa) feng shui. It was the task of the master to find the place, nestled between the creatures that represented heaven on earth. He did this using a shipan (described in Chapter 6, "The Principle of the Five Phases"). Over time, this divine instrument was replaced by the luopan, the compass used by feng shui masters today.

In Search of the Dragon's Lair

The earliest textual documentation underlying the theories of Form School feng shui surface in the fifth century B.C.E. in *Guanzi*, purportedly written by Guan Zhong, the prime minister of the state of Qi. However, a fully developed theory discussing the relationship of the terrestrial plane and qi isn't seen for another six centuries. As we already mentioned, the fourth century C.E. *Book of Burial* (*Zhangshu*) was the bible of landforms, the text describing in detail how to locate the *dragon's lair* (long xue)—the place where qi converges. Many scholars believe Guo Pu's (276–324 C.E.) *Book of Burial* clarifies the *Classic of Burial*, a text purportedly dating to the Han dynasty. It states: "Qi flows according to the shape of the earth. With qi's nourishment, all living things come into existence. Qi flows within the ground. Its motion follows the shape of the terrain, accumulating where the terrain stops."

Wise Words

The **dragon's lair** (long xue) is the common point of intersection between the southern landform of the crimson bird, the eastern landform of the azure dragon, the northern black turtle, and the western white tiger. The dragon's lair is considered the most auspicious site on which to build a home or to bury the dead.

Locating the cave of the lair, a metaphor for the place where sheng qi pools, is what Form School feng shui is about. When the deceased are buried in this spot, the yin (dead) bones are activated by or charged with yang (living) qi. When a home is built on this auspicious site, the occupants are blessed with good health and wealth.

Climb Every Mountain

Besides being associated with a direction, the bird, dragon, turtle, and tiger landforms correspond to a season, a five phase color, and a yin and yang polarity, as shown in the following illustration.

Beginning with the *crimson bird* and traveling clockwise, the bird represents the south, summer, the color red, and yang qi. Since birds are more abundant in warmer climates, it makes sense why the bird deity was placed in the southern sky. Terrestrially, the bird's features must be lower than the others. The bird doesn't have to be a landform; it can also represent a body of water.

Master Class

What type of feathered friend is the crimson bird? In its earliest version, it was a sparrow. However, later on, the sparrow was replaced by an antlered phoenix.

The *white tiger* represents the west, autumn, the color white, and yin qi. The tiger is indigenous and plentiful the farther west toward India you travel. Terrestrially, the tiger's peak is traditionally longer and lower than its eastern counterpart, the dragon.

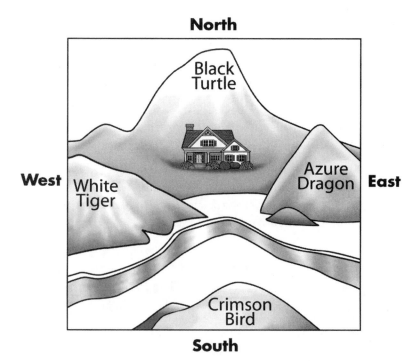

North

Black Turtle

West

White Tiger

Azure Dragon

East

Crimson Bird

South

The terrestrial configurations of the four celestial deities.

The *black turtle* represents the north, winter, the color black, and yin qi. Not to be confused with the amphibious tortoise, the land creature boasts the highest terrestrial landform feature. Why a turtle? Why the north? Well, all we know is that turtle shell divination was a northern tradition. In fact, divination using the plastrons or bottom shells of turtles (plastomancy) led to a type of divination called sortilege, where a person drew lots (stone, sticks, or straws, for example) to determine his or her fate. The ancient Chinese used stalks from the yarrow plant, a method directly tied to the development of the *Yijing*, considered the oldest system of divination still in use today.

Wise Words

The lowest of the landforms, the southern **crimson bird** can also represent a body of water. This is balanced by the highest northern landform, the **black turtle**. To the east, the high **azure dragon** is balanced by the long and low **white tiger** of the west.

Finally, the *azure dragon* represents the east, spring, the color green, and yang qi. Traditionally, the dragon's terrestrial features are higher than the western tiger. Meteorologically, the azure dragon is equivalent to the Greco-Roman constellation Scorpious.

Together, the crimson bird, white tiger, black turtle, and azure dragon form the dragon's lair. Regardless of their stature, each component plays a vital role in nourishing the land of the living and the realm of the dead. Let's find out what role each plays.

Have a Seat

Imagine the lair as an armchair. The tiger and dragon represent the arms, the turtle is the back, and the bird, the foot stool. The fortunate site for a grave, building, or settlement rests in the middle, the seat of the chair. Now, imagine sitting in the chair. How would you feel if the left (azure dragon) or right (white tiger) arm was missing? Would you feel uncomfortable? Exposed? Unbalanced, perhaps? In feng shui, the dragon and the tiger protect the lair just as the arms of the chair protect your body.

The black turtle provides support and protection. In China, the turtle blocked bitter Arctic winds and helped to battle against barbaric attacks. Continuing with our chair analogy, don't you feel safer and more secure with your back supported? Of course you do! This idea also gives rise to the phrase "Watch your back."

Master Class

Traditionally, the Chinese believe the left is more important than the right. For this reason, the highest-ranking prime minister always appeared on the left side of the emperor. In part, this has to do with how our brain functions. For people who are right-handed, the left side of the brain controls the right side of the body. The ancient Chinese understood this, honoring the brain's importance by ranking its officials accordingly.

What about the crimson bird? While not offering protection, this low-lying landform or body of water buffers you from incoming forces. Also, this area provides an unobstructed view of the site in question.

Although traditionally, the four terrestrial creatures correspond to one of the four directions, we mustn't be so strict when we judge our home's location. Regardless of magnetic orientation, just know it's most favorable to have the landforms of the turtle supporting your back, the dragon on your left, the white tiger on your right, and the crimson bird in front.

City Slickers

Let's say you live on flat terrain with no dragon, turtle, or tiger landform in sight. Does this mean your home brings you misfortune? Absolutely not! Symbolically, the four terrestrial creatures can represent buildings. For example, most of us have neighboring structures on the left and right sides of our home. Looking outside from within our dwelling, these structures represent the dragon (left side) and tiger (right side). To determine which side bears the greatest strength you must consider …

Master Class

Suitably placed and appropriately sized trees, hedges, bushes, or even fences are a valid substitute for landforms and buildings. If your home backs onto a park, for example, you could plant a grove of trees or a hedge to protect your back side. A fence will also do.

- The size of the buildings: the bigger and more imposing, the stronger.
- The proximity of each to your home: the closer, the more powerful.
- The density on each side: the side with a greater number of buildings has more influence.

If the neighboring buildings on the left side are more prominent than on the right side, your home favors the male occupants. This is because the left side, the dragon side, corresponds to yang (male) qi. If the neighboring buildings on the right side are more prominent, your home favors the yin female occupants.

The back side of your home can also be supported by a building. While offering security and protection, the structure in question must not overwhelm your home. Also, it must not block sunlight.

Rolling on the River; Ease on Down the Road

In feng shui, river courses and roadways are evaluated in the same way. A meandering river is similar to a winding road. A sharp current is like heavy rushing traffic. Depending on their patterns, rivers and roads can bring you benevolent sheng qi, inspiring good fortune, or malicious sha qi, causing misfortune and illness.

So, if you're in the market to buy a new home or would just like to assess your current situation, what we offer here should be considered. In some measure, our health and livelihood depend on the very paths we take for granted.

Notable Quotable

Qi rides the wind and disperses until it encounters water.
—Guo (276–324 C.E.), *Book of Burial*

Consider the following illustrations. Before reading our analysis, try to form your own conclusion. Staying oblivious to all other factors, consider only how the road's contour makes you feel.

In feng shui, river courses and roadways are evaluated the same way.

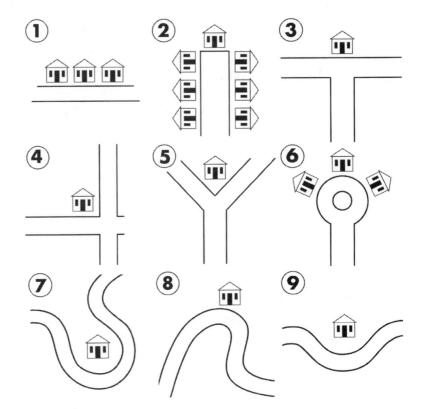

Let's consider each illustration separately:

1. **A straight road.** Generally, most homes are positioned along this type of road pattern. Is this a bad thing? Only if the road is a main thoroughfare, where you're subjected to extra noise, dirt, and other things possibly causing fatigue and illness. Is it more peaceful listening to sirens or song birds? In the same vein, if you live alongside an aqueduct or river rapids, you may feel out of control, as if you're being buffeted downstream. Now, if the straight road in question is not frequented by traffic, it resembles a lazy stream—quiet, peaceful, balanced.

2. **A dead-end street.** Here, this dwelling is a recipient of poison arrow qi rushing up the street into the occupant's front door. Most inauspicious, indeed. It's also unfavorable to live in an apartment or work in an office at the end of a long hall.

3. **A T-junction.** Once again, poison arrow qi intrudes. Like a runaway locomotive, it will stop only on impact, enveloping your home in its destructive forces.

4. **A corner lot.** You may feel unbalanced living on a corner lot. This is because one side of your dwelling's protection is separated by the street. Also, traffic, noise, and glaring headlights are a consideration.

5. **A Y-junction.** Similar to a dead-end and T-junction pattern, a home residing in a Y-junction is subjected to two torrents of unfavorable qi. Further, this configuration is cause for accidents due to cars careening off the path into your home.

6. **A cul-de-sac.** Unlike the dead-end street depicted in illustration 2, a house situated on a cul-de-sac containing an island is fortunate. Why? If you imagine the street as a water course, the island (in this situation) is the crimson bird—the buffer dispersing sha qi's ill effects. What about a cul-de-sac that doesn't have a protective island? This, too, is favorable because qi can flow, moving in a circular motion, dispersing its benevolent energy.

7. **A U-shape.** It stands to reason you may feel suffocated living in a house positioned inside a noose! Although atypical to city streetscape, avoid purchasing a country or mountain home where this type of pattern is more common.

8. **A sharp bend.** Maneuvering a car around sharp bends is tricky business. The screech of brakes and the glare of headlights add extra anxiety. Would you want to live on such a danger-prone street?

9. **A meandering path.** Cradled inside an open U-junction, you are protected from the threat of accidents, glaring lights, and poison arrow qi. A house situated here is considered lucky—the benevolent, winding qi bringing prosperity, good health, and promotion.

Master Class

If you live along a straight roadway, the most auspicious house is in the middle supported by the tiger and dragon. In feng shui, the corner dwelling (or the one at the end of the lane) is considered unfavorable because the qi has dispersed. Also the house's support is unbalanced with the street coming between the protection of the tiger/dragon.

Feng Alert

If you live at a T- or Y-junction, can anything be done to protect you from the affects of poison arrow qi? Install a high fence or plant a wall of shrubbery to block qi's destructive path. However, it's best to avoid choosing locations requiring such action.

Some final points: Although not illustrated here, living on the same level or below a freeway is inauspicious. So is living between parallel roads. So, what then are the most favorable locations? Simply, a meandering path (9), followed by a cul-de-sac (6), and a straight road (1) not frequented by traffic. Remember, when evaluating your situation, roadways and water courses are equivalent.

The Least You Need to Know

- The foundation of Form School feng shui stems from ancient cosmology.
- In feng shui, landforms are referred to as the bird, dragon, turtle, and tiger shapes.
- Buildings, trees, and fences can represent the four terrestrial creatures.
- Rivers and roads are evaluated in the same way.
- The patterns of river courses and roadways can bring either fortune or misfortune to your dwelling.

Chapter 9

Home Sweet Home: Evaluating Your House and Its Surroundings

In This Chapter

- ◆ How neighboring facilities can be a health risk
- ◆ Recognizing favorable lot shapes
- ◆ Houses of all shapes and sizes
- ◆ Laying out your bedroom and office

This chapter continues where Chapter 8, "Turtles, Tigers, and Dragons, Oh My: Evaluating Your Environment," left off. Here, you'll learn more about your environment, and how the proximity of a school, church, power plant—among other things—affects how you feel, relate, and even sleep. You'll discover how the land your house is built on plays a role in your well-being.

This chapter is also about practical application—things you can do now to improve your living space, such as the best way to position your bed to gain a restful night's sleep, or where to station your desk to increase your productivity. By making simple adjustments and being mindful of potential qi-inspired hazards, you'll feel more balanced and centered. You'll feel strong and in control instead of butting heads with the elements.

Church Bells and Power Poles

There is a host of man-made factors that can influence your health and livelihood. While some are obvious hazards, others are less so. Take living next to a school. Would you think its proximity poses a health risk? Aside from the school bus exhaust fumes, the area is charged with the high energy of youth. Just being in your own children's presence can wear you out. Now, multiply this by say, a thousand. Over time, the voltage of kid qi may cause insomnia, anxiety, and muscle tension.

Conversely, how about living next to a hospital, funeral parlor, or even a place of worship? Here, you're enveloped with trauma, depression, sorrow, illness, and death. But wait, aren't churches, synagogues, and the like peaceful places? They can be. However, you're still subjected to the maladies of others. Here are more sites you should avoid living in close proximity to the following:

- Garbage dump
- Landfill
- Cemetery
- Police station
- Fire station
- Airport
- Railroad
- Factory
- Military camp
- High-tension power lines

If you live next to one of these places, can a five phase remedy offer protection? Unfortunately, no. The presence is simply too overwhelming. If you're a soldier stationed in a military camp or a minister living in the parsonage next to the church, take extra precautions to safeguard your health. A proper diet and exercise will help to defend against the inherently inauspicious site you must live in. However, it's best to try to avoid it altogether.

Land Sakes Alive!

There's much to consider when choosing or evaluating a house. You've already learned you can create a veritable heaven on earth just by identifying and situating yourself in an area that protects your back and left and right sides. Even if you don't live in a mountainous region, you can still find security and protection among neighboring structures.

Also, don't forget the fourth component—river and/or road patterns (and foothills, if applicable). Do the river courses and roadways surrounding your house bring sheng qi, promoting good health, wealth, and happiness? Or is your house the object of sha qi, bringing potential money loss, illness, and failed relationships?

Let's examine the land your house is situated on. Later, we'll look at other favorable and unfavorable factors that influence your state of being.

Over Hill, Over Dale

Where's the best place to live? On top of a hill? On a steep incline? How about on sloping land or flat terrain? Look at the following illustration. What do you believe to be the most favorable terrain?

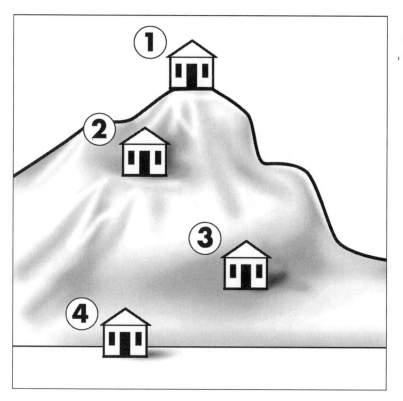

The geophysical plane your house sits on can affect your livelihood.

1. **A hilltop.** While offering a spectacular view, this is not an auspicious site. Left unprotected, you're subjected not only to nature's forces but also to psychological vulnerability. People who live on hilltops are known to feel insecure and exposed.

Wise Words

According to the *Professional Hypnotism Manual* by John G. Kappas, the **fight or flight** instinct is a primitive and involuntary reaction triggered during moments of danger or anxiety. As humankind (and animals) evolved, some developed greater strength and aggressiveness (fight), while others developed agility, speed, and a sensitivity to the senses of smell, sight, and hearing (flight). Those who remained passive eventually became extinct.

Feng Alert

While generally it's favorable to have a natural mountain formation supporting your back and a body of water in front, there are circumstances where this configuration can be detrimental to your health and livelihood. You'll learn more about this in Chapter 16, "The Flying Stars, Part 4."

Often, these individuals are prone to insomnia and nervousness. Imagine yourself camping out on a hilltop. It's just you and your sleeping bag. You have an unobstructed view of the stars. After a while, you doze off. But your sleep is not restful. On guard, you summon up the *fight or flight* reaction understood by primitive man. While the inhabitants of Masada and Machu Picchu may have been skilled at sleeping with one eye open, ultimately, they did not withstand the test of time. Again, choose a secure haven over a scenic view.

2. **A steep incline.** A mountain view in back, a panoramic view in front. Sound ideal? Imagine standing on a vertical incline. Naturally, you tend to lean back and widen your stance—anything to offer stability to prevent you from toppling over. Psychological effects aside, how about the threat of landslides? In feng shui, those who live on a steep incline are unable to retain wealth. Like a house on top of a hill, a house on a steep incline does not allow sheng qi to accumulate and settle. It's carried downhill. So is your hard-earned money.

3. **A sloping hill.** Classical feng shui doctrines tell us that living on a gently sloping hill is ideal. This is because the soil on this terrain is fertile and rich. Here, your house is less likely to flood. Depending on the grade of the slope, the upward incline can represent the black turtle, protecting and supporting your back.

4. **Flat terrain.** Although the ancient Chinese classics tell us flat, low-lying areas are best avoided (because of the threat of flooding and poor soil quality), these texts spoke to an agricultural society. Today, most urban dwellers live on flat terrain. Offering a solid foundation and security, this type of site is favorable.

Armed with this information, you'll think twice before purchasing your dream house on a hilltop or steep incline. As mama says, "It's better to be safe than sorry!"

Lots of Plots

Now that you understand what kind of terrain is considered favorable, let's see how the shape of your lot affects your well-being. Much of what we have presented so far relies on plain old common sense, a factor we're more accustomed to dealing with than complicated environmental concerns. We've discussed where you should seek a lot, now let's talk about the individual lot itself. Disregarding all other external details, look at the following illustrations. Which lots do you think are most favorable?

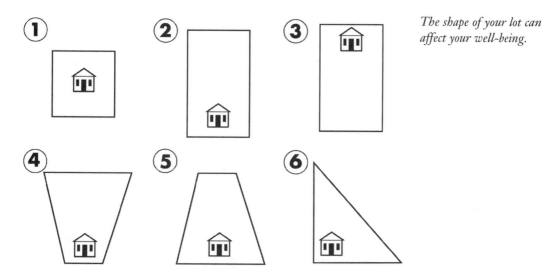

The shape of your lot can affect your well-being.

1. **Square lot.** In feng shui, a square shape, be it a lot, a room, or a table, denotes stability and balance. Qi is able to flow freely, unobstructed. Ideally, your house should be situated in the center of a lot, allowing qi to circulate around the structure and through its windows and doors, nourishing the occupants.

2. **Rectangular lot.** In this example, the dwelling is positioned at the front of the lot. Qi flows in and accumulates in the back, your wealth and health safeguarded. It's similar to a wealthy individual having "deep pockets." Investors have *backers*— ensuring support behind them.

3. **Deep front yard, shallow backyard.** In feng shui, if the space behind your house is significantly less than the space in front, you will have difficulty retaining money.

4. **Trapezoid lot.** Here, sheng qi inspiring good health and monetary gain must squeeze in. Like a bottleneck, the object in question must maneuver through the tight opening in order to accumulate in back. Because qi will have difficulty entering, this shape is not considered favorable.

5. **Inverted trapezoid lot.** In this example, qi has no trouble entering, but a difficult time staying. Imagine a cone-shaped paper cup. Flatten the bottom so that it's able to stand on its end, then fill it with water. More than likely, before the water reaches the rim, the cup will fall over. Its support base is too weak to retain the liquid. Similarly, sheng qi is unable to collect and settle.

6. **Triangular lot.** This is the most unfavorable of all the lot shapes. Simply, angular lots are disorienting.

Most likely, the shape of your lot corresponds to one of the illustrations just offered. Of course, there are other shapes. Take an L configuration. This shape is considered unfavorable because qi has a difficult time maneuvering around corners. Also, the junction of walls and/or fences produces angle sha, which impacts negatively on the well-being of the occupants. But, what if you live on a lot with no visible boundaries? Common in the Midwest, this situation features adjoining multiple lots with little, if any, visible division. The suggestion here is of one great yard. As long as qi is able to flow unobstructed, nourishing each structure, this housing configuration does not pose a problem. However, do be mindful of wind tunnels. We suggest planting shrubs and trees to prevent possible negative effects.

Regarding apartment-dwellers, while the external lot the building sits on is certainly a consideration, the shape of your unit within the building takes precedence. In other words, think of the floor your unit is located on as the lot. Where your unit is situated plays a role in the overall auspiciousness of your dwelling. Traditionally, side and back units don't receive as much light as front units. To offset the lack of yang qi, make sure your unit is amply lit.

House of Shapes

As we mentioned in Chapter 6, "The Principle of the Five Phases," each of the five phases corresponds to a shape: fire is triangular, earth is square, metal is round, water is wavy, and wood is rectangular. How does the shape affect qi's course? Consider each individually:

◆ **A triangle.** Most of us don't live in a teepee or a church. But some of us live in A-framed houses, or have some rooms whose walls are angular. Attic rooms are a good example. What does this mean? Well, again, you may feel disoriented, out of control, as if the room might cave in on you. Some people feel claustrophobic. Also, if two protruding walls come together to form an angle, this troublesome juncture creates sha qi.

Regarding qi's flow in a triangular dwelling, imagine bouncing a Super Ball in this room. What happens? The angular walls cause it to bounce in a crazy, haphazard fashion. It is the same with qi. After awhile, this dizzying effect will take its toll on your well-being.

- ◆ **A square.** This shape is your best friend. Square lots, square house, square rooms. No fuss, no muss. Here, qi flows freely. So abstain from an architecturally challenged structure in favor of something nice and normal. You'll be better off.

- ◆ **A circle.** This shape is ideal for sports coliseums, but would you want to be caught up in a whirlwind of qi? Imagine how water drains. Imagine the power a hurricane or tornado creates. Caught in the path, it's nearly impossible to free yourself. People who live in circular houses or who spend a lot of time in domed or circular rooms have trouble concentrating and sleeping.

- ◆ **Wavy.** A house conforming to this horizontal shape has variegated roof/ceiling lines. Like a ship at sea, the up-and-down motion of qi waves can cause you to feel unstable. Many castles and modern houses correspond to this shape.

- ◆ **A rectangle.** Symbolic of wood's expansion and growth, living in this type of structure is considered favorable. Like a square shape, rectangles don't present any odd angles to which qi will have difficulty maneuvering. Ranch houses and trailers are examples of rectangular dwellings. Now, a rectangle standing on its end is also considered a wood shape. High-rise buildings are good examples.

Feng Alert

Many modern houses are designed in a W- or lightning-bolt shape. While these houses may be the subject of interesting conversation, the sharp angles created by the juncture of these walls can cause misfortune and illness.

What about other configurations? While there are myriad different shapes, here are two common ones that, from our experience, affect the occupants differently.

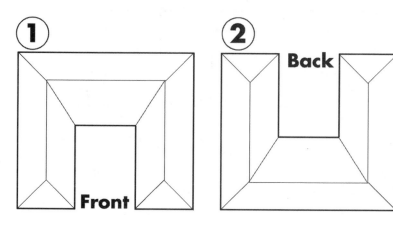

Two common shapes that affect the occupants differently.

1. People who live in a house with a receding central section are known to be of humble means and content. But in this case, you can't judge a book by its cover. While subconsciously they may appear to others to lack wealth, it's more likely the owners are financially secure. This is because the back of their house is solid, providing support and security.

2. People who live in a house that forms a U-shape, its central back section missing, subconsciously appear to others to be well off. In fact, these people are subjected to possible divorce, money loss, and other misfortune. This is because the sitting side of their dwelling does not provide uniform protection. Occupants feel as if they're exposed.

When judging a structure's form and layout, disregard furniture, doors, and windows, concentrating only on the shape of the dwelling and rooms. How do they make you feel? Remember, the external and internal environment should nurture, not deplete, you.

A Grand Entrance

As you'll soon find out in upcoming chapters, the most important part of a house is the entrance. It represents who we are. Similar to the car we drive or the clothes we wear, much can be said about the outward appearance of the main entrance. Yet, aside from visual factors, the front door is the primary location for the invisible qi force to enter. Later, you'll learn to determine if the entrance is inherently auspicious. But for now, let's concentrate on factors that can influence how you and your guests feel.

The size of the entrance affects occupants.

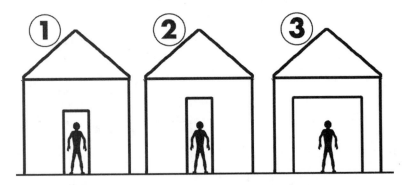

The size of your front door should be proportionate to the size of an average person (see illustration 1). Illustrations 2 and 3 show an entrance that is too tall and too large, respectively. Doors of this size encourage valuable qi to escape. In feng shui, it is believed you may experience financial loss by having such a grand entrance.

Conversely, if your entrance is too small (not illustrated here), you are restricting qi from entering. Here are some other considerations:

- The front door should not be impeded by things like a single tree or utility pole placed curbside in direct alignment with your entrance.

- The front door should be protected against any poison arrow qi coming from T-junctions, Y-junctions, or other sha qi emitted by neighboring structures.

- The path leading to your front door should be curved, forming a right angle just before the door.

- Ideally, the main entrance should be at the top of a flight of stairs. Sub-consciously, the occupants feel safer above street level.

- The main entrance should not be below street level. Qi is not able to enter easily; the occupants feel trapped.

- The main entrance should be inviting. Your front lawn should be mowed and bushes trimmed. In general, you should feel good about entering your own house; your guests should feel welcome. Your house shouldn't be an eyesore of weeds, overgrown plants, and peeling paint!

- The front entrance should not open onto a stairway positioned directly opposite the door. Similar to living on a hilltop or a steep incline, your potential to accumulate wealth will flow out the door.

- The front door and back door should not be in alignment. Literally, qi will enter in one door, and exit from the other.

- The front entrance should be well lit. By protecting the main entrance, you'll be promoting better health, wealth, and happiness.

You may be wondering if these considerations only apply to your main entrance. They apply to the front door and any other door (such as the back or side entrances) you use most often.

Feng Alert

Many public buildings, places of business, houses of worship, and large residential houses feature impressive double doors. If you're the owner of such a dwelling and are experiencing financial troubles, the size of the door may be a contributing factor to your hardship. We suggest using only one side of the door, disabling qi from gushing out.

Master Class

Unfortunately, many houses are constructed such that a long hallway connects the front and back doors. Considering the appropriate five phase remedy (and space provided), block negative qi's path by placing a screen, piece of furniture, or plant near the main entrance.

Room for Improvement

You may have heard that you should sleep with your head positioned toward the north. But as you'll soon learn, the direction you should sleep is determined by the trigram you belong to—knowledge you'll acquire in Chapter 10, "The Eight Houses, Part 1." This same method will also describe which directions are best for work and study. But until then, other factors contribute to the quality of your sleep, work, and study. Even though auspicious bed and desk positions are evaluated in the same way, we will separate the two to facilitate easier learning.

Now I Lay Me Down to Sleep

It stands to reason we should do everything possible to ensure a restful sleep. After all, we spend a third of our lifetime in our bedroom. Disregarding factors such as the shape of the room and the color of the room, here are some bed positions you should avoid:

Unfavorable bed placement.

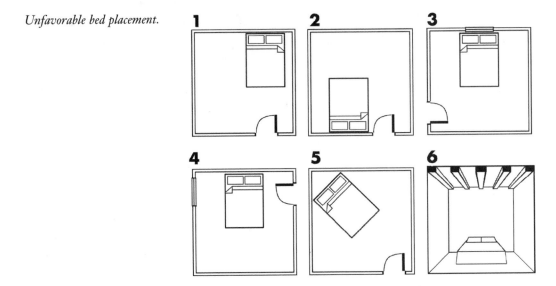

1. The foot of your bed should not face the door. Qi's flow will disrupt your sleep.

2. For the same reason, your bed should not be placed on the same wall as the door.

3. Your bed should not be positioned under a window. The elements will prevent a peaceful rest.

4. Your bed should not be positioned between a doorway and window, or a combination thereof. The wind tunnel will cause a disturbance.

5. Your bed should not be placed on an angle. Having the solid support of the black turtle will make you feel more secure, preventing the boogeyman from lurking in the black crevices.

6. You should not sleep under ceiling beams. The beams cause qi to create a ripple effect, the downward pressure impacting not only your sleep but also your health.

Feng Alert

While bunk beds save space, they don't promote quality sleep. The occupant on the bottom feels threatened by the looming top bunk; the occupant at top feels unconsciously susceptible to an inevitable fall. If a room is too small for two beds, consider a trundle bed (a bed that slides out from under a bed).

So, where is the ideal place to position your bed? Referring to the following illustrations, the bed should be placed on an unobstructed wall diagonally across from the door, as far enough away from the window such that you aren't bothered by the direct hit of incoming qi. Also, the bed should be accessible from both sides.

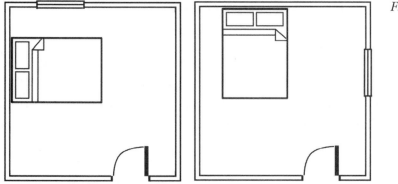

Favorable bed placement.

Now, before you begin to move furniture, you must first learn to determine which directions favor you (an important factor you'll learn about in the next chapter). Only then can you make a competent evaluation.

Working Nine to Five

The time we spend in our bedrooms may reign, but the time we spend at our desks follows closely. So, again, it behooves us to harness sheng qi to promote a better livelihood. Look at the following illustrations:

Unfavorable desk placement.

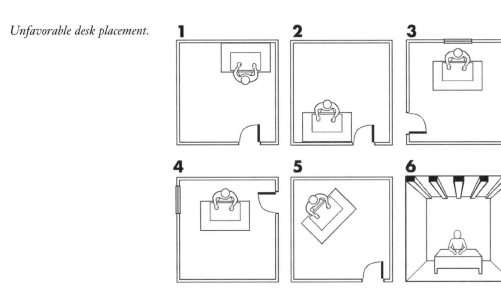

1. Your back should not face a doorway. It's important that you see anyone who enters. More importantly, your back must be supported by a wall.

2. The desk must not be placed on the same wall as the doorway. Qi flows directly toward you, causing a lack of concentration.

3. Your back must not be exposed to a window. Again, you need support. Besides, incoming sunlight will cause a glare on your computer screen.

4. The desk should not be positioned between two doors or two windows, or a combination thereof. The wind tunnel creates a lack of concentration and need for paperweights.

5. The desk should not be placed on an angle. You need support to get the job done.

6. The desk should not be positioned under overhead beams. The bombardment of the hammerlike qi pattern created by the beams will negatively affect you over time.

Now for the favorable positions. The following illustrations show a desk placed so that the person's back is supported by a wall. How close should your back be to the wall? Close enough so that you feel it's solidity. Also, you must be far enough away from qi's direct path entering through the window and door. And, the occupant must have a clear view of anyone entering.

Again, don't move anything just yet. First, you must learn how to determine your favorable directions. When all factors are considered, then you can begin the laborious task of rearranging the furniture. Hey, while you're at it, why not apply a fresh coat of paint (using the appropriate color, of course), and get rid of clutter? Qi will flow more smoothly. You'll feel more organized, confident, and motivated.

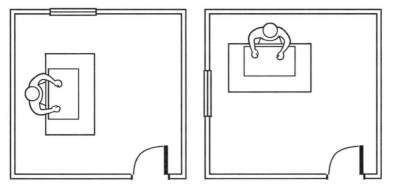

Favorable desk placement.

Moving Day

What about the rest of your house? What about arranging your living room, den, and kitchen according to feng shui principles? Follow these simple guidelines and you'll be on your way to achieving harmony, balance, good health, and prosperity:

♦ The furniture in the room should be a mixture of yin and yang. Balance dark with light; angled corners with round.

♦ The furniture should be proportionate to the room. The pieces should be arranged evenly to facilitate easy access.

♦ Sofas are best placed against a wall.

♦ The backs of sofas or chairs should not face any entrances.

♦ All areas should be free of clutter.

♦ Objets d'art should be balanced.

It's a good idea to plot out different furniture arrangements on graph paper. Study each design and choose the one best corresponding to our suggestions. Sometimes change can be difficult. So, have a friend or family member help you. A well-informed, objective opinion can present options you may not have considered.

In the next part, we'll introduce you to the Eight House method of feng shui.

The Least You Need to Know

♦ Living next to a place of worship, school, hospital, or fire station can cause health risks.

♦ Living on gently sloping or flat terrain is better than living on a hill or a steep incline.

◆ The shape of your lot and house affects how vital sheng qi is able to accumulate and settle.

◆ To ensure a restful sleep, your bed should be supported by a wall and positioned away from doors and windows.

◆ To increase productivity, your back should be supported by a wall; the desk should be stationed away from doors and windows.

Part 4

Feng Shui Mechanics 101

Part 4 is all about the Eight House system, the most popular method of feng shui in Asia. Why is it so popular? Probably because it's relatively easy to master, requiring minimal calculations. Also, this method offers a black-and-white analysis. No variables. No shades of gray. It's a cinch.

Want to know if you're compatible with your house? Or if you're compatible with your significant other? You'll learn how to determine this here. Also, you'll learn which direction affords you the best sleep and which direction promotes productivity at your work or study station. By making simple adjustments, at no expense, you can improve your living situation.

Chapter 10

The Eight Houses, Part 1

In This Chapter

- What is the Eight House system?
- Calculate your personal trigram
- Determine your best sitting direction
- Determine your best sleeping direction
- Determine your compatibility with your significant other, friends, and family members

Are there certain people who, for no apparent reason, "rub you the wrong way"? Are there people with whom you immediately bond? Do you find you sleep better facing a certain direction? Are there rooms in your home that invite relaxation, peace, and comfort? Are there rooms that make you feel uncomfortable, anxious, or depressed? Have you ever wondered about all of this?

This chapter will answer these questions. So, sharpen your pencil—you're about to learn some basic feng shui mechanics. You'll also be putting to good use everything you've learned thus far.

About Face: The Eight House System

Eight House feng shui proposes that each of the eight cardinal directions holds a different kind of qi to which people and buildings react either positively or negatively. Stated another way, Eight House is used to determine your four lucky and four unlucky directions (or areas within your home). Also, the system is used to determine your home's favorable and unfavorable directions. The object of Eight House is to ascertain a person's compatibility with his dwelling and then (using the five phases of qi that you learned about in Chapter 6, "The Principle of the Five Phases") remedy or enhance the qi in his or her living and/or working space to provide a productive atmosphere conducive to good health, harmony, and success.

While we'll expand upon these ideas in this chapter and in successive ones about Eight House, for now understand the eight "houses" or trigrams that you learned about in Chapter 7, "The Principle of the Eight Trigrams," are divided into two groups of four trigrams—the East Group and the West Group:

♦ East Group: Zhen (east), Xun (southeast), Kan (north), Li (south)

♦ West Group: Qian (northwest), Kun (southwest), Gen (northeast), Dui (west)

Upon closer examination, you might wonder why each division contains a trigram that is not directionally appropriate. Why does Kan (north) belong to the East Group? Why does Gen (northeast) belong to the West Group? The traditional explanation cited in the *Yijing* says that each group forms a family. This is easily demonstrated in the West Group: father (Qian), mother (Kun), youngest son (Gen), and youngest daughter (Dui). But the composition of the East Group familial unit requires a stretch of your imagination: The middle son (Kan) and middle daughter (Li) are supported by the oldest son (Zhen) and oldest daughter (Xun). Get the idea?

Wise Words _____

Eight House (Bazhai, in Chinese) is a method of determining your four lucky and unlucky directions for you and your home. Also, it can be used to determine how compatible you are with any given person. Eight House is also known as Yigua (Changing Trigrams) feng shui, Eight Mansions, and the East/West System.

Generally, for those belonging to the East Group, all four of its associated directions are favorable, while all the directions of the West Group are unfavorable. For those belonging to the West Group, all four of its associated directions are favorable, while all the directions in the East Group are unfavorable. People born in the same group are more compatible than with those belonging to opposing groups. How can you determine to which East or West Group you belong? You'll find out soon enough! By understanding and practicing Eight House you'll be able to …

Feng Facts

According to legend, Yi Xing (673–727 C.E.), a Chan Buddhist monk, astronomer, and royal advisor to the Tang dynasty, created the Eight House method at the request of Emperor Xuan Zong (685–762 C.E.). However, while the emperor ordered Yi Xing to devise a false method for the "barbarian" neighbors, the monk instead created a simple one based on feng shui's fundamental principles. While written documentation of Yi Xing's methodology no longer exists, the system is described in a few texts. First, there's the Ming dynasty (1368–1644 C.E.) text of unknown authorship called *Yangzhai Shishu* (*Ten Books on Residential Feng Shui*). Then, there's the *Bazhai Mingjing* (*A Clear Treatise on the Eight Houses*), which is also known as the *Bazhai Zhoushu* (*The Complete Book of Eight Houses*). Attributed to Ruo Guan ("bamboo hat") Daoren ("Daoist") of the Qing dynasty (1644–1911 C.E.), the *Bazhai Mingjing* was included in Emperor Qian Long's imperial library.

- ◆ Determine your personal trigram.
- ◆ Determine your home's trigram.
- ◆ Understand how the same house can affect people differently.
- ◆ Locate an auspicious home and/or office.
- ◆ Locate the productive (and unproductive) areas in your home.
- ◆ Locate your best sleeping direction.
- ◆ Determine if a potential mate is right for you.
- ◆ Understand why you get along better with some people than with others.

Eight House is ideal for beginners because it's relatively easy to master. Once you understand its principles, application is a snap. You'll be analyzing your home and your friends' homes before you know it!

What's Your Trigram?

Xun, Li, Kun, Zhen, Dui, Gen, Kan, or Qian? Don't know your personal trigram? Well, there's a special formula that determines which trigram and its associations belong to you. You need only to know two things: your year of birth and gender. Once you figure out your personal trigram, you can then determine which of the eight magnetic directions are beneficial and which are detrimental to your well-being. You'll also understand how you affect—and are affected by—other people. Are you the controlled or the controller? Do you support or are you supported?

 **Master Class**

Your personal trigram is determined by your birth year and gender.

Generally, those of the same gender born in a given year will share the same trigram—but there's an exception to this rule. If you were born between January 1 and February 2 of a given year, you'll use the year prior to your birth year to determine your personal trigram. If you were born on February 3, 4, or 5, you must consult the table in Chapter 21, "Introducing the Twelve Animals of the Chinese Zodiac," to determine to which year you belong (instructions and examples are provided to ensure an accurate calculation). Why all the fuss? This is because feng shui uses the Chinese solar calendar, which variously marks February 3, 4, or 5 as the first day of the new year, the midpoint between the winter solstice and spring equinox. For example, let's take a woman born on January 3, 1962. She would use the year 1961 to calculate her personal trigram.

Personal Trigram Formula: Male

Use the following formula to determine a male's personal trigram. The blank spaces after each sample calculation are for you to calculate your own personal trigram. If you're a female, you have to use the formula for female (in the following section)—use the formula below to calculate the trigrams of the men in your family. Why are there different formulas for a male and female? Because yang (male) and yin (female) qi tend to flow in opposing directions. Although it is beyond our scope to investigate this further, know that each formula is determined by movement of qi.

1. Add the digits in your birth year. As an example, let's use a male born in 1954.

   $1 + 9 + 5 + 4 = 19$

   _____ + _____ + _____ + _____ = _____

2. Add the resulting number until you get a single-digit number.

   $1 + 9 = 10; 1 + 0 = 1$

   _____ + _____ = _____

3. Subtract the resulting number from 11. If the result is 10, add the digits until you get a single-digit number.

   $11 - 1 = 10; 1 + 0 = 1$

   _____ - _____ = _____

The resulting number is your ming gua, your natal or personal trigram, which is matched with a number from the Luoshu magic square (something you'll learn about in Chapter 13, "The Flying Stars, Part 1").

In the example's case, Kan (1) is his personal trigram. Kan is associated with the water phase.

Note: If your personal trigram is 5, use number 2 as your trigram.

Personal Trigram Formula: Female

Use the following formula to determine a female's personal trigram. The blank spaces are for you to calculate your own personal trigram, assuming, of course, that you're female.

1. Add the digits in the birth year. As an example, let's continue with the woman. As we have already concluded, the example would use 1961 as her Chinese birth year.

   $1 + 9 + 6 + 1 = 17$

   _1_ + _9_ + _6_ + _5_ = _21_

2. Add the resulting number until you get a single-digit number.

   $1 + 7 = 8$

   _2_ + _1_ = _3_

3. Add 4 to the resulting number.

   $8 + 4 = 12$

   _3_ + _4_ = _7_

4. The resulting number is your personal trigram. Because the example's resulting number is a two-digit number, she must add up the digits. The sum is the example's personal trigram. Therefore:

   $1 + 2 = 3.$

In the example's case, Zhen (3) is her trigram. Zhen is associated with the wood phase.

Note: If your personal trigram is 5, use the number 8 as your trigram.

Now you know your personal trigram.

Master Class _____

Remember, if you were born between January 1 and February 2, use the year prior to your birth year to determine your personal trigram. If you were born on February 3, 4, or 5, you must consult the table in Chapter 21 to determine your Chinese birth year.

The Personal Trigram Quick Reference Chart

Anxious that you may have made a mistake? Don't worry. The following quick reference chart gives you everything you need to know right at your fingertips.

Table 1 - Personal Trigram Quick Reference Chart

Year	Male	Gua	Phase	Female	Gua	Phase	Year	Male	Gua	Phase	Female	Gua	Phase
1924	Xun	4	Wood	Kun	2	Earth	1964	Li	9	Fire	Qian	6	Metal
1925	Zhen	3	Wood	Zhen	3	Wood	1965	Gen	8	Earth	Dui	7	Metal
1926	Kun	2	Earth	Xun	4	Wood	1966	Dui	7	Metal	Gen	8	Earth
1927	Kan	1	Water	Gen	8	Earth	1967	Qian	6	Metal	Li	9	Fire
1928	Li	9	Fire	Qian	6	Metal	1968	Kun	2	Earth	Kan	1	Water
1929	Gen	8	Earth	Dui	7	Metal	1969	Xun	4	Wood	Kun	2	Earth
1930	Dui	7	Metal	Gen	8	Earth	1970	Zhen	3	Wood	Zhen	3	Wood
1931	Qian	6	Metal	Li	9	Fire	1971	Kun	2	Earth	Xun	4	Wood
1932	Kun	2	Earth	Kan	1	Water	1972	Kan	1	Water	Gen	8	Earth
1933	Xun	4	Wood	Kun	2	Earth	1973	Li	9	Fire	Qian	6	Metal
1934	Zhen	3	Wood	Zhen	3	Wood	1974	Gen	8	Earth	Dui	7	Metal
1935	Kun	2	Earth	Xun	4	Wood	1975	Dui	7	Metal	Gen	8	Earth
1936	Kan	1	Water	Gen	8	Earth	1976	Qian	6	Metal	Li	9	Fire
1937	Li	9	Fire	Qian	6	Metal	1977	Kun	2	Earth	Kan	1	Water
1938	Gen	8	Earth	Dui	7	Metal	1978	Xun	4	Wood	Kun	2	Earth
1939	Dui	7	Metal	Gen	8	Earth	1979	Zhen	3	Wood	Zhen	3	Wood
1940	Qian	6	Metal	Li	9	Fire	1980	Kun	2	Earth	Xun	4	Wood
1941	Kun	2	Earth	Kan	1	Water	1981	Kan	1	Water	Gen	8	Earth
1942	Xun	4	Wood	Kun	2	Earth	1982	Li	9	Fire	Qian	6	Metal
1943	Zhen	3	Wood	Zhen	3	Wood	1983	Gen	8	Earth	Dui	7	Metal
1944	Kun	2	Earth	Xun	4	Wood	1984	Dui	7	Metal	Gen	8	Earth
1945	Kan	1	Water	Gen	8	Earth	1985	Qian	6	Metal	Li	9	Fire
1946	Li	9	Fire	Qian	6	Metal	1986	Kun	2	Earth	Kan	1	Water
1947	Gen	8	Earth	Dui	7	Metal	1987	Xun	4	Wood	Kun	2	Earth
1948	Dui	7	Metal	Gen	8	Earth	1988	Zhen	3	Wood	Zhen	3	Wood
1949	Qian	6	Metal	Li	9	Fire	1989	Kun	2	Earth	Xun	4	Wood
1950	Kun	2	Earth	Kan	1	Water	1990	Kan	1	Water	Gen	8	Earth
1951	Xun	4	Wood	Kun	2	Earth	1991	Li	9	Fire	Qian	6	Metal
1952	Zhen	3	Wood	Zhen	3	Wood	1992	Gen	8	Earth	Dui	7	Metal
1953	Kun	2	Earth	Xun	4	Wood	1993	Dui	7	Metal	Gen	8	Earth
1954	Kan	1	Water	Gen	8	Earth	1994	Qian	6	Metal	Li	9	Fire
1955	Li	9	Fire	Qian	6	Metal	1995	Kun	2	Earth	Kan	1	Water
1956	Gen	8	Earth	Dui	7	Metal	1996	Xun	4	Wood	Kun	2	Earth
1957	Dui	7	Metal	Gen	8	Earth	1997	Zhen	3	Wood	Zhen	3	Wood
1958	Qian	6	Metal	Li	9	Fire	1998	Kun	2	Earth	Xun	4	Wood
1959	Kun	2	Earth	Kan	1	Water	1999	Kan	1	Water	Gen	8	Earth
1960	Xun	4	Wood	Kun	2	Earth	2000	Li	9	Fire	Qian	6	Metal
1961	Zhen	3	Wood	Zhen	3	Wood	2001	Gen	8	Earth	Dui	7	Metal
1962	Kun	2	Earth	Xun	4	Wood	2002	Dui	7	Metal	Gen	8	Earth
1963	Kan	1	Water	Gen	8	Earth	2003	Qian	6	Metal	Li	9	Fire

Dui 7 Metal

Table 1 - Personal Trigram Quick Reference Chart

Year	Male	Gua	Phase	Female	Gua	Phase	Year	Male	Gua	Phase	Female	Gua	Phase
2004	Kun	2	Earth	Kan	1	Water	2014	Xun	4	Wood	Kun	2	Earth
2005	Xun	4	Wood	Kun	2	Earth	2015	Zhen	3	Wood	Zhen	3	Wood
2006	Zhen	3	Wood	Zhen	3	Wood	2016	Kun	2	Earth	Xun	4	Wood
2007	Kun	2	Earth	Xun	4	Wood	2017	Kan	1	Water	Gen	8	Earth
2008	Kan	1	Water	Gen	8	Earth	2018	Li	9	Fire	Qian	6	Metal
2009	Li	9	Fire	Qian	6	Metal	2019	Gen	8	Earth	Dui	7	Metal
2010	Gen	8	Earth	Dui	7	Metal	2020	Dui	7	Metal	Gen	8	Earth
2011	Dui	7	Metal	Gen	8	Earth	2021	Qian	6	Metal	Li	9	Fire
2012	Qian	6	Metal	Li	9	Fire	2022	Kun	2	Earth	Kan	1	Water
2013	Kun	2	Earth	Kan	1	Water	2023	Xun	4	Wood	Kun	2	Earth

Before you proceed with this chapter, you must determine your personal trigram. Take a moment to calculate it now if you haven't done so. A personal trigram chart can also be found on the back of the tear-out card in front of this book.

Master Class

The question often arises: "Does wearing the color or decorating my room in the color associated with my personal trigram bring me good luck?" For example, if you belong to the Zhen trigram, is green your best color? Or, if you belong to the Kan trigram, are blue and black your best colors? The answer is: not necessarily. The colors that represent your innate qi can only be determined by calculating your Four Pillars, a method of Chinese astrology that you'll learn about in Part 7, "Fate or Free Will: What's Your Destiny?"

The Eight Wandering Stars

The eight types of qi are collectively known as the Eight Wandering Stars (You Xing). Referring to the following table, we've included each star's Chinese name and English translation, its associated phase, a level of fortune, and a description of its qi. The letter F stands for Fortunate Qi, with F1 being the most favorable star and F4 being the fourth most favorable star. Conversely, the letter H stands for Harmful Qi, with H1 representing the least harmful star and H4 the most harmful star. Depending to which trigram you belong, each of the eight directions is either fortunate or harmful to you in varying degrees. So how can you determine which direction corresponds to Sheng Qi (F1), you ask? Keep reading!

Table 2 - The Eight Wandering Stars

Star	English Translation	Phase	Level of Fortune	Auspice
Sheng Qi	Life Qi	Wood	F1	Prosperity & Respectability
Yan Nian	Prolonged Years	Metal	F2	Longevity & Romantic Relationships
Tian Yi	Heavenly Doctor	Earth	F3	Good Health & Harmonious Relationships
Fu Wei	Stooping Position	Wood	F4	Peace & Stability
Hou Hai	Misfortune	Earth	H1	Accidents, Arguments & Injury
Liu Sha	Six Devils	Water	H2	Malicious Encounters & Failed Relationships
Wu Gui	Five Ghosts	Fire	H3	Litigation, Accidents, Injury & Fire
Jue Ming	Ultimate End of Life	Metal	H4	Disease, Misfortune & Unproductive Careers

Master Class

The phase associated with each star (along with the phase associated with the Hou Tian palaces or eight cardinal directions) will become particularly important when you learn to balance the qi in your living/working space (the subject of Chapter 12, "The Eight Houses, Part 3"). For a reminder about what phase governs a particular direction, see Chapter 7, "The Principle of the Eight Trigrams," or the front of the tear-out card at the beginning of this book.

Changing Your Fortune

To determine your most favorable directions, you need your personal trigram and its symbol. (This method is also used to determine your home's most favorable directions. But to do this, you must first determine your home's trigram, which you'll learn in the next chapter.) Again, follow along and compute your favorable directions using the space provided.

Your F1 direction corresponds to Sheng Qi, the qi energy that brings about heightened prosperity and respectability. It's your most favorable magnetic direction for conducting business, studying, or anything else of importance. To determine your F1 direction, change line 3. Let's take the male example who belongs to the Kan trigram. In this case, line 3 of the Kan trigram is yin (broken line). He would then change it to yang (solid line).

Master Class

Remember, trigrams are read from the bottom line up.

The example's Kan trigram changes to the Xun trigram, located in the southeast.

Your F2 direction corresponds to Yan Nian, the qi energy that brings about longevity and romantic relationships. The F2 direction is your second most favorable direction. To determine your F2 direction, change all three lines.

The example's Kan trigram changes to the Li trigram, located in the south.

Your F3 direction corresponds to Tian Yi, the qi energy that brings about good health and harmonious relationships. The F3 direction is your third most favorable direction. To determine your F3 direction, change lines 1 and 2. In the example's case, line 1 is yin, which now changes to yang; line 2 is yang, which becomes yin.

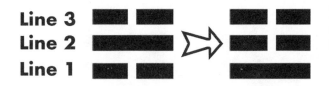

The example's Kan trigram changes to the Zhen trigram, located in the east.

Your F4 direction corresponds to Fu Wei, the qi energy that brings about peace and stability. F4 is your fourth most favorable direction. You will get your best sleep if the crown of your head points toward F4. To determine your F4 direction, no lines are changed.

The example's Kan (north) trigram remains the same.

Your H1 direction corresponds to Hou Hai, the qi energy that is considered the first least harmful. If located at your entrance or bedroom, H1 qi has been known to cause accidents, arguments, and injury. To determine your H1 direction, change line 1. The example's yin line becomes a yang line.

The example's Kan trigram changes to Dui, located in the west.

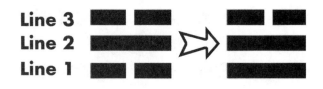

Your H2 direction corresponds with Liu Sha, the qi energy that is considered the second least harmful. H2 qi has been known to cause malicious encounters or sexual entanglements and failed relationships. To determine your H2 direction, change lines 1 and 3. In the example's case, lines 1 and 3 are yin, which now becomes yang.

The example's Kan trigram changes to Qian, located in the northwest.

Your H3 direction corresponds with Wu Gui, the qi energy that is third least harmful. H3 qi has been known to cause fires, accidents, and abandonment of friends and family. To determine your H3 direction, change lines 2 and 3. The example's line 2 becomes yin; line 3 becomes yang.

The example's Kan trigram changes to Gen, located in the northeast.

Your H4 direction corresponds with Jue Ming, the qi energy that is the most harmful and dangerous. You should spend the least amount of time in or avoid this area altogether. H4 qi brings about disease, misfortune, and unproductive careers. Using entrances or bedrooms with H4 qi will weaken your health, wealth, and relationships. To determine your H4 direction, change line 2. The example's line 2 now becomes yin.

The example's Kan trigram changes to Kun, located in the southwest.

If you're wondering how a particular star is associated with the changing trigram formula, there is a reason behind the methodology. For example, why is a person's Sheng Qi (F1) and not, say, the qi associated with the star Hou Hai, determined by changing line 3 of his or her trigram? Unfortunately, space prevents us from offering an explanation here. However, one explanation can be found in Chapter 14 of *The Complete Idiot's Guide to the I Ching.*

Master Class

The Eight Wandering Stars are matched with the nine stars of the Big Dipper as follows: Sheng Qi is matched with Tan Lang (Ravenous Wolf); Yan Nian is matched with Wu Qu (The Military); Tian Yi with Ju Men (Great Gate); Fu Wei with the two stars comprising the Big Dipper's handle, Zou Fu and You Bi (Left and Right Assistants); Hou Hai with Lu Cun (Prosperity Reserved); Liu Sha with Wen Qu (The Scholars); Wu Gui with Lian Zhen (Chastity); and Jue Ming with Po Jun (Destructive Army). Although it is not clear how the concept of the Nine Stars developed, many scholars believe the names comprising the seven stars of the Big Dipper (excluding the two stars forming its handle) came from India.

East Meets West

Notice how the example's four most favorable directions belong to the same trigram group: Xun (F1), Li (F2), Zhen (F3), and Kan (F4). They represent the East Group of trigrams we first defined at the beginning of this chapter. The example's most unfavorable directions belong to this opposing trigram group: Dui (H1), Qian (H2), Gen (H3), and Kun (H4). They represent the West Group of trigrams.

This is a lot of work! How can you be sure you've calculated your favorable and unfavorable directions correctly? No fear, another quick reference table is here! The Wandering Star Auspice chart can also be found on the front of the tear-out card in the beginning of this book.

The following table (divided into East and West Groups) shows how each of the eight Wandering Stars affects the trigram in question. For example, take the Kun trigram (West Group). A Kun person's favorable directions are northeast (F1), northwest (F2), west (F3), and southwest (F4). Conversely, the Kun person's unfavorable directions are east (H1), south (H2), southeast (H3), and north (H4). Before you proceed, find your personal trigram and learn the directions that are beneficial and detrimental to your well-being.

The eight trigrams and their corresponding good and bad directions.

Table 3

WANDERING STAR AUSPICE

		EAST GROUP				WEST GROUP			
		Zhen	Xun	Kan	Li	Qian	Kun	Gen	Dui
		Wood	Wood	Water	Fire	Metal	Earth	Earth	Metal
		3	4	1	9	6	2	8	7
		D	I	R	E	C	T	I	O	N	S
Great Prosperity & Respectability	F1	S	N	SE	E	W	NE	SW	NW
Longevity & Romantic Relationships	F2	SE	E	S	N	SW	NW	W	NE
Good Health & Harmonious Relationships	F3	N	S	E	SE	NE	W	NW	SW
Peace & Stability	F4	E	SE	N	S	NW	SW	NE	W
Accidents, Arguments & Injury	H1	SW	NW	W	NE	SE	E	S	N
Possible Malicious Encounters & Failed Relationships	H2	NE	W	NW	SW	N	S	E	SE
Litigation, Accidents, Injury & Fire	H3	NW	SW	NE	W	E	SE	N	S
Possible Disease, Misfortune & Unproductive Careers	H4	W	NE	SW	NW	S	N	SE	E

At this point you may be thinking, "Okay, I understand this table. But how can the letter designations help to improve my health, livelihood, and relationships?" Well, you can benefit from the auspicious qi (designations F1 to F4) appropriate to your personal trigram by making simple adjustments now. Referring to the illustration below, it is most advantageous to face your F1 direction, followed by your F2 and F3 directions. Although F4 is more favorable than H1 to H4, you might experience drowsiness or a sense of procrastination.

Facing your favorable directions F1 to F3 will promote good fortune and productivity.

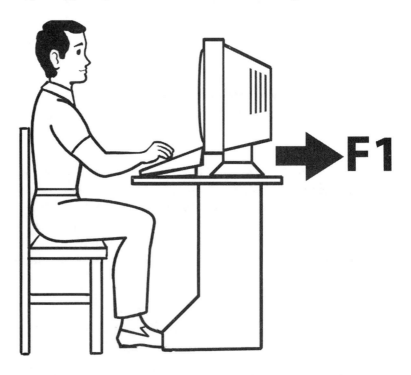

Now, let's discuss your most favorable sleeping directions. Referring to the following illustration, the position promoting the most restful night's sleep is to have the crown of your head pointing toward your F4 direction. This is followed by F3 (your second choice) and F2 (your third choice). Although F1 is more favorable than H1 to H4, sleeping toward your F1 direction may cause insomnia. This is because your subconscious mind will continue to work at the same pace as when you are awake. The inability of the subconscious mind to relax often causes insomnia.

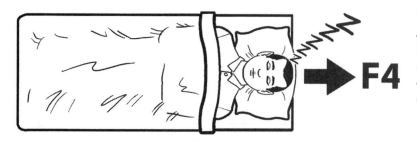

To promote a restful night, sleep with your head pointed toward your F4 direction ideally, then F3, F2, and F1 directions in order of decreasing preferences.

Now that you understand how to determine the directions most beneficial to you, feel free to don your work gloves and move your bed and desk positions accordingly. But, be careful! You must also consider door and window alignment. As a reminder, consult Chapter 9, "Home Sweet Home: Evaluating Your House and Its Surroundings."

Are You Compatible?

As we mentioned earlier in this chapter, those belonging to the same East or West Group are generally compatible and those belonging to opposing groups are not. While this is a broad statement, let's fine-tune the level of compatibility. First, determine the ming gua (personal trigram) of the person in question. If his or her ming gua falls on the F1 or F2 sections of your chart (consult the Wandering Star Auspice table 3), the relationship (marriage, friend, family member, boss, significant other, for example) is excellent. If his or her gua falls on the F3 section of your chart, the relationship is very good. If it falls on the F4 section of your chart, the relationship is good. On the other hand, if the person's gua is located on your H1 section, the relationship is unsatisfactory. If the person's gua is located on your H2 section, the relationship is bad. And, if it is located on the H3 or H4 sections of your chart, the relationship is disastrous.

For example, take a Zhen (3) person married to a Xun (4) person. The number 3 is located in the east section of the Hou Tian (After Heaven) sequence of trigrams. Consulting the previous Wandering Star Auspice table 3, east for a Xun person is F2. Therefore, their relationship is excellent. Take a Zhen person married to a Kan (1) person. East (Zhen) for a Kan person is F3—their marriage is very good. Take a Zhen person married to a Kun (2) person. East (Zhen) for a Kun person is H1—their marriage is bad. Get the idea?

Feng Facts

George W. Bush (Li/East Group) and Laura Welch Bush (Qian/West Group) belong to opposing trigrams. They are H4 to each other. Bill Clinton (Li/East Group) and Hillary Clinton (Dui/West Group) also belong to opposing trigrams. They are H3 to each other. Prince Charles (Dui/West Group) and the former Princess Diana (Zhen/East Group) were also incompatible. They were H4 to each other. On the positive side, JFK (Kun/West Group) and Jacqueline Kennedy (Dui/West Group) were F3 to each other; Richard (Dui/West Group) and Pat Nixon (Gen/West Group) were F2 to each other; and Ronald (Gen/West Group) and Nancy Reagan (Gen/West Group) are F4 to each other. According to an old Chinese proverb, if you believe everything you read in a book, it is better to be without the book. While we believe Eight House is 75 percent accurate, there is a margin for error. Hence, some of these examples may not be entirely accurate.

The following People Compatibility table 4 illustrates the procedure we just described. Considering the first example—the Zhen person married to a Xun person—the point where the two trigrams intersect designates the quality of their relationship. Zhen and Xun are F2 to each other. Note: If you're F1 or F2 to each other, the relationship is excellent. If you're F3 to each other, the relationship is very good. If you're F4 to each other, the relationship is good. If you're H1 to each other, the relationship is unsatisfactory. If you're H2 to each other, the relationship is bad. And, if you're H3 or H4 to each other, the relationship is disastrous.

People Compatibility table.

Table 4

		EAST GROUP				WEST GROUP			
Personal Trigram ▶▼		**Zhen**	**Xun**	**Kan**	**Li**	**Qian**	**Kun**	**Gen**	**Dui**
		3	4	1	9	6	2	8	7
Zhen	3	F4	F2	F3	F1	H3	H1	H2	H4
Xun	4	F2	F4	F1	F3	H1	H3	H4	H2
Kan	1	F3	F1	F4	F2	H2	H4	H3	H1
Li	9	F1	F3	F2	F4	H4	H2	H1	H3
Qian	6	H3	H1	H2	H4	F4	F2	F3	F1
Kun	2	H1	H3	H4	H2	F2	F4	F1	F3
Gen	8	H2	H4	H3	H1	F3	F1	F4	F2
Dui	7	H4	H2	H1	H3	F1	F3	F2	F4

(Left side labels: EAST GROUP for Zhen, Xun, Kan, Li; WEST GROUP for Qian, Kun, Gen, Dui)

As an experiment, determine the personal trigrams of individuals you like and dislike. More often than not, those with whom you share an affinity belong to the same East or West Group as you. Those who "rub you the wrong way" probably belong to an opposing group.

The next chapter continues with the Eight House system. Focusing on determining your home's trigram, you'll learn how to choose the dwelling best suited to you.

The Least You Need to Know

- ◆ Your personal trigram is determined by your birth year and gender.
- ◆ Your personal trigram reflects how you affect—and are affected by—other people.
- ◆ Your personal trigram determines your favorable and unfavorable directions.
- ◆ Your personal trigram can determine which direction is best for work, study, and sleep.

Chapter 11

The Eight Houses, Part 2

In This Chapter

- ◆ Determining your home's trigram
- ◆ Determining your home's facing direction
- ◆ Using a compass to determine your home's sitting direction
- ◆ Comparing your personal trigram to your home's trigram
- ◆ Dividing your house into eight equal sections
- ◆ Comparing your personal trigram to your home's trigram

In the previous chapter, we introduced you to the Eight House system and told you how your personal trigram determines your favorable and unfavorable directions. Now let's continue our discussion of Eight House methodology.

This chapter's all about your living and working space. You'll learn why certain places make you feel uncomfortable, while other places make you feel "at home." You'll learn how to identify homes, apartments, and offices that are compatible with your personal trigram. So have your compass ready—you'll be using it later on in this chapter.

Your House Has a Trigram, Too

Just as you have a personal trigram, so does your home, building, apartment, and office unit. Although their trigrams are determined using a different technique, the other rules still apply:

- The trigrams are divided into the same set of East and West Groups.

- Trigrams belonging to the same group are compatible, whereas trigrams belonging to opposing groups are not.

- The trigram F through H symbologies remain the same.

The following illustrations show the eight types of dwellings that can be determined by using the Eight House system. The ⊔ symbol represents the sitting direction of the house. The ↑ symbol represents the facing direction of the house. The sections outlined in bold represent each group's favorable directions.

The East Group House Trigrams

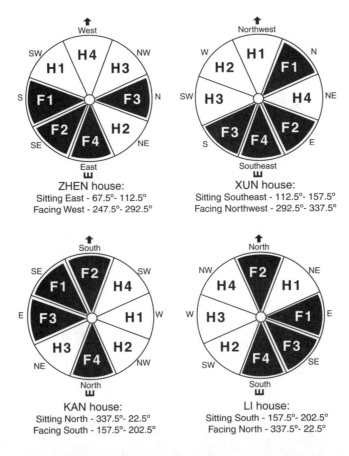

ZHEN house:
Sitting East - 67.5°- 112.5°
Facing West - 247.5°- 292.5°

XUN house:
Sitting Southeast - 112.5°- 157.5°
Facing Northwest - 292.5°- 337.5°

KAN house:
Sitting North - 337.5°- 22.5°
Facing South - 157.5°- 202.5°

LI house:
Sitting South - 157.5°- 202.5°
Facing North - 337.5°- 22.5°

The West Group House Trigrams

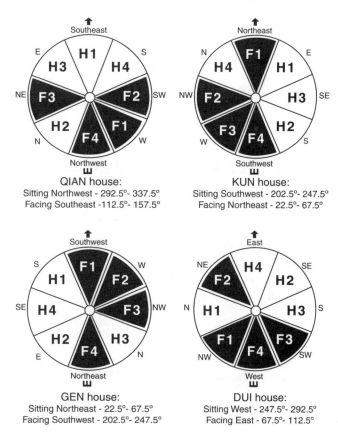

QIAN house:
Sitting Northwest - 292.5°- 337.5°
Facing Southeast -112.5°- 157.5°

KUN house:
Sitting Southwest - 202.5°- 247.5°
Facing Northeast - 22.5°- 67.5°

GEN house:
Sitting Northeast - 22.5°- 67.5°
Facing Southwest - 202.5°- 247.5°

DUI house:
Sitting West - 247.5°- 292.5°
Facing East - 67.5°- 112.5°

Notice how the F4 direction, or F4 qi, is in the same position in each of the eight trigrams. In feng shui, this position is called the *sitting direction*. The sitting direction determines the trigram. For example, Zhen is associated with the direction east. East is in Zhen's F4 direction. Dui is associated with the direction west. West is in Dui's F4 direction. Li is associated with the direction south. South is in Li's F4 direction. And so forth.

A house also has a *facing direction*. While we will learn how to determine this later on in this chapter, know that the facing direction is magnetically opposite the sitting direction. If this may seem like an obvious assumption, determining a home's sitting and facing sides is often a confusing task—even to an experienced practitioner. Evaluating apartment units is perhaps the most difficult. But, don't fret. We've provided

Wise Words

A home's **sitting direction** determines its trigram. The sitting direction usually corresponds to the backside of a dwelling. A home's **facing direction** is magnetically opposite its sitting direction.

detailed instructions on how to make a competent evaluation of your home's sitting and facing directions.

Ideally, your home's main entrance, your bedroom, and other rooms where you spend the most amount of time (living/family room, kitchen, home office) should hold favorable qi represented by the designations F1, F2, F3, and F4. The unfavorable qi areas represented by the designations H1, H2, H3, and H4 should be designated to rooms like the laundry room, bathrooms, guest bedrooms, and the basement—areas in which you spend less time.

Comparing Your Personal Trigram to a Home's Trigram

It stands to reason that the same can affect people in different ways. For example, while you may feel comfortable in a particular place, another might feel on edge, unable to relax. This "feeling" has to do with your innate compatibility with your dwelling. So, how can you find a home that is the most compatible with your personal trigram? Simple. We'll use the same chart in the previous chapter that determined a person's compatibility with another person. For a reminder about what each F or H designation stands for, please see Chapter 10, "The Eight Houses, Part 1," or the front of the tear-out card in the beginning of this book.

For example, a Zhen person is compatible with a Li house (F1), a Xun house (F2), a Kan house (F3) and a Zhen house (F4). A Zhen person is not compatible with a Kun house (H1), Gen house (H2), Qian house (H3), and a Dui house (H4).

Person to House Compatibility Chart.

TRIGRAMS House ▶ People ▼		EAST GROUP				WEST GROUP			
		Zhen	Xun	Kan	Li	Qian	Kun	Gen	Dui
EAST GROUP	Zhen	F4	F2	F3	F1	H3	H1	H2	H4
	Xun	F2	F4	F1	F3	H1	H3	H4	H2
	Kan	F3	F1	F4	F2	H2	H4	H3	H1
	Li	F1	F3	F2	F4	H4	H2	H1	H3
WEST GROUP	Qian	H3	H1	H2	H4	F4	F2	F3	F1
	Kun	H1	H3	H4	H2	F2	F4	F1	F3
	Gen	H2	H4	H3	H1	F3	F1	F4	F2
	Dui	H4	H2	H1	H3	F1	F3	F2	F4

You might ask, "Why not just locate the house whose F1 qi matches my personal trigram? Why settle for second, third, or fourth best?" Referring to the previous table, if you're a Li person, then your first choice would be to live in a Zhen house. Right? Not necessarily. While F1 qi brings great prosperity and respectability, it also brings an atmosphere charged with activity. F1 qi motivates, making it an ideal house for those in their earning years. But what if you're retired? In this case, a Li person's best choice would be to live in a home matching his own personal trigram.

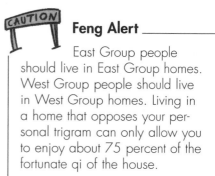

Feng Alert

East Group people should live in East Group homes. West Group people should live in West Group homes. Living in a home that opposes your personal trigram can only allow you to enjoy about 75 percent of the fortunate qi of the house.

A Li house would bring a Li person peace and stability, represented by the designation F4. Your best choice is to choose a home suited to your needs.

Now that you've located the homes that are compatible with your personal trigram, you're probably wondering which trigram your own home belongs to. Good question. Let's find out!

Determine Your Home's Sitting and Facing Directions

As you've learned, your house/building/apartment/office unit's trigram is determined by its sitting direction. The sitting direction is the direction your house or apartment unit leans against. Imagine your house or unit sitting in an armchair. Now, what direction corresponds with its backside? For a house, this is pretty easy to figure out. It's the side corresponding to the backyard or alley. For an apartment, determining the sitting side is a little tricky. It's the yin side of the unit, the part containing the bedrooms—the less active areas.

Once you've located the sitting or backside of your dwelling, the facing side is magnetically opposite. Don't allow the position of the front door to cloud your judgment. In classical feng shui, the front door plays no role in determining the sitting and facing sides of the building or unit in question. Using the chair analogy again. If you're sitting in a chair, your back represents the sitting direction and your front side represents the facing direction, right? Now, say that your face represents the main entrance. While the main entrance usually correlates with the facing side, in some cases, the front door may represent neither the sitting nor the facing side. For example, if you turn your head (front door) to the right, your front or facing side hasn't changed. Get the idea?

Before you whip out your compass to take a reading of your dwelling, assess the whole situation. It's not enough to simply locate and study a component of the building. Understanding the whole layout is essential to preparing an accurate feng shui analysis. By making an incorrect judgment, your reading will be based on the wrong trigram for that dwelling.

There are many factors you must consider when determining your home's orientation, but again, the fundamental rule to remember is that the *sitting and facing directions are magnetically opposite*. Here are some general guidelines to keep in mind as you determine your home's orientation:

◆ The backyard corresponds to the sitting direction.

◆ A back alleyway usually corresponds to the sitting direction.

◆ The main entrance is usually on the facing direction.

◆ The street address corresponds to the facing direction.

◆ Traffic is heaviest on the facing direction.

◆ Large windows may indicate the facing direction.

◆ Room location may help determine the sitting and facing directions. Usually, the living/family rooms (the yang areas) are located on the facing side, while the bedrooms and kitchen (the yin areas) are located on the sitting side.

◆ For apartments and offices, furniture arrangement is a strong indicator of its facing direction.

Understanding how to locate the sitting and facing directions is the most important aspect of performing a precise feng shui reading. But try not to overanalyze each situation. Instead, *feel* how the dwelling is oriented. Use your common sense. Go with your gut. Determining the sitting and facing directions requires keen observation, practice, groundwork, and patience.

Using a Compass to Determine Your Home's Trigram

You can obtain an accurate reading of your home's sitting direction using an ordinary Western-style compass. For our purposes here, we'll use the Silva Explorer Model 203 compass that's pictured in Chapter 1, "What Is Feng Shui?" (See Chapter 1 for more detailed instructions regarding compass selection.) If you are unfamiliar with using a compass, spend a few minutes to become comfortable with it. While it will probably be obvious to you, a little patience and caution will prevent inaccurate readings.

To determine your home's trigram, refer to the following illustration as you follow these simple procedures.

To determine the facing and sitting direction:

1. As indicated by the illustration, first stand in front of your house, the side corresponding to the facing side. Make sure your back is perfectly square with the house.

2. Holding your compass at waist level, rotate the compass dial until the red portion of the magnetic arrow aligns with north.

3. Read the compass grade at the index line (labeled the "bearing" line on the Silva Explorer Model 203). This is the facing direction. The grade magnetically opposite is the sitting direction.

4. Repeat steps 1, 2, and 3, taking a reading at two other locations parallel to the sitting side of your home as indicated by illustrations B and C.

Master Class _____

To ensure an accurate compass reading, remove any metal adornments—including watches, cufflinks, belt buckles, and jewelry—that may influence the compass's magnetic arrow. Also, make sure you distance yourself from parking meters, cars, and even the building itself. Generally, a distance of five feet should be sufficient to ensure an accurate reading.

If you live in an apartment, you must take a reading of your unit *outside* the dwelling. Likewise, if you are analyzing your own office unit, take a reading of the space outside the building.

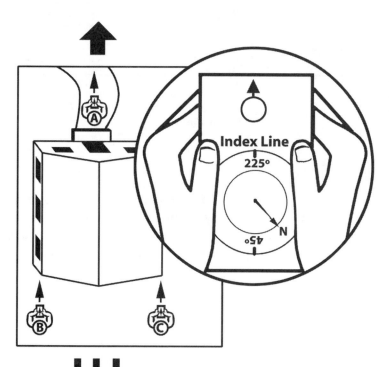

Take several compass readings until you are sure of an accurate one. The example shows a Gen house facing southwest 225 degrees and sitting northeast 45 degrees.

What's Your House Trigram?

Now that you've determined the compass grade, consult the following table to determine which trigram your home belongs to. Referring to the previous illustration, the house sits 45 degrees northeast and faces 225 degrees southwest. Based on the *sitting* direction, the house belongs to the Gen trigram. If your index (facing) line reads 180 degrees, your house would belong to the Kan trigram. It sits north and faces south. If your index line reads 330 degrees, your house would belong to the Li trigram. It sits south and faces north. If your index line reads 125 degrees, your house belongs to the Qian trigram. It sits northwest and faces southeast. It's simple once you get the hang of it!

Western Compass Gradations and Their Corresponding House Trigrams.

Trigram	Sitting Direction	Compass Designation	Facing Direction	Compass Designation
Kan	N	337.5º - 22.5º	S	157.5º - 202.5º
Gen	NE	22.5º - 67.5º	SW	202.5º - 247.5º
Zhen	E	67.5º - 112.5º	W	247.5º - 292.5º
Xun	SE	112.5º - 157.5º	NW	292.5º - 337.5º
Li	S	157.5º - 202.5º	N	337.5º - 22.5º
Kun	SW	202.5º - 247.5º	NE	22.5º - 67.5º
Dui	W	247.5º - 292.5º	E	67.5º - 112.5º
Qian	NW	292.5º - 337.5º	SE	112.5º - 157.5º

Now that you've learned how to calculate a building's trigram, you can use the tables in this chapter to see how compatible you are with that building.

Assembling a Simple Floor Plan

If you're lucky enough to have a to-scale floor plan of your home, you're ahead of the game. But most of you probably don't. Assembling one is no big deal. Your goal is to draw a *simple* plan with the sitting direction oriented on the *bottom* of the page. To get a better idea of your task at hand, refer to the following illustration. Your floor plan should include …

◆ All exterior and interior entrances and doorways.

◆ All windows.

◆ All beds.

◆ All desks.

To avoid wasting time, don't try to eyeball the measurements. Why not? Because ultimately, you're going to divide the whole of your dwelling into eight equal wedges—each wedge corresponding to the F1 to F4 and H1 to H4 qi fields you learned about in the previous chapter. An inaccurate measurement will ensure an incorrect analysis of which areas hold positive and negative qi. Instead, spend an extra 15 minutes to measure the length and width of your dwelling. There are a few ways you can do this:

- Get one of those nifty electronic measuring devices found in most hardware or building supply stores. The one we use is the Starrett DigiTape, which costs about $24. All you have to do is run the tape measure. The measurement will illuminate in the display window.

- Use a plain old tape measure or ruler. It'll take a couple more minutes, but what's the hurry?

- Use the tried-and-true, one-foot-in-front-of-the-other method. It's a little less exact, but it gets the job done. Counting one step as a measurement of one foot in length, just place your right heel parallel to the wall, then place your left foot at the right's toe. Continue walking, heel to toe, counting the number of steps to the end of the wall.

We suggest first measuring the length of each room. Begin with the back wall connected to the sitting side of your dwelling. Jot down its measurement. Next, measure the room adjacent to the length of the wall you just measured. (Don't forget to consider the wall space separating each room.) Jot down its measurement. Continue this procedure until the last room adjacent to the length of the wall in question is measured. Repeat this procedure to obtain the width of each room. Based on these measurements, you can now draw a simple to-scale floor plan. We suggest using a pencil as you may have to make changes.

If your home is more than one story, you must draw a plan for each floor. But believe us, it's worth the effort.

The next step is to divide your dwelling into eight equal wedges. First, find the center of the house by dividing the total length and width by two. For example, if the total length is 60 feet, the midpoint is 30 feet. If the total width is 45 feet, the midpoint is 22½ feet. The point where the midsections converge corresponds to the center of your dwelling. Your final step is to label the plan. Inside, label each room. Outside, label each of the eight directions. To note the sitting and facing directions use the sitting ⊔ and facing ⬆ symbols. Finally, write down the name of your house

Feng Alert _____

For teaching purposes, we have divided the sample floor plan into eight equal wedges. Yet, please understand the real dividing lines are the walls! You must not be so rigid when applying classical feng shui methods. Remember, the qi fields are interconnected, not separate and distinct parts!

trigram (Kan, Zhen, Dui, etc.) and its associated East or West Group. Write down each family member, his or her trigram and East or West Group association. A completed sample floor plan is shown in the following figure.

A simple floor plan. Note the sitting direction is oriented on the bottom of the page, and the plan is labeled both inside and outside.

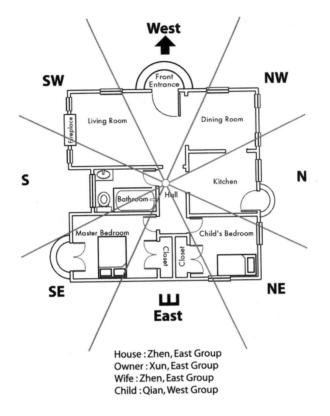

House : Zhen, East Group
Owner : Xun, East Group
Wife : Zhen, East Group
Child : Qian, West Group

Great Grids!

But, you ask, what if my house isn't square? What if it's a rectangle, an L-shape, or it has some funky alcoves? What if my house is missing a section? The following illustrations show some examples of irregularly shaped houses divided properly.

The first illustration, A, shows a house with a missing section. Is this bad luck? No! A missing section is a missing section. It is not unlucky. End of story.

Illustration B also has sections missing to varying degrees. Again, you can't make something out of nothing. To find the center of a house with a trapezoid shape, connect the midpoint of the upper and lower sides. Because the house is broader at the base (or sitting side), the center is one-third to halfway from the base.

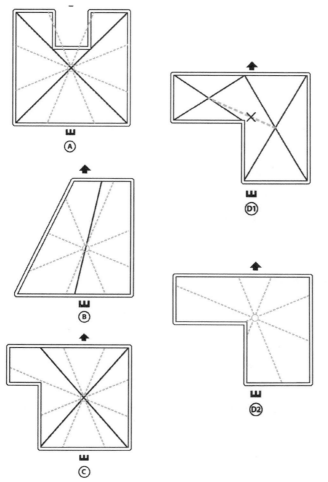

Proper division of irregularly shaped houses.

Illustration C shows a house with a small extension. If an extended area is one-quarter or less than the main body of the house, then the extension becomes part of the wedge in question, as in illustration C. However, if an extended area is greater than one-quarter of the main body of the house, then it is representative of an L-shaped house. Follow the instructions provided for illustration D following.

Illustration D shows an L-shaped house. To locate the center of the house, first find the center of each wing (figure D1). The center of the house will be along the line joining the centers of the wings. But be careful. If the two wings comprising the L-shape are equal, the center would be the exact midpoint of this line. However, in this example, the north-south wing is bigger than its smaller east-west counterpart. Therefore, the center will be closer to center of the larger rectangle. Represented by an "x," the point marks the center for the whole house (figure D2).

Master Class _____

Some feng shui masters divide a house by creating a grid of nine equal cells—an idea that conforms to the nine-celled Luoshu numeric diagram (you'll learn about this in Chapter 12, "The Eight Houses, Part 3"). While this is an acceptable practice, we believe the pie-shaped wedges conform to the movement of qi through the perpetual cycle of nature (birth, growth, decay, and death). Also, as you'll learn in Chapter 14, "The Flying Stars, Part 2," the Chinese believe time is cyclic rather than linear.

Now that you've properly divided and labeled your house or apartment unit, we bet you're eager to analyze and remedy your dwelling's qi! This is the subject of the next chapter.

The Least You Need to Know

- By matching your personal trigram to a home's trigram, you can determine your compatibility with that dwelling.
- A home's sitting and facing directions can sometimes be difficult to ascertain.
- A home's trigram is determined by its sitting direction.
- The sitting direction is determined by a compass reading.
- Creating a to-scale floor plan ensures an accurate reading.

Chapter 12

The Eight Houses, Part 3

In This Chapter

♦ Understanding how the palace phase qi affects the house

♦ Understanding how the wandering star phase qi affects the house

♦ Understanding how to balance the wandering star phase qi to promote a better well-being

If you wanted to, you could just determine those areas within your home that bring benevolent qi and arrange your house accordingly. For example, let's say your house belongs to the East Group trigram Kan. Its good areas are the southeast, south, east, and north. Ideally, your front door, bedroom, and any other room where you spend a lot of time in, should be situated in these four areas. If you belong to an East Group trigram (Zhen, Xun, Kan, or Li), your qi would be compatible with a Kan house. In other words, your four favorable directions are the same as those within your dwelling. If you are incompatible with your home, well, at the very least, orient your bed and desk so that you face your sheng qi—your beneficial qi.

What we've just described is the first layer of Eight House. The next layer is to examine how the palace qi (the phases associated with the eight cardinal directions) and wandering star qi (the phases associated with the F to H levels of auspice) interact. This is what this chapter is all about. Here, you'll need your divided floor plan that you constructed in the previous chapter.

Do You Know Where Your Palace Is?

Eight House requires knowledge of the bagua, the Hou Tian (After Heaven) sequence of trigrams and its affiliations. While you may want to review Chapter 7, "The Principle of the Eight Trigrams," we'll provide a short review here. Each of the eight directions is ruled by a palace. Each palace is assigned a phase. Referring to the following table, the fire palace is related to the south and the fire phase; the earth palace is related to the southwest and the earth phase; the lake palace is related to the west and the metal phase; the heaven palace is related to the northwest and the metal phase, and so forth. Later on, you'll be applying this information to your floor plan. But, don't do anything just yet! We need to assemble more information.

The eight palaces and their directional and phase associations.

Table 1 D i r e c t i o n s

	S	SW	W	NW	N	NE	E	SE
Palace	Fire	Earth	Lake	Heaven	Water	Mountain	Thunder	Wind
Phase	Fire	Earth	Metal	Metal	Water	Earth	Wood	Wood

The palace qi map represents the foundation. It's the base qi, the bedrock or stable qi permeating each of the eight directional areas within your home.

Do You Know Where Your Wandering Star Is?

In Chapter 10, "The Eight Houses, Part 1," you learned about the Eight Wandering Stars. Again, while a review of the chapter will help facilitate easier learning, we'll offer an overview here. Referring to the following table, the wandering star called Sheng Qi is affiliated with F1, the most fortunate level of auspice related to the wood phase; the star Yan Nian is affiliated with F2, the second most fortunate qi related to the metal phase; the star Tian Yi is affiliated with F3, the third most fortunate qi related to the earth phase; the star Fu Wei is affiliated with F4, the fourth most fortunate qi related to the wood phase, and so forth. Like the palace qi, you will be applying this information to your floor plan. But not just yet!

Table 2   L e v e l   o f   A u s p i c e

	F1	F2	F3	F4	H1	H2	H3	H4
Wandering Star	Sheng Qi	Yan Nian	Tian Yi	Fu Wei	Hou Hai	Liu Sha	Wu Gui	Jue Ming
Phase	Wood	Metal	Earth	Wood	Earth	Water	Fire	Metal

The Eight Wandering Stars and their auspice and phase associations.

The wandering star qi map is the working force, the energy that actively affects the health, livelihood, and harmony of the occupants. Unlike the palace qi map that is constant and stable, the wandering star qi map varies according to the magnetic orientation of your house (a subject we covered in Chapter 11, "The Eight Houses, Part 2"). Stated another way, a dwelling's sitting direction determines which of the eight different wandering star qi maps your home belongs to. For our purposes, we will carry over the Zhen house floor plan from the previous chapter. Belonging to the East Group set of trigrams, the wandering star qi distribution is a follows:

Zhen House   (East Group)

	F1	F2	F3	F4	H1	H2	H3	H4
Direction	S	SE	N	E	SW	NE	NW	W
Phase	Wood	Metal	Earth	Wood	Earth	Water	Fire	Metal

The qi distribution of a Zhen house, sitting east and facing west.

To make your task a little easier, here are charts appropriate to the remaining seven trigrams.

Xun House   (East Group)

	F1	F2	F3	F4	H1	H2	H3	H4
Direction	N	E	S	SE	NW	W	SW	NE
Phase	Wood	Metal	Earth	Wood	Earth	Water	Fire	Metal

Kan House   (East Group)

	F1	F2	F3	F4	H1	H2	H3	H4
Direction	SE	S	E	N	W	NW	NE	SW
Phase	Wood	Metal	Earth	Wood	Earth	Water	Fire	Metal

Li House   (East Group)

	F1	F2	F3	F4	H1	H2	H3	H4
Direction	E	N	SE	S	NE	SW	W	NW
Phase	Wood	Metal	Earth	Wood	Earth	Water	Fire	Metal

Qian House   (West Group)

	F1	F2	F3	F4	H1	H2	H3	H4
Direction	W	SW	NE	NW	SE	N	E	S
Phase	Wood	Metal	Earth	Wood	Earth	Water	Fire	Metal

Kun House   (West Group)

	F1	F2	F3	F4	H1	H2	H3	H4
Direction	NE	NW	W	SW	E	S	SE	N
Phase	Wood	Metal	Earth	Wood	Earth	Water	Fire	Metal

Gen House   (West Group)

	F1	F2	F3	F4	H1	H2	H3	H4
Direction	SW	W	NW	NE	S	E	N	SE
Phase	Wood	Metal	Earth	Wood	Earth	Water	Fire	Metal

Dui House   (West Group)

	F1	F2	F3	F4	H1	H2	H3	H4
Direction	NW	NE	SW	W	N	SE	S	E
Phase	Wood	Metal	Earth	Wood	Earth	Water	Fire	Metal

Did you locate the wandering star chart corresponding to your house? Good. Let's move on.

Qi-ing In on Qi

The next step is to determine the areas within the house that are favorable and unfavorable to each occupant. Continuing with our case study of the Zhen house, let the owner Peter belong to the Xun trigram. Let his wife, Mary, belong to the Zhen trigram, and their son Jacob to the Qian trigram. The qi that is beneficial and detrimental to their well-being breaks out as follows:

		F1	F2	F3	F4	H1	H2	H3	H4
Peter	Xun	N	E	S	SE	NW	W	SW	NE
Mary	Zhen	S	SE	N	E	SW	NE	NW	W
Jacob	Qian	W	SW	NE	NW	SE	N	E	S

The qi distribution of those living in a Zhen house.

If you haven't already done so, take this time now to determine the good and bad directions affiliated with your ming gua, your personal trigram. If you don't know your personal trigram, and those belonging to your family, consult Chapter 10 or look on the back of the tear-out card at the front of this book.

The Good, the Bad, and the Possibilities

Okay, it's now time to apply all the information we've assembled so far onto the floor plan. So that we're all on the same page, so to speak, first study the following floor plan, and then write down the information appropriate to your house in the same way.

A Zhen house and the phases associated with each palace and wandering star.

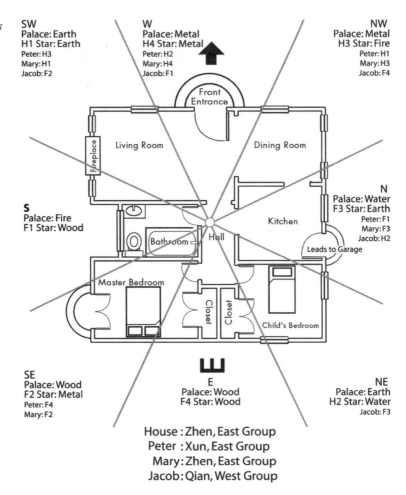

SW
Palace: Earth
H1 Star: Earth
Peter: H3
Mary: H1
Jacob: F2

W
Palace: Metal
H4 Star: Metal
Peter: H2
Mary: H4
Jacob: F1

NW
Palace: Metal
H3 Star: Fire
Peter: H1
Mary: H3
Jacob: F4

S
Palace: Fire
F1 Star: Wood

N
Palace: Water
F3 Star: Earth
Peter: F1
Mary: F3
Jacob: H2

SE
Palace: Wood
F2 Star: Metal
Peter: F4
Mary: F2

E
Palace: Wood
F4 Star: Wood

NE
Palace: Earth
H2 Star: Water
Jacob: F3

Front Entrance

Living Room

Dining Room

Fireplace

Kitchen

Hall

Bathroom

Leads to Garage

Master Bedroom

Closet

Closet

Child's Bedroom

House : Zhen, East Group
Peter : Xun, East Group
Mary : Zhen, East Group
Jacob : Qian, West Group

Feng Facts

If your bedroom is located in an inauspicious area and you cannot move to another room that is more favorable, at least orient your bed so that the crown of your head points toward a favorable direction. Also, make sure your desk is positioned so that you face a favorable direction.

Upon closer examination, note that while Peter and Mary are inherently compatible with their home (the couple and the dwelling belonging to East Group trigrams Xun, Zhen, and Zhen respectively), Jacob is not. He belongs to the West Group trigram Qian. Despite the couple's innate compatibility with their home, the main entrance is inauspicious for them (H2 for Peter; H4 for Mary). Yet, for their son Jacob, the main entrance promotes the likelihood of good fortune (F1). To mitigate the possibility of misfortune, Peter and Mary should use an alternate entrance, the one leading from the garage (not illustrated) to the kitchen. This entrance envelopes Peter in F1 qi and Mary in F3 qi.

Regarding the bedrooms, Peter and Mary sleep in a favorable area (F4 and F2 respectively), their heads pointed toward an auspicious direction—east for Peter corresponds to his F2 qi and for Mary, F4. Also, while Jacob sleeps in an area compatible with his innate qi (F3), his bed is pointed toward the north, his H2 qi. If we position the bed toward the east wall, it corresponds to his H3 qi. This leaves the west wall between the doorway and the window. Although the bed position corresponds to his F1 qi, Jacob must be mindful of a potential wind tunnel produced by an open window and an open door. To prevent illness and sleeplessness associated with this inauspicious surge of qi, Peter must keep either the door or the window closed when he sleeps.

Master Class

What if you and your spouse belong to opposing groups? While one solution would be to sleep in different bedrooms, this is not feasible for most couples. In this case, the spouse whose trigram opposes the home's trigram should be favored.

The Rules of the Eight House Game

Now, that you've determined your lucky and unlucky areas within your home and have positioned your bed and desk to take advantage of your good qi, we can begin to examine and remedy the qi phases associated with the palace and wandering star. But, first, let's set up some rules:

Rule 1: If a good wandering star (F1, F2, F3, F4) enhances (produces) the palace, install the phase that enhances the star. This is because the palace is weakening the star. For example, while wood (F1) is enhancing the southern fire palace, fire is weakening wood's power. Add water to fortify wood's strength.

Rule 2: If a good wandering star (F1, F2, F3, F4) assists (is the same as) the palace, install the phase that enhances them. For example, if F1 (wood) resides in a wood palace (east or southeast), add water.

Rule 3: If a good wandering star (F1, F2, F3, F4) controls the palace, do nothing. For example, if wood's F1 qi controls an earth palace (southwest or northeast), leave it alone. Adding a phase to enhance or assist the star will not help matters. Weakening it will deplete the favorable star's power.

Rule 4: If a good wandering star (F1, F2, F3, F4) is being controlled by the palace, add the phase that restores balance to the cycle. Although the palace will be weakened, the star will be strengthened. For example, if wood's F1 qi is being controlled by a metal palace (west or northwest), add water to reinstate the natural sequence of qi.

Rule 5: If a bad wandering star (H1, H2, H3, H4) enhances (produces), assists (is the same as), or controls the palace, install the phase that weakens the star. The idea is to lessen the bad star's unfavorable affect.

Master Class

But what of the phase associated with a person's ming gua? It is not considered in an Eight House analysis. In fact, a person's ming gua phase is not really representative of his or her innate qi. In Chapter 23, "The Four Pillars of Destiny, Part 2," and Chapter 24, "The Four Pillars of Destiny, Part 3," you'll learn how to determine the phases most beneficial to you.

Rule 6: If a bad wandering star (H1, H2, H3, H4) is being controlled by the palace, do nothing. Adding the phase to weaken the inauspicious star will control the palace. For example, if H4's metal is being controlled by the southern fire palace, water will deplete the bad metal's zeal, but also dominate the palace. Therefore, leave it alone. If possible, avoid the area.

As you can see, the focus is on the wandering star and not the palace. The star is the qi force that directly affects the occupants and thus, it must be remedied accordingly. Using an analogy, the palace can be likened to the plate we eat on. A plate can't affect your well-being, right? The wandering star is the food. Good food nourishes and bad food causes an upset stomach or even food poisoning.

The Analysis

To help bolster your understanding of the five phase relationships, please refer to Chapter 6, "The Principle of the Five Phases," for a refresher. Also, the front of the tear-out card is invaluable. We've condensed the productive, controlling, and weakening cycles into one illustration. For quick reference, you can consult the following table:

The five phases of qi and their enhancing, assisting, controlling, and weakening agents.

	Fire	Earth	Metal	Water	Wood
Enhancer	Wood	Fire	Earth	Metal	Water
Assister	Fire	Earth	Metal	Water	Wood
Controller	Water	Wood	Fire	Earth	Metal
Weakener	Earth	Metal	Water	Wood	Fire

Referring to the previous illustration of the Zhen house, let's examine each room. We'll begin in the west and travel clockwise around the house.

West Entrance: palace (metal) H4 star (metal)

An inauspicious metal star (H4) is assisting the metal palace. According to Rule 5, we must weaken the wandering star. Therefore, the main entrance needs the water phase. A table fountain or an aquarium will do nicely.

Northwest Dining Room: palace (metal) H3 star (fire)

An inauspicious fire star (H3) is controlling the metal palace. According to Rule 5, we must add the phase that weakens the star. In this case, earth will deplete fire's unfavorable effect. Ceramic, clay, or stone table bases, vases, or statuary will work. This area shouldn't contain plants as the wood phase will empower fire's bad nature.

North Kitchen: palace (water) F3 star (earth)

A favorable earth star (F3) is controlling the water palace. According to Rule 3, do nothing.

Northeast Jacob's Bedroom: palace (earth) H2 star (water)

According to Rule 6, nothing can be done to remedy an inauspicious star being controlled by a palace. Here, the water H2 star is being controlled by an earth palace. Yet, despite the innate inauspiciousness, the northeast area is good for Jacob (F3). Again, this is because he belongs to the West Group; the house belonging to the East Group set of trigrams.

East Closets: palace (wood) F4 star (wood)

Although it is not necessary to remedy closet space, for sake of learning we'll pretend it's another room. Here, a favorable wood star (F4) is assisting the wood palace. According to Rule 2, we must add the phase that enhances them. In this case, water enhances or produces wood. It would not be wise to burn candles or decorate this room with red tones as the fire phase will weaken wood's good nature.

Southeast Master Bedroom: palace (wood) F2 star (metal)

A favorable metal star (F2) is controlling the wood palace. According to Rule 3, do nothing.

South Bathroom: palace (fire) F1 star (wood)

A favorable wood star (F1) is enhancing the fire palace. According to Rule 1, add the water phase to strength wood's benevolent qi. Because this is the bathroom, the area is self-remedied.

Southwest Living Room: palace (earth) H1 star (earth)

An inauspicious earth star (H1) is assisting the earth palace. According to Rule 5, add the phase that weakens the star. Here, metal weakens earth. Metal table bases, picture frames, a chiming clock, or statuary will work well. Avoid burning candles and using the fireplace excessively here. This is because fire will empower the wandering star's bad nature.

Master Class _____

When remedying or enhancing, the actual phase is more powerful than its representative color. For example, water is more effective than blue and black; a working fireplace and a burning candle are more effective than red, purple, and pink; a plant is more effective than green. Yet, if possible, incorporate the appropriate color scheme into the remedy/enhancement in question. A little extra edge goes a long way toward a balanced environment.

In Part 5, "Feng Shui Mechanics 201," you'll learn about a more sophisticated method of feng shui called Flying Star. Why is it more sophisticated? Because it includes the element of time. Specifically, a Flying Star analysis studies the time your home was "born" and the magnetic space it sits on. As you'll soon learn, the eight fundamental directions are divided into three finer distinctions each. Therefore, instead of your dwelling belonging to one of eight directions, it will belong to one of twenty-four directions.

The Least You Need to Know

- The palace star is the qi force affiliated with the eight cardinal directions.
- The wandering star is the qi force that directly affects the well-being of the occupants.
- Eight House methodology seeks to enhance the good stars and weaken the bad stars by using the appropriate phase fire, earth, metal, water, or wood.
- The phase associated with a person's ming gua (personal trigram) is not considered.

Part 5

Feng Shui Mechanics 201

A bit more complex, but well worth your while, Part 5 teaches you the Flying Star System. Here, you'll use those mysterious numbers correlated to the five phases and eight trigrams. Although numerology is the gist of this method, mathematics isn't involved. So put away your calculator and put on your thinking cap. Understanding a number's inherent nature and its life cycle, among other things, can be tricky business.

Part 5 also give you step-by-step instruction about performing a Flying Star analysis. You'll learn what the number combinations mean and how you can remedy or enhance the qi in a particular area to encourage favorable events and discourage unfavorable ones. We know you'll find this sophisticated technique interesting and enlightening.

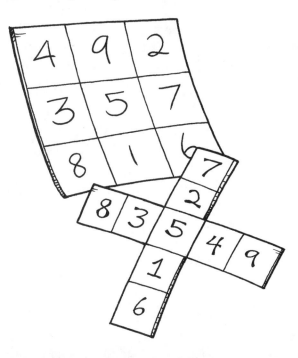

Chapter 13

The Flying Stars, Part 1

In This Chapter

- It's all in the stars: introducing the Flying Star system
- Understanding the Hetu and Luoshu diagrams
- The Magic Square of Three
- The significance of the number nine in cultures throughout the world

You've come this far. You've learned the three fundamental principles governing feng shui: yin and yang, the five phases, and the eight trigrams. You've learned the simple, yet profound Eight House system of determining your home's qi essence and your compatibility with it. You've learned how to use this system to make the most out of your living space. Now you're ready to learn Flying Star, a more sophisticated technique that uses factors associated with both time and space to describe your dwelling's qi. Yet, before you apply this method, you must first acquire some background knowledge. This will help you to better understand this complex, yet fascinating system of feng shui. This chapter's all about learning the history behind the "stars," or numbers, that govern your well-being.

What Is the Flying Star System?

The system of *Flying Star* addresses questions you may have asked while learning the Eight House system. Why does the Eight House system paint a static picture of our living and/or working space? Why haven't we incorporated the element of time into the equation? These are typical questions concerning the Eight House system.

Wise Words

Flying Star is a sophisticated and complex system of analyzing how time and space affect a building. The magnetic orientation of the dwelling, along with the year the home was built, are important factors that determine the innate character of the house.

Feng Facts

In Chinese, Flying Star is called Xuankong Feixing, which means "Time and Space Flying Stars." While there exists no textual evidence to support the system's authorship, Flying Star was probably developed during the Tang dynasty (618–907 C.E.) and no later than the Song dynasty (960–1279 C.E.). Jiang Da Hong, an officer in the Ming dynasty (1368-1644 C.E.), is credited as being the first feng shui master on record to use Flying Star.

Taken together, Eight House and Flying Star provide a more detailed analysis of your living and/or working situation. Considered individually, one system isn't superior over the other. In feng shui, we look at how the whole of its principles work together. Everything you've learned, all the components that make up feng shui, are necessary tools for conducting an accurate reading. Neglecting a component would be like driving a car with three wheels! It simply can't be done.

Ancient Beginnings

You might be wondering about the word "star" in Flying Star. Are the numbers 1 to 9 affiliated with nine celestial stars? Yes and no. The stars in question are the seven stars that form the Big Dipper (Beidou), plus the two adjacent stars at its handle. Like the principle of the five phases, it's not the object (the stars) that is important but the movement and transformation of its associated qi.

But what is the meaning behind each star? Unfortunately, this is not known. Like so much of feng shui, the original documentation is lost in history. Only the methods remain. Yet, suffice it to say, the ancient Chinese recognized mathematical patterns in nature. The Flying Star system is based on their observation of the macrocosmic world and its influence on us, the microcosmic world. These observations gave rise to two specific mathematical diagrams of the universe, as you are about to learn.

The Hetu River Map

The fifth century B.C.E. text called the *Shangshu* (*Classic of History*) tells how Fuxi, one of China's legendary figures who is credited with inventing the bagua (the eight fundamental trigrams), among other things, received a gift from heaven. But, it was no ordinary gift, for it described an ideal world where all is in perfect harmony. According to legend, the gift appeared as a pattern of black

Wise Words _____

The **Hetu,** or **River Map,** is a pattern of black (yin) and white (yang) dots purportedly found on a fantastic dragon-horse emerging from the Yellow River. The Hetu symbolizes the ideal world.

and white dots on the flank of a mystical dragon-horse emerging from the Yellow River. Hence, the diagram is also known as the *Hetu* (also spelled Ho-t'u) or *River Map.* In the following diagram of the Hetu, the markings illustrate structure and balance, with the white dots representing yang, the black dots, yin. This scheme becomes clearer when numbers are applied to the dot patterns. For example, the 7 white dots found at the top of the diagram correspond to the number 7 in the numeric structure of the Hetu. The 2 black dots beneath the 7 white dots correspond to the numeric value of 2, and so forth. Disregarding the central 5 white dots and surrounding 10 black ones, you can see how the odd (yang) numbers are perfectly balanced by an opposing even (yin) number: 1 (yang) is opposite 2 (yin); 3 (yang) is opposite 4 (yin); 6 (yin) is opposite 7 (yang), and 8 (yin) is opposite 9 (yang).

Upon closer examination (again, disregarding the central 5), notice how all of the odd (yang) numbers and even (yin) numbers add up to 20: 1 + 3 + 7 + 9 = 20; 2 + 4 + 6 + 8 = 20.

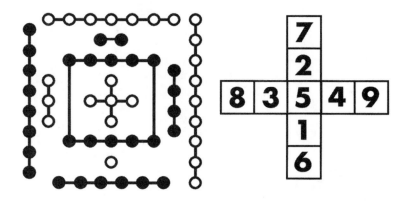

The Hetu River map.

Does this diagram of an ideal, perfect, and sedentary world remind you of anything? Perhaps the Before Heaven sequence of trigrams that we discussed in Chapter 7, "The Principle of the Eight Trigrams"? Although the Hetu diagram was correlated with the trigram sequence in the Song dynasty (960–1279 C.E.), there is much debate about whether this correlation is meaningful. In fact, some contemporary scholars believe there is no connection between the Hetu number sequence and the Before Heaven trigram sequence.

So, you might ask, what's so special about the Hetu diagram? Its link with the turtle's offering, the Luoshu diagram.

The Luoshu Writing

A second gift was bestowed on Yu the Great, founder of China's first dynasty Xia (c. 2100–1600 B.C.E.) This one was another pattern of black (yin) and white (yang) dots inscribed on a turtle's shell, an arrangement that came to be known as the *Luo River Writing*. Simply called the Luoshu (also spelled Lo-shu), this diagram was correlated to the After Heaven sequence of trigrams (again see Chapter 7 for a reminder) conceivably as early as the Han dynasty (206 B.C.E.–220 C.E.), some 2,000 years after its purported discovery by Yu. As a reminder, the After Heaven sequence of trigrams denotes motion, transformation, and interaction of natural and human qi forces. The Luoshu/After Heaven sequence is the antithesis of the motionless Hetu and Before Heaven sequence of trigrams.

The Luo River Writing.

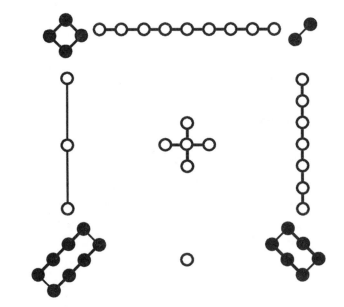

We all know these diagrams couldn't have really appeared on the backs of two animals. So what's the real story? The fact is, the origins of the Hetu and Luoshu sequence of numbers are unknown. Although their antiquity is unquestioned, contemporary scholars can't prove the Luoshu existed before the time of Confucius (551–479 B.C.E.). This is because the Luoshu is first mentioned in the *Confucian Analects* (sayings of Confucius compiled by his students). The origin of the Hetu diagram, on the other hand, is a bit more mysterious. It isn't mentioned until the early Han dynasty, some 400 years after Confucius. And, the configuration of numbers it represents can't be dated until the Song dynasty (960–1279 C.E.), some 1,000 years later. So, until new discoveries are made, or scholars put forth new evidence, we will never know the diagrams' true inventor(s) or date of origin.

Despite the mysterious origins of the Hetu and Luoshu diagrams, we can surmise they were a product of astute observations by the ancients—that they recognized and recorded patterns made manifest in the celestial heavens, patterns that revealed the secrets of the universe. The legend of the miraculous appearance of the Hetu and Luoshu points to their power. The fact that the ancient Chinese had forgotten what they meant by the time scholars began to analyze the diagrams increases their mysterious nature. Nevertheless, because they are considered magical and because their meanings were elusive, they were thought to be divine in origin.

Wise Words

Also known as the **Luo River Writing**, the **Luoshu** is a pattern of black (yin) and white (yang) dots said to be inscribed on a turtle's shell. The Luoshu correlates to the After Heaven sequence of trigrams denoting motion, transformation, and interaction of natural and human qi.

The Magic Square of Three

Just as the black (yin) and white (yang) dots of the Hetu correspond to a numeric value, so, too, do the Luoshu's dots. Referring back to the illustration of the Luo River Writing, look at the top configuration of dots: A pattern of 4 black dots and 2 black dots is separated by a pattern of 9 white dots. Numerically, the dot values equal 4, 9, and 2, respectively—a factor that is illustrated in the following diagram of the Magic Square of Three. Before you continue, take a minute to consider how all the other dot patterns correspond to the numbers in the following illustration.

The Luoshu is also known as the *Magic Square of Three*. This is because 3 cells add up to 15 along any diagonal, vertical, or horizontal line:

Diagonally $4 + 5 + 6 = 15$
              $2 + 5 + 8 = 15$

Vertically $4 + 3 + 8 = 15$
              $9 + 5 + 1 = 15$
              $2 + 7 + 6 = 15$

Horizontally $4 + 9 + 2 = 15$
              $3 + 5 + 7 = 15$
              $8 + 1 + 6 = 15$

The Magic Square of Three.

4	**9**	**2**
3	**5**	**7**
8	**1**	**6**

Wise Words

The **Magic Square of Three** is considered magical because 3 cells along any diagonal, vertical, or horizontal line add up to 15. The Magic Square of Three represents the numeric value of the black (yin) and white (yang) dots of the Luoshu.

The magic doesn't stop here. Like the After Heaven trigram sequence, the Luoshu diagram moves, symbolizing a world in flux, in constant transformation. Although the diagram is square, it is also inherently cyclic. How so, you ask? First, connect the 2 pairs of odd (yang) numbers: 1 and 9, and 3 and 7. Next, draw a line through the 2 northern cells 6 and 1. In the same fashion, draw lines through the 2 eastern cells 8 and 3, the 2 southern cells 4 and 9, and the 2 western cells 2 and 7. The end result should look similar to the following illustration, a counterclockwise swastika—each arm connecting the 9 cells of the Magic Square.

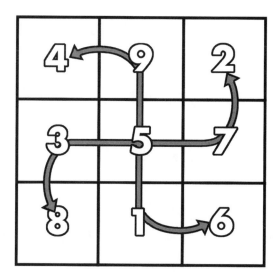

The cyclic nature of the Magic Square of Three.

Notice how the odd (yang) numbers forming the cross and the 4 extending arms of even (yin) numbers add up to 10: 9 + 1 = 10, 3 + 7 = 10, 4 + 6 = 10, and 2 + 8 = 10. The sums differ by a factor of 5, the number of the central cell. Impressed? There's more. Upon closer examination, you'll notice that central number 5 is the factor that links the extending pairs:

> 1 (North) and 6 (Northwest), or 1 + 5 = 6
>
> 3 (East) and 8 (Northeast), or 3 + 5 = 8
>
> 4 (Southeast) and 9 (South), or 4 + 5 = 9
>
> 2 (Southwest) and 7 (West), or 2 + 5 = 7

Finally, you'll notice these directional pairs are none other than the arms forming the Hetu cross! This connection suggests the Hetu is probably a by-product of the Luoshu diagram.

You might be wondering why the swastika revolves counterclockwise. This is because the clockwise movement expresses passing time, while the counterclockwise movement expresses future time. Richard Wilhelm in his preface to the *I Ching or Book of Changes* (Princeton University Press, 1950) explains it this way: "The usual clockwise movement, cumulative and expanding as time goes on, determines the events that are passing; an opposite, backward movement, folding up and contracting as time goes, through which the seeds of the future take form. To know this movement is to know the future. In figurative terms, if we understand how a tree is contracted into a seed, we understand the future unfolding of the seed into a tree."

Feng shui is concerned with predicting the probability of future events. Moreover, feng shui seeks to promote good events and dissuade bad events.

> **Feng Facts**
>
> Today, the swastika is a symbol widely associated with anti-Semitism and Hitler's Third Reich. But did you know the swastika predates Hitler's empire of evil? That it is one of the oldest symbols of humankind? Virtually every ancient culture has a remarkably similar version of what is generally accepted to be a solar emblem. The swastika has been used by the indigenous peoples of North, Central, and South America, and the French, Greek, Swiss, Japanese, and Irish.
>
> However, many scholars believe the swastika was probably first used by the Hindus. In fact, the word swastika comes from the Sanskrit *svastika* meaning "lucky" and "fortunate." The most distinctly identifiable ancient use of the swastika was by the Jains, a Hindu religious doctrine closely resembling Buddhism, founded about 500 B.C.E. The Jains used the symbol as an emblem of Buddha. Always represented with its arms in a counterclockwise fashion, the swastika was introduced to China in about 200 B.C.E. The Chinese called the swastika Lei Wen, meaning "thunder scroll," a name suggesting it was a symbol associated with celestial activity.
>
> How did Hitler contaminate such a kindly sign? Actually, the Viennese racial theorist and founder of the Order of the New Templars, Dr. Jorge Lanz von Liebenfels (a.k.a. Adolf Lanz), adopted the swastika in 1907. Symbolizing his irrational belief in establishing a pure master race, the swastika was probably mistaken by Lanz to be a symbol of Germanic origin. The clockwise version adopted by Hitler in 1920 was designed by a dentist, Dr. Freidrich Krohn.

The Nine Imperial Palaces

The nine cells, or nine "halls," of the Magic Square describe the layout of the Imperial Palace in China, what venerated scholar Joseph Needham in *Science and Civilization in China* (Cambridge University Press, 1956) calls "the mystical temple-dwelling which the emperor was supposed to frequent, carrying out the rites appropriate to the season."

What does this mean exactly? Well, the emperor, the Son of Heaven, petitioned heaven (composed of a group of his illustrious forebears) on behalf of his people, rendering thanks and appreciation for fine weather, good health, and prosperity. It was also his duty to ask heaven to continue its benevolence. Specifically, requests were made for the upcoming year. Each rite would be carried out in the appropriate hall of the emperor's palace. Each hall corresponded to the one of the twelve lunar months. Each lunar month lasted approximately 29½ days; each lunar year, 360 days.

But there are 9 cells and 12 months. How does this figure? Good question. Basically, it worked like this. The emperor would live in each of the central rooms (north, south, east, and west) for one month. Because the corner rooms corresponded to two directions (for example, southeast = south and east), the emperor would live in these rooms for two months. So, during the spring, he would presumably live in the northeast room for one month, the east room for one month, and the southeast room for one month. In the summer, he would spend one more month in the southeast room, followed by a month in the south room, and a month in the southwest room, and so forth. Thus, the emperor was able to complete a tour of the lunar calendar, cycling around each of the nine halls.

As if this wasn't enough, the emperor also had to symbolically harmonize with each season's distinct affiliations (color, animal, smell, sound, cereal, etc.). For example, in summer, the emperor donned red garments and feasted on peas and chicken. In autumn, he dressed in white and ate sesame and dog. In winter, he wore black and ate millet and pork. And, in spring, the emperor chose green clothing and ate mutton and wheat. Sounds exhausting, doesn't it? Such were the duties and obligations of imperial privilege.

Here's to the Nines

Before we move on to providing step-by-step instructions for performing a Flying Stars audit, let's explore for a moment the significance of the number nine, the highest single-digit number. Interestingly, nine is revered globally, its symbology strikingly similar. It symbolizes completeness, the end of a cycle before returning to number one. To the Chinese, the number nine represents heaven and perfection. It is the supreme yang (male) number. But, that's not all. Here are a few more examples of how the number nine has been incorporated into Chinese culture:

- In early Chinese mythology, the number nine figures often: nine fields of heaven, nine terraces of the sacred mountain Kunlun, and nine songs of heaven.
- *The Book of Rituals*, compiled in the later Han dynasty, speaks of nine ceremonies: puberty rite for men, wedding, audience, ambassadorship, burial, sacrifice, hospitality, drinking, and military.
- The center of Peking (now Beijing) has eight roads leading to the collective ninth, the city.
- The Forbidden City is said to have 9,999 rooms.
- Nine dragons are incorporated into the emperor's throne.
- Nine mythical animals adorn palace and temple buildings.
- Many pagodas have nine stories.

The number nine is significant in other cultures, too: In Egypt, nine, or the higher power of three, was very important to the religious and cosmological order. A group of nine gods was called a pesedjet, or ennead. Flip back a couple of pages to the illustration of the swastika formation inside the Magic Square. The cross connecting the odd numbers (1 and 9, 3 and 7), together with the "X" connecting the even numbers (4 and 6, 8 and 2), forms the 3000 B.C.E. Egyptian hieroglyph for "heaven."

To the Hebrews, the ninth letter of their alphabet is Tet. Tet symbolizes completeness. At the next level, the Zadi (90) represents righteousness, and the completeness of the human spirit. The final Zadi (900) represents the outer world.

In Christianity, hell has nine gates (three of brass, three of iron, and three of adamantine). Furthermore, the hierarchy of hell is divided into nine sections. Also, there are nine choirs of angels in heaven. Christ died at the ninth hour.

To the Bahá'í, nine represents culmination, comprehensiveness. In the numerology connected with the Arabic alphabet, nine is the numeric value of the letters making up the name "Baha," the revealer of the Bahá'í faith—considered by its followers to be the ninth existing independent religion.

Western numerologists believe if the total number of letters in your first name is nine, you are a person of great talent. You possess global consciousness.

In sorcery, a magic circle must be nine feet in diameter. Magical formulas generally must be repeated nine times. The human gestation period is nine months. Cats are said to have nine lives. We dress to the "nines." Mathematicians check their calculations by "casting out nines." There are nine judges on the Supreme Court, nine players on a baseball team. Shopkeepers will forever charge $9.99. Finally, who can forget the Beatles' song, "Revolution 9"?

Feng Shui and Nine

In feng shui, the nine cells of the Luoshu are connected by the counterclockwise swastika. Also, the number nine enhances the number it's combined with, as you shall soon see. What does this mean? If the number 9 combines with an auspicious number (you'll learn all about favorable and unfavorable numbers in the next chapter), expect the possibility of promotion, financial gain, and happy events. However, if 9 combines with an inauspicious number, beware! The threat of eye disease, fire, litigation, and insanity is likely.

In the next chapter, you'll learn about the 24 directions and the Chinese concept of time. Also, we'll talk more about numbers. Specifically, how they relate to human events, characteristics, and health.

The Least You Need to Know

- Flying Star is a system that calculates the qi pattern of a building according to the way the dwelling is oriented and the date of construction.
- The Hetu diagram of black and white dots represents the ideal world.
- The Luoshu diagram of black and white dots represents motion, transformation, and the interaction of qi.

◆ The Chinese believe the Magic Square of Three is a divine gift. Each number along any diagonal, vertical, or horizontal line adds to 15.

◆ The number nine is significant in many cultures around the world.

Chapter 14

The Flying Stars, Part 2

In This Chapter

- ◆ Space: the 24 mountains
- ◆ Time: three cycles and nine periods
- ◆ The personalities of the nine stars
- ◆ The ruling number

In this chapter, you'll learn more about time and space. Here, you'll learn that your home corresponds to 1 of 24 directions (space), instead of the 8 you used in the Eight House method. Also, you'll understand that the nine "stars" or numbers of the Luoshu relate to specific periods time. And that, like a person, each star has a personality that changes over time.

Space: The 24 Mountains

Undeniably, mountains are part of physical reality. They take up space. And, space is one of the two primary components of classical feng shui, with time being the other one. In ancient China, the idea was to study not only the physical features of the terrain (to select the most auspicious site on which to build a settlement or bury the dead), but also to evaluate and measure its magnetic space.

As you learned in Part 4, "Feng Shui Mechanics 101," each of the eight trigrams and their correlative directions hold a different kind of qi that describe a building's inherent personality. In Flying Star methodology, the 8 fundamental directions are divided into 3 components each for a total of 24 directions (8 trigrams × 3 parts = 24 directions). Called the *24 mountains*, these finer directional distinctions, coupled with the time your home was constructed, hold a lot of valuable information, as you shall soon learn.

Wise Words

The **24 mountains** or directions of a luopan compass derive from the 8 fundamental trigrams: Each trigram constitutes 45 degrees of the compass (8 trigrams × 45 degrees = 360 degrees). Each trigram is subdivided into 3 equal parts of 15 degrees each (3 parts × 15 degrees = 45 degrees). The total number of subdivided parts (3 parts × 8 trigrams) comprises the 24 mountains, each of which has a Chinese name.

A simplified luopan compass.

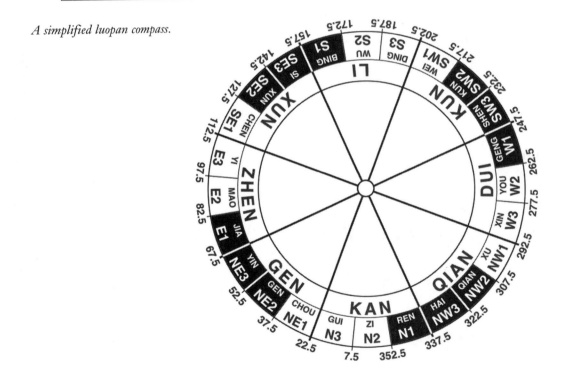

Referring to the preceding illustration of a simplified loupan compass, let's take a closer look. Beginning with the Kan trigram at the bottom, notice that this northern trigram is divided into three mountains: Ren (north 1) at 337.5 degrees to 352.5 degrees, Zi (north 2) at 352.5 degrees to 7.5 degrees, and Gui (north 3) at 7.5 degrees to 22.5 degrees. Moving clockwise around the luopan, the northeastern trigram Gen follows. It's comprised of Chou (northeast 1) at 22.5 to 37.5 degrees, Gen (northeast 2) at 37.5 degrees to 52.5 degrees, and Yin (northeast 3) at 52.5 degrees to 67.5 degrees. The 24 mountains and their magnetic affiliations continue around the luopan in this fashion.

But, why are some mountains black and some white? Simply, the mountains in black are yang, the white ones yin. We include these designations for sake of completeness.

Do You Know Where Your House Is?

In the system of the Flying Stars, it is not enough to determine to which trigram your home belongs. Here, we need to be more exact. For example, say your home belongs to the Zhen trigram. You need to determine what *type* of Zhen house you have: Jia, Mao, or Yi. After taking a compass reading (refer to Chapter 11, "The Eight Houses, Part 2," for a refresher), say you determine that your home sits at ⊔⊔ 87 degrees and ⬆ faces 267 degrees. According to this measurement, your home sits in E2 and faces W2.

Let's take another example. Say your home belongs to the Qian trigram. According to a precise compass reading, you find that it sits at ⊔⊔ 330 degrees (NW3) and ⬆ faces 150 degrees (SE3). Get the idea?

Feng Alert _____

If the compass reading corresponding to your home is on the boundary between two mountains (at 292.5, 307.5, 322.5, for example), you may want to find a digital compass that can provide a more precise reading. If the reading is still on the line, then you cannot proceed. In these cases, there is a special treatment that is beyond the scope of this book.

The Luopan Charted

Here's a charted version (see following table) of the luopan compass. You may find it "easier on your eye" than the circular representation.

Before we proceed, please determine to which mountain your home sits in and faces toward. For our purposes, once you have determined to which mountain your home corresponds, the magnetic designations are no longer needed. Record your information as follows:

Example: My home belongs to the Dui trigram. It sits 凵 in W2 and faces ⬆ toward E2.

My home belongs to the _____ trigram. It sits 凵 in _____ and faces ⬆ toward _____.

You have now determined the magnetic space your home occupies. Now, we will need to link this information with the time your home was constructed.

Trigram	Mountain	Sitting Direction	Compass Designation	Facing Direction	Compass Designation
KAN	REN	N1	337.5° - 352.5°	S1	157.5° - 172.5°
	ZI	N2	352.5° - 7.5°	S2	172.5° - 187.5°
	GUI	N3	7.5° - 22.5°	S3	187.5° - 202.5°
GEN	CHOU	NE1	22.5° - 37.5°	SW1	202.5° - 217.5°
	GEN	NE2	37.5° - 52.5°	SW2	217.5° - 232.5°
	YIN	NE3	52.5° - 67.5°	SW3	232.5° - 247.5°
ZHEN	JIA	E1	67.5° - 82.5°	W1	247.5° - 262.5°
	MAO	E2	82.5° - 97.5°	W2	262.5° - 277.5°
	YI	E3	97.5° - 112.5°	W3	277.5° - 292.5°
XUN	CHEN	SE1	112.5° - 127.5°	NW1	292.5° - 307.5°
	XUN	SE2	127.5° - 142.5°	NW2	307.5° - 322.5°
	SI	SE3	142.5° - 157.5°	NW3	322.5° - 337.5°
LI	BING	S1	157.5° - 172.5°	N1	337.5° - 352.5°
	WU	S2	172.5° - 187.5°	N2	352.5° - 7.5°
	DING	S3	187.5° - 202.5°	N3	7.5° - 22.5°
KUN	WEI	SW1	202.5° - 217.5°	NE1	22.5° - 37.5°
	KUN	SW2	217.5° - 232.5°	NE2	37.5° - 52.5°
	SHEN	SW3	232.5° - 247.5°	NE3	52.5° - 67.5°
DUI	GENG	W1	247.5° - 262.5°	E1	67.5° - 82.5°
	YOU	W2	262.5° - 277.5°	E2	82.5° - 97.5°
	XIN	W3	277.5° - 292.5°	E3	97.5° - 112.5°
QIAN	XU	NW1	292.5° - 307.5°	SE1	112.5° - 127.5°
	QIAN	NW2	307.5° - 322.5°	SE2	127.5° - 142.5°
	HAI	NW3	322.5° - 337.5°	SE3	142.5° - 157.5°

Time: Three Cycles and Nine Periods

To Westerners, the Chinese concept of time may seem very peculiar. Time isn't linear, but spiral-shaped. Following the laws of yin and yang, time repeats itself. Because time repeats, events are also likely to repeat. This idea is the central premise of the *Yijing*, considered the oldest book of divination still in use. Basically, when you ask the oracle a question, you are projecting your situation into a time-space model, the *Yijing*. Since your situation has occurred before, the *Yijing* can foretell a probable solution. To learn more about the *Yijing* and how you can use it to help you solve a dilemma, concern, or problem, please see *The Complete Idiot's Guide to the I Ching* (Alpha Books, 2001).

Referring to the following table, the largest unit of time consists of 180 years. Called the *Great Cycle* (Da Yun), February 4, 1864, marked the beginning of the 180 cycle we are currently in. The cycle officially ends on February 4, 2044, with the new one beginning immediately thereafter.

CYCLE	UPPER			MIDDLE			LOWER		
PERIOD	1	2	3	4	5	6	7	8	9
YEAR BEGIN	Feb.4 1864	Feb.4 1884	Feb.5 1904	Feb.5 1924	Feb.5 1944	Feb.5 1964	Feb.4 1984	Feb.4 2004	Feb.4 2024

The Great Cycle is divided equally into 3 cycles of 60 years each: the Upper Cycle (1864–1924), the Middle Cycle (1924–1984), and the Lower Cycle (1984–2044). The Great Cycle is also divided into 9 luck periods composed of 20 years each. Notice that the Upper Cycle consists of Period 1 (1864–1884), Period 2 (1884–1904), and Period 3 (1904–1924). The Middle Cycle consists of Period 4 (1924–1944), Period 5 (1944–1964), and Period 6 (1964–1984). Finally, the Lower Cycle consists of Period 7 (1984–2004), Period 8 (2004–2024), and Period 9 (2024–2044). Can you guess what period we are now in? If you guessed the seventh 20-year period, you are correct. Period 8 will not begin until February 4, 2004.

Feng Alert

Remember, in feng shui we use the Chinese solar year that begins variously on February 3, 4, or 5 of each year. This is because feng shui studies how qi changes over the year as marked by the position of the sun on the ecliptic path.

So, where is all this leading, you ask? The year the construction of your house was completed determines which 20-year period it was "born into." For example, if your house was completed in 1927, it falls in Period 4 of the Great Cycle. If your house was completed in 1985, then it shares the period we are currently in—Period 7.

The key words here are "construction completed." This is because construction may have begun in one year and ended in the next, a factor that becomes especially crucial if the 20-year period is changing. How can you find out when your house was built? What if you live in an apartment complex? No sweat. This information is a phone call away. The county recorder's office, the tax assessor's office, your building supervisor, or rental office should be able to help you.

Wise Words

A **Great Cycle** (Da Yun) lasts 180 years. It is divided into three 60-year cycles (Yuan) called the Upper, Middle, and Lower Cycles (Shang Yuan, Zhong Yuan, Xia Yuan). The Great Cycle is also divided into nine 20-year luck periods. We are currently in Period 7 (1984–2004) of the Lower Cycle (1984–2044).

Before we proceed, determine to which 20-year period your home was built. Record the information here:

My home was built in Period _____.

Now, let's step back for a minute and talk more about numbers and their characteristics as they relate to human events. The idea behind this concept is central to evaluating your numeric-based Flying Star chart.

It's All in the Numbers

As you're coming to learn, numbers express more than their values—they express ideas and beliefs. And, somehow, nature and humankind conform to this man-made abstraction, an idea we talked about in Chapter 2, "Western Intellectual Heritage and the Holy Grail." In classical feng shui, numbers also express probabilities: the probability an event may happen within a given time and space. It could be a good event, such as a promotion or wedding, or a bad event, suggesting misfortune or illness. But how can these events be determined?

In the West, we've learned to determine the outcome of events by applying the laws of cause and effect. This has been the basis of Western scientific thinking for centuries. Causality is the name of the game—nothing is left to chance, a very unscientific process. The Chinese, on the other hand, are concerned with acausal probabilities, chance happenings and coincidences that are connected by seemingly unrelated events. Nature, or more precisely, the macrocosm, plays a starring role in their acausal theory. They believe human events aren't necessarily caused by natural phenomena, only connected in an acausal relationship. Countless hours through countless centuries were spent correlating acausal events between the outer world and our well-being. Numbers became a method of recording and predicting, forming the basis of the *Yijing*, from which feng shui is partially derived.

In Sync with Greater Nature

This acausal connecting principle is actually known as *synchronicity*, a word coined by renowned Swiss psychologist Carl Jung (1875–1961). Simply, synchronicity can be described as a pattern of coincidences in which thoughts, ideas, objects, and events (or a combination) are linked to form a theme of meaning to the observer(s).

We've all experienced synchronicity. For example, we (Elizabeth Moran and Val Biktashev) experienced a meaningless type of synchronicity, a happening that was more of an oddity than a life-altering event. Late one night we were driving home. The street was quiet, the road was empty, the radio off. Suddenly, at the same time, we started to sing the same line from the Elton John song "Goodbye Yellow Brick Road." Shocked at this unlikely incident, we stared at each other. Then, I (Elizabeth) turned on the radio. Guess what was playing? We and the radio station were "in sync." What's the probability of this happening? What caused this striking coincidence? While we won't get into the "why" here, we talk at great length about the scientific reasoning behind synchronicity in Chapter 11 of *The Complete Idiot's Guide to the I Ching* (Alpha Books, 2001).

Wise Words

Developed by Swiss psychologist Carl Jung (1875–1961), **synchronicity** expresses the connection of acausal (random) events within a limited time frame. The Chinese believe human events are linked with nature in an acausal relationship. Feng shui seeks to determine probabilities of synchronistic events within a certain time period. Numerology is one method classical feng shui uses.

The Attack on America

Yet, there are synchronistic events that are meaningful to the observer(s). For instance, take the September 11, 2001, terrorist attack on New York City's World Trade Center and the Pentagon, the governmental complex for the Department of Defense, located just outside Washington, D.C. A number of seeming unrelated facts came together on this particular day within a specific space. The synchronicities involve the number 11. They are downright chilling:

- The attack occurred on 9/11: $9 + 1 + 1 = 11$
- September 11 marks the two hundred fifty-fourth day of the year: $2 + 5 + 4 = 11$.
- After September 11, 111 days are left in the year.
- From afar, the Twin Towers (part of the World Trade Center complex) resembled a gigantic number 11.
- The first airplane that crashed into the North Tower was American Airlines flight 11.
- In 1788, New York was the eleventh state to join the Union.

- The words "New York City" contain 11 letters.
- The words "The Pentagon" contain 11 letters.
- The word "Afghanistan" contains 11 letters.

Pretty amazing, huh? You may wonder what the number 11 means. According to retired Harvard professor Annemarie Schimmel, as she states in her well-researched book, *The Mystery of Numbers* (Oxford University Press, 1993), "Larger than 10 and smaller than 12, it stands between two very important round numbers and therefore, while every other number had at least one positive aspect, 11 was always interpreted in medieval exegesis *ad malam partem*, in a purely negative sense. The sixteenth-century numerologist Petrus Bungus went so far as to claim that 11 'has no connection with divine things, no ladder reaching up to things above, nor any merit.' He considered it to be the number of sinners and penance."

We need not dwell on the symbolic meaning of the number 11 and the extraordinary facts linking it with the World Trade Center attack. You can formulate your own conclusion. Here, our point is to illustrate a recent, albeit catastrophic, example of numeric synchronicity.

In classical feng shui, the combination of numbers generated by a Flying Star qi chart represents synchronistic probabilities. For example, the Chinese recognized that a 2-1 combination was often linked with spousal conflict, separation, or divorce. An 8-9 combination spawned the likelihood of weddings and pregnancy. A 5-1 combination meant the probability of ear, kidney, or genital disorders. Get the idea? You'll be learning more about interpreting number combinations in later chapters.

A Number Is Worth a Thousand Words

Each number of the Luoshu (please refer to Chapter 13, "The Flying Stars, Part 1," for a reminder) reflects a certain kind of qi. It's important to understand that numbers, too, follow the laws of yin and yang. No number can be favorable or unfavorable all the time. Rather, the auspiciousness of each number is cyclic. But before you learn how to determine a number's timeliness, you must first understand the inherent nature of each number. Remember, we're talking about the numbers comprising a Flying Star qi map, which is generated by the period your home was built in along with its magnetic orientation. Other numbers such as those signifying your birth date, address, age, and the like, have no significance in feng shui. The following are the nine numbers of the Luoshu and their innate characteristics.

Luoshu Number	Inherent Characteristics
1	Wisdom, fame, and fortune
2	Fertility and health (favorable and unfavorable)
3	Misfortune, quarrels, and robbery
4	Writing, academic achievement, creativity, romance, and low morals (extramarital affairs)
5	Power, catastrophe, death, lawsuits, and illness
6	Authority and respect
7	Competition and destruction
8	Happiness and wealth
9	Enhances accompanied number whether favorable or unfavorable

In general, the numbers 1, 6, and 8 are considered good-natured and auspicious. The numbers 2, 3, and 7 are harmful and inauspicious. The number 4 is neutral. The number 5 is best avoided—it shows its power by being sinister, by hurting others.

The Ruler Principle

In the Luoshu, the number 5 occupies the central square of the nine-part grid. It "rules" the earth. Thus, the number 5 represents the stable matter of earth qi and its gravitational force, pulling everything toward the center.

Conversely, there's heaven qi. It moves and changes over time. Each of the nine "stars" or numbers takes turns to rule heaven. Each star rules for 20 years or for one period. As you learned earlier on in this chapter, we are now in Period 7, with the number 7 ruling from 1984 to 2004. The ruling star is the most powerful star, followed by the star that is next in line. Using an analogy, think of number 7 as United States President George W. Bush or Britain's Prime Minister Tony Blair. While we don't yet know who the president/prime minister elect will be, the stars are more orderly. The successor of number 7 is number 8, the next ruling star for the time period 2004 to 2024.

What about the immediate past ruler, the number 6 governing 1964 to 1984? Consider this star like former president Bill Clinton. While he is no longer president, he is still influential.

Wheel of Fortune

Looking at the following illustration, notice how the life cycle wheel revolves in a counterclockwise fashion: that which rules retires, then dies, only to grow again. Numerically, 7 rules; 6 is retired; 5, 4, 3, 2, and 1 are dead; 9 is growing into the apprentice ruler; and 8 is the future ruler.

The life cycle of numbers.

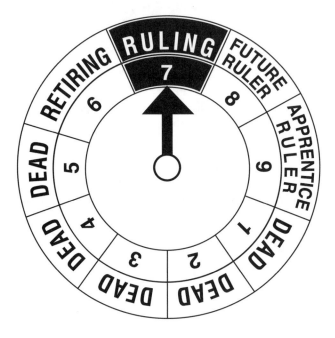

To determine the ruling star for the 20-year period beginning on February 4, 2004, simply turn the wheel one position to the left. The number 8 now rules, and 7 retires. The other numbers follow suit.

Master Class _____

Numbers should be defined in terms of the aging process with their inherent characteristics taken into consideration. For example, the number 1 is inherently a good number representing fame and fortune. If we let number 1 represent Miss America, her reign marks the height of her glory. When she has completed her term, she retires. She is still attractive, but as she ages, she becomes prone to illness and hardship. In other words, when a star ages and then dies, it no longer has the strength to help you.

In Sickness and in Health: The Timeliness of the Stars

How does each number individually embody a ruling, retired, dead, or apprentice/future ruler star? Consult the following table. Pertaining to Period 7 (1984–2004), take the number 1. An inherently favorable number, it is currently dead. In its death cycle, the number 1 has been known to cause marital troubles. Referring to the illustration of the life cycle, you'll see that number 1 will "rise" from the dead and become the apprentice future ruler in 2004, when number 8 becomes the ruler. During its productive years, the number 1 promotes wisdom, fame, and fortune. Let's take the number 7. Currently, it's the ruling star. Referring to the chart, when the number 7 is in its ruling or apprentice/future ruler cycle, it ushers in the possibility of greater financial success and fertility. However, beginning on February 4, 2004, it retires. It exhibits both its good and bad qualities (just like the number 6 does during Period 7).

The Nature of Timely and Untimely Stars for the 20 Year Period, Feb. 4, 1984 - Feb. 3, 2004

NUMBER	TIMELY CHARACTERISTICS	NUMBER	UNTIMELY CHARACTERISTICS
	Wisdom, Fame & Fortune	1	Spousal Conflict, Separation & Divorce
	Good Health & Fertility	2	Sickness & Miscarriage
	Abundance of Wealth	3	Lawsuits, Robbery & Asthma
	Academic Achiement, Creativity, Writing, Romance	4	Affairs, Sexual Entanglements
	Success, Power & Prosperity	5	Catastrophes, Casualties Lawsuits & Sickness
6	Great Authority, Dignity & Fame	6	Loneliness & Lawsuits
7	Financial Gain & Fertility		Fire, Theft & Casualties
8	Steady Progress in Finance, Good Fortune		Harmful to Youth & Solitude
9	Success & Promotion		Eye Desease, Fire, Litigation & Insanity

We suggest placing a paper clip on this page. Until you have memorized each number's inherent nature and life cycles, you'll be referring to this table often.

In this chapter, you've determined the two most important factors that will generate a numeric qi pattern of your home—the magnetic orientation (space) and the period (time) it was born into. In the next chapter, you'll learn how to "fly" the stars, to create the numeric qi pattern.

The Least You Need to Know

- In a Flying Star reading, 24 mountains or directions are considered instead of the 8 you used in the Eight House system.

- The Chinese view time as cyclic. The largest unit of time is made up of 180 years. Called the Great Cycle, it is divided into three equal parts of 60 years each. Each 60-year cycle is subdivided into three equal parts of 20 years each.

- Currently, we are in Period 7 (1984–2004) of the Great Cycle. Period 8 begins on February 4, 2004, and ends on February 3, 2024.

- Each of the nine "stars" or numbers of the Luoshu has distinct personalities that change over time.

- In Flying Star methodology, numbers and combinations of numbers express the probability of events occurring.

Chapter

15

The Flying Stars, Part 3

In This Chapter

- ◆ Flying the period or time star
- ◆ Flying the stars forward
- ◆ Flying the stars backward

Flying Star is a very challenging system. It's a bit technical so we suggest you undertake this chapter and successive ones regarding the mechanics of the Flying Star system only when you are energetic, clearheaded, and free of time constraints. An alert mind, a positive attitude, and an insatiable curiosity are all it takes to advance toward more sophisticated feng shui techniques.

Do Stars Fly?

To fly a star means to move numbers around the nine cells of the Luoshu in a specific sequence. What you're actually doing here is calculating the movement of qi; determining the qi pattern made manifest by the building's construction date (time) and its magnetic orientation (space). So, instead of saying, "I'll run the numbers," you say, "I'll fly the numbers." In doing so, you'll sound cool using feng shui lingo!

Flying Stars!

In the last chapter, you learned about the Chinese concept of time—that the construction year of your home relates to a specific 20-year period. For example, if your home was completed in 1985, it belongs to Period 7 (1984–2004), the cycle we're currently in. If your home was completed in 1950, it belongs to Period 5 (1944–1964). Whatever period your home belongs to is the number that represents the star that ruled when your home was "born." In other words, if your home was built between 1984 and 2004 (Period 7), the number 7 prevailed; it ruled heaven's qi.

Also called the *time star*, the ruling or period number is placed in the central palace of the nine-part Luoshu grid. In an ascending manner, the other numbers will fill the remaining eight cells by following a precise directional sequence: NW, W, NE, S, N, SW, E, SE. For example, let's take a house built during Period 4 (1924–1944). Placing the time star number 4 in the center, the other numbers "fly" as shown in the figures following.

Example of flying the time star for a house built in Period 4. Note: While technically, the Luoshu diagram is a square configuration, we have rounded the diagram to match the circular Hou Tian (After Heaven) sequence to which the Luoshu numbers are correlated.

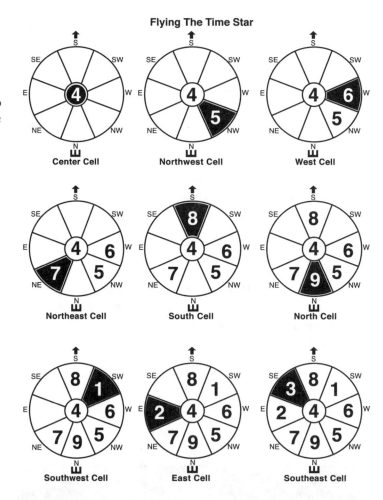

Next, you must check your work. An easy way to determine if the numbers have been flown correctly is to check the number in the last, or southeast cell. If it precedes the number in the center palace, there should be no mistake. In this example, the number 3 is in the southeast cell. Three precedes four.

Flying the Stars

As the saying goes, "Practice makes perfect." To fully comprehend Flying Star, it's best that you take an active role. Participate. Be proactive and not passive. What follows are eight empty charts (representing Period 2 through Period 9) for you to complete. At this stage, the directions corresponding to your home's sitting and facing sides are not a consideration. This aspect comes into play later on in this chapter. Here, we're only concerned with your dwelling's construction date. To give you a head start, we've filled out the first chart (Period 1) for you. Remember, the sequence is:

Center, NW, W, NE, S, N, SW, E, SE

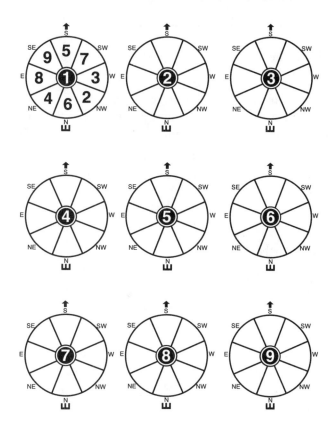

That wasn't so difficult, was it? Did you remember to check the southeast cell? Does the number in this cell precede that which is in the center palace? See. What seemed complicated is, in fact, simple—a piece of cake, a walk in the park.

Constructing a Flying Star Chart

You've just completed step one of constructing a Flying Star chart, manifesting the heaven or time qi governing your home. Now, things get more complicated.

Step two is to calculate the house's qi pattern, which relates to its magnetic space. Let's take a house built in Period 7, sitting N1 and facing S1. Referring to the following illustration of House 1, the star (or number) corresponding to the sitting direction (number 3) is copied and moved to the top, left side of the central palace. This star is called the *sitting star*. Next, the *facing star*, the number corresponding to the dwelling's facing direction, is copied and moved to the top, right side of the central palace. In this example, number 2 represents the facing star.

Let's take another example. House 2 represents a dwelling built in Period 4, sitting SW2 and facing NE2. As indicated, the sitting star 1 is copied and moved to the top, left side of the central palace. The facing star 7 is copied and moved to the top, right side of the central palace.

Finally, one more example. House 3 represents a dwelling built in Period 1, sitting E1 and facing W1. Here, the sitting star 8 is copied and moved to the top, left side of the central palace. The facing star 3 is copied and moved to the top, right side of the central palace.

Using the preceding empty chart (My House), fly the time star (period or ruling star) affiliated with your own home. Then, transfer the sitting and facing stars to their appropriate positions in the central palace.

Wise Words _____

The **time star** (period star) is the number that ruled when your house was built. The **sitting star** (zuo xing) is the number that corresponds to your dwelling's sitting direction. The **facing star** (xiang xing) is the number that corresponds to your dwelling's facing direction. These numbers "fly" to the top left and top right of the central palace, respectively. The sitting star is also called the mountain star (shan xing) or people star (ding xing). The facing star is also called the water star (shui xing) or money star (cai xing).

House 1

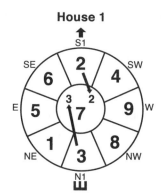

House 2

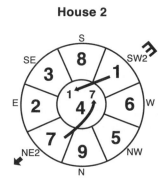

After you have determined to which period your home belongs, the next step is to transfer the sitting and facing stars to the left and right sides of the central cell respectively. The empty chart is for you to record the information appropriate to your own home.

House 3

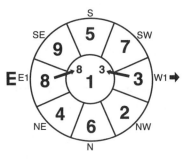

My House

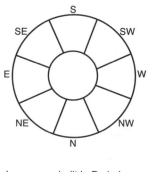

My house was built in Period: _____.

It ⊔ sits _____ and ↑ faces _____.

Flying Forward, Flying Backward

Step three requires you to fly the sitting and facing stars either forward (just like you did for the time star) or backward. Logically, if flying forward (1, 2, 3, 4, 5, 6, 7, 8, 9) means the numbers ascend, then flying backward (9, 8, 7, 6, 5, 4, 3, 2, 1) means the numbers descend while following the directional sequence (center, NW, W, NE, S, N, SW, E, SE). Whether the sitting and facing star flies forward or backward depends on two factors:

◆ If the star in question is odd or even.

◆ If the mountain the house sits in and faces toward is the first, second, or third mountain of the trigram in question.

Now, following the five rules below, determine if the sitting and facing stars in the center palace fly forward or backward:

> **Rule 1:** If your house sits in and faces toward the first mountain (N1 to S1; NE1 to SW1; E1 to W1, for example) and if the sitting or facing star is odd (except the number 5), then the star in question flies forward.

> **Rule 2:** If your house sits in and faces toward the first mountain (N1 to S1; NE1 to SW1; E1 to W1, for example) and if the sitting or facing star is even, then the star in question flies backward.

> **Rule 3:** If your house sits in and faces toward the second or third mountains (N2 to S2; N3 to S3; W2 to E2; W3 to E3, for example) and if the sitting or facing star is odd (except the number 5), then the star in question flies backward.

> **Rule 4:** If your house sits in and faces toward the second or third mountains (N2 to S2; N3 to S3; W2 to E2; W3 to E3, for example) and if the sitting or facing star is even, then the star in question flies forward.

> **Rule 5:** The number 5 flies forward or backward according to whether the ruling star in the center palace is odd or even. In other words, if the ruling star is 1, 3, 7, or 9, the number 5 in the sitting or facing position flies according to rule 1 or rule 3. If the ruling star is 2, 4, 6, or 8, the number 5 in the sitting or facing position flies according to rule 2 or rule 4.

Referring to the following examples, let's look at House 1. Built in Period 7, it sits N1 and faces S1. According to Rule 1, the sitting star 3 (located in the top, left position of the central cell) flies forward: 3 (center), 4 (NW), 5 (W), 6 (NE), 7 (S), 8 (N), 9 (SW), 1 (E), and 2 (SE). According to Rule 2, the facing star 2 (located in the top, right position of the central cell) flies backward: 2 (center), 1 (NW), 9 (W), 8 (NE), 7 (S), 6 (N), 5 (SW), 4 (E), and 3 (SE). Referring to House 2, it sits N3 and faces S3. According to Rule 3, the sitting star 3 flies backward. According to Rule 4, the facing star 2 flies forward. Get the idea?

According to Rule 1, the sitting star 3 flies forward. According to Rule 2, the facing star 2 flies backward.

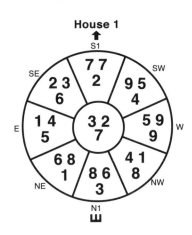

House 1

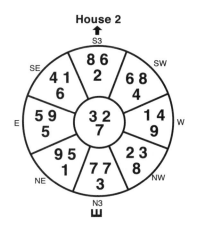

According to Rule 3, the sitting star 3 flies backward. According to Rule 4, the facing star 2 flies forward.

Now, it's your turn. Take this time to complete your chart (My House) by flying the sitting and facing stars in the central cell.

Master Class

Another method similar to Xuankong Feixing (Time and Space Flying Stars), which we present here, is called Zibai Feigong or Purple-White Flying Palace. Basically, this technique flies the Luoshu number that correlates to your dwelling's sitting trigram and then compares the eight other numbers to the central one. Dating to the Ming dynasty (1368–1644), the system is also called Zibai Jiuxing or Purple-White Nine Stars. Why purple-white? Because each number is associated with a color. The colors white (1, 6, 8) and purple (9) are considered auspicious numbers. Since the colors were used as mnemonics to aid learning, we will not discuss the Zibai Feigong colors, which are not related to the five phase colors.

More Flying Forward, More Flying Backward

To facilitate learning, let's review this intricate procedure one more time. House 3 (following) sits at W2 and faces E2. It was built in 1950. Take this time now to fly the stars. To help you, check off each task as you complete it:

❏ Using the sitting ⛰ and facing ⬆ symbols, notate the directional orientation of the dwelling.

❏ Determine the 20-year period the home was constructed in. Consult Chapter 14, "The Flying Stars, Part 2," for a reminder. Write this number (the time star) in the central palace.

❏ Fly the time star forward. Remember, the directional sequence is: Center, NW, W, NE, S, N, SW, E, SE.

❏ Copy and move the sitting star to the top, left side of the central palace. Copy and move the facing star to the top, right side of the central palace.

❏ Refer to the five rules to determine if the sitting and facing stars fly forward or backward. Fly the stars.

So, how did you do? Compare your result to the answer at the end of the chapter.

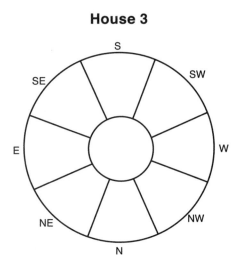

House 3

Charted Floor Plan

Let's not lose sight of the fact that the nine numeric cells represent the qi distribution coming from the eight cardinal directions, with the central palace representing the home's innate essence. Once you have created a Flying Star chart appropriate to your home, you must overlay the numeric qi map onto your floor plan. Divide the home into eight equal wedges, with the sitting side at the bottom of the page and the facing side at the top of the page. (More information about dividing a home using the 24 mountains is available in Appendix E, "Learn More About Taking a Proper Compass Reading Using the 24 Mountains.") For instance, Figure 1 shows a house constructed in Period 6, sitting NW2 and facing SE2. To orient the house such that the sitting side is flush with the bottom of the page, rotate the diagram one position clockwise. By doing this, you will avoid having to analyze your home on an angle.

Orient your home so that the sitting side corresponds to the bottom of the page.

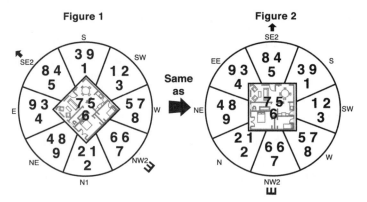

You may want to flip forward to Part 6, "Practical Application," to get a better idea about how a home is divided. You'll notice that the central palace is not an area, but a mere dot representing a dwelling's inherent personality. We'll be discussing this notion in more detail later on. Also, take care not to run dividing lines through the floor plan. The walls are the real dividing lines. Again, the idea is not to compartmentalize your home into distinct sections (like in Life Aspirations and Black Sect methodology), but to study how qi coming from the eight directions affects the whole of your living and/or working space. This will become clearer as you progress through the case studies in Chapters 18, "The Flying Stars, Part 6," 19, "A House Hunting We Will Go," and 20, "Does Your Office Measure Up?"

 Notable Quotable

"The so-called internal qi does not come from within. It is actually the qi that flows from outside."

—Jiang Da Hong, seventeenth-century feng shui master in his annotation of *Qing Nang Jing*.

Great Charts!

We stated in Chapter 1, "What Is Feng Shui?" that there are 216 types of houses. How did we come to this conclusion? There are 24 mountains x 9 periods = 216. If you found that flying the stars is a laborious task, don't fear—we've done all the work for you. In fact, we've even oriented the charts so that the sitting is at the bottom of the page and the facing is at the top of the page. All you need to do is look up the chart corresponding to your home! First, find the period in which your house was constructed. Then, find the chart correlating to its sitting direction.

In the next chapter, you'll learn how the position of the sitting and facing stars affects the auspiciousness of a house.

Houses Built in Period 1 (Feb. 4, 1864 - Feb. 3, 1884)

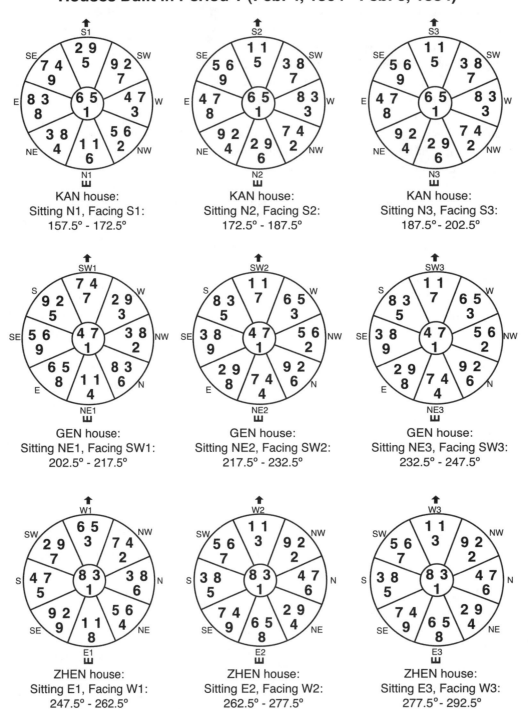

KAN house:
Sitting N1, Facing S1:
157.5° - 172.5°

KAN house:
Sitting N2, Facing S2:
172.5° - 187.5°

KAN house:
Sitting N3, Facing S3:
187.5° - 202.5°

GEN house:
Sitting NE1, Facing SW1:
202.5° - 217.5°

GEN house:
Sitting NE2, Facing SW2:
217.5° - 232.5°

GEN house:
Sitting NE3, Facing SW3:
232.5° - 247.5°

ZHEN house:
Sitting E1, Facing W1:
247.5° - 262.5°

ZHEN house:
Sitting E2, Facing W2:
262.5° - 277.5°

ZHEN house:
Sitting E3, Facing W3:
277.5° - 292.5°

Houses Built in Period 1 (Feb. 4, 1864 - Feb. 3, 1884)

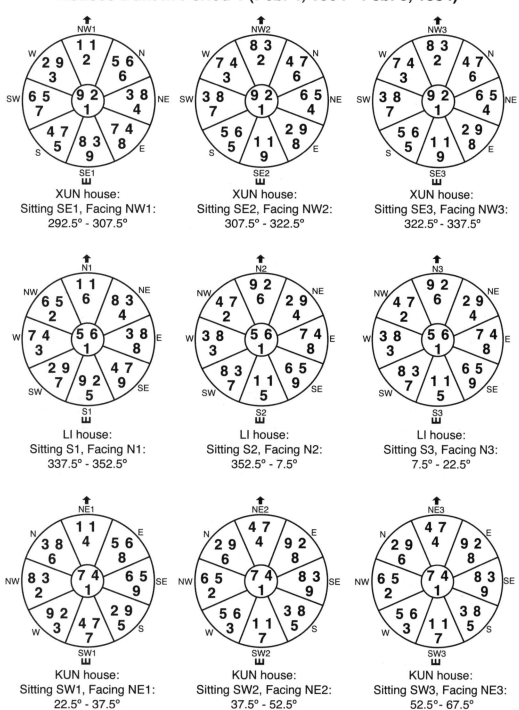

XUN house:
Sitting SE1, Facing NW1:
292.5° - 307.5°

XUN house:
Sitting SE2, Facing NW2:
307.5° - 322.5°

XUN house:
Sitting SE3, Facing NW3:
322.5° - 337.5°

LI house:
Sitting S1, Facing N1:
337.5° - 352.5°

LI house:
Sitting S2, Facing N2:
352.5° - 7.5°

LI house:
Sitting S3, Facing N3:
7.5° - 22.5°

KUN house:
Sitting SW1, Facing NE1:
22.5° - 37.5°

KUN house:
Sitting SW2, Facing NE2:
37.5° - 52.5°

KUN house:
Sitting SW3, Facing NE3:
52.5°- 67.5°

Houses Built in Period 1 (Feb. 4, 1864 - Feb. 3, 1884)

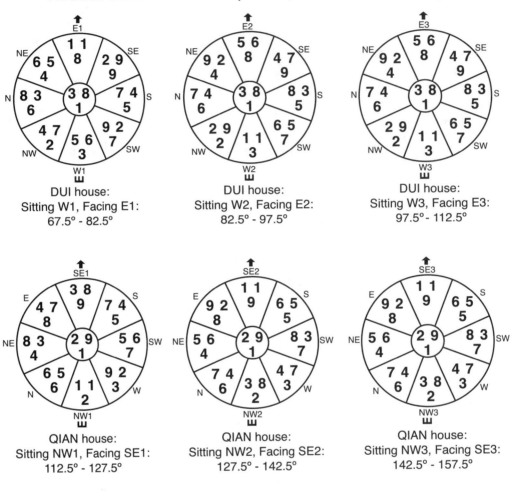

DUI house:
Sitting W1, Facing E1:
67.5° - 82.5°

DUI house:
Sitting W2, Facing E2:
82.5° - 97.5°

DUI house:
Sitting W3, Facing E3:
97.5° - 112.5°

QIAN house:
Sitting NW1, Facing SE1:
112.5° - 127.5°

QIAN house:
Sitting NW2, Facing SE2:
127.5° - 142.5°

QIAN house:
Sitting NW3, Facing SE3:
142.5° - 157.5°

Houses Built in Period 2 (Feb. 4, 1884 - Feb. 4, 1904)

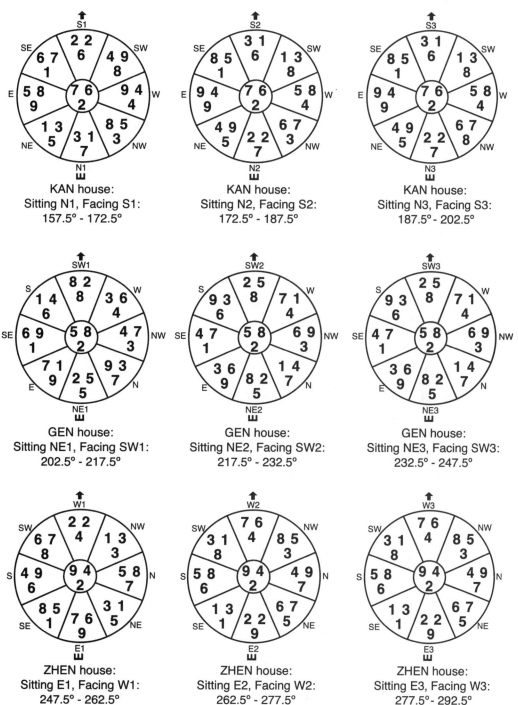

KAN house:
Sitting N1, Facing S1:
157.5° - 172.5°

KAN house:
Sitting N2, Facing S2:
172.5° - 187.5°

KAN house:
Sitting N3, Facing S3:
187.5° - 202.5°

GEN house:
Sitting NE1, Facing SW1:
202.5° - 217.5°

GEN house:
Sitting NE2, Facing SW2:
217.5° - 232.5°

GEN house:
Sitting NE3, Facing SW3:
232.5° - 247.5°

ZHEN house:
Sitting E1, Facing W1:
247.5° - 262.5°

ZHEN house:
Sitting E2, Facing W2:
262.5° - 277.5°

ZHEN house:
Sitting E3, Facing W3:
277.5° - 292.5°

Houses Built in Period 2 (Feb. 4, 1884 - Feb. 4, 1904)

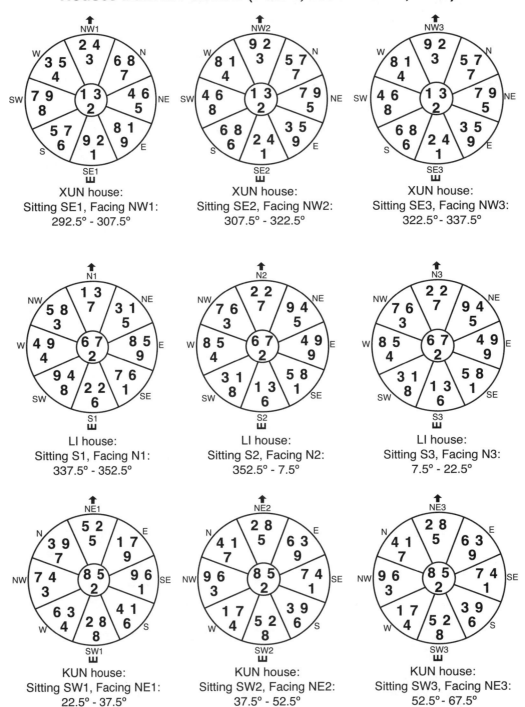

XUN house:
Sitting SE1, Facing NW1:
292.5° - 307.5°

XUN house:
Sitting SE2, Facing NW2:
307.5° - 322.5°

XUN house:
Sitting SE3, Facing NW3:
322.5° - 337.5°

LI house:
Sitting S1, Facing N1:
337.5° - 352.5°

LI house:
Sitting S2, Facing N2:
352.5° - 7.5°

LI house:
Sitting S3, Facing N3:
7.5° - 22.5°

KUN house:
Sitting SW1, Facing NE1:
22.5° - 37.5°

KUN house:
Sitting SW2, Facing NE2:
37.5° - 52.5°

KUN house:
Sitting SW3, Facing NE3:
52.5° - 67.5°

Houses Built in Period 2 (Feb. 4, 1884 - Feb. 4, 1904)

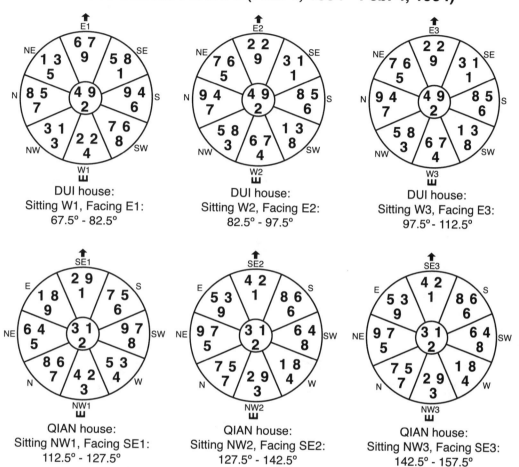

DUI house:
Sitting W1, Facing E1:
67.5° - 82.5°

DUI house:
Sitting W2, Facing E2:
82.5° - 97.5°

DUI house:
Sitting W3, Facing E3:
97.5° - 112.5°

QIAN house:
Sitting NW1, Facing SE1:
112.5° - 127.5°

QIAN house:
Sitting NW2, Facing SE2:
127.5° - 142.5°

QIAN house:
Sitting NW3, Facing SE3:
142.5° - 157.5°

Houses Built in Period 3 (Feb. 5, 1904 - Feb. 4, 1924)

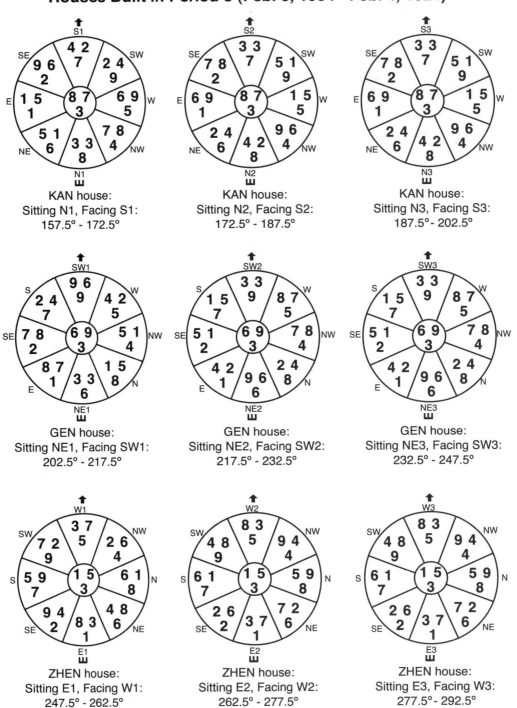

KAN house:
Sitting N1, Facing S1:
157.5° - 172.5°

KAN house:
Sitting N2, Facing S2:
172.5° - 187.5°

KAN house:
Sitting N3, Facing S3:
187.5° - 202.5°

GEN house:
Sitting NE1, Facing SW1:
202.5° - 217.5°

GEN house:
Sitting NE2, Facing SW2:
217.5° - 232.5°

GEN house:
Sitting NE3, Facing SW3:
232.5° - 247.5°

ZHEN house:
Sitting E1, Facing W1:
247.5° - 262.5°

ZHEN house:
Sitting E2, Facing W2:
262.5° - 277.5°

ZHEN house:
Sitting E3, Facing W3:
277.5° - 292.5°

Houses Built in Period 3 (Feb. 5, 1904 - Feb. 4, 1924)

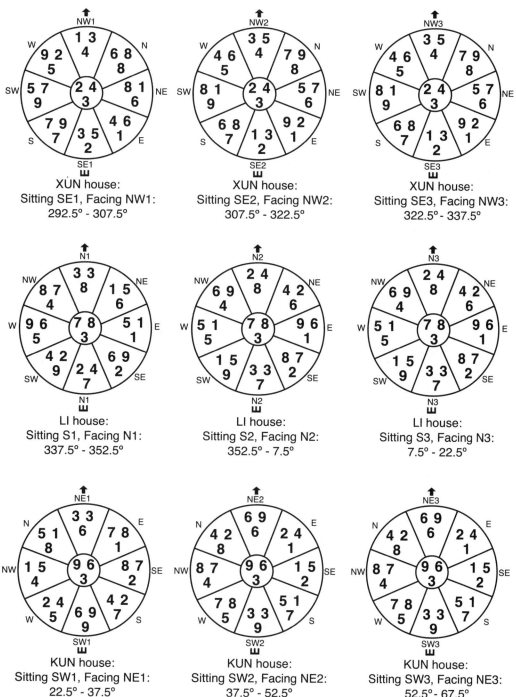

XUN house:
Sitting SE1, Facing NW1:
292.5° - 307.5°

XUN house:
Sitting SE2, Facing NW2:
307.5° - 322.5°

XUN house:
Sitting SE3, Facing NW3:
322.5° - 337.5°

LI house:
Sitting S1, Facing N1:
337.5° - 352.5°

LI house:
Sitting S2, Facing N2:
352.5° - 7.5°

LI house:
Sitting S3, Facing N3:
7.5° - 22.5°

KUN house:
Sitting SW1, Facing NE1:
22.5° - 37.5°

KUN house:
Sitting SW2, Facing NE2:
37.5° - 52.5°

KUN house:
Sitting SW3, Facing NE3:
52.5° - 67.5°

Houses Built in Period 3 (Feb. 5, 1904 - Feb. 4, 1924)

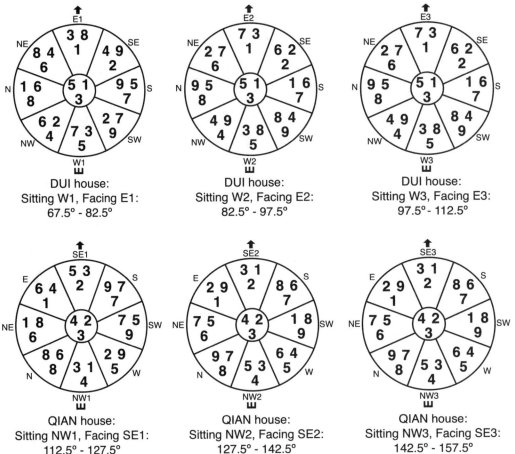

DUI house:
Sitting W1, Facing E1:
67.5° - 82.5°

DUI house:
Sitting W2, Facing E2:
82.5° - 97.5°

DUI house:
Sitting W3, Facing E3:
97.5° - 112.5°

QIAN house:
Sitting NW1, Facing SE1:
112.5° - 127.5°

QIAN house:
Sitting NW2, Facing SE2:
127.5° - 142.5°

QIAN house:
Sitting NW3, Facing SE3:
142.5° - 157.5°

Houses Built in Period 4 (Feb. 5, 1924 - Feb. 4, 1944)

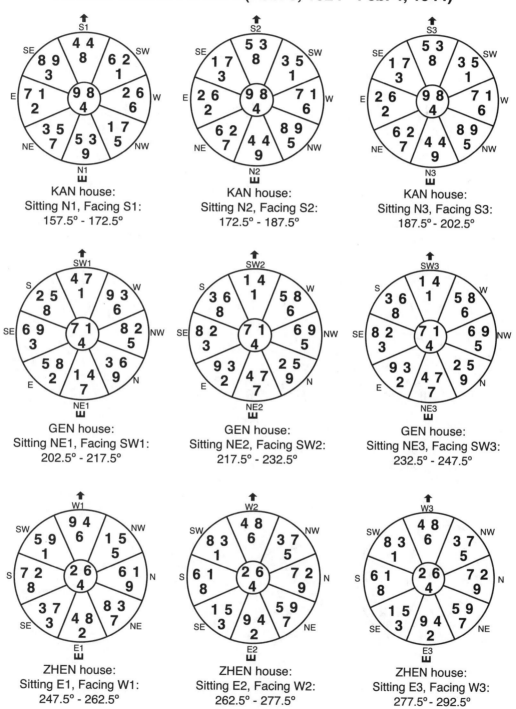

KAN house:
Sitting N1, Facing S1:
157.5° - 172.5°

KAN house:
Sitting N2, Facing S2:
172.5° - 187.5°

KAN house:
Sitting N3, Facing S3:
187.5° - 202.5°

GEN house:
Sitting NE1, Facing SW1:
202.5° - 217.5°

GEN house:
Sitting NE2, Facing SW2:
217.5° - 232.5°

GEN house:
Sitting NE3, Facing SW3:
232.5° - 247.5°

ZHEN house:
Sitting E1, Facing W1:
247.5° - 262.5°

ZHEN house:
Sitting E2, Facing W2:
262.5° - 277.5°

ZHEN house:
Sitting E3, Facing W3:
277.5° - 292.5°

Houses Built in Period 4 (Feb. 5, 1924 - Feb. 4, 1944)

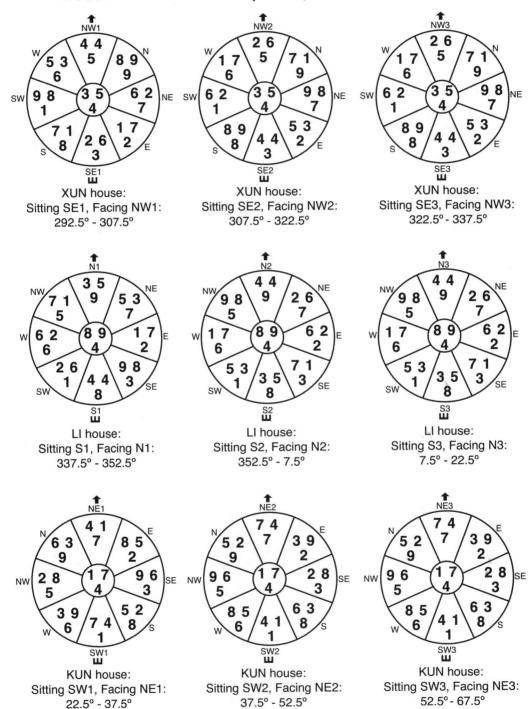

XUN house:
Sitting SE1, Facing NW1:
292.5° - 307.5°

XUN house:
Sitting SE2, Facing NW2:
307.5° - 322.5°

XUN house:
Sitting SE3, Facing NW3:
322.5° - 337.5°

LI house:
Sitting S1, Facing N1:
337.5° - 352.5°

LI house:
Sitting S2, Facing N2:
352.5° - 7.5°

LI house:
Sitting S3, Facing N3:
7.5° - 22.5°

KUN house:
Sitting SW1, Facing NE1:
22.5° - 37.5°

KUN house:
Sitting SW2, Facing NE2:
37.5° - 52.5°

KUN house:
Sitting SW3, Facing NE3:
52.5° - 67.5°

Houses Built in Period 4 (Feb. 5, 1924 - Feb. 4, 1944)

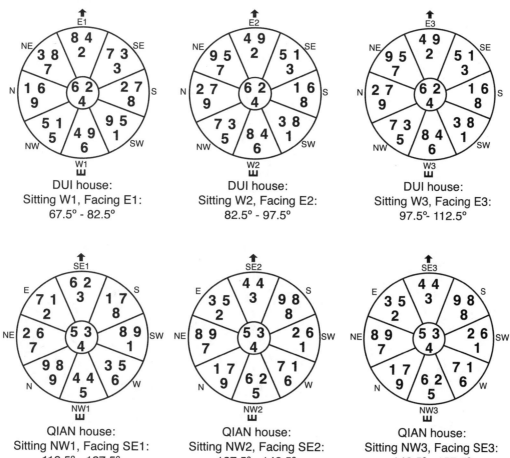

DUI house:
Sitting W1, Facing E1:
67.5° - 82.5°

DUI house:
Sitting W2, Facing E2:
82.5° - 97.5°

DUI house:
Sitting W3, Facing E3:
97.5°- 112.5°

QIAN house:
Sitting NW1, Facing SE1:
112.5° - 127.5°

QIAN house:
Sitting NW2, Facing SE2:
127.5° - 142.5°

QIAN house:
Sitting NW3, Facing SE3:
142.5° - 157.5°

Houses Built in Period 5 (Feb. 5, 1944 - Feb. 4, 1964)

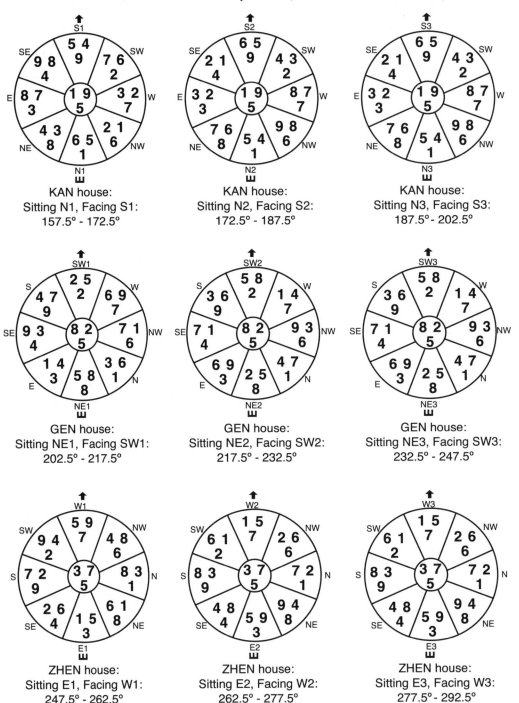

KAN house:
Sitting N1, Facing S1:
157.5° - 172.5°

KAN house:
Sitting N2, Facing S2:
172.5° - 187.5°

KAN house:
Sitting N3, Facing S3:
187.5° - 202.5°

GEN house:
Sitting NE1, Facing SW1:
202.5° - 217.5°

GEN house:
Sitting NE2, Facing SW2:
217.5° - 232.5°

GEN house:
Sitting NE3, Facing SW3:
232.5° - 247.5°

ZHEN house:
Sitting E1, Facing W1:
247.5° - 262.5°

ZHEN house:
Sitting E2, Facing W2:
262.5° - 277.5°

ZHEN house:
Sitting E3, Facing W3:
277.5° - 292.5°

Houses Built in Period 5 (Feb. 5, 1944 - Feb. 4, 1964)

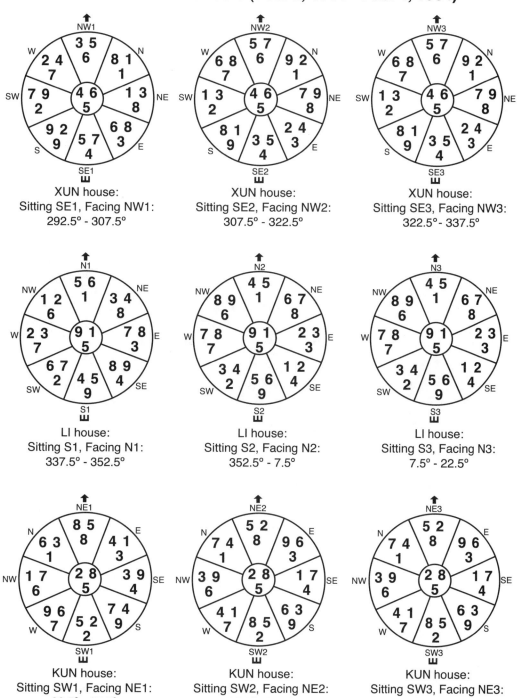

XUN house:
Sitting SE1, Facing NW1:
292.5° - 307.5°

XUN house:
Sitting SE2, Facing NW2:
307.5° - 322.5°

XUN house:
Sitting SE3, Facing NW3:
322.5°- 337.5°

LI house:
Sitting S1, Facing N1:
337.5° - 352.5°

LI house:
Sitting S2, Facing N2:
352.5° - 7.5°

LI house:
Sitting S3, Facing N3:
7.5° - 22.5°

KUN house:
Sitting SW1, Facing NE1:
22.5° - 37.5°

KUN house:
Sitting SW2, Facing NE2:
37.5° - 52.5°

KUN house:
Sitting SW3, Facing NE3:
52.5°- 67.5°

Houses Built in Period 5 (Feb. 5, 1944 - Feb. 4, 1964)

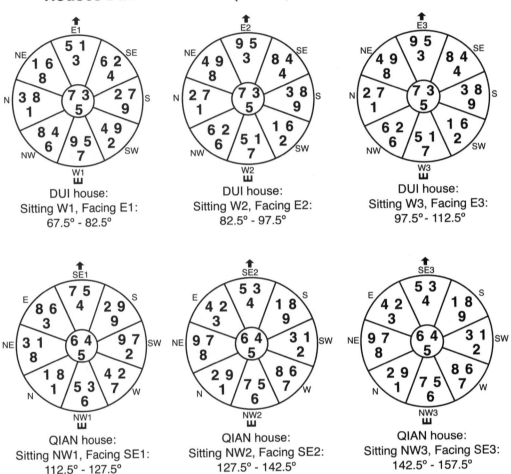

DUI house:
Sitting W1, Facing E1:
67.5° - 82.5°

DUI house:
Sitting W2, Facing E2:
82.5° - 97.5°

DUI house:
Sitting W3, Facing E3:
97.5°- 112.5°

QIAN house:
Sitting NW1, Facing SE1:
112.5° - 127.5°

QIAN house:
Sitting NW2, Facing SE2:
127.5° - 142.5°

QIAN house:
Sitting NW3, Facing SE3:
142.5° - 157.5°

Houses Built in Period 6 (Feb. 5, 1964 - Feb. 3, 1984)

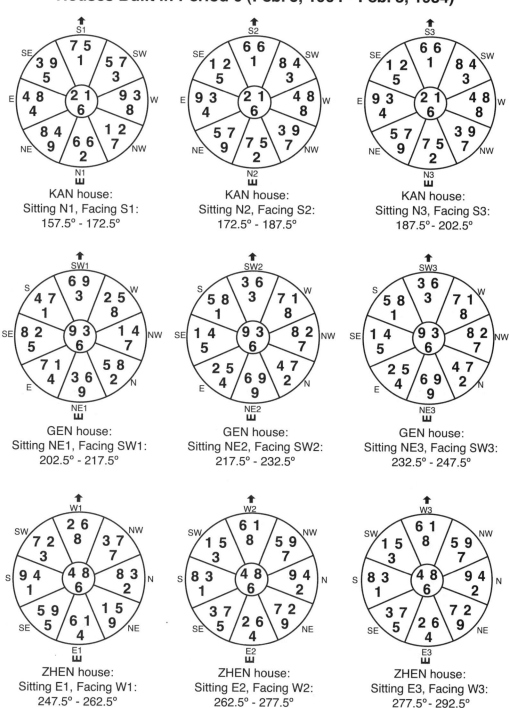

KAN house:
Sitting N1, Facing S1:
157.5° - 172.5°

KAN house:
Sitting N2, Facing S2:
172.5° - 187.5°

KAN house:
Sitting N3, Facing S3:
187.5° - 202.5°

GEN house:
Sitting NE1, Facing SW1:
202.5° - 217.5°

GEN house:
Sitting NE2, Facing SW2:
217.5° - 232.5°

GEN house:
Sitting NE3, Facing SW3:
232.5° - 247.5°

ZHEN house:
Sitting E1, Facing W1:
247.5° - 262.5°

ZHEN house:
Sitting E2, Facing W2:
262.5° - 277.5°

ZHEN house:
Sitting E3, Facing W3:
277.5° - 292.5°

Houses Built in Period 6 (Feb. 5, 1964 - Feb. 3, 1984)

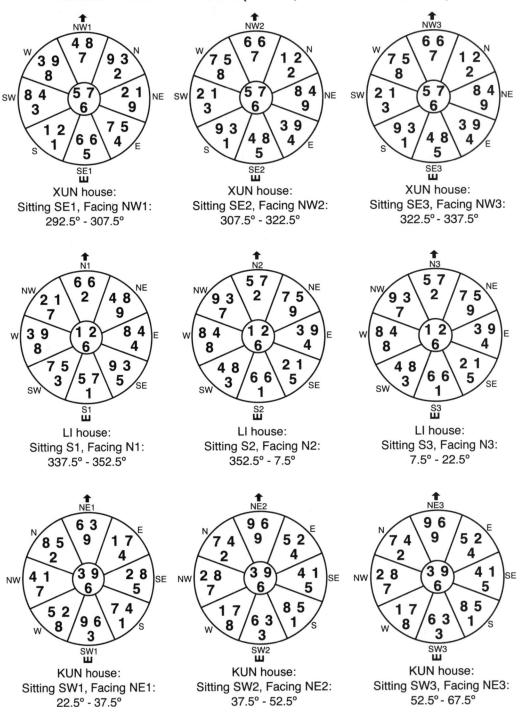

XUN house:
Sitting SE1, Facing NW1:
292.5° - 307.5°

XUN house:
Sitting SE2, Facing NW2:
307.5° - 322.5°

XUN house:
Sitting SE3, Facing NW3:
322.5° - 337.5°

LI house:
Sitting S1, Facing N1:
337.5° - 352.5°

LI house:
Sitting S2, Facing N2:
352.5° - 7.5°

LI house:
Sitting S3, Facing N3:
7.5° - 22.5°

KUN house:
Sitting SW1, Facing NE1:
22.5° - 37.5°

KUN house:
Sitting SW2, Facing NE2:
37.5° - 52.5°

KUN house:
Sitting SW3, Facing NE3:
52.5° - 67.5°

Houses Built in Period 6 (Feb. 5, 1964 - Feb. 3, 1984)

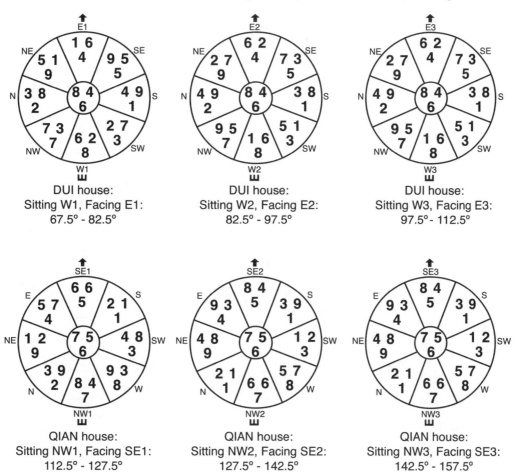

DUI house:
Sitting W1, Facing E1:
67.5° - 82.5°

DUI house:
Sitting W2, Facing E2:
82.5° - 97.5°

DUI house:
Sitting W3, Facing E3:
97.5° - 112.5°

QIAN house:
Sitting NW1, Facing SE1:
112.5° - 127.5°

QIAN house:
Sitting NW2, Facing SE2:
127.5° - 142.5°

QIAN house:
Sitting NW3, Facing SE3:
142.5° - 157.5°

Houses Built in Period 7 (Feb. 4, 1984 - Feb. 3, 2004)

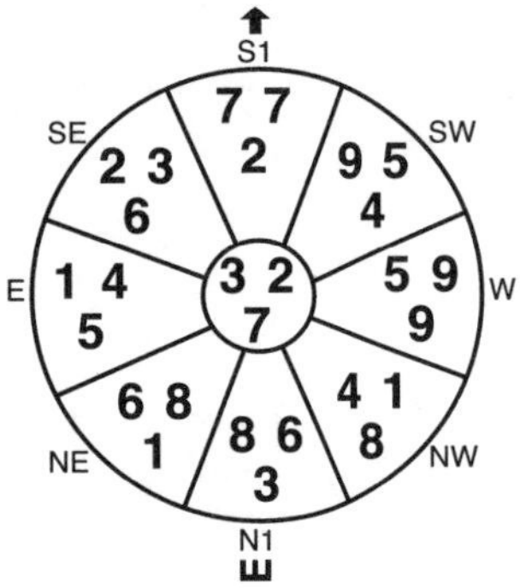

KAN house:
Sitting N1, Facing S1:
157.5° - 172.5°

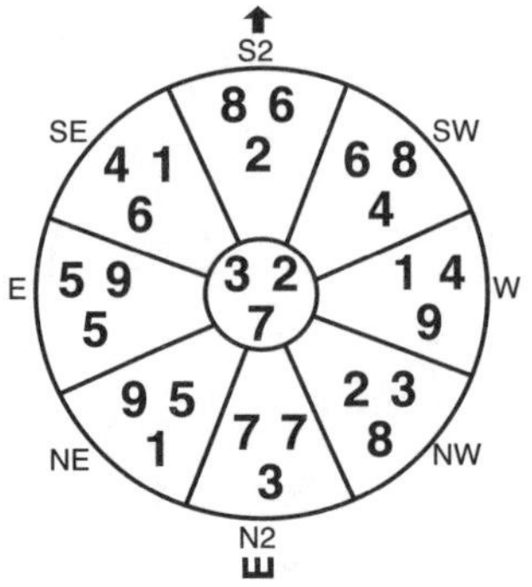

KAN house:
Sitting N2, Facing S2:
172.5° - 187.5°

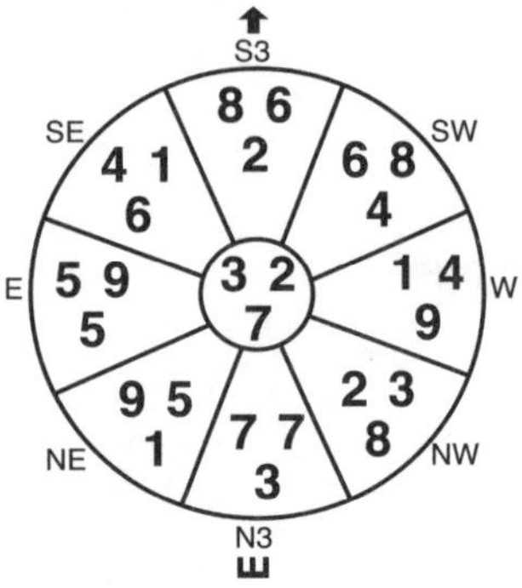

KAN house:
Sitting N3, Facing S3:
187.5° - 202.5°

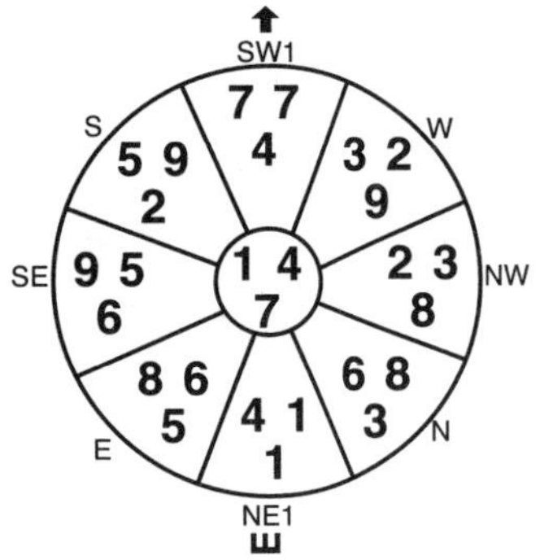

GEN house:
Sitting NE1, Facing SW1:
202.5° - 217.5°

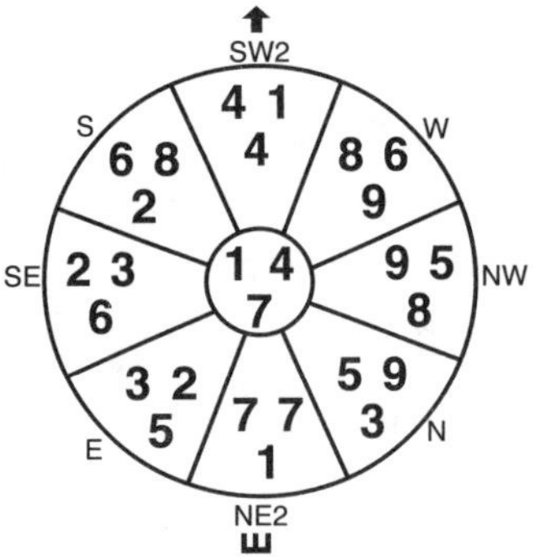

GEN house:
Sitting NE2, Facing SW2:
217.5° - 232.5°

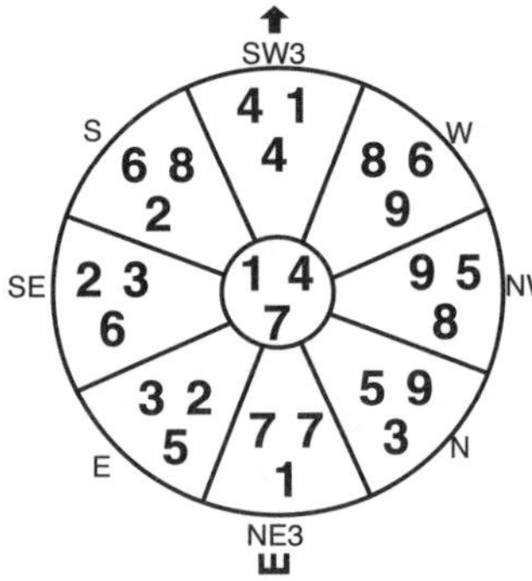

GEN house:
Sitting NE3, Facing SW3:
232.5° - 247.5°

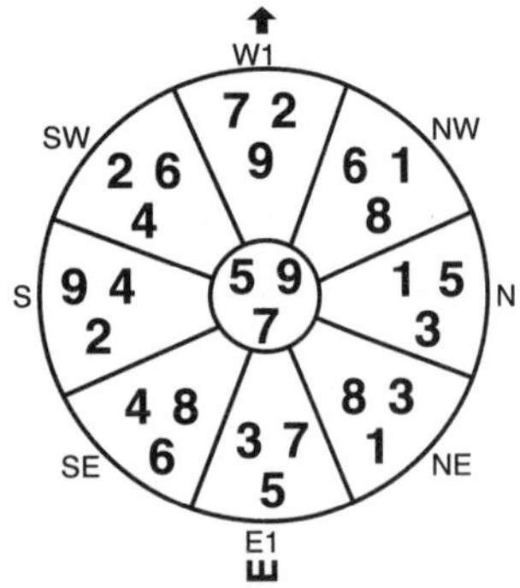

ZHEN house:
Sitting E1, Facing W1:
247.5° - 262.5°

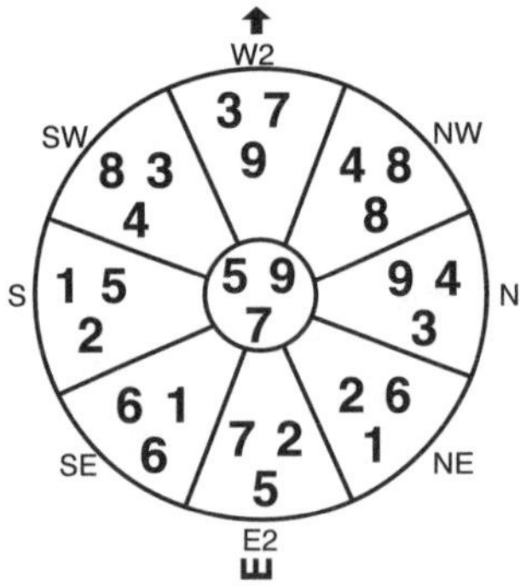

ZHEN house:
Sitting E2, Facing W2:
262.5° - 277.5°

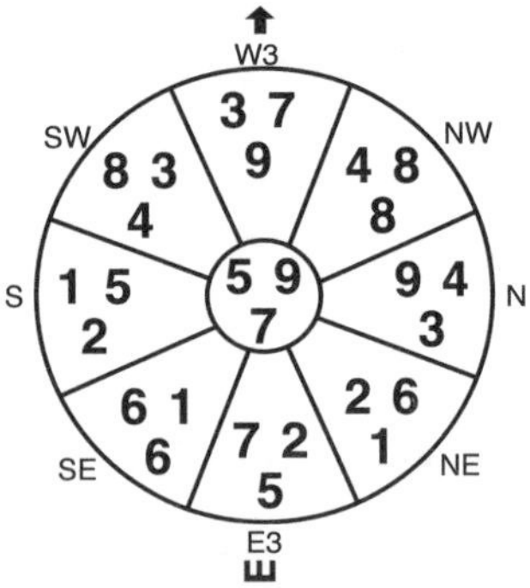

ZHEN house:
Sitting E3, Facing W3:
277.5° - 292.5°

Houses Built in Period 7 (Feb. 4, 1984 - Feb. 3, 2004)

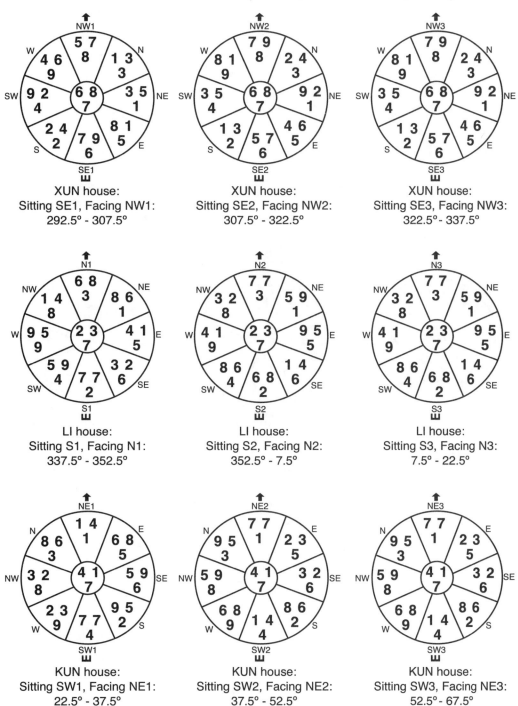

XUN house:
Sitting SE1, Facing NW1:
292.5° - 307.5°

XUN house:
Sitting SE2, Facing NW2:
307.5° - 322.5°

XUN house:
Sitting SE3, Facing NW3:
322.5° - 337.5°

LI house:
Sitting S1, Facing N1:
337.5° - 352.5°

LI house:
Sitting S2, Facing N2:
352.5° - 7.5°

LI house:
Sitting S3, Facing N3:
7.5° - 22.5°

KUN house:
Sitting SW1, Facing NE1:
22.5° - 37.5°

KUN house:
Sitting SW2, Facing NE2:
37.5° - 52.5°

KUN house:
Sitting SW3, Facing NE3:
52.5° - 67.5°

Houses Built in Period 7 (Feb. 4, 1984 - Feb. 3, 2004)

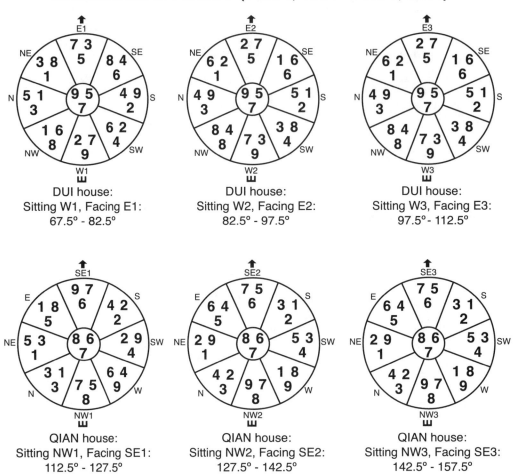

DUI house:
Sitting W1, Facing E1:
67.5° - 82.5°

DUI house:
Sitting W2, Facing E2:
82.5° - 97.5°

DUI house:
Sitting W3, Facing E3:
97.5° - 112.5°

QIAN house:
Sitting NW1, Facing SE1:
112.5° - 127.5°

QIAN house:
Sitting NW2, Facing SE2:
127.5° - 142.5°

QIAN house:
Sitting NW3, Facing SE3:
142.5° - 157.5°

Houses Built in Period 8 (Feb. 4, 2004 - Feb. 3, 2024)

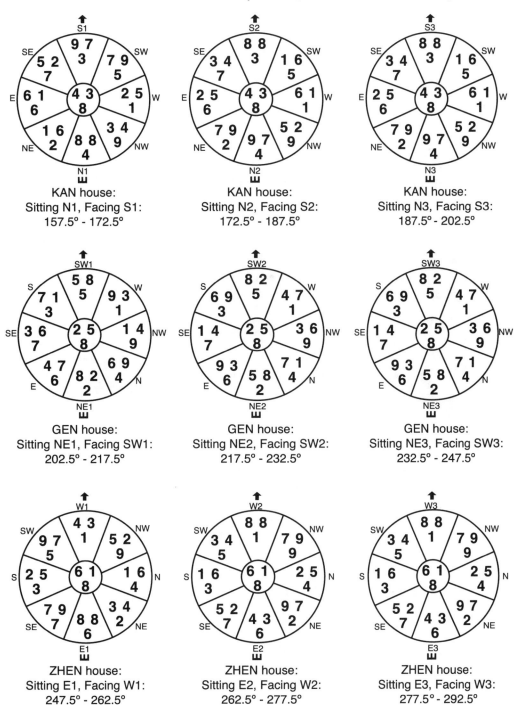

KAN house:
Sitting N1, Facing S1:
157.5° - 172.5°

KAN house:
Sitting N2, Facing S2:
172.5° - 187.5°

KAN house:
Sitting N3, Facing S3:
187.5° - 202.5°

GEN house:
Sitting NE1, Facing SW1:
202.5° - 217.5°

GEN house:
Sitting NE2, Facing SW2:
217.5° - 232.5°

GEN house:
Sitting NE3, Facing SW3:
232.5° - 247.5°

ZHEN house:
Sitting E1, Facing W1:
247.5° - 262.5°

ZHEN house:
Sitting E2, Facing W2:
262.5° - 277.5°

ZHEN house:
Sitting E3, Facing W3:
277.5° - 292.5°

Houses Built in Period 8 (Feb. 4, 2004 - Feb. 3, 2024)

XUN house:
Sitting SE1, Facing NW1:
292.5° - 307.5°

XUN house:
Sitting SE2, Facing NW2:
307.5° - 322.5°

XUN house:
Sitting SE3, Facing NW3:
322.5° - 337.5°

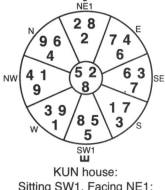

LI house:
Sitting S1, Facing N1:
337.5° - 352.5°

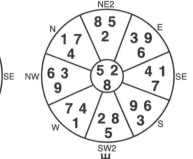

LI house:
Sitting S2, Facing N2:
352.5° - 7.5°

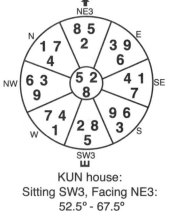

LI house:
Sitting S3, Facing N3:
7.5° - 22.5°

KUN house:
Sitting SW1, Facing NE1:
22.5° - 37.5°

KUN house:
Sitting SW2, Facing NE2:
37.5° - 52.5°

KUN house:
Sitting SW3, Facing NE3:
52.5° - 67.5°

Houses Built in Period 8 (Feb. 4, 2004 - Feb. 3, 2024)

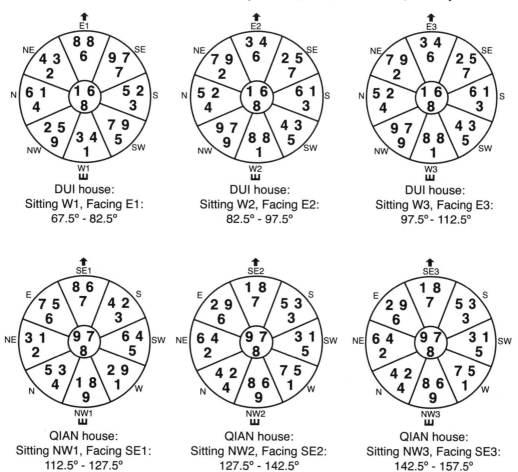

DUI house:
Sitting W1, Facing E1:
67.5° - 82.5°

DUI house:
Sitting W2, Facing E2:
82.5° - 97.5°

DUI house:
Sitting W3, Facing E3:
97.5° - 112.5°

QIAN house:
Sitting NW1, Facing SE1:
112.5° - 127.5°

QIAN house:
Sitting NW2, Facing SE2:
127.5° - 142.5°

QIAN house:
Sitting NW3, Facing SE3:
142.5° - 157.5°

Houses Built in Period 9 (Feb. 4, 2024 - Feb. 4, 2044)

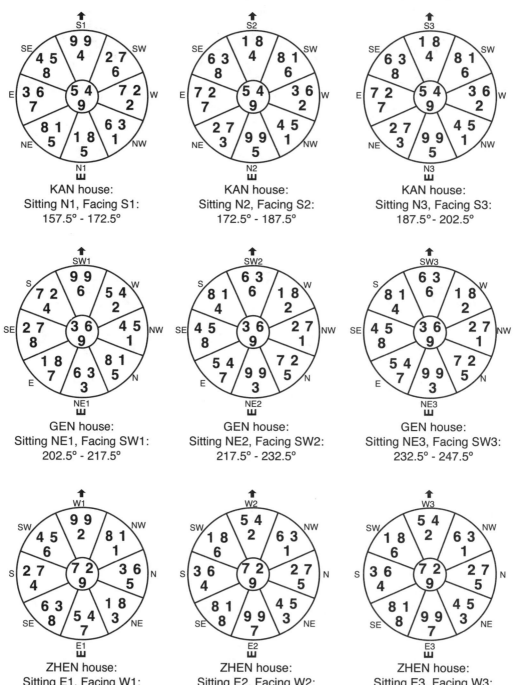

KAN house:
Sitting N1, Facing S1:
157.5° - 172.5°

KAN house:
Sitting N2, Facing S2:
172.5° - 187.5°

KAN house:
Sitting N3, Facing S3:
187.5° - 202.5°

GEN house:
Sitting NE1, Facing SW1:
202.5° - 217.5°

GEN house:
Sitting NE2, Facing SW2:
217.5° - 232.5°

GEN house:
Sitting NE3, Facing SW3:
232.5° - 247.5°

ZHEN house:
Sitting E1, Facing W1:
247.5° - 262.5°

ZHEN house:
Sitting E2, Facing W2:
262.5° - 277.5°

ZHEN house:
Sitting E3, Facing W3:
277.5° - 292.5°

Houses Built in Period 9 (Feb. 4, 2024 - Feb. 4, 2044)

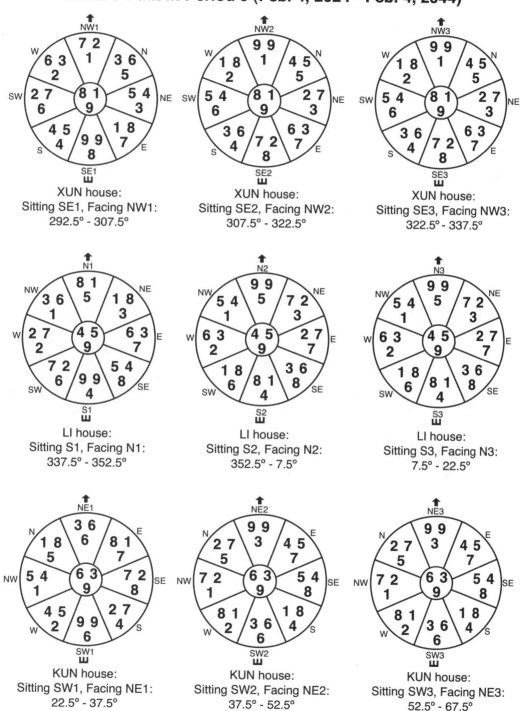

XUN house:
Sitting SE1, Facing NW1:
292.5° - 307.5°

XUN house:
Sitting SE2, Facing NW2:
307.5° - 322.5°

XUN house:
Sitting SE3, Facing NW3:
322.5° - 337.5°

LI house:
Sitting S1, Facing N1:
337.5° - 352.5°

LI house:
Sitting S2, Facing N2:
352.5° - 7.5°

LI house:
Sitting S3, Facing N3:
7.5° - 22.5°

KUN house:
Sitting SW1, Facing NE1:
22.5° - 37.5°

KUN house:
Sitting SW2, Facing NE2:
37.5° - 52.5°

KUN house:
Sitting SW3, Facing NE3:
52.5° - 67.5°

Houses Built in Period 9 (Feb. 4, 2024 - Feb. 4, 2044)

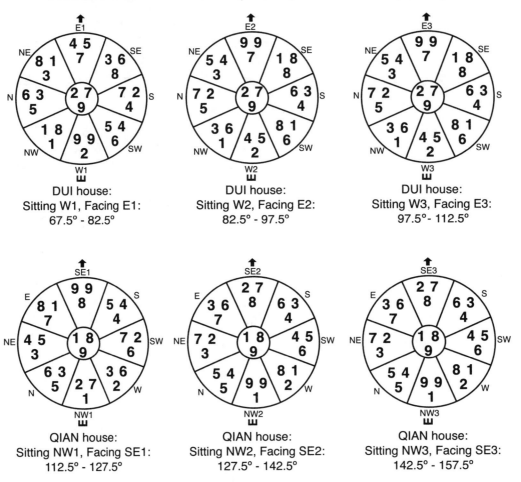

DUI house:
Sitting W1, Facing E1:
67.5° - 82.5°

DUI house:
Sitting W2, Facing E2:
82.5° - 97.5°

DUI house:
Sitting W3, Facing E3:
97.5°- 112.5°

QIAN house:
Sitting NW1, Facing SE1:
112.5° - 127.5°

QIAN house:
Sitting NW2, Facing SE2:
127.5° - 142.5°

QIAN house:
Sitting NW3, Facing SE3:
142.5° - 157.5°

The Least You Need to Know

- The set of three stars (numbers) in the central palace (the time star, sitting star, and facing star) dictate where the other stars are located.
- The stars always fly in a specific directional sequence: Center, NW, W, NE, S, N, SW, E, SE.
- The set of three stars in each of the eight cells surrounding the central cell represents the qi distribution coming from the eight cardinal directions.
- Orient your dwelling so that the sitting side corresponds to the bottom of the page.

House 3

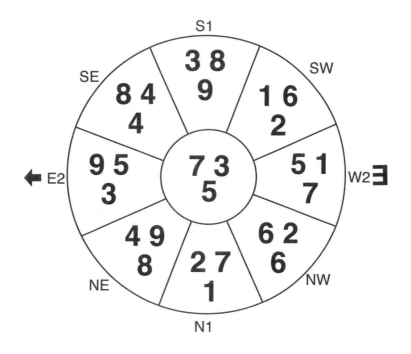

A house built in period 5 (1944-1964)
山 sitting W2, ↑ facing E2.

To double-check your work, consult the appropriate chart we've provided in this chapter.

Chapter **16**

The Flying Stars, Part 4

In This Chapter

◆ Identifying a Fortunate Mountain Fortunate Water house

◆ Identifying a Reversed Mountain and Water house

◆ Identifying a Double Facing star house

◆ Identifying a Double Sitting star house

Now that you've assembled a Flying Star chart appropriate to your home, it's time to begin interpreting the patterns of numbers that relate to your wealth, health, and relationships. In this chapter, you'll learn that your home may have special characteristics, a type of personality that can favorably or unfavorably affect the quality of your health and livelihood.

Yin and Yang, Mountain and Water

As you learned in Chapter 5, "The Principle of Yin and Yang," yin and yang are two dynamic and opposing forces of nature. The premise of feng shui is to study how these qi forces affect the quality of your health, livelihood, and relations with other people.

In Flying Star methodology, yin qi and everything it represents is expressed as the *mountain force*, the qi force that oversees a person's health and relationships. If you think about it, this idea makes perfect sense. Yin qi, associated with the female, is nurturing. Yin qi is quiet, restful, still, and stable—qualities encouraging rejuvenation, a peaceful spirit, and harmonious interaction with other people. Like a mother's yearning to protect her children, yin qi or mountain qi, shields its inhabitants from strong winds and harsh rains. Without this protective shield, you are prone to sickness and subject to arguments and disagreements.

While the landscape surrounding your house is certainly an important consideration in a feng shui evaluation, in your home the walls are the mountains that govern your health. The walls not only contain valuable qi, but they also allow yin qi coming from the eight fundamental directions to penetrate through them, infusing the occupants with its essence. We'll be talking more about this idea in the next chapter.

Wise Words

Associated with yin, the **mountain force** administers a person's health and relationships. Its qi enters a home through the walls, the building's mountainlike structures protecting the occupants. Associated with yang, the **water force** governs a person's wealth. Its qi enters a home through the windows and doors, the building's free-flowing waterlike edifices. In classical feng shui terminology, the **mountain star** is synonymous with the sitting star and the stars on the top, left side of each cell. The **water star** is synonymous with the facing star and the stars on the top, right side of each cell.

Conversely, yang qi governs a person's wealth. Associated with the male, yang qi is equated with the *water force*. It's on the move. Like the streams, rivers, and seas, water qi nourishes the soil, bringing life to vegetation. Water is also an effective mode of transport. Indeed, before the advent of airplanes, societies were economically dependent on the flowing substance to help foster the exchange of goods and services. Likewise, while watercourses and streetways (virtual watercourses) are important factors in an accurate feng shui assessment, in Flying Star methodology, water qi is that which flows into your dwelling through windows and doors. Again, this idea will be discussed in more detail in the next chapter.

For now, understand that the mountain force is embodied in the *mountain star*, which is identical to the sitting star (the number affiliated with the sitting direction of your home) and all of the other stars (numbers) occupying the top, left side of each cell. On the other hand, the water force is embodied in the *water star*, which is identical to the facing star (the number affiliated with the facing direction of your home) and all of the other stars occupying the top, right side of each cell. To be perfectly clear, the mountain stars govern your health and relationships; the water stars govern your finances.

Fortunate Mountain Fortunate Water

As of this writing, we are in Period 7 with the number 7 ruling from February 4, 1984, to February 3, 2004. You learned in Chapter 14, "The Flying Stars, Part 2," that the ruling star reigns supreme. It is the king star, the president, and prime minister. It rules over all other stars for a 20-year period. The ruling star is timely, bestowing its auspicious characteristics onto its subjects, the occupants.

When a ruling mountain star is located in the top, left position of the sitting cell and a ruling water star is located in the top, right position of the facing cell (the mountain and water positions respectively), it is most fortunate. This type of house is called *Fortunate Mountain Fortunate Water* or Wang Shan Wang Shui, in Chinese. Basically, it means the occupants have the highest probability of attaining good fortune, good health, and beneficial relationships. They have a leg up, if you will. To illustrate this idea, look at the following figures. House 1 represents a Zhen dwelling constructed in Period 7, sitting E2 and facing W2. House 2 represents a Gen dwelling constructed in Period 8, sitting NE1 and facing SW1. Both houses are Fortunate Mountain Fortunate Water. (We have oriented the charts so that the sitting side corresponds to the bottom of the page.)

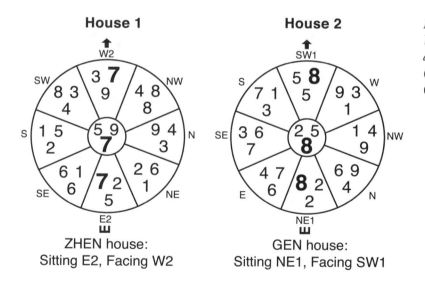

House 1

ZHEN house:
Sitting E2, Facing W2

House 2

GEN house:
Sitting NE1, Facing SW1

Examples of Fortunate Water Fortunate Mountain dwellings for Period 7 (House 1) and Period 8 (House 2).

However, regardless of the auspicious positions of the mountain and water stars in the sitting and facing cells, the stars must be supported environmentally. A mountain or a man-made "mountain" such as a building, tall hedge, or forest must support the ruling mountain star in the sitting or back side of the dwelling. A watercourse (ocean, river, swimming pool, fountain, for example), or a virtual waterway like a road, must support the water star in the facing or front side of the dwelling. How close should these supporting structures be to the house so that it still qualifies as Fortunate Mountain Fortunate Water? The general rule of thumb is that the supporting structure must be in eyesight distance. You must "feel" its essence. For most urban dwellers these factors are easily satisfied. But, what if the converse is true? What if a body of water is located on the sitting or back side and a mountain is located on the facing side or front side of the dwelling? In this case, the house is not considered Fortunate Mountain Fortunate Water. It loses its special quality, its leg up.

Wise Words _____

In Chinese, a **Fortunate Mountain Fortunate Water** dwelling is considered Wang Shan Wang Shui if the ruling mountain and water numbers are in their proper places. The ruling mountain star must be situated in the top, left position of the sitting cell. The ruling water star must be situated in the top, right position of the facing cell. This type of house is most favorable, bringing the highest possibility of fame, fortune, and good health.

When Period 8 arrives on February 4, 2004, and the ruling star 7 leaves office, star charts with the Fortunate Mountain Fortunate Water configuration are rendered invalid. The house no longer possesses that extra edge, that something special because the ruling mountain star 8 is not at the sitting and the ruling water star 8 is not at the facing.

Master Class _____

Fortunate Mountain Fortunate Water houses built in Period 7 (February 4, 1984–February 3, 2004) include the Zhen houses sitting E2 and E3; the Xun house sitting SE1; the Dui houses sitting W2 and W3; and the Qian house sitting NW1. Fortunate Mountain Fortunate Water houses built in Period 8 (February 4, 2004–February 3, 2024) include the Gen house sitting NE1; the Xun houses sitting SE2 and SE3; the Kun house sitting SW1; and the Qian houses sitting NW2 and NW3.

Reversed Mountain and Water

When the ruling mountain and ruling water star in question (the number 7 for Period 7 or the number 8 for Period 8, for example) are improperly placed, then the star chart is called *Reversed Mountain and Water*. It is most unfortunate. Stated another way, if the ruling water star (governing wealth) is located on the mountain (top, left) side of the sitting cell and the ruling mountain star (governing health and relationships) is located on the water (top, right) side of the facing cell, the house is potentially less fortunate in wealth and health for the 20-year period.

Wise Words _____

In Chinese, a **Reversed Mountain and Water** dwelling is considered Shang Shan Xia Shui if the mountain and water stars are improperly placed, reversed. Here, the ruling mountain star is improperly located in the facing cell. The ruling water star is improperly located in the sitting cell. A Reversed Mountain and Water star chart brings the probability of misfortune and illness for the 20-year period to which the ruling star corresponds.

Simply, the stars are misaligned. Mountain's yin force is preventing your finances from growing and water's yang force is causing a whirlwind of heightened activity resulting in anxiety, sleeplessness, and illness. Like living in close proximity to a freeway, the overabundance of yang qi embodied by the heavy traffic can wear you out.

Here are examples of Reversed Mountain and Water houses. House 1 was built in Period 7. It sits W1 and faces E1. House 2 was built in Period 8 and sits SE1 and faces NW1.

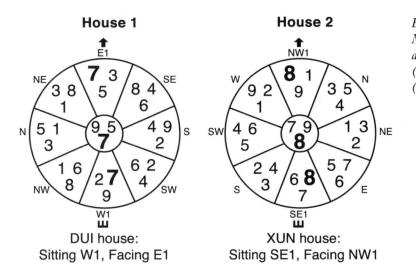

House 1

DUI house:
Sitting W1, Facing E1

House 2

XUN house:
Sitting SE1, Facing NW1

Examples of Reversed Mountain and Water dwellings for Period 7 (House 1) and Period 8 (House 2).

Can anything be done to remedy the dire prospects? Yes! In this case, a mountain or mountainlike structure (tall hedge, forest, building) must support the misaligned mountain star on the facing or front side of the dwelling. Likewise, a body of water or a roadway must support the misaligned water star on the sitting or back side of the dwelling.

When Period 8 arrives on February 4, 2004, and the ruling star 7 leaves office, star-crossed charts are relieved from their hazardous duties. The havoc they wreak is thwarted.

Master Class _____

Reversed Mountain and Water houses built in Period 7 (February 4, 1984–February 3, 2004) include the Zhen house sitting E1; the Xun houses sitting SE2 and SE3; the Dui house sitting W1; and the Qian houses sitting NW2 and NW3. Reversed Mountain and Water houses built in Period 8 (February 4, 2004–February 3, 2024) include the Gen houses sitting NE2 and NE3; the Xun house sitting SE1; the Kun houses sitting SW2 and SW3; and the Qian house sitting NW1.

The Double Facing Star Chart

When both the ruling mountain and the ruling water stars are located in the facing cell, the chart is called *Double Ruling Star at Facing* or Shuang Ling Xing Dou Xiang, in Chinese. In this case, the ruling water star (governing wealth) situated in the top, right side of the facing cell is in its proper place. Because of this, the house inspires financial gain. However, the ruling mountain star (governing health and relationships) is improperly placed. Here, it is located in the yang or facing side of the dwelling. Because of the misalignment, the house brings the likelihood of poor health and difficult relationships.

Here are examples of Double Facing star charts. House 1 was built in Period 7, sitting SW2 and facing NE2. House 2 was built in Period 8, sitting W1 and facing E1.

Examples of Double Ruling Star at Facing dwellings for Period 7 (House 1) and Period 8 (House 2).

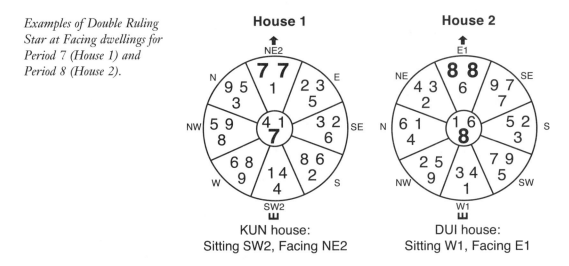

House 1

KUN house:
Sitting SW2, Facing NE2

House 2

DUI house:
Sitting W1, Facing E1

To remedy a Double Facing situation, a body of water or virtual water like a roadway must support the facing or front side of the dwelling. The facing side must also contain a mountain or a man-made "mountain" structure such as a tall hedge or building to support the misaligned mountain star. That which exists at the sitting or backside of the dwelling is not considered.

When Period 8 arrives on February 4, 2004, and the ruling star 7 leaves office, the charts of houses conforming to a Double Facing configuration are rendered invalid.

Wise Words

In Chinese, a **Double Ruling Star at Facing** is considered Shuang Ling Xing Dou Xiang if both the ruling mountain and ruling water stars are located in the facing cell. In this case, it is easy for the occupants to make and retain money, but it is difficult for them to form stable relationships and maintain good health.

The Double Sitting Star Chart

When both the ruling mountain and the ruling water stars are located in the sitting cell, the star chart is called *Double Ruling Star at Sitting* or Shuang Ling Xing Dou Zuo, in Chinese. In this case, the ruling mountain star (governing health and relationships) situated in the top, left side of the sitting cell is in its proper place. Because of this auspicious orientation, the house inspires robust health and productive relations with other people. However, the ruling water star (governing wealth) is improperly placed. Here, it is located in the yin or sitting side of the dwelling. Because of the misalignment, the house brings the probability of money loss.

Here are examples of Double Sitting star charts. House 1 was built in Period 7, sitting N2 and facing S2. House 2 was built in Period 8, sitting E1 and facing W1.

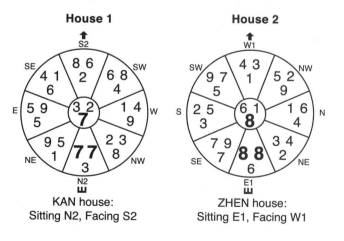

House 1
KAN house:
Sitting N2, Facing S2

House 2
ZHEN house:
Sitting E1, Facing W1

Examples of Double Ruling Star at Sitting dwellings for Period 7 (House 1) and Period 8 (House 2).

To remedy a Double Sitting situation, a mountain or a man-made "mountain" such as a tall hedge or building must support the sitting or back side of the dwelling. The sitting side must also contain a body of water or a roadway to support the misaligned water star. That which exists at the facing or front side of the dwelling is irrelevant.

When Period 8 arrives on February 4, 2004, and the ruling star 7 leaves office, charts of houses conforming to a Double Sitting configuration are rendered invalid.

Feng Alert _____

It's important to understand that the four types of houses described in this chapter are only valid if the period the house was constructed in matches the ruling period. For example, take a house constructed in Period 4 (1924–1944). Even if the number configurations conform to a Fortunate Mountain and Water, Reversed Mountain and Water, Double Facing, or Double Sitting situation, the house wouldn't qualify as one of the four special cases until Period 4 arrives again in the year 2104.

In the next chapter, you'll learn how to interpret and remedy the number combinations made manifest in the central palace and the remaining eight cells.

The Least You Need to Know

- The numbers located on the top, left side of each cell are called the mountain stars. They govern a person's health and relationships. The numbers located on the top, right side of each cell are called the water stars. They govern a person's wealth.

- There are four types of star charts that hold special characteristics valid only if the period the house was constructed in matches the ruling period in question.

- The auspicious characteristics manifest only when the appropriate forms (mountain, building, water, road) support the stars.

- The inauspicious characteristics manifest only when the appropriate forms (mountain, building, water, road) do not exist to thwart the ill affects.

Chapter

The Flying Stars, Part 5

In This Chapter

- More about the mountain, water, and time stars
- A Flying Star chart analysis
- Star combinations and their meanings

Congratulations for assembling a Flying Star chart appropriate to your home. Give yourself a round of applause, a pat on the back for a job well done. In this chapter, you'll learn how to interpret your star chart. Don't be intimidated by the 27 stars (9 cells × 3 stars each) composing a chart. Understanding their meanings, enhancing their positive aspects, and discouraging the negative ones, will lead to a productive environment fostering better wealth, good health, and beneficial relationships.

The Mountain, Water, and Time Stars

Before you proceed with understanding and remedying the number combinations, let's take a moment to fully comprehend the three stars comprising each cell—the mountain, water, and time stars:

- **The Water Star.** Governing wealth, the water star is located on the top, right side of each cell. If your home conforms to one of the four special cases discussed in the previous chapter, follow the advice to activate the ruling star for the chart in question. If your home does not belong to one of the four special cases, locate the ruling water number in your chart (the number 7 for Period 7 or the number 8 for Period 8). Support the star environmentally, allowing the yang qi essence of the nearby water/roadway to flow into the house through an open window or door. Use the space containing the ruling money star for a home office—any area where you conduct money-related business.

Regarding the remaining nonruling money stars, *timely* stars (the numbers 9, 8, and 7 for Period 7; the numbers 1, 9, and 8 for Period 8) located only in *active* areas can bolster financial gain. Because of their negative characteristics, untimely (retired/ dead) stars (the numbers 6, 5, 4, 3, 2, and 1 for Period 7; the numbers 7, 6, 5, 4, 3, and 2 for Period 8) cannot foster wealth. Diminish an untimely water star's negative aspects by keeping the windows and doors closed in the area in question, at least during the night. Also, as you'll soon learn, employ a five-phase remedy to ward off an unfavorable projection.

Master Class _____

In an active (yang) area within a home (family room, home office, kitchen), focus on the water star and how it reacts with the mountain star. If the time star is productive to or belongs to the same phase as the water star, the possibility of financial gain is even greater. In an inactive (yin) area (bedroom, guest bedroom, living room), focus on the mountain star and how it reacts with the water star. If the time star is productive to or belongs to the same phase as the mountain star, the probability of good health increases. Why not remedy the entire dwelling for wealth? Because poor health leads to a poor financial outlook! Remember, feng shui is about balancing the yin and yang qi forces.

◆ **The Mountain Star.** Governing health and relationships, the mountain star is located on the top, left side of each cell. If your home conforms to one of the four special cases discussed in the previous chapter, follow the advice to activate the mountain star for the chart in question. If your home does not belong to one of the four special cases, locate the ruling mountain number in your chart (the number 7 for Period 7 or the number 8 for Period 8). Support the star, allowing the yin qi essence of the nearby mountain/building to enter the house by infusing and charging the walls. Windows should be kept closed, particularly if the water (yang) star is not favorable. If the water star is favorable, make sure the wind does not disperse yin's (health and relationship) qi. Use the space containing the ruling health and relationship star for your bedroom and other areas promoting rest and relaxation.

Regarding the remaining nonruling mountain stars, *timely* stars (the numbers 9, 8, and 7 for Period 7; the numbers 1, 9, and 8 for Period 8) located only in *inactive* areas can foster good health and beneficial relationships. Because of their negative characteristics, untimely (retired/dead) stars (the numbers 6, 5, 4, 3, 2, and 1 for Period 7; the numbers 7, 6, 5, 4, 3, and 2 for Period 8) cannot bolster your health and relations. In this case, diminish an untimely mountain star's inauspicious aspects by employing a five-phase remedy.

◆ **The Time Star.** The time star provides a base for the mountain and water stars. Using an analogy, the water star is like steak, the protein fortifying your strength and determination to succeed. The mountain star is like a vegetable, the vitamins nourishing your health. The time star is the plate on which your dinner is served. You do not eat the plate, do you? Yet, the plate must be clean and beautiful otherwise you cannot enjoy the meal. While the time star itself does not foster fortune or misfortune, it either supports or does not support the water and mountain star. It depends on the phase (fire, earth, metal, water, and wood) relationship between the time star and the mountain star, and the time star and the water star. If the relationship is productive, the water or mountain star in question is enhanced. If the time star controls or reduces the water or mountain star's power, the star in question loses its zeal.

Before you proceed, it's a good idea to have the Flying Star chart corresponding to your home in front of you.

Master Class _____

Flying Star is about balancing the mountain (yin) and water (yang) forces. External to a house, there are mountains, buildings, rivers, lakes, and streets. Inside a house, there are also mountains and waterways. Walls and large furniture are interior mountains. Doors, windows, and hallways are interior watercourses. When activating a yang area for wealth, keep windows open and make sure the hallways are unobstructed. When activating a yin area for health and relationships, make sure the qi is not dispersed by wind. High-back chairs and a bed with its headboard against a solid wall are ways to make good use of a timely mountain star.

The Central Palace

Now that you understand more thoroughly what the water and mountain stars represent and how you can use them to your advantage, let's take a look at the central palace. A feng shui assessment begins here. Heaven's qi (associated with the time the dwelling was "born" into) and earth's qi (associated with the magnetic orientation of the building) merge to produce a house with a specific type of personality made manifest by the numbers in the central palace. When the sitting (mountain) and facing (water) stars are compatible, chances are the innate essence fosters harmony. However, when the sitting and facing stars conflict, chances are the innate essence fosters discord. Because the central palace does not represent an area, the stars here cannot be balanced with one of the five phases of qi. Great care must be taken, then, to balance the stars comprising the surrounding eight cells.

Feng Alert _____

Don't forget to consider the exterior and interior environment. What can be done to allow qi to flow productively, easily, and uninhibited? Consult Chapter 8, "Turtles, Tigers, and Dragons, Oh My: Evaluating Your Environment," and Chapter 9, "Home Sweet Home: Evaluating Your House and Its Surroundings," about assessing the surrounding terrain, the lot on which your house sits, the alignment of roads and watercourses, and the orientation of furniture.

It's All in the Stars: The Star Combination Chart

The following number combinations reflect the possibility that the favorable or unfavorable event in question may occur if proper remedies/enhancements are not installed. As you become more familiar with each number combination, you'll notice that some combinations contain both good and bad aspects. You may be wondering, then, how to promote the good and dissuade the bad? While space doesn't permit us to get into a detailed analysis of the number combinations, remember that timely stars bring out the good characteristics and untimely stars bring out the bad ones. A general rule of thumb is to enhance timely stars and weaken untimely stars. You may want to review Chapter 14, "The Flying Stars, Part 2," about the characteristics of untimely and timely stars. The following effects are valid for the Lower Cycle (1984–2044).

The Effects of Combinations of Stars (Numbers)

Mountain Star	Phase	Water Star	Phase	Effect
1	Water	1	Water	Academic, artistic, and monetary achievement. Ear-, blood-, and kidney-related diseases caused by alcohol.
1	Water	2	Earth	Spousal conflict, separation, or divorce. Miscarriage and abdominal pain. Traffic accident likely.

Mountain Star	Phase	Water Star	Phase	Effect
1	Water	3	Wood	Theft and legal entanglements. Exhaustion due to competition.
1	Water	4	Wood	Gaining fame through writing or artistic work. Romance.
1	Water	5	Earth	Illness of the ears, kidney, and genital organs.
1	Water	6	Metal	Promotion and career success. Probability of nervous breakdown.
1	Water	7	Metal	Financial gain. Injury by knife. Flirtation.
1	Water	8	Earth	Health and wealth. Dispute among siblings and colleagues.
1	Water	9	Fire	Career advancement and financial gain. Eye disease.
2	Earth	1	Water	Spousal conflict, separation, or divorce. Miscarriage and abdominal pain. Traffic accidents.
2	Earth	2	Earth	Sickness and injury due to an accident.
2	Earth	3	Wood	Conflict, gossip, litigation, and accidents.
2	Earth	4	Wood	Romance. Woman harassing her mother. Abdominal disease.
2	Earth	5	Earth	Bankruptcy, serious illness, and possible death.
2	Earth	6	Metal	Wealth and power. Abdominal disease.
2	Earth	7	Metal	Financial gain. Abdominal and mouth-related illness.
2	Earth	8	Earth	Great wealth. Frequent minor illness.

continues

The Effects of Combinations of Stars (Numbers) (continued)

Mountain Star	Phase	Water Star	Phase	Effect
2	Earth	9	Fire	Stupidity and mental disorder. Bad for a bedroom.
3	Wood	1	Water	Theft and legal entanglements. Injury due to an accident.
3	Wood	2	Earth	Conflict, gossip, lawsuits, and accidents.
3	Wood	3	Wood	Arguments, disagreements, and assault. Robbery.
3	Wood	4	Wood	Creativity and romance. Unruly behavior.
3	Wood	5	Earth	Financial delinquency. Liver disease and leg injury.
3	Wood	6	Metal	Gaining recognition. Leg injury for a man.
3	Wood	7	Metal	Financial success. Injury by a metal object. Lawsuit.
3	Wood	8	Earth	Monetary gain. Limb injury, especially for children.
3	Wood	9	Fire	Birth of intelligent son. Man easily loses temper. Financial gain through career promotion.
4	Wood	1	Water	Gaining fame through writing or artistic work. Romance.
4	Wood	2	Earth	Woman harassing her mother. Abdominal disease.
4	Wood	3	Wood	Robbery and litigation. Disruptive behavior.
4	Wood	4	Wood	Great artistic achievement. Inappropriate romance.
4	Wood	5	Earth	Loss of wealth. Breast tumor. Plagiarism.
4	Wood	6	Metal	Gaining recognition. Physical injuries for a woman.

Mountain Star	Phase	Water Star	Phase	Effect
4	Wood	7	Metal	Financial gain. Flirtation. Injury to a woman.
4	Wood	8	Earth	Financial success. Injury to children.
4	Wood	9	Fire	Birth of an intelligent child. Failure in examination.
5	Earth	1	Water	Illness of the ears, kidney and genital organs.
5	Earth	2	Earth	Bankruptcy, serious illness, and possible death.
5	Earth	3	Wood	Financial delinquency. Liver disease and leg injury.
5	Earth	4	Wood	Breast tumor. Entangled in plagiarism. Failed relationship.
5	Earth	5	Earth	Disastrous in wealth and health.
5	Earth	6	Metal	Gaining power, but at the expense of headaches.
5	Earth	7	Metal	Gaining wealth. Food poisoning and mouth-related disease.
5	Earth	8	Earth	Financial gain. Broken bones and injured tendon.
5	Earth	9	Fire	Confusion of the mind. Financial and health hazard due to impulsive behavior.
6	Metal	1	Water	Promotion and career success. Possibility of nervous breakdown.
6	Metal	2	Earth	Financial loss due to sickness.
6	Metal	3	Wood	Robbery resulting in injury. Accident causing leg injury.
6	Metal	4	Wood	Troubled relationship. Woman hurt by a metal object.

continues

The Effects of Combinations of Stars (Numbers) (continued)

Mountain Star	Phase	Water Star	Phase	Effect
6	Metal	5	Earth	Financial loss due to loss of power.
6	Metal	6	Metal	Gaining power. Lawsuit and arguments.
6	Metal	7	Metal	Conflicts, disagreements, and fighting. Injury by a metal object.
6	Metal	8	Earth	Financial success. Promotion. Obstinacy.
6	Metal	9	Fire	Financial gain. Lung and head disease. Authority challenged.
7	Metal	1	Water	Flirtation. Bleeding. Success by traveling overseas.
7	Metal	2	Earth	Financial loss. Physical fitness.
7	Metal	3	Wood	Robbery. Litigation over money.
7	Metal	4	Wood	Flirtation. Injury to a woman.
7	Metal	5	Earth	Financial disaster. Food poisoning.
7	Metal	6	Metal	Conflicts and fighting. Injury by a metal object.
7	Metal	7	Metal	Wealth through competition. Good health.
7	Metal	8	Earth	Great wealth and blossoming romance.
7	Metal	9	Fire	Gaining recognition and wealth. Fire hazard.
8	Earth	1	Water	Health and wealth. Disputes among siblings and colleagues.
8	Earth	2	Earth	Healthy but not quite wealthy. Good for bedroom.
8	Earth	3	Wood	Robbery and arguments. Injury to children.

Mountain Star	Phase	Water Star	Phase	Effect
8	Earth	4	Wood	Inappropriate romance. Injury to children.
8	Earth	5	Earth	Financial loss. Good health.
8	Earth	6	Metal	Gaining authority. Good for a bedroom.
8	Earth	7	Metal	Great monetary gain. Successful romance.
8	Earth	8	Earth	Good for wealth and health. Loneliness.
8	Earth	9	Fire	Happy events, wedding and birth of a child.
9	Fire	1	Water	Career advancement and financial gain. Eye disease.
9	Fire	2	Earth	Stupidity and mental disorder. Financial loss due to illness.
9	Fire	3	Wood	Birth of an intelligent child. Bad temper.
9	Fire	4	Wood	Birth of an intelligent child. Failure in examination.
9	Fire	5	Earth	Confusion of the mind. Financial and health hazard due to impulsive behavior.
9	Fire	6	Metal	Lung and head disease. Authority challenged.
9	Fire	7	Metal	Financial gain. Fire hazard. Arguments and fighting.
9	Fire	8	Earth	Happy events, wedding, and birth of a child.
9	Fire	9	Fire	Celebrations for success in career and romance.

In order to begin analyzing and remedying/enhancing the number combinations, make sure you fully understand the relationships between the five phases. If the productive, controlling, and weakening cycles aren't firmly embedded into your mind, review Chapter 6, "The Principle of the Five Phases." Also, the front of the tear-out card will come in handy. It includes an illustration of the three natural cycles along with the Luoshu number each phase is correlated with.

A Simple Analysis

Considering only the stars, let's examine a Flying Star chart for a Dui house built in Period 7, sitting W2 and facing E2. We'll begin with the central palace, then move up to the facing cell, and travel clockwise around the chart. Note: M stands for mountain star; W for water star; and T for time star.

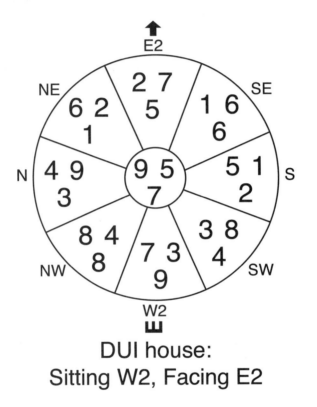

DUI house:
Sitting W2, Facing E2

Center: 9M (fire) 5W (earth) 7T (metal)

Fire produces earth. Although a productive relationship, it is not a healthy one. Here, the number 9 is not only encouraging the highly inauspicious number 5's proclivity for misfortune, but it is also melting the ruling star 7's benevolence. (Remember, the number 9 enhances any number it's paired with.) While the numbers comprising the central palace cannot cause fortune or misfortune, they represent the innate nature of the dwelling. In this case, it is inharmonious, causing the possibility of financial and health hazards.

East: 2M (earth) 7W (metal) 5T (earth)

Earth produces metal. Because this is the facing and yang side of the dwelling, it is appropriate to focus on the money star 7. It is advantageous to have the main entrance here. Make sure there is a body of water (a fountain, river, roadway) outside to support number 7. Inside, metal will bolster 7's prospects for financial gain and lessen the negative affects brought on by the innate evil numbers 2 and 5. Be mindful of abdominal and mouth-related disorders.

Southeast: 1M (water) 6W (metal) 6T (metal)

Metal produces water. This is a productive combination heralding prospects for promotion and career success. Thus, no remedy is needed. However, the stress associated with more responsibility may cause an abundance of nervousness. This is because the number 1's water is draining the 6's energy, a number associated with the head.

South: 5M (earth) 1W (water) 2T (earth)

Earth blocks water. This is a controlling relationship, with the combination bringing the possibility of ear-, kidney-, and genital-related disorders. Moving metal (a chiming clock with a metal pendulum or playing the piano) is needed here to thwart the occurrence of an ailment. Metal will reduce the affects of the untimely and inherently inauspicious numbers 2 and 5. Metal will bridge earth and water, reverting the cycle to a productive one. Since the water (wealth) star is also untimely, this area should be avoided.

Southwest: 3M (wood) 8W (earth) 4T (wood)

Wood burdens earth. The highly favorable number 8 is located on the water or wealth side, making this area terrific for a home office. To increase the chance for financial success, install a fire remedy here to connect the wood and earth phases. Doing so will discourage wood from depleting 8's auspicious nature. The possibility of limb injuries for a child makes this area unsuitable for a playroom or child's bedroom.

West: 7M (metal) 3W (wood) 9T (fire)

Metal pierces wood. Because this is the sitting and yin side of the dwelling, it is appropriate to focus on the mountain star 7. This area is suitable for a bedroom. Outside, make sure a mountain or a building supports the sitting star. Inside, the number 9 is melting metal's favorable nature. To remedy the possibility of robbery and legal entanglements, earth is needed to restore the cycle to a productive one: wood produces fire, fire produces earth, earth produces metal.

> **Feng Facts**
>
> Don't forget to consider how each number affects parts of the body. As a reminder, here are the number/body correlations: 1) ears, blood, kidneys; 2) abdomen, stomach; 3) feet, lower leg; 4) thighs, buttocks, lower back; 5) N/A; 6) head, lungs; 7) mouth, teeth, tongue, chest; 8) hands, fingers; 9) eyes, heart. A disorder arises only if the number in question is untimely or if it is being attacked by another phase.

Northwest: 8M (earth) 4W (wood) 8T (earth)

Wood burdens earth. The advantageous number 8 is situated on the mountain (health and relationships) side, making the area favorable for a bedroom. To thwart possible spousal affairs (brought on by the untimely number 4), install the fire phase to revert the cycle to a productive one. The combination is unfavorable for young children.

North: 4M (wood) 9W (fire) 3T (wood)

Wood produces fire. The auspicious combination 4-9 is known as "fire makes wood glowing and glamorous." In other words, fire brightens 4's romantic nature, making the area good for a bedroom (particularly for a couple seeking a pregnancy). Because 9 is a timely money star, the area also makes a favorable home office. No remedy is needed.

Northeast: 6M (metal) 2W (earth) 1T (water)

Earth produces metal. Although this is a productive relationship, metal is needed to suppress the unfavorable and untimely number 2's promotion of illness and money loss. Metal will also strengthen 6's inherently auspicious quality of bringing authority and fame, which is being corroded by the time (water) star.

Conclusion: Although the dwelling's innate personality is inharmonious, there are several favorable star combinations that, if properly remedied, can offset the inauspicious combination in the central palace. The areas that should be actively used and which inspire financial gain are the east, southeast, southwest, and north. The areas promoting good health and good relations are located in the west, north, northwest, and northeast. In this case, the south is an inauspicious area.

Take this time now to evaluate and remedy the eight cells comprising your living and/or working space. However, things may change when we add the annual star. This is the subject of the next chapter.

The Least You Need to Know

♦ Begin a feng shui assessment by studying the numbers comprising the central palace. They represent the dwelling's inherent essence.

♦ Locate the areas containing the ruling and timely water (wealth) stars. If needed, remedy or enhance the area in question with one of the five phases to increase the possibility of financial success.

♦ Locate the areas containing the ruling and timely mountain (health and relationship) stars. If needed, remedy or enhance the area in question with one of the five phases to ensure good health and beneficial relations with other people.

♦ A Flying Star chart must be supported by the proper forms (mountains, buildings, water, and the like) outside.

Qin dynasty's Meng Tian, the builder of the Great Wall, confessed: "I could not make the Great Wall without cutting through the [qi] veins of the earth." Supposedly, this explains the short reign of the Qin dynasty (221–206 B.C.E.) and the early demise of Shihuangdi, the First Emperor of Qin.

(Image copyright ©1998 PhotoDisc, Inc.)

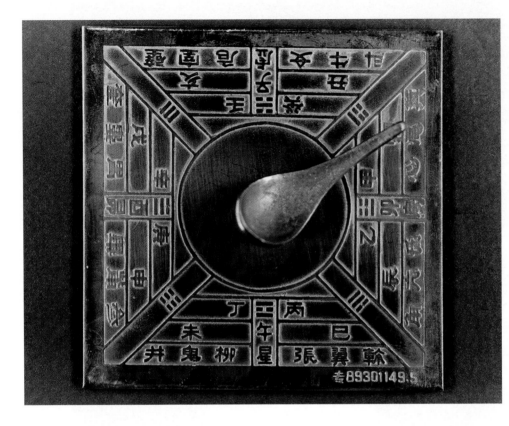

Precursor to the modern luopan compass, this early version, dating to about 83 C.E., was a two-part, south-pointing instrument—a metal spoon made of magnetic lodestone and a square base-plate.

(Photo by Val Biktashev)

These ancient coins reflect the Chinese idea of the cosmos. The central square represents the earth; the circular disc, heaven.

(Image copyright ©1998 PhotoDisc, Inc.)

Behind Russia and Canada, China is the third largest country in the world. Featuring impressive landscapes, it was the task of the feng shui master to find the "dragon's lair," the most auspicious site on which to build a dwelling or bury the dead.

(Image copyright ©1998 PhotoDisc, Inc.)

Situated between Aberdeen Harbor and Victoria Peak, Hong Kong residents believe their well-being is protected because the harbor resembles a sack of money. Also, Victoria Peak offers the inhabitants both psychological and physical security and protection.

(Image copyright ©1998 PhotoDisc, Inc.)

Guarding the Forbidden City (so-called because it was off-limits for 500 years) is the symbol of the emperor, the dragon. Also, a symbol of wealth and power, dragon artifacts are prolific throughout China and ethnic Chinese communities worldwide.

(Image copyright ©1998 PhotoDisc, Inc.)

Like an arrow pointed at you, the angle sha of the Sony Music building in Santa Monica, California, could cause misfortune to those in its path.

(Photo by Lorraine Wilcox)

A model of the Concorde pointed toward the Condé Nast building in New York City's Times Square may have caused scaffolding to collapse, killing an elderly woman.

(Photo by Arkadiy Yagudaev)

Located on the shores of Lake Michigan west of Chicago is the impressive Bahá'í House of Worship. Recognized as a national landmark, the building's circular architecture, nine entrances, and manicured gardens inspire prayer and meditation.

(Photo courtesy of Bahá'í Publishing Trust)

Located on Hollywood Boulevard, California, this complex has been void of business since it opened several years ago. Two trees, two planters, and a light pole block qi's path into the complex. Also, notice the angle sha created by the monstrous metal structure.

(Photo by Val Biktashev)

One block away from the Hollywood Galaxy you'll find the prosperous Mann's Chinese Theatre. Here, movie sales may improve if the box office in front and the connective awning were removed, allowing qi to flow freely within the circular court.

(Photo by Val Biktashev)

Taken some two years later (2001) at Mann's Chinese Theatre (in early morning before the tourists arrive), notice the area has been cleaned up. The frontal box office has been relocated, the trees removed.

(Photo by Val Biktashev)

Italy's Leaning Tower of Pisa may cause those under its shadow to feel insecure and unstable, as if the famous building might topple on them at any moment.

(Image copyright ©1998 PhotoDisc, Inc.)

Chapter

18

The Flying Stars, Part 6

In This Chapter

◆ Flying the annual star

◆ The annual star chart

◆ Learning how the annual star affects the mountain, water, and time stars

This is the final chapter about the Flying Star system. Here, you'll receive the last piece of the puzzle—the annual star. Once you've incorporated the annual star into your chart, you can fully evaluate your chart to create a productive atmosphere fostering better well-being.

The Annual Star

Each year, the nine heavenly stars visit earth. One of the stars is the leader and is stationed in the central palace along with the mountain, water, and time stars governing the chart. Who's the leader of the annual stars? The nine stars take turns being leader, with the term of office being one solar year beginning variously on the third, fourth, or fifth day of February. Because there are nine stars, it takes nine years to complete a cycle. The cycle we're currently in began in the year 2000, with the number 9 as leader. In 2001, the leader is the number 8. In 2002, the leader is the number 7. The other numbers follow suit in a descending order.

To determine the annual star for any particular year, there's a simple formula:

1. Add up all the digits for the year in question. For example, let's calculate the annual star for 2009: 2 + 0 + 0 + 9 = 11.

2. Add the resulting number until you get a single-digit number. Continuing with our example: 1 + 1 = 2.

3. Subtract the resulting number from 11. The answer is the annual star number. In the case of 2009, 11 − 2 = 9.

> **Feng Facts**
>
> Have you notice that the annual star formula is the same for the ming gua of a male? The only difference is that for the annual star you do not convert the number 5 to a 2.

Let's calculate another year. How about 2004?

$$2 + 0 + 0 + 4 = 6$$
$$11 - 6 = 5$$

The number 5 is the annual star for 2004.

Get the idea? What star prevailed during your birth year?

The Annual Star Chart

For your convenience, we've assembled the following quick-reference table. Notice how the numbers descend with the progression of years.

The Annual Star Chart

Year	Star	Year	Star	Year	Star	Year	Star
1980	2	1989	2	1998	2	2007	2
1981	1	1990	1	1999	1	2008	1
1982	9	1991	9	2000	9	2009	9
1983	8	1992	8	2001	8	2010	8
1984	7	1993	7	2002	7	2011	7
1985	6	1994	6	2003	6	2012	6
1986	5	1995	5	2004	5	2013	5
1987	4	1996	4	2005	4	2014	4
1988	3	1997	3	2006	3	2015	3

To figure out the annual stars previous to 1980, count up. To figure out the annual stars beyond 2015, count down.

Flying the Annual Star

The annual star, or number, flies in exactly the same manner as the time star (the period star). It flies forward, the ascending numbers filling the remaining eight cells by following the directional sequence: NW, W, NE, S, N, SW, E, SE.

When a star occupies the central palace, it's less influential than the other stars because it's "locked" or "imprisoned" in the chart. However, if the design of the house leaves the center open (if there's an atrium, patio, or courtyard in the center, for example), then the numbers are freed. The heaven qi from the facing palace (the water star) will positively or negatively affect the numbers situated in the facing cell and the heaven qi from the sitting palace (the mountain star) will positively or negatively affect the numbers situated in the sitting cell.

As a visiting star, there are three ways an annual star can affect a house:

♦ An annual star can act on its own to affect the relationship between the mountain, water, and time stars in question. If an annual star is timely, it will affect the area positively. If the annual star is untimely, it will affect the area negatively.

♦ An annual star can activate a combination (mountain-water, mountain-time, water-time) if the phase it's correlated with produces the phase attached to the mountain or water star in question.

♦ An annual star can activate a combination (mountain-water, mountain-time, water-time) if the number is the same as the mountain or the water star in question. In this case, the annual star assists the mountain and/or time star.

We will demonstrate this idea by carrying over the example from the previous chapter of the house built in Period 7, sitting W2 and facing E2. If you're uncertain about the relationship between the phases and to which number each phases corresponds, it's a good idea to use the illustration on the front of the tear-out card for a handy reminder.

The Annual Star for 2002

Beginning in the central palace, moving up to the facing cell, and traveling clockwise around the chart, let's take a look at how the annual star affects the other stars. Again, M stands for mountain star, W for water star, T for time star, and A for annual star. The number in bold adjacent to the time star corresponds to the annual star.

The annual star 7 (2002) and how it relates to a Dui house built in Period 7, sitting W2 and facing E2.

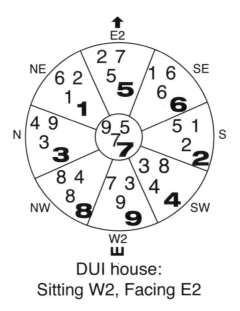

DUI house:
Sitting W2, Facing E2

Center: 9M (fire) 5W (earth) 7T (metal) 7A (metal)

Fire (9M) produces earth (5W). Although a productive relationship, it is not a healthy one. Here, the number 9 is not only encouraging the highly inauspicious number 5's proclivity for misfortune, it is also melting the ruling star 7's benevolence. While the numbers comprising the central cell cannot cause fortune or misfortune, they represent the innate nature of the dwelling. In this case, it is inharmonious. In this example, the 7 annual star, which just happens be the same as the auspicious ruling star 7, is a good omen. While its influence is minimal within the confines of the central cell, the annual 7 can help lessen 5's unfavorable effect.

East: 2M (earth) 7W (metal) 5T (earth) 5A (earth)

Earth (2M) produces metal (7W). In the last chapter, we determined that metal is needed to strengthen the money star 7's likelihood of fostering financial gain. Metal will also reduce 2 and 5, the innately evil star's propensity for misfortune and illness. The addition of another 5 makes matters worse because it activates the 2M-7W and 2M-5T combinations. More metal is needed in the area in question.

Southeast: 1M (water) 6W (metal) 6T (metal) 6A (metal)

Metal (6W) produces water (1M). This is a productive combination heralding the possibility of promotion and career success. Thus, no remedy is needed. However, the stress associated with more responsibility may cause an abundance of nervousness. This is because 1's water is draining 6's energy, a number associated with the head. The annual 6 (an inherently auspicious number) activates the 1M-6W and 6W-6T combinations. Again, a remedy is not needed this year. Annual 6 will only enhance the positive prospects.

South: 5M (earth) 1W (water) 2T (earth) 2A (earth)

Earth (5M) blocks water (1W). This is a controlling relationship, the combination bringing the probability of ear-, kidney-, and genital-related disorders. In the last chapter, we determined moving metal is needed here to thwart the untimely and inherently inauspicious numbers 2 and 5. Also, metal will bridge earth and water, reverting the cycle to a productive one. The annual 2 activates the 5M-2T and 1W-2T combinations. More metal is needed here.

Southwest: 3M (wood) 8W (earth) 4T (wood) 4A (wood)

Wood (3M) burdens earth (8W). The highly favorable number 8 is located on the water or wealth side. To increase the chance for financial success, install a fire remedy here to connect the wood and earth phases. The visiting 4 activates the 3M-4T and 8W-4T combinations, effectively hurting or depleting earth's auspicious power. More fire is needed here.

West: 7M (metal) 3W (wood) 9T (fire) 9A (fire)

Metal (7M) pierces wood (3W). In the last chapter, we determined earth was needed to diminish the possibility of robbery and legal entanglements. Earth would restore the cycle to a productive one: wood produces fire, fire produces earth, earth produces metal. However, the annual 9 makes the 7M-9T combination brighter. While a person's recognition and money prospects may flourish, the probability of fire also increases. Earth will diminish fire's intensity. Avoid using red, purple, or pink in this area. While water colors such as blue or black will help cool things down, you must not use real water here. This is because water will drown the ruling mountain star 7.

Northwest: 8M (earth) 4W (wood) 8T (earth) 8A (earth)

Wood (4W) burdens earth (8M). Because the advantageous number 8 is situated on the mountain (health and relationships) side, we must thwart the possibility of spousal affairs (brought on by the untimely number 4) by installing the fire phase. Fire will revert the cycle to a productive one. The annual 8 (an inherently auspicious number) activates the 8M-8T relationship, ushering in the strong possibility of good fortune and good health. Fire (a red décor, for example) will only heighten the favorable prospects.

North: 4M (wood) 9W (fire) 3T (wood) 3A (wood)

Wood (4M) produces fire (9W). In the previous chapter, we determined that a remedy is not needed because 9's fire would intensify 4's romantic nature, making the area good for a couple seeking a pregnancy. Because 9 is a timely money star, the area also makes a favorable home office. The annual 3 activates all three combinations. With the additional wood, the fire phase is needed to keep the flame burning.

Northeast: 6M (metal) 2W (earth) 1T (water) 1A (water)

Earth (2W) produces metal (6M). Although this is a productive relationship, in the previous chapter we determined metal is needed to suppress the unfavorable and untimely number 2's promotion of illness and money loss. Metal will also strengthen 6's inherently auspicious quality of bringing authority and fame, which is being corroded by the time (water) star. While the annual 1 will not activate the 6M-2W combination, it will activate the 6M-1T and 2W-1T combinations. Metal is still needed to strengthen the innately favorable numbers 6 and 1 and to weaken the innately unfavorable 2.

Conclusion: In 2002, the only area the annual star affects is the West sector where the visiting star's fire makes things too intense. Now, let's see how the annual star 6 for the year 2003 affects the same home.

The Annual Star for 2003

Beginning in the central palace, moving up to the facing cell, and traveling clockwise around the chart, let's take a look at how the annual star affects the other stars. Again, M stands for mountain star, W for water star, T for time star, and A for annual star. The numbers in bold adjacent to the time star corresponds to the annual star.

The annual star 6 (2003) and how it relates to a Dui house built in Period 7, sitting W2 and facing E2.

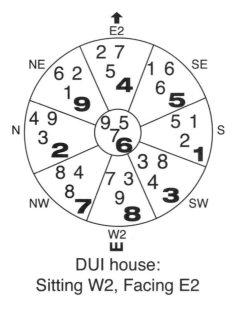

DUI house:
Sitting W2, Facing E2

Center: 9M (fire) 5W (earth) 7T (metal) 6A (metal)

Fire (9M) produces earth (5W). Although a productive relationship, it is not a healthy one. The number 9 is not only encouraging the highly inauspicious number 5's penchant for misfortune, it is also melting the ruling star 7's benevolence. While the numbers comprising the central cell cannot cause fortune or misfortune, they represent the innate nature of the dwelling. In this case, it's inharmonious. For 2003, the annual 6 star does not activate a combination. On its own, its affect is minimal. Here, 6 will help diminish 5's unfavorable aspects (metal reduces earth).

East: 2M (earth) 7W (metal) 5T (earth) 4A (wood)

Earth (2M) produces metal (7W). Metal is needed to strengthen the money star 7's likelihood of monetary gain. Metal will also reduce 2 and 5, the innately evil star's propensity for misfortune and illness. The annual star 4 doesn't active a combination. Thus, 4's wood will act on its own, bringing the possibility of sexual entanglements. Metal will help chop some of the untimely 4's wood.

Southeast: 1M (water) 6W (metal) 6T (metal) 5A (earth)

Metal (6W) produces water (1M). This is a productive combination fostering the likelihood of promotion and career success. No remedy is needed. However, the stress associated with more responsibility may be accompanied by a nervous breakdown. This is because 1's water is draining 6's energy, a number associated with the head. The visiting and evil-natured 5 activates the 1M-6W and 6W-6T combinations. This year, metal is needed to lessen 5's ugly disposition and bolter 6's favorable, but weakened influence.

South: 5M (earth) 1W (water) 2T (earth) 1A (water)

Earth (5M) blocks water (1W). This is a controlling relationship, the combination bringing the possibility of ear-, kidney-, and genital-related disorders. Moving metal is needed here to thwart the untimely and inherently inauspicious numbers 2 and 5. Also, metal will connect earth and water, reverting the cycle to a productive one. The annual 1 activates the 5M-1W and 1W-2T combinations. More metal is needed here to revert these cycles to productive ones.

Southwest: 3M (wood) 8W (earth) 4T (wood) 3A (wood)

Wood (3M) burdens earth (8W). The highly favorable number 8 is located on the water or wealth side. To increase the chance for financial achievement, install a fire remedy to connect the wood and earth phases. The visiting 3 activates the 3M-8W and 3M-4T combinations, effectively depleting earth's auspicious power. Fire is needed here this year, too.

West: 7M (metal) 3W (wood) 9T (fire) 8A (earth)

Metal (7M) pierces wood (3W). Although water would restore the phase balance, you cannot put a ruling mountain star in water. Therefore, add earth to diminish the possibility of robbery and lawsuits. Earth will also restore the cycle to a productive one: wood produces fire, fire produces earth, earth produces metal. The visiting 8 activates the 7M-3W combination only.

Northwest: 8M (earth) 4W (wood) 8T (earth) 7A (metal)

Wood (4W) burdens earth (8M). The advantageous number 8 is situated on the mountain (health and relationships) side. Fire will thwart the possibility of spousal affairs (brought on by the untimely number 4) and revert the cycle to a productive one. The annual 7 doesn't activate a combination. Thus, it will act on its own. Because it's still the ruling star, it will help positive prospects materialize.

North: North: 4M (wood) 9W (fire) 3T (wood) 2A (earth)

Wood (4M) produces fire (9W). A remedy is not needed here because 9's fire would intensify 4's romantic nature, making the area good for a couple seeking a pregnancy. Because 9 is a timely money star, the area also makes an auspicious home office. The annual and evil-natured 2 doesn't activate a combination. Thus, it will act on its own to bring sickness. Install metal to mitigate its nasty effects.

Northeast: 6M (metal) 2W (earth) 1T (water) 9A (fire)

Earth (2W) produces metal (6M). Although this is a productive relationship, metal is needed to suppress the unfavorable and untimely number 2's promotion of illness and money loss. Metal will also strengthen 6's inherently auspicious quality of bringing authority and fame, which is being corroded by the time (water) star. While the annual 9 doesn't activate a combination, it does enhance the numbers it's with. Enhancing 2's evilness must be thwarted. More metal is need in this area this year.

Conclusion: In 2003, things change in the southeast and north sections. While a remedy was not needed in 2002, metal is needed in the southeast. Metal also replaces fire in the north.

Okay, feng shui enthusiasts, go to it! You now have all the tools. You understand how to use them. Take this time now to review your own chart. Implement the appropriate five-phase remedy to balance your dwelling's qi.

In the next part, we'll present three case studies to help facilitate your comprehension of Flying Star.

The Least You Need to Know

- The annual stars change each year beginning variously on the third, fourth, or fifth of February.
- The annual star's reign lasts for one solar year.
- The annual star can activate a combination by sharing the same number as the mountain or water star or by producing the mountain or water phase in question.

Part **6**

Practical Application

Part 6 puts you in the driver's seat, offering you the chance to test-drive your feng shui skills. You'll meet folks just like you who seek to benefit from feng shui. Using Flying Star, you'll examine a home and a business, each with a unique situation and a particular solution. We'll show you how simple modifications, such as repositioning beds and desks and changing color schemes, can make a big difference in how you feel.

We'll be there to assist you every step of the way. So buckle up and enjoy the fruits of your labors. This is one ride you don't want to miss!

A House Hunting We Will Go

In This Chapter

◆ Choosing a house

◆ Incorporating elements of the Eight House system

◆ Using Flying Star to remedy/enhance the dwelling's qi

If buying your first house is stressful, the process of looking for a house is even worse. Unlike shopping for a car where you can rent a contender for a weekend, try it out, and get to know the car's design features and flaws before plunking down your hard-earned savings, shopping for a house often doesn't present such luxuries. In this chapter, we won't be checking for leaks, cracks, or termites. We won't be checking on your neighbors or the school system. We'll be checking the qi, determining the auspiciousness of the house, inside and out, before making a purchase.

Doing Your Homework

The search for a house begins at home. Before you scrutinize the Open House listings, you must determine what type of house suits you. We're not talking about a ranch, colonial, or Mediterranean-type house. We're referring to the house's essence, the compatibility of its qi to yours. Let's take an example. Alex, a lawyer, and his wife Anna, a part-time librarian, are looking for their dream home. Having saved $50,000 for a down payment, they don't want to make a mistake. After all, it's probably the biggest investment they'll ever make. To help find a house best suited to them, the couple uses the Eight House and Flying Star systems. Let's see what they did.

Putting Your Best Direction Forward

The first step toward finding the right house is determining to which set of East or West Group trigrams you belong. The next step is to determine your four favorable and four unfavorable directions.

Name		Alex	Anna
Birthdate		7/4/69	3/5/68
Trigram		Xun	Kan
Number		4	1
East/West Group		East	East
D i r e c t i o n s			
F1	G O O D	N	SE
F2		E	S
F3		S	E
F4		SE	N
H1	B A D	NW	W
H2		W	NW
H3		SW	NE
H4		NE	SW

Both Alex (Xun) and Anna (Kan) belong to the East Group set of trigrams. They are F1 to each other (please consult the following chart that's also used to determine a person's compatibility with a particular type of dwelling), their relationship representing the highest level of compatibility. Alex's best directions are north (F1), east (F2), south (F3), and southeast (F4). Anna's best directions are southeast (F1), south (F2), east (F3), and north (F4). Based on their compatibility criteria, they can now narrow the field to look for only those houses belonging to the East Group: Zhen, Xun, Kan, and Li. Furthermore, they know the East Group house best suited to them should have …

- An entrance located at their F1, F2, F3, F4 directions.
- An auspicious bedroom.
- A favorable wall where their bed can be positioned.
- A productive office for Alex.
- A favorable wall where Alex's desk can be positioned.

There are four East Group dwellings. Is there a way to ascertain which of the four is best? Absolutely.

Homeward Bound

Referring to the following table, here's how the couple is compatible with the four East Group houses:

TRIGRAMS House ▶ People ▼		EAST GROUP				WEST GROUP			
		Zhen	Xun	Kan	Li	Qian	Kun	Gen	Dui
EAST GROUP	Zhen	F4	F2	F3	F1	H3	H1	H2	H4
	Xun	F2	F4	F1	F3	H1	H3	H4	H2
	Kan	F3	F1	F4	F2	H2	H4	H3	H1
	Li	F1	F3	F2	F4	H4	H2	H1	H3
WEST GROUP	Qian	H3	H1	H2	H4	F4	F2	F3	F1
	Kun	H1	H3	H4	H2	F2	F4	F1	F3
	Gen	H2	H4	H3	H1	F3	F1	F4	F2
	Dui	H4	H2	H1	H3	F1	F3	F2	F4

To facilitate easier learning, their compatibility with the Zhen, Xun, Kan, and Li house is as follows:

- ◆ *Zhen House:* F2, Alex; F3, Anna
- ◆ *Xun House:* F4, Alex; F1, Anna
- ◆ *Kan House:* F1, Alex; F4, Anna
- ◆ *Li House:* F3, Alex; F2, Anna

While Alex and Anna would benefit from all four East Group houses, ideally, they should try to find a house favoring Alex. This is because he is the breadwinner, providing the primary source of income. Therefore, the couple should look for a Kan house (F1 for Alex), followed by a Zhen (F2 for Alex), Li (F3 for Alex), and Xun house (F4 for Alex). If, on the other hand, Anna supplied the main source of income, they would look for a Xun house, followed by a Li house, Zhen house, and Kan house.

Master Class _____

What if you and your spouse belong to opposite East/West Groups? Which party should the house favor? It depends on the situation. If one person has or is more susceptible to health problems, find a house favoring that person. If a woman plans to start a family, the house should support her well-being. If children are not a factor and both people are healthy, choose a house supporting the breadwinner.

There's No Place Like Home

Of course, environmental factors must be considered even before stepping foot inside a prospective dwelling. There's no point in examining closet space if the house rests on a steep slope, an inauspicious-shaped lot, or is the object of sha qi (refer to Chapter 8, "Turtles, Tigers, and Dragons, Oh My: Evaluating Your Environment," and Chapter 9, "Home Sweet Home: Evaluating Your House and Its Surroundings," for a reminder of these negative influences). Move on. Don't waste your valuable time. The external environment is just as important as the internal space. Say this 10 times before you fall in love with the house on the hill enveloped by potentially cancerous electromagnetic fields emitted by the power plant next door.

So, did Alex and Anna find their dream home? Well, they found two identical side-by-side Kan houses within a new community. Because the dwellings are situated on a curved street, they aren't perfectly aligned. They are situated at 30 degree angles from one another.

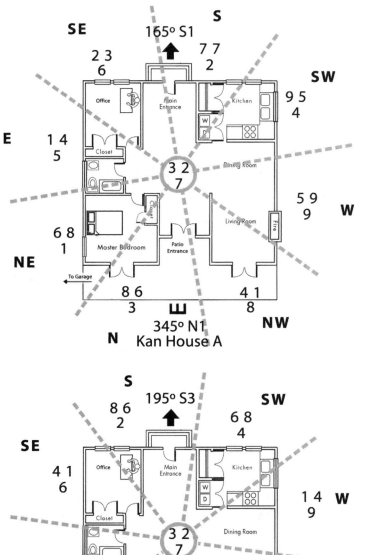

Two identical Kan houses built in Period 7 and oriented at 30 degree angles from each other. House A sits N1 and faces S1; House B sits N3 and faces S3.

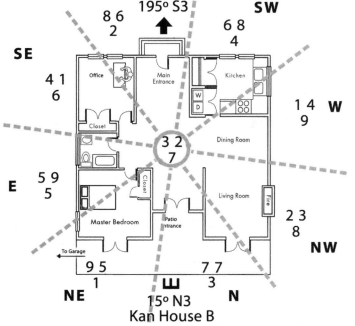

Built in Period 7 (anytime from February 4, 1984 to February 3, 2004), Kan house A sits N1 and faces S1 at 165 degrees. It's a Double Facing house because the ruling mountain (health and relationships) and water (wealth) stars (7) are located in the facing cell.

According to what you've learned in Chapter 16, "The Flying Stars, Part 4," until Period 7 ends, it's easy for the occupants to make and retain money, but it's difficult for them to form stable relationships and maintain good health. To rectify the misaligned position of the ruling mountain star (which should be located on the left side of the sitting cell), a mountain or a man-made mountain such as a building or tall hedge must support the ruling mountain star at the facing or front side of the dwelling. The facing side must also support the properly placed ruling water or money star. A body of water or virtual water such as a roadway will ensure the likelihood of increased wealth. In this case, the opposing dwelling serves as the mountain remedy (not illustrated). While the street serves as the water enhancement, it's also a good idea to install a fountain, pond, or lawn sprinklers.

Feng Alert

Remember, your dwelling only conforms to a Fortunate Mountain Fortunate Water, Reversed Mountain and Water, Double Facing, or Double Sitting situation if the period it was built in matches the period we are currently in. For example, take a Kan house built in Period 6 (1964–1984) sitting N2 and facing S2. While the number configuration conforms to a Double Facing scheme, it has lost its quality as a Double Facing dwelling because the period number (6) does not match the current period number (7 until February 3, 2004; 8 from February 4, 2004 to February 3, 2024). The Period 6 Double Facing dwelling will be activated only when Period 6 arrives again in the year 2144.

Also built in Period 7, Kan house B sits N3 and faces S3 at 195 degrees. It's a Double Sitting house because the ruling mountain (health and relationships) and water (wealth) stars (7) are located in the sitting cell. According to what you've learned in Chapter 16, until Period 7 ends, it's easy for the occupants to form stable relationships and maintain good health, but it's difficult for them to retain and make money. To rectify the improperly placed ruling water star (which should be located on the right side of the facing cell), a body of water or virtual water like a roadway must support the star at the sitting or back side of the dwelling. A swimming pool, fountain, or koi pond in the backyard would do nicely. To ensure the probability of good health, a mountain or a man-made mountain such as a building or tall hedge must support the ruling mountain star at the sitting side. In this case, let's assume a tall hedge separates the property from the one it backs up against.

Master Class

When Period 7 is over on February 3, 2004, the number 8 will become the ruling star. Activate the 8 money star with water and the 8 people star with a mountain. So, if you installed a fountain in the east to correspond with the 7 money star, move it to where the money 8 star is located. If it's impossible to place forms outside the house, use them inside (if you live in an apartment, for example). Although the effect isn't as powerful as an exterior form, it is satisfactory.

Side-by-Side, Qi-by-Qi

So, which house should Alex and Anna choose? Let's run the numbers and compare the two dwellings. Until they select which home best suits them, we'll leave out the time star in this cursory evaluation.

		Kan House A ш N1 ↟S1		Kan House B ш N3 ↟S3	
S	Main Entrance	7M 7W	Wealth Through Competition	8M 6W	Authority
SW	Kitchen	9M 5W	Financial & Health Hazard	6M 8W	Financial Success
W	Dining Room	5M 9W	Financial & Health Hazard	1M 4W	Writing, Creativity & Romance
NW	Living Room	4M 1W	Writing, Creativity & Romance	2M 3W	Conflict, Gossip, Litigation & Accidents
N	Patio Entrance	8M 6W	Authority	7M 7W	Wealth Through Competition
NE	Master Bedroom	6M 8W	Financial Success	9M 5W	Financial & Health Hazard
E	Bathroom	1M 4W	Writing, Creativity & Romance	5M 9W	Financial & Health Hazard
SE	Guest Bedroom/ Office	2M 3W	Conflict, Gossip, Litigation & Accidents	4M 1W	Writing, Creativity & Romance

A side-by-side comparison of the qi distribution for Kan houses A and B.

For a preliminary check, first study the numbers occupying the entrances, master bedroom, and office. The remaining rooms are not as important. Thus, it isn't necessary to scrutinize them at this early stage. Referring to the previous table, let's concentrate on the rooms that count!

♦ **Main Entrance:** Auspicious for both homes during Period 7. Regarding House A, when Period 8 arrives on February 4, 2004, the ruling number 7 retires. When it leaves office, the innately inauspicious star's untimely characteristics bring the threat of fire, theft, and casualties. Regarding House B, it boasts two inherently auspicious numbers 8 and 6. Bringing authority and respect, when Period 8 comes, the number 8 is advantageously located on the mountain (health and relationships) side of the entrance. It must be supported environmentally by a mountain, building, tall hedge, or forest to increase the likelihood of good relations and robust health.

◆ **Patio Entrance:** Auspicious for both homes during Period 7. Regarding House A, the 8M-6W combination is favorable, especially when Period 8 arrives. The occupants must take care not to dissipate the mountain star's (health and relationships) yin energy. Ideally, the patio door on the left side of the double door, as well as the outside doors located in the master bedroom, should be kept closed (at least at night) to allow the auspicious yin qi to permeate the dwelling by infusing the walls. Regarding House B, the back entrance is only usable during Period 7. For reasons that were explained above, the number 7 becomes untimely and problematic.

◆ **Master Bedroom:** For House A, the 6M-8W combination is extremely favorable, especially in Period 8 where the number 8 is located on the water or money side. To take advantage of the ruling money star, support it environmentally by leaving the window open. Doing so will allow the yang essence of the driveway to flow into the dwelling, increasing the probability of financial gain. This area can double as an office, too. Regarding House B, the numbers aren't as favorable, with a 9M-5W bringing the possibility of financial and health hazards due to impulsive behavior. Not a great place for a bedroom.

Feng Alert

Remember, when assessing number configurations you must consider the position of the numbers, where they are located within the dwelling, the number's innate nature, whether it's timely or not (and the characteristics each embodies), and what happens when numbers are paired with other numbers. For a reminder about these aspects, consult Chapter 14, "The Flying Stars, Part 2," and Chapter 17, "The Flying Stars, Part 5."

◆ **Guest Bedroom/Office:** Considering that Alex is a lawyer, House A's 2M-3W combination (conflict, litigation) may be favorable, the area increasing his skill in devising arguments and rebuttals. That said, he would be better off working in the master bedroom, where the qi is much more favorable. House B, on the other hand, contains a benevolent combination, with 4M-1W being a great place for a writer, artist, or a person looking to find romance. This area makes a fine bedroom or office.

All things considered, Alex and Anna decide on Kan house A. Although the main entrance will become inauspicious in Period 8, they'll use the back entrance more frequently anyway. This is because a pathway leads directly from the garage to either the master bedroom or patio door.

The Analysis

Alex and Anna use Flying Star methodology to remedy and enhance the stars in their new home. Beginning in the center, moving up to the facing cell, then traveling clockwise around the floor plan, let's examine the number combinations:

Center: 3M (wood) 2W (earth) 7T (metal)

Wood controls earth. Innately, the qi for the entire home carries an inauspicious force fostering conflict, lawsuits, gossip, and accidents. Great care must be taken to properly balance all areas to mitigate misfortune.

South Main Entrance: 7M (metal) 7W (metal) 2T (earth)

Metal assists metal. A great area for an entrance, bedroom, or office for Period 7. Although a remedy is not needed now, when Period 8 arrives, add water to lessen 7's untimely qualities, which are being encouraged by the time star (earth produces metal). A table fountain would work nicely here.

Southwest Kitchen: 9M (fire) 5W (earth) 4T (wood)

Fire produces earth. Although a productive relationship, it is not a healthy one. Here, the number 9 is empowering the highly inauspicious number 5's propensity for misfortune. Moreover, the wood time star is adding fuel to the fire (literally), increasing the likelihood for financial and health hazards. Because this is the kitchen, an inherently "hot" place, moving metal is needed to thwart impending threats (metal reduces earth). A chiming clock will do the trick.

West Dining Room: 5M (earth) 9W (fire) 9T (fire)

Fire produces earth. An inauspicious scenario described above. In fact, the situation is worse here because the number 9 (represented by both the water and time stars) enhances any number it's with. Again, moving metal is preferable. A chiming clock, a piano that is played, metal statuary, table bases, and the like, will help diminish unfavorable prospects.

Northwest Living Room: 4M (wood) 1W (water) 8T (earth)

Water produces wood. This is a productive relationship fostering creativity, writing, and romance. While a remedy is not needed, water will strengthen the inherently favorable number 1 that is being controlled by the earth time star. Since the living and dining rooms are one space, water will also help quench the raging fire in the dining area. A table fountain or an aquarium will work nicely. This is a good area for Anna (a librarian) to read and write.

North Patio Entrance: 8M (earth) 6W (metal) 3T (wood)

Earth produces metal. While the combination brings authority, be mindful of the inherently good, but untimely number 6. Because 6 is the money star located in an entrance, it becomes the focus. During Period 7, 6's favorable (authority and dignity) and unfavorable (loneliness and lawsuits) aspects manifest. The remedy is to bridge the wood time star and the earth mountain star with fire. Thus, the sequence will be balanced: wood-fire-earth-metal. Fire will keep the untimely number 6 in check (fire controls metal) and support the mountain star (fire produces earth) at the same time. Yet, too much fire will brighten 6's unfavorable qualities. A small rug inside the entryway with warm tones or a small red decorative object will do. When Period 8 arrives on February 4, 2004, the 8 mountain star must be supported by a mountain, tall hedge, or fence, to bring good health and beneficial relationships.

Northeast Master Bedroom: 6M (metal) 8W (earth) 1T (water)

Earth produces metal. Described above, the only difference here is how the time star affects the mountain-water combination. In this case, water is corroding 6's innately aus-picious, but untimely qualities. With more responsibility due to increased authority and possible promotion, the couple may suffer from stress and headaches. Remedy with a little fire. It will enhance the auspicious money star and control the mountain star's negative aspects. When Period 8 arrives, keep the window open during the day. Doing so will allow the yang qi essence of the driveway (not illustrated) to increase the likelihood of better financial prospects. At night, the 6 mountain star will charge the walls, bringing possible career advancement. Regarding bed placement, they should position it against the eastern wall (as illustrated). For Alex, east corresponds to his F2 qi; for Anna, her F3 qi. The bedroom door should be closed while they sleep. Alex should also consider using this room as an office. They should orient the desk toward the east, his F2 qi.

East Bathroom: 1M (water) 4W (wood) 5T (earth)

Water produces wood. A productive relationship fostering creativity, writing, and romance. They should install metal to connect earth (5) to water (1) to wood (4). While you may think to add water to promote the favorable possibilities, water will actually activate the untimely number 4 known to bring inappropriate romances! A metal-framed mirror and/or bathroom accessories will do the job.

Southeast Office: 2M (earth) 3W (wood) 6T (metal)

Wood controls earth. This is an unlucky relationship coupling two inherently inauspicious numbers. Adding a little fire will restore balance to the cycle (wood-fire-earth). However, the remedy causes a side effect by enhancing the sickness-provoking star 2 (fire produces earth). The reductive phase metal is needed to weaken the mountain star (metal reduces earth). Metal filing cabinets, statuary, picture frames, and the like, are suggestions. Yet, because of the destructive nature of both the mountain and water stars, the remedies will not transform the room to a good one. It's best that Alex and Anna avoid this room, rele-gating it to a storage area or guest bedroom. Alex would be better off installing a desk in the master bedroom. If however, he needed the southeast room as an office, he may bene-fit from the propensity of arguments triggered by the 2M-3W combination. With his desk facing east (F2), he could harness the area's qi to help him devise appeals and rebuttals.

Conclusion: Overall, Alex and Anna have selected a fine home. As you're learning, no home can be completely good or completely bad. Following the concept of yin and yang, in one there's always the hint of the other! Of course, before installing the remedies, the couple must consider how the annual star affects the star combinations.

In the next chapter, we'll examine an office.

The Least You Need to Know

- First determine the type of East or West Group house most compatible with your qi.
- If the surrounding environmental factors are favorable, examine the stars in the entrances, bedroom, and office. Consider purchasing or renting the space only if they're favorable.
- Remedy or enhance the qi in each section of the dwelling.
- Use the Eight House system to determine your most auspicious directions. Place your bed and desk accordingly.

Chapter 20

Does Your Office Measure Up?

In This Chapter

- ◆ Gaining a competitive edge is easier than you think
- ◆ Reorganizing your office space
- ◆ Incorporating Eight House and Flying Star methodology

Whether you own a large corporation or a small business, your primary goal is to generate revenue. Yet, to do this, you must first create a welcoming and comfortable working environment: a place where employees will be driven to succeed and that encourages camaraderie and teamwork. Often, we set aside this notion, viewing the design and layout factors as incidental and low priority. In this chapter, you'll understand how quite the opposite is true—promoting a harmonious environment is an essential consideration, a positively golden means to a lucrative end.

Labor Pains

Mr. Smith owns and operates a small insurance agency. He has nine full-time employees on his payroll: five sales associates, one accountant, two secretaries, and a receptionist. All are paid competitive salaries. After six months of service, each is eligible to participate in a retirement program and receive medical and dental benefits. Also, Mr. Smith rewards each member of his staff with a three-week paid vacation per year. He reimburses accrued sick days not taken at the end of the year. He provides holiday parties, tickets to sporting events, and other niceties. By most company standards, Mr. Smith offers a very generous package.

So why is his staff listless? Why is Mr. Smith himself sluggish? Why must he mediate frequent arguments? Why, despite all the incentives, is his staff unmotivated and unhappy? Desperate and frustrated, Mr. Smith seeks your advice.

First Things First

Even before you can determine favorable directions and appropriate remedies, you must first walk around the outside of Mr. Smith's facility. Determine the building's sitting direction. Take a compass reading. Evaluate the environment. In this case, there are no external factors influencing the owner and his staff. Now, go inside. Scope it out. Draw up a simple floor plan and divide it into eight equal sections. Ask yourself if the layout, in some measure, is responsible for poor performance and troublesome relations.

Mr. Smith's previous floor plan. A Dui building constructed in 1920 (Period 3), it sits W2 and facing E2 at 90 degrees.

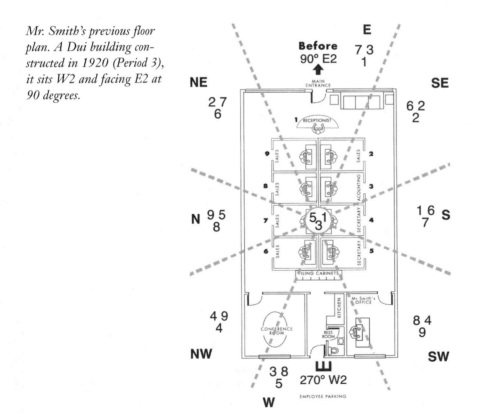

Disregarding the numeric qi map for the moment, focus on the floor plan. Upon entering through the eastern main entrance, you are greeted by a receptionist. Is there a problem here? Well, as you learned in Chapter 8, "Turtles, Tigers, and Dragons, Oh My: Evaluating Your Environment," you should not sit directly opposite a door. Here, the receptionist is subjected to a surge of qi hitting her each time the door opens. But take a closer look. The wall in back of the receptionist, formed by two adjoined cubicles, prevents qi from circulating throughout the interior. No wonder Mr. Smith and his staff feel stagnant and tired. They aren't being nourished by life's breath.

Furthermore, the eight cubicles are set up so that the desks face each other. Even though the cubicle walls offer the staff privacy, they still, in effect, are "in each other's face." Also, is it good feng shui to sit with your back exposed to a doorway? Of course not! Plus, despite the close proximity, the staff is dissuaded from interacting with each other, with their cubicle entrances on opposing sides of the room. These factors could quite possibly contribute to the bickering and tension.

Regarding the western areas of the business, Mr. Smith's desk is seemingly situated in an advantageous position against an unobstructed wall (we'll examine this later). The back entrance, adjacent to the employee parking lot, opens into a tidy restroom/kitchen area. The conference room? It holds a proportionate oval table and chairs.

> **Feng Alert**
>
> It is not favorable to sit with your back exposed to a door. You are subjected to a surge of qi, which can cause a lack of concentration, unproductivity, and illness. This position offers only unfavorable psychological and physical effects. Ideally, your back, like your home, must be supported by a wall or a mountain.

Let's Get Compatible

Wow! There's much to consider. Where do you begin? First determine Mr. Smith's innate compatibility with his building. Based on this information, examine the auspiciousness of the entrances. Then determine the owner's and employee's best directions. Because you'll be using Flying Star, don't don your work gloves until a conclusion has been reached.

Dui Have a Match?

Born on April 2, 1948, Mr. Smith belongs to the Dui and West Group set of trigrams. His west-sitting building also corresponds to Dui. An exact match, Mr. Smith and his structure are compatible. Referring to the following table, you'll find that a Dui person living or working in a Dui building benefits from F4 qi's peace and stability.

Mr. Smith and his building belong to the Dui trigram. They are F4 to each other.

TRIGRAMS House People		EAST GROUP				WEST GROUP			
		Zhen	Xun	Kan	Li	Qian	Kun	Gen	Dui
EAST GROUP	Zhen	F4	F2	F3	F1	H3	H1	H2	H4
	Xun	F2	F4	F1	F3	H1	H3	H4	H2
	Kan	F3	F1	F4	F2	H2	H4	H3	H1
	Li	F1	F3	F2	F4	H4	H2	H1	H3
WEST GROUP	Qian	H3	H1	H2	H4	F4	F2	F3	F1
	Kun	H1	H3	H4	H2	F2	F4	F1	F3
	Gen	H2	H4	H3	H1	F3	F1	F4	F2
	Dui	H4	H2	H1	H3	F1	F3	F2	F4

If Mr. Smith was inclined to relocate, he should choose a Qian (F1) building, followed by a Gen (F2) and Kun (F3) building. Despite F4's lackluster business acumen, the space is still harmonious to Mr. Smith's nature.

Won't You Please Come In?

Before we make any changes, let's consider what the Flying Stars have to say. Beginning in the center, traveling up to the facing cell, we'll move clockwise around the floor plan:

Note: M stands for Mountain Star; W for Water Star; and T for Time Star.

Center: 5M (earth) 1W (water) 3T (wood)

Earth controls water. A dominating relationship promoting the likelihood of ear-, kidney-, and genital-related illness. Install a golden (metal) rug along the central pathway (see after floor plan). This will weaken the ill-natured 5 earth star (metal reduces earth) and strengthen the 1 water star (metal produces water), an innately auspicious number.

East: 7M (metal) 3W (wood) 1T (water)

Metal controls wood. A dominating combination bringing potential robberies and litigation. During Period 7 (1984 to February 3, 2004), the ruling mountain star 7 must be supported by a mountain. The building directly across the street serves as the remedy and will help bring good health and beneficial relationships to Mr. Smith and his staff. Moving on, while you might think to add water to restore balance, and thus, diminish the unfavorable forecast, the reductive phase water isn't strong enough to thwart the untimely and inherently bad number 3. Here, metal is needed to control the water star and assist the mountain star.

Southeast: 6M (metal) 2W (earth) 2T (earth)

Earth produces metal. Although productive, the relationship fosters financial loss due to illness, an unfortunate mishap that is being encouraged by the ill-natured earth time star. Add metal to weaken the disadvantageous water star.

South: 1M (water) 6W (metal) 7T (metal)

Metal produces water. A productive relationship bringing career advancement. No remedy is needed.

Southwest: 8M (earth) 4W (wood) 9T (fire)

Wood controls earth. A dominating relationship bringing creativity and harmony only if the conflicting situation is remedied. Install the fire phase to revert the cycle to a balanced one: wood-fire-earth. Fire will brighten 4 wood's creativity and lessen the possibility of inappropriate affairs. Also, fire will enhance the mountain star's ability to elicit teamwork and harmony among co-workers.

West: 3M (wood) 8W (earth) 5T (earth)

Wood controls earth. A combination bringing monetary gain only if the dominating relationship is remedied. A bridge (fire) is needed to connect the mountain and water stars. A red rug inside the entryway is recommended. The number 8 water (money) star will become especially advantageous during Period 8, where it must be supported by water or virtual water such as a roadway. The back entrance should be used more in Period 8.

Northwest: 4M (wood) 9W (fire) 4T (wood)

Wood produces fire. A productive combination fostering writing and creativity. In this case, notice that the area contains two highly auspicious money numbers—9W in the northwest and 8W in the west. As you'll soon learn, we recommend that Mr. Smith move his office here. Install a table fountain to activate the money (water) stars. Disregarding the phase relationships between water (the enhancement), 9 fire and 8 earth (the water stars), remember that water activates usable water stars (7, 8, and 9 for Period 7; 8, 9, and 1 for Period 8).

North: 9M (fire) 5W (earth) 8T (earth)

Fire produces earth. Although a productive relationship, it is not a healthy one. Here, the number 9 is encouraging the highly unfavorable number 5's propensity for misfortune. Moving metal is needed to reduce the possibility of financial and health hazards.

Northeast: 2M (earth) 7W (metal) 6T (metal)

Earth produces metal. A combination bringing financial gain. Moreover, the ruling water star (for Period 7) heightens the probability. During Period 7, the water star must be supported environmentally by a body of water or virtual water such as a roadway. Here, the street serves as the enhancement.

Sitting Pretty

Now that you've determined the remedy or enhancement appropriate for each area of the office, you can put the final piece in place. Look at how the desks of Mr. Smith's staff are positioned. Depending on which East or West Group each staff member belongs to, you'll reposition their desk so they face either the east or west wall.

Determining the staff's most favorable desk positions.

Name	Period 3 Building	Mr. Smith	Female 1	Male 2	Female 3	Female 4	Female 5	Male 6	Male 7	Female 8	Male 9
Birthdate	1920	1948	1979	1960	1955	1982	1966	1970	1962	1958	1955
Trigram	Dui	Dui	Zhen	Xun	Qian	Qian	Gen	Zhen	Kun	Li	Li
East/West Group	West	West	East	East	West	West	West	East	West	East	East
D i r e c t i o n s											
F1	NW	NW	S	N	W	W	SW	S	NE	E	E
F2	NE	NE	SE	E	SW	SW	W	SE	NW	N	N
F3	SW	SW	N	S	NE	NE	NW	N	W	SE	SE
F4	W	W	E	SE	NW	NW	NE	E	SW	S	S
H1	N	N	SW	NW	SE	SE	S	SW	E	NE	NE
H2	SE	SE	NE	W	N	N	E	NE	S	SW	SW
H3	S	S	NW	SW	E	E	N	NW	SE	W	W
H4	E	E	W	NE	S	S	SE	W	N	NW	NW

Moving clockwise around the room, let's look at each employee, beginning with the receptionist:

1. **Zhen, female.** The receptionist faces F4. As there is only one choice here, she's fortunate.

2. **Xun, male.** Currently, this sales person faces north, his F1 qi. While auspicious, his back is exposed. We'll move him to face the east, his F2 qi.

3. **Qian, female.** Facing her H2 direction (north), position the accountant's desk to face her F1 direction, west.

4. **Qian, female.** Currently, this secretary faces north, her H2 direction. Reposition her desk to face west, her F1 direction.

5. **Gen, female.** Facing north activates the secretary's H3 qi. Move her desk to face west, her F2 qi.

6. **Zhen, male.** While facing his F1 qi (south) is auspicious, his back cannot be exposed. Reposition the sales associate's desk against the east wall, facing his F4 qi.

7. **Kun, male.** Currently, this sales associate faces his H2 qi (south). We'll move him so that he faces west, his F3 qi.

8. **Li, female.** While south (F4) is favorable for this sales person, we cannot expose her back to the door. Reposition her desk toward the east wall, her F1 qi.

9. **Li, male.** Now, this sales associate faces south, his F4 qi. Move his desk to the east wall, his F1 qi.

By making some simple adjustments, Mr. Smith and his staff should think and feel better.

A Means to an End

Taking into account the interior layout and the Eight House and Flying Star systems, form a conclusion. What recommendations would you suggest? Consider …

♦ Whether the entrance should be relocated.

♦ Now that you've determined a favorable sitting direction for everyone (we'll discuss Mr. Smith later on), how the cubicles can be positioned such that the design fosters harmony among the co-workers.

♦ How the cubicles can be positioned so qi can easily circulate.

♦ Given what the Flying Stars destine, whether some employees should switch desk positions.

♦ Whether Mr. Smith's office best suited to him.

The following illustration shows our recommendations.

Based on this new floor plan, we suggest …

♦ Relocating the main entrance—it is *the* key feng shui solution in this case study. We suggest moving it to the northeast wall. Currently, the door's location corresponds to the building's and Mr. Smith's H4 qi. By moving the entrance, it will bathe the owner, staff, and clients in auspicious an qi combination (2M-7W) inspiring financial gain. Northeast also corresponds to the building's and Mr. Smith's F3 qi.

♦ The cubicles should be arranged such that a middle corridor allows qi to circulate freely. The corridor will also give the staff more privacy.

♦ To facilitate harmony among the co-workers, entrances should be along the corridor.

♦ The accountant in Room 3 should switch with the sales person in Room 6. The auspicious water stars (8 in the west and 9 in the northwest) are great for administering the company's finances.

◆ Mr. Smith should occupy the west-northwest office. Corresponding to his F4 and F1 qi respectively, orient his desk so his back is against the north wall (as illustrated). Although he'll face his H3 qi (south), he'll also face the 8 water (money) star. This takes precedence.

Mr. Smith's improved floor plan.

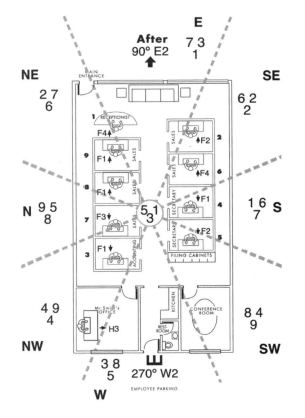

In theory, if Mr. Smith applies our suggestions, he and his staff should coexist peacefully. He should notice an increase in motivation and production!

In Part 7, "Fate or Free Will: What's Your Destiny?" you'll learn about the Chinese zodiac and a method of Chinese astrology called The Four Pillars of Destiny.

The Least You Need to Know

◆ Design and layout play an important role in a business's success.

◆ An employee's desk position within a particular design/layout can affect his or her job motivation and productivity.

◆ Preventing qi from circulating fosters misfortune and illness.

Part 7

Fate or Free Will: What's Your Destiny?

Part 7 is all about Chinese astrology. First, you'll learn about the Chinese zodiac, a popular method involving 12 animals. You know, the ones featured on Chinese restaurant place mats. Based on your birth date, you'll learn which animals make your best friends and which are best avoided. Also, there's a personality profile of each animal. So, you'll know a horse is a horse, of course, of course!

Next, we'll tell you about The Four Pillars of Destiny. Unlike Western astrology, which calculates the movement of heavenly bodies to determine your destiny, The Four Pillars calculates the type of qi you inhaled at birth. That's right, the Chinese believe you inhale your destiny. Besides calculating and interpreting your fate, you'll also understand how a world humanitarian met hers—an interesting study, to be sure!

Chapter 21

Introducing the Twelve Animals of the Chinese Zodiac

In This Chapter

◆ What is the Chinese zodiac?

◆ The 12 animals and their compatibility

◆ What's your animal sign?

◆ Personality profiles of each animal sign

You're in a Chinese restaurant waiting for your food to arrive. What else is there to do but read your horoscope, which is printed on virtually every place mat? You can learn all kinds of things from the Chinese zodiac. Which of the 12 animal signs were you born under? Are you a sociable but crafty rat, or a proud and unpredictable tiger? Perhaps you're a nurturing and benevolent rabbit? Whatever your sign, your paper place mat will undoubtedly inform you which animals are your friends and which are your foes. You'll also learn which creature rules the current year and how its sign affects your prospects.

So, what does Chinese astrology have to do with feng shui? Not a whole lot. But, a good feng shui practitioner will incorporate elements of Chinese astrology into his or her feng shui analysis. Things like determining compatibility, your lucky colors, careers and environments best suited to you are best described using astrology.

This chapter will take an elementary look into the popular system of Chinese astrology. But know, while the animal zodiac can provide cursory insights into your personality, it is rarely considered in more sophisticated systems of Chinese fate calculation (you'll learn about one such method, the Four Pillars of Destiny, in Chapters 22 through 25). Nevertheless, it's fun! Even on a superficial level, the results are amazingly accurate.

What Is the Chinese Zodiac?

Legend has it, just before entering Nirvana, Buddha (563–483 B.C.E.) summoned the animal kingdom. For some reason, only 12 animals answered his call. To reward the respondents, Buddha named a year after each animal in the order of its arrival. The rat arrived first, so it was honored with the first year. Then came the ox, followed by the tiger, rabbit, dragon, snake, horse, sheep, monkey, rooster, dog, and pig. Thus, we have the 12 animals that make up the Chinese zodiac.

But this is a legend. The truth is, no one really knows where the animal signs came from. Sima Qian (163–85 B.C.E.), considered to be one of the greatest scholars of the Han dynasty, and the Grand Astrologer to the emperor, never mentioned the animal cycle. Nor is it mentioned in the astronomical chapters of the *Jin Shu*, the history of the Jin dynasty (265–420 C.E.). But, somehow, toward the end of the tenth century, the animal cycle was in full use. Interestingly, contemporary scholars agree its origins are probably not even Chinese. We'll leave it up to the scholars to discover the true origins. Let's move on.

Twelve Animals, Twelve Earthly Branches

Not one of the 12 animal signs represents a star or a constellation. Rather, the animals represent the movement of earthly qi expressed in cycles of time. Called the *Twelve Earthly Branches*, each of the 12 animal signs corresponds to a branch, or component, of 12 two-hour increments, 12 months, and 12 years.

Most zodiac astrologers consider only the year, month, and hour of birth when determining a client's astrological chart. But, what of the day you were born? Determining the day branch requires a series of mathematical calculations that is either ignored by, or not known by, astrologers who practice this system. As you'll soon learn in Chapter 22, "The Four Pillars of Destiny, Part 1," the Chinese believe we have eight components to our personality. If the day/animal branch is ignored, then this analysis will account for only three-eighths, or less than half, of our overall makeup.

So, what purpose do the animals serve? The animal signs attached to each branch are merely mnemonics to aid learning the different types of qi and their associated natural and human phenomena.

Take the rat, for example. A nocturnal and social creature, the rat is an ideal emblem for yin's midnight hour, for winter, and for north. The rat person is at his best at night and in a crowd. Directly opposite the rat is the horse, the emblem of noon, summer, and south. The horse symbolizes independence, passion, and masculinity—all characteristics of yang's force at its highest. This gives added meaning to the steadfast Marlboro ads, doesn't it?

Wise Words _____

The **Twelve Earthly Branches** (Di Zhi) represent a cycle of the earth's qi expressed by the year, the month, the day, and the time of day.

Governing the earthly branches, or animal cycle, are the five phases of fire, earth, metal, water, and wood. Also, each branch corresponds to a yin and yang polarity. The following illustration shows the interplay of everything we've discussed so far.

The Chinese zodiac and its relationship to the earth's qi.

Notice that the earth phase separates each of the other phase elements. This is because the qi represented by fire, metal, water, and wood returns to earth before transforming into another phase.

What's Your Animal Sign?

Suppose you're a rooster. Are you a fire rooster, earth rooster, metal rooster, water rooster, or wood rooster? You could also be a fire rooster born in a water rat month, on an earth tiger day, at the time of the metal dragon. See, this stuff is a lot more complex than you thought! Even the experienced fortune-teller has much to consider. But learning to analyze each component of your destiny is beyond the scope of this chapter. We'll leave that task to Chapter 23, "The Four Pillars of Destiny, Part 2." For our purposes here, we'll concern ourselves with only your year sign.

The following table lists the Chinese solar years from 1924 to 2023, along with the exact time the year began. If you were born *after* the fifth of February, determining your sign is simple. However, if you were born on the third, fourth, or fifth day of February, the hour of your birth determines your Chinese birth year. Let's say you were born at 3:30 P.M. on February 4, 1925. You would use 1924 as your year of birth because 1925 didn't begin until 3:37 P.M. If you were born at 5:00 P.M. on February 4, 1925, then you would stay with 1925. Let's take another example. If you were born at 7:00 A.M. on February 5, 1940, would you use 1940, the year of the Dragon, as your Chinese birth year? No. This is because 1940 didn't actually begin until 7:08 A.M.—eight minutes after you were born. Your Chinese birth year would be 1939, the year of the Rabbit.

The question arises, why are we using the solar calendar instead of the lunar calendar to mark the beginning of the year? While traditionally, Chinese New Year (which can occur variously on a date in late January through mid February) marks the change in animal sign, scholars and serious students of feng shui and the Four Pillars of Destiny (a method of Chinese astrology that you'll learn about in Chapters 22–25) consider the beginning of spring as the new year.

Feng Facts

The Chinese solar year begins variously on February 3, 4, or 5. It is the midpoint between the Winter Solstice (the day when daylight is at its minimum) and Spring Equinox (one of two days when day and night are of equal length). The solar calendar is based on the rotation of the earth on its axis (the solar day) and the revolution of the earth around the sun (the solar year). The ancients also measured the interval between the successive full moons, the lunar months.

Table 1

Solar Year	Date	Time Year Began	Phase	Animal	Solar Year	Date	Time Year Began	Phase	Animal
1924	Feb 5	9:50 am	Wood	Rat	1964	Feb 5	3:05 am	Wood	Dragon
1925	Feb 4	3:37 pm	Wood	Ox	1965	Feb 4	8:46 am	Wood	Snake
1926	Feb 4	9:39 am	Fire	Tiger	1966	Feb 4	2:38 pm	Fire	Horse
1927	Feb 5	3:31 am	Fire	Rabbit	1967	Feb 4	8:31 pm	Fire	Sheep
1928	Feb 5	9:17 am	Earth	Dragon	1968	Feb 5	2:08 am	Earth	Monkey
1929	Feb 4	3:09 pm	Earth	Snake	1969	Feb 4	7:59 am	Earth	Rooster
1930	Feb 4	8:52 pm	Metal	Horse	1970	Feb 4	1:46 pm	Metal	Dog
1931	Feb 5	2:41 am	Metal	Sheep	1971	Feb 4	7:26 pm	Metal	Pig
1932	Feb 5	8:30 am	Water	Monkey	1972	Feb 5	1:20 am	Water	Rat
1933	Feb 4	2:10 pm	Water	Rooster	1973	Feb 4	7:04 am	Water	Ox
1934	Feb 4	8:04 pm	Wood	Dog	1974	Feb 4	1:00 pm	Wood	Tiger
1935	Feb 5	1:49 am	Wood	Pig	1975	Feb 4	6:59 pm	Wood	Rabbit
1936	Feb 5	7:30 am	Fire	Rat	1976	Feb 5	12:40 am	Fire	Dragon
1937	Feb 4	1:26 pm	Fire	Ox	1977	Feb 4	6:34 am	Fire	Snake
1938	Feb 4	7:15 pm	Earth	Tiger	1978	Feb 4	12:27 pm	Earth	Horse
1939	Feb 5	1:11 am	Earth	Rabbit	1979	Feb 4	6:13 pm	Earth	Sheep
1940	Feb 5	7:08 am	Metal	Dragon	1980	Feb 5	12:10 am	Metal	Monkey
1941	Feb 4	12:50 pm	Metal	Snake	1981	Feb 4	5:56 am	Metal	Rooster
1942	Feb 4	6:49 pm	Water	Horse	1982	Feb 4	11:46 am	Water	Dog
1943	Feb 5	12:41 am	Water	Sheep	1983	Feb 4	5:40 pm	Water	Pig
1944	Feb 5	6:23 am	Wood	Monkey	1984	Feb 4	11:19 pm	Wood	Rat
1945	Feb 4	12:20 pm	Wood	Rooster	1985	Feb 4	5:12 am	Wood	Ox
1946	Feb 4	6:05 pm	Fire	Dog	1986	Feb 4	11:09 am	Fire	Tiger
1947	Feb 4	11:55 pm	Fire	Pig	1987	Feb 4	4:52 pm	Fire	Rabbit
1948	Feb 5	5:43 am	Earth	Rat	1988	Feb 4	10:43 pm	Earth	Dragon
1949	Feb 4	11:23 am	Earth	Ox	1989	Feb 4	4:27 am	Earth	Snake
1950	Feb 4	5:21 pm	Metal	Tiger	1990	Feb 4	10:15 am	Metal	Horse
1951	Feb 4	11:14 pm	Metal	Rabbit	1991	Feb 4	4:08 pm	Metal	Sheep
1952	Feb 5	4:54 am	Water	Dragon	1992	Feb 4	9:48 pm	Water	Monkey
1953	Feb 4	10:46 am	Water	Snake	1993	Feb 4	3:38 am	Water	Rooster
1954	Feb 4	4:31 pm	Wood	Horse	1994	Feb 4	9:31 am	Wood	Dog
1955	Feb 4	10:18 pm	Wood	Sheep	1995	Feb 4	3:14 pm	Wood	Pig
1956	Feb 5	4:13 am	Fire	Monkey	1996	Feb 4	9:08 pm	Fire	Rat
1957	Feb 4	9:55 am	Fire	Rooster	1997	Feb 4	3:04 am	Fire	Ox
1958	Feb 4	3:50 pm	Earth	Dog	1998	Feb 4	8:53 am	Earth	Tiger
1959	Feb 4	9:43 pm	Earth	Pig	1999	Feb 4	2:42 pm	Earth	Rabbit
1960	Feb 5	3:23 am	Metal	Rat	2000	Feb 4	8:32 pm	Metal	Dragon
1961	Feb 4	9:23 am	Metal	Ox	2001	Feb 4	2:20 am	Metal	Snake
1962	Feb 4	3:18 pm	Water	Tiger	2002	Feb 4	8:08 am	Water	Horse
1963	Feb 4	9:08 pm	Water	Rabbit	2003	Feb 4	1:57 pm	Water	Sheep

Table 1

Solar Year	Date	Time Year Began	Phase	Animal
2004	Feb 4	7:46 pm	Wood	Monkey
2005	Feb 4	1:34 am	Wood	Rooster
2006	Feb 4	7:25 am	Fire	Dog
2007	Feb 4	1:14 pm	Fire	Pig
2008	Feb 4	7:03 pm	Earth	Rat
2009	Feb 4	12:52 am	Earth	Ox
2010	Feb 4	6:42 am	Metal	Tiger
2011	Feb 4	12:32 pm	Metal	Rabbit
2012	Feb 4	6:40 pm	Water	Dragon
2013	Feb 4	12:24 am	Water	Snake

Solar Year	Date	Time Year Began	Phase	Animal
2014	Feb 4	6:21 am	Wood	Horse
2015	Feb 4	12:09 pm	Wood	Sheep
2016	Feb 4	6:00 pm	Fire	Monkey
2017	Feb 3	11:49 pm	Fire	Rooster
2018	Feb 4	5:38 am	Earth	Dog
2019	Feb 4	11:28 am	Earth	Pig
2020	Feb 4	5:18 pm	Metal	Rat
2021	Feb 3	11:08 pm	Metal	Ox
2022	Feb 4	4:58 am	Water	Tiger
2023	Feb 4	10:47 am	Water	Rabbit

Considered individually, it takes 60 years for each phase's sign to reappear (5 phases × 12 branch animals = 60 years). The last complete cycle began in 1924 (the year of the wood rat), and ended in 1983 (the year of the water pig). The year 1984 ushered in a new cycle of 60 years, which will end in 2043.

Who Are Your Friends?

Many Chinese wouldn't think of proceeding with a ceremony, partnership, or anything else of importance without first seeking guidance from an astrologer. As a cursory check for compatibility, you too can determine the auspiciousness of a relationship.

Compatibility among the 12 animal signs.

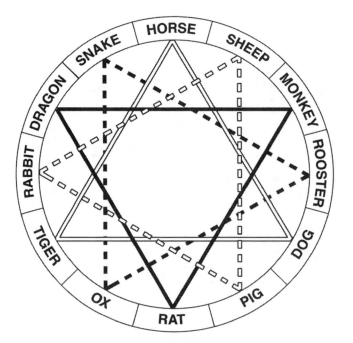

The signs that form a triangle are considered your most harmonious relationships (see the preceding figure). The rat-dragon-monkey are the best of friends, as are the ox-snake-rooster, the tiger-horse-dog, and the rabbit-sheep-pig. Upon closer examination, you'll notice each sign is four away from its compatible partner.

If you have some time on your hands, jot down the birth dates of your best friends and family members. You'll find that your affinity for your loved ones is more than a coincidence.

Who Are Your Foes?

For every two allies, you have one dangerous rival. You can determine yours by locating the animal directly opposite your sign. These are inauspicious relationships resulting in conflict, tension, and even disaster.

The animal signs that do not appear opposite each other and are not part of an affinity triad are considered compatible to varying degrees.

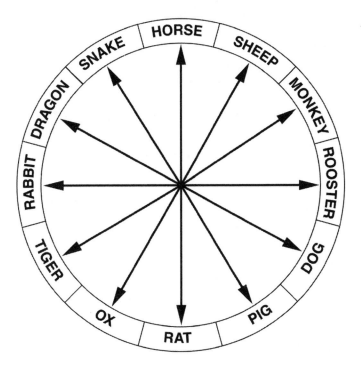

Incompatibility among the 12 animal signs.

Good Year/Bad Year

To check if the current year is auspicious for you—or whether the upcoming year will be—simply compare your phase sign to the year in question. For example, 2002 marks the year of the water horse. If your element is the same as, or productive to, water and your animal sign is compatible with a horse, then 2002 will not feature unfavorable qi for you. Yet, remember, this is a generality. Your year branch represents only one-eighth of your personality.

Feng Alert _____

If you're wondering why the phase associated with your personal trigram is different than the phase assigned to your animal sign, there is a reason. The personal trigram represents the East or West *Group* you belong to. The phase is the phase of the group, not the individual. The phase associated with your animal sign denotes the year of birth. However, the year phase also does not represent the individual. As you'll learn in the next chapter, the phase associated with the day stem characterizes a person.

Personality Profiles

Unlike other systems of Chinese fortune-telling where prediction and precautionary measures are the cornerstones, the system of the animal zodiac offers nothing more than general characteristics shared by people born under a specific sign. In the following sections, we'll discuss the aspects of each of the 12 animals in the Chinese zodiac.

The Industrious Rat

Famous Rats: William Shakespeare, Mozart, George Washington, Mata Hari, Jimmy Carter, Prince Charles, Doris Day, Sidney Poitier, Peggy Fleming, and Sean Penn

Everyone loves a rat. Charming, social, and quick-witted, those born during a rat year are generally popular people. Always on the move, rats find safety in numbers, giving credence to the phrases "the rat race" and "the rat pack." Rats also have good business acumen. Self-motivated, detail oriented, hard working, and overambitious, rats are able to accumulate wealth effortlessly. Their thrifty nature and shrewdness pays off during a recession. If you have a rat boss—beware! You'll have to do a lot of negotiating to make this rat part with his reserves. Rat women make excellent wives and mothers. Budgeting, bargaining, delegating duties, and organizing hoards of stuff are her best qualities. Negatively, the rat person loves to gossip and criticize. He is often self-obsessed, and greedy.

The Methodical Ox

Famous Oxen: Walt Disney, Emperor Hirohito, Richard Nixon, Vincent van Gogh, Margaret Thatcher, Robert Redford, Dustin Hoffman, Adolf Hitler, Charlie Chaplin, Saddam Hussein

The ox person succeeds by his own merits. Hard working, logical, meticulous, and tenacious, the ox can be trusted to get the job done. By nature, he is methodical, sticking to routines and tradition. It's almost impossible to get the ox to budge. His rigidity and militant style often result in an unapproachable and intimidating manner. At home, the ox man is the disciplinarian, the decision maker, and the rule setter. Disobeying an ox is cause for a rampage. Stay clear if he charges you! But, he is an excellent provider and his family will never do without. An ox wife excels on the job and in her domestic duties. The bills are paid, the checkbook is balanced, the dinner is made, the shirts are ironed, and the kids are tucked in. Although the ox lacks a sense of humor, his affairs governed by his head rather than his heart, he is an intensely loyal creature.

The Unpredictable Tiger

Famous Tigers: Beethoven, Ho Chi Minh, Queen Elizabeth II, Dwight D. Eisenhower, Hugh Hefner, Marilyn Monroe, Rudolf Nureyev, Stevie Wonder, Jodie Foster, Tom Cruise

Tigers are romantic, charismatic, and independent. They're also fiercely adventurous, moody, impulsive, and reckless. An ardent optimist, tigers live life to the fullest and on their terms! Although he gives 110 percent to whatever catches his attention at that moment, he is notoriously unreliable. The tiger man is brash, rash, and extremely possessive. If he sees you with his lady, look out. The tiger woman is vain and indecisive. She is playful with her children, but enforces good behavior. In all, tigers are unpredictable creatures.

The Lucky Rabbit

Famous Rabbits: Albert Einstein, Orson Welles, John Dillinger, David Rockefeller, King Olav V of Norway, Jane Seymour, Nicholas Cage, Fidel Castro, Francis Ford Coppola, Sting

Rabbits are affable, even-tempered, and diplomatic. Known for their discriminating taste, rabbits are refined, cultured, and a bit snobbish! They thrive on fine wine, gourmet food, designer clothes, and stimulating conversation. In business, a rabbit is a deft negotiator. His good judgment, sound advice, and graciousness will move him up the career track—fast. Because he has few enemies he rarely gets into trouble. Rabbits live by the Golden Rule and wouldn't think of burning a bridge. Lady rabbits are kind, considerate, and caring, but superficial.

The Dynamic Dragon

Famous Dragons: Joan of Arc, John Lennon, Jimmy Connors, Salvador Dali, Shirley Temple Black, Fred (Mr.) Rogers, Al Pacino, Pee Wee Herman, Christopher Reeves, Robin Williams

Master Class

In China, the dragon is the guardian of wealth and power. It is the symbol of the emperor. This is why there is an abundance of dragon artifacts throughout China and ethnic Chinese communities worldwide. If you have a keen eye, you'll notice that the dragon emblems used by the commoners have four claws on each paw. Only the emperor's emblems depict a dragon with five claws.

Among the 12 animals, dragons are the most fortunate. In fact, they're downright lucky! They're energetic, self-assured, grandiose, and egocentric. Dragons are the doers of the world. They don't sit around waiting for things to happen, they make them happen. You can always count on the no-nonsense dragon to take charge—and take risks. Their fiery enthusiasm and forceful nature rule. Dragons want things done their way. They demand perfection from themselves, and from others. Even though the dragon must have the last word, he is quick to forgive. Holding grudges will slow him down. While the dragon's magnanimous spirit draws a crowd, he has few close friends.

The Wise Snake

Famous Snakes: Picasso, Mao Tse-tung, J. Paul Getty, Brooke Shields, John F. Kennedy, Abraham Lincoln, Ryan O'Neal, Jacqueline Onassis, Oprah Winfrey

Those born under the sign of the snake are governed by their innate wisdom and intuition. Snake people think a lot. They mull things over before forming an opinion. They're intensely philosophical and make excellent listeners. Snake people are fast learners and will never make the same mistake twice. Highly skeptical and secretive creatures, snakes prefer to keep matters to themselves. They cherish their privacy, concealing their innermost wants and needs. Distrustful and somewhat unforgiving, they tend to be paranoid, even neurotic. Cross a snake and you can be sure he'll strike at you. Most of the world's beautiful and powerful people are snakes.

The Independent Horse

Famous Horses: Rembrandt, Leonid Brezhnev, Theodore Roosevelt, Franklin Roosevelt, Billy Graham, Laura Dern, Clint Eastwood, Roger Ebert, Paul McCartney, Barbra Streisand

A horse person loves freedom. Freedom to keep his own hours. Freedom from routine. And, freedom from anyone intending to rope him in. So, if you're married to a horse, give him space or he'll bolt. Incredibly industrious and self-reliant, horses love a challenge. Horses tend to be show-offs and self-centered, and will compliment to get a compliment. Finances are never an issue. Horses are hard-working and creative. Also, they are very headstrong, quick-minded, and don't tolerate those who are not "up to speed." Able to do 10 things at once, the horse abhors idleness. Horses are poor savers, thinking of the now and not the future.

Feng Alert

For unknown reasons, the Chinese dread the year of the fire horse, believing that children born under this sign will bring disaster to the family. In 1966, it was reported that many Asians opted to abort, causing the birthrate to plummet. The year of the fire horse returns in 2026.

The Sensitive Sheep

Famous Sheep: Andy Warhol, Andrew Carnegie, Michelangelo, Bruce Willis, Barbara Walters, Julia Roberts, John Wayne, Malcolm Forbes, Dan Rather, Robert DeNiro

Ultra-sensitive, altruistic, compliant, sincere, gentle: This is a sheep. Although they make excellent sounding boards, don't expect the sheep to help you solve your dilemma. They're there to listen only! Prone to stress and depression, sheep prefer tranquil environments. At their worst, sheep can be pessimistic, withdrawn, and lazy. Any kind of criticism will cause them to brood for days. In the end, their self-pity will give rise to encouragement and support from friends and colleagues. Don't let a sheep manage your finances. They overspend what they have due to their generous nature. Sheep individuals follow the crowd, seldom lead.

The Mischievous Monkey

Famous Monkeys: Leonardo da Vinci, Charles Dickens, Mick Jagger, Danny De Vito, Tom Hanks, Macauley Culkin, Elizabeth Taylor, Nelson Rockefeller, Princess Caroline of Monaco, Ted Kennedy

Insatiably curious, monkeys will try anything once. Eager to learn new skills, a monkey will enthusiastically perform it over and over until he's mastered it. This gives credence to the phrase, "Monkey see, monkey do." Also, monkeys are intensely competitive. They make it their mission to do things better than anyone else. Failure is not in the monkey's vocabulary. Extremely intelligent, clever, and innovative, the monkey person will excel in any field. He truly believes he is "the top banana." On the negative side, monkeys are difficult to trust. They tend to be too self-centered to care about anyone else.

The Meticulous Rooster

Famous Roosters: Sergei Rachmaninoff, Elton John, Dolly Parton, Gene Siskel, Prince Phillip, Quincy Jones, Joan Rivers, Pope Paul VI, Emperor Akihito, Katharine Hepburn

Cocky and pretentious, the rooster loves to strut his stuff, showing off his fine feathers. Roosters are proud creatures. Their world is black and white, void of gray. Brutally honest, forthright, and candid; ask a rooster his opinion and he'll tell you exactly what he thinks. When he wants your opinion, he'll give it to you! He is definitely not a diplomat. If the rooster could learn to sweeten his criticism, he'd be much better off. On the positive side, roosters are detail-oriented and perfectionists. Give a rooster your money and he will account for every penny. Also, roosters are extremely focused. Their organizational skills are superlative.

The Devoted Dog

Famous Dogs: Sir Winston Churchill, Harry Houdini, Elvis Presley, Cher, Bill Moyers, Kevin Bacon, George Gershwin, Andre Agassi, Donald Sutherland, Bill Clinton

A dog is truly a person's best friend. Compatible, compromising, loyal, and unprejudiced, dogs are there when you need them. The dog person is trustworthy and dutiful, making an excellent (albeit reluctant) leader. Contrary to what you may think, dogs form friendships slowly. First, they must check you out, watch, and wait. You must win their affection. For the most part, dogs are humble animals, caring little about money. While they can lavish you with unconditional devotion and love, when provoked, a dog can be fiercely mean-spirited, downright nasty. Of all the signs in the Chinese zodiac, the dog is the most likeable.

The Nurturing Pig

Famous Pigs: Al Capone, Prince Rainier, Ronald Reagan, Lucille Ball, Woody Allen, Alfred Hitchcock, Kevin Kline, Billy Crystal, Arnold Schwarzenegger, Hillary Clinton

Bottom line, pigs are the nicest people on the planet. With hearts of gold, they are honest, patient, and will take every measure to ensure your safety and comfort. A pig will remain your friend for life. But, pigs are often taken for granted. Only when they're not around do you realize how dependent you are on them. Naturally naive, pigs can be gullible, falling prey to charlatans and swindlers. In all, pigs of both genders are selfless, devoted, and loving. They just can't say "no." Because of their overzealous generosity, the pig person has little money. Nevertheless, he has enough, giving credence to the phrase, "the more you give, the more you shall receive."

These are the general characteristics of the 12 animals of the Chinese zodiac. If you're interested in a more detailed account, there are many books on the subject. One we suggest is Theodora Lau's *The Handbook of Chinese Horoscopes* (HarperCollins, 1991).

In the next chapter, you'll learn about The Four Pillars of Destiny, a method of Chinese astrology that can help you determine your lucky days, as well as the environments, careers, and colors best suited to your own qi.

The Least You Need to Know

- The 12 animals of the Chinese zodiac represent cycles of earthly qi.
- The Chinese zodiac system of astrology is superficial, but fun.
- Once you determine your animal sign, you'll know who are your animal friends and foes.
- This system is concerned more with personality profiles than fate prediction and prevention.

Chapter 22

The Four Pillars of Destiny, Part 1

In This Chapter

- ◆ Is our destiny determined by fate or free will?
- ◆ The Ten Heavenly Stems
- ◆ The Twelve Earthly Branches
- ◆ Assembling your life chart

There are two main schools of Chinese astrology. One is The Four Pillars of Destiny (Ziping Bazi), a system of analyzing "pillars" of our fate made manifest in the year, month, day, and hour of our birth. The other school is Purple Constellation Fate Computation, or Ziwei Doushu in Chinese. A bit more complex, this system analyzes anywhere from 36 to 157 stars in accordance with our birth information (and beyond our scope here).

In this chapter, you'll learn the former, and more popular, method of fate calculation, The Four Pillars of Destiny. You'll learn how to assemble your own chart just like a Chinese astrologer would have done over 1,000 years ago. Don't be intimidated by the seemingly complicated charts. They're easy to read.

We have a lot to do, so let's get busy!

How Free Is Free Will?

We all know what free will means. It's what sets us apart from any other living, breathing thing on earth. Free will allows us to make choices, to actively participate in building our life's path. But are we totally free? Of course not. No one has absolute free will. Not even America—"the land of the free." Physical limitations and psychological conditioning restrict most of us from making choices that are harmful, or socially and morally unacceptable. For example, we have the freedom to jump off a cliff. But would you want to? Also, we have the freedom to say just about anything. It's our constitutional right. But would you want to? Do you really want to tell your best friend that you hate her new hairdo? Do you really want to tell your spouse he or she is not your soul mate? We think not.

Clearly, our decisions in some measure reflect the belief systems of our parents, society, and country. But our decisions are also influenced by our character or personality, the part of us that is largely inexplicable. Some believe our fundamental character is determined by our genetic composition. Some believe God or a Higher Power grants us our innate character, talents, and circumstances. Then there's reincarnation, the belief that cause and effect, or karma, determines the outcome of our lives. Basically, reincarnation holds that we are continually reborn until we achieve our full potential.

The Chinese believe that our destiny is a blend of fate and free will, a harmony of heavenly, earthly, and human qi. They believe our character is a by-product of our fate. Our fate is determined by the first breath we take. Literally, we inhale our destiny, a composite of qi present at that exact moment.

What Is The Four Pillars of Destiny?

Simply, *The Four Pillars of Destiny* is a method of calculating and interpreting the five phase components of the qi you inhaled at birth. Like feng shui, it is an accurate system of predicting possibilities. For example, the chart you will soon create may indicate a potential for great wealth, thus creating an innate urge to succeed. But how you act on this urge is where your free choice comes into play. In other words, regardless of what your chart may indicate, free will helps to determine the outcome of your fate.

Wise Words

Called Bazi ("eight characters") in Chinese, **The Four Pillars of Destiny** is a method of calculating and interpreting the five phase elements present at your birth. Each pillar represents a year, month, day, and hour. The Four Pillars of Destiny measures probabilities, not certainties, of your life's path.

So, if good fortune prevails in your chart, waiting for Publisher's Clearinghouse to come knocking at your door isn't an answer. The onus is on you to act on your inborn talents and desires—to force the hand, so to speak. If you are blessed with advantageous possibility, it's up to you to bring it to fruition!

What do the "pillars" of The Four Pillars of Destiny mean? Well, each pillar is actually a time component. One pillar represents the year, one the month, one the day, and one the hour. Each time component describes the five-phase element structure present at the moment of your birth (when you took your first, qi-inspired breath). The relationship and position of each phase helps to determine your probable life path. The following chart shows the Four Pillars, which you'll be assembling later on in this chapter.

	Hour	Day	Month	Year
Stem	Yi	Yi	Jia	Xin
Branch	You	Wei	Wu	Chou
Stem Phase	Wood	Wood	Wood	Metal
Branch Phase	Metal	Earth	Fire	Earth

An example of The Four Pillars of Destiny life chart.

Notice that each pillar is divided into a stem-branch component. Actually, stem is short for Ten Heavenly Stems, and branch is short for Twelve Earthly Branches, which we'll discuss a little later in this chapter.

Master Class

There's a fundamental difference between Western and Chinese astrology. Western astrology considers the positions of the planets, sun, and moon at your birth—a truly astral method. Chinese astrology is concerned with types of qi (heavenly, earthly, and human) and, therefore, isn't exclusively astral.

Time, Chinese Style

Before we can get into the mechanics, let's take a moment to talk about, well, time. As we mentioned in Chapter 14, "The Flying Stars, Part 2," Westerners view time as linear. The year begins on January 1 and ends on December 31. The month begins on the first and generally ends on the thirtieth. The day begins and ends at midnight. Times proceeds along a straight line.

The Chinese, on the other hand, think cyclically. Time is a continuous spiral. What goes around, comes around. Time does repeat itself—sort of.

The Ten Heavenly Stems

How did the Chinese develop their concept of time? As the story goes, the legendary Huang Di, known as the Yellow Emperor (2697–2597 B.C.E.), ordered a wise man named Da Nao to invent a system of recording time. To achieve this, Da Nao set about observing the intricacies of the five phases of qi, how they transformed over the course of the year. From this observation, Da Nao developed what he called the *Ten Heavenly Stems*, shown in Table 1.

Why are the stems "heavenly"? Harkening back to Chapter 4, "Qi Wiz! It's Life's Force!" the Chinese people use the word "heaven" to mean "time." Hence, the heavenly stems record how qi changes with time.

Wise Words

The **Ten Heavenly Stems** (Tian Gan) represent how the five phases alter with the passage of a year. One type of qi undergoes growth, then declines while yielding to another type. The growing stage is yang qi (as described in Chapter 5, "The Principle of Yin and Yang," yang is associated with the land of the living, summer, heat). The declining stage, yin qi is related to the realm of the dead, winter, cold.

The Ten Heavenly Stems.

Table 1

PINYIN	NUMBER	PHASE	POLARITY
Jia	1	Wood	Yang
Yi	2	Wood	Yin
Bing	3	Fire	Yang
Ding	4	Fire	Yin
Wu	5	Earth	Yang
Ji	6	Earth	Yin
Geng	7	Metal	Yang
Xin	8	Metal	Yin
Ren	9	Water	Yang
Gui	10	Water	Yin

The Twelve Earthly Branches

Just as the words "heaven" and "time" are interchangeable, so, too, are the words "earth" and "space." As you learned in the previous chapter, the *Twelve Earthly Branches* denote the location where different qi prevails on earth. In the north, water qi prevails. In the east, wood qi prevails. Fire qi prevails in the south, and metal qi in the west. Although this idea is illustrated in Chapter 21, "Introducing the Twelve Animals of the Chinese Zodiac," it does not include the branch names and numbers as indicated in the following Table 2.

Table 2

PINYIN	NUMBER	ANIMAL	PHASE	POLARITY
Zi	1	Rat	Water	Yang
Chou	2	Ox	Earth	Yin
Yin	3	Tiger	Wood	Yang
Mao	4	Rabbit	Wood	Yin
Chen	5	Dragon	Earth	Yang
Si	6	Snake	Fire	Yin
Wu	7	Horse	Fire	Yang
Wei	8	Sheep	Earth	Yin
Shen	9	Monkey	Metal	Yang
You	10	Rooster	Metal	Yin
Xu	11	Dog	Earth	Yang
Hai	12	Pig	Water	Yin

The Twelve Earthly Branches.

We won't be using the zodiac animals that we talked about in the previous chapter in the Four Pillars calculations. We've included them here merely for amusement. After all, Chinese zodiac astrology is derived, in some measure, from the Twelve Earthly Branches—each animal being associated with a branch.

The Cycle of Sixty

The Ten Heavenly Stems and the Twelve Earthly Branches combine into a *Cycle of Sixty* stem-branch pairs, shown in the following Table 3. If you imagine two gears—one with 10 teeth and the other with 12 teeth—and allow them to rotate and interlock, the gear with 10 teeth would complete its rotation before the gear with 12 teeth. If you mark the first tooth of each gear and begin the rotation, you'll note that it takes six rotations of the 10 and five rotations of the 12 before the first teeth of the respective gears are aligned as they were at the start. Thus, the sixtieth interlocking will start the repeating of the cycle. Therefore, there are 60 possible pairs when the stems and branches are combined.

Beginning with Jia Zi, the year 2697 B.C.E. marked the first of the 60-year, or 60-stem-branch cycle. Why does the cycle begin with Jia (wood) Zi (water)? This is because the branch (Zi/water) is at the end of yin. The beginning of yang is marked by the growth of wood. It is a time of birth and renewal. What cycle are we currently in, you ask? You'll find out in a moment.

Wise Words

The **Cycle of Sixty** represents all possible combinations (60) of the Ten Heavenly Stems and Twelve Earthly Branches. The year 2697 B.C.E. marked the first of the 60-year, or 60-stem-branch cycle.

Table 3

NUMBERS		STEM/BRANCH	PHASE	POLARITY	NUMBERS		STEM/BRANCH	PHASE	POLARITY
1	S1B1	Jia Zi	Wood Water	Yang	31	S1B7	Jia Wu	Wood Fire	Yang
2	S2B2	Yi Chou	Wood Earth	Yin	32	S2B8	Yi Wei	Wood Earth	Yin
3	S3B3	Bing Yin	Fire Wood	Yang	33	S3B9	Bing Shen	Fire Metal	Yang
4	S4B4	Ding Mao	Fire Wood	Yin	34	S4B10	Ding You	Fire Metal	Yin
5	S5B5	Wu Chen	Earth Earth	Yang	35	S5B11	Wu Xu	Earth Earth	Yang
6	S6B6	Ji Si	Earth Fire	Yin	36	S6B12	Ji Hai	Earth Water	Yin
7	S7B7	Geng Wu	Metal Fire	Yang	37	S7B1	Geng Zi	Metal Water	Yang
8	S8B8	Xin Wei	Metal Earth	Yin	38	S8B2	Xin Chou	Metal Earth	Yin
9	S9B9	Ren Shen	Water Metal	Yang	39	S9B3	Ren Yin	Water Wood	Yang
10	S10B10	Gui You	Water Metal	Yin	40	S10B4	Gui Mao	Water Wood	Yin
11	S1B11	Jia Xu	Wood Earth	Yang	41	S1B5	Jia Chen	Wood Earth	Yang
12	S2B12	Yi Hai	Wood Water	Yin	42	S2B6	Yi Si	Wood Fire	Yin
13	S3B1	Bing Zi	Fire Water	Yang	43	S3B7	Bing Wu	Fire Fire	Yang
14	S4B2	Ding Chou	Fire Earth	Yin	44	S4B8	Ding Wei	Fire Earth	Yin
15	S5B3	Wu Yin	Earth Wood	Yang	45	S5B9	Wu Shen	Earth Metal	Yang
16	S6B4	Ji Mao	Earth Wood	Yin	46	S6B10	Ji You	Earth Metal	Yin
17	S7B5	Geng Chen	Metal Earth	Yang	47	S7B11	Geng Xu	Metal Earth	Yang
18	S8B6	Xin Si	Metal Earth	Yin	48	S8B12	Xin Hai	Metal Water	Yin
19	S9B7	Ren Wu	Water Fire	Yang	49	S9B1	Ren Zi	Water Water	Yang
20	S10B8	Gui Wei	Water Earth	Yin	50	S10B2	Gui Chou	Water Earth	Yin
21	S1B9	Jia Shen	Wood Metal	Yang	51	S1B3	Jia Yin	Wood Wood	Yang
22	S2B10	Yi You	Wood Metal	Yin	52	S2B4	Yi Mao	Wood Wood	Yin
23	S3B11	Bing Xu	Fire Earth	Yang	53	S3B5	Bing Chen	Fire Earth	Yang
24	S4B12	Ding Hai	Fire Water	Yin	54	S4B6	Ding Si	Fire Fire	Yin
25	S5B1	Wu Zi	Earth Water	Yang	55	S5B7	Wu Wu	Earth Fire	Yang
26	S6B2	Ji Chou	Earth Earth	Yin	56	S6B8	Ji Wei	Earth Earth	Yin
27	S7B3	Geng Yin	Metal Wood	Yang	57	S7B9	Geng Shen	Metal Metal	Yang
28	S8B4	Xin Mao	Metal Wood	Yin	58	S8B10	Xin You	Metal Metal	Yin
29	S9B5	Ren Chen	Water Earth	Yang	59	S9B11	Ren Xu	Water Earth	Yang
30	S10B6	Gui Si	Water Fire	Yin	60	S10B12	Gui Hai	Water Water	Yin

The Cycle of Sixty.

Calculating Your Four Pillars

Determining your Four Pillars is as easy as one-two-three-four. We've provided an empty chart for you to fill out at the end of the chapter. All you have to do is plug in the information. If you'd rather, you may write each pillar's components on a separate sheet of paper, transferring the information to the chart at the end. This may save time flipping back and forth between pages.

The Year Pillar

To determine your year pillar, locate your birth year on Table 4. Remember, if you were born between January 1 and February 2, you must use the year prior to your actual birth year. If you were born on February, 3, February 4, or February 5, you must look in the "Time" column to determine your Chinese birth year. For example, if you were born on February 4, 1970, at 3:00 P.M., your birth year is 1970. But if you were born at 1:00 P.M., you would use 1969, as February 4 did not begin yet.

Let's take an example to help you assemble your chart. A woman was born on July 1, 1961, at 7:45 P.M. As you can see in Table 4, the year 1961 is a Xin Chou year. Xin (stem) represents the metal phase; Chou (branch), the earth phase. How do we know this? Just consult the Ten Heavenly Stems and Twelve Earthly Branches tables that we presented a little earlier. Although the yin and yang polarity is a consideration, for your purposes, we will not be fussing with this.

Thus, your chart should look something like this:

	Hour	**Day**	**Month**	**Year**
	7:45p	1	July	1961
Stem				Xin
Branch				Chou
Stem Phase				Metal
Branch Phase				Earth

Table 4

YEAR	DATE	TIME	STEM / BRANCH	YEAR	DATE	TIME	STEM / BRANCH
1924	February 5	9:50a	Jia Zi	1964	February 5	3:05a	Jia Chen
1925	February 4	3:37p	Yi Chou	1965	February 4	8:46a	Yi Si
1926	February 4	9:39p	Bing Yin	1966	February 4	2:38p	Bing Wu
1927	February 5	3:31a	Ding Mao	1967	February 4	8:31p	Ding Wei
1928	February 5	9:17a	Wu Chen	1968	February 5	2:08a	Wu Shen
1929	February 4	3:09p	Ji Si	1969	February 4	7:59a	Ji You
1930	February 4	8:52p	Geng Wu	1970	February 4	1:46p	Geng Xu
1931	February 5	2:41a	Xin Wei	1971	February 4	7:26p	Xin Hai
1932	February 5	8:30a	Ren Shen	1972	February 5	1:20a	Ren Zi
1933	February 4	2:10p	Gui You	1973	February 4	7:04a	Gui Chou
1934	February 4	8:04p	Jia Xu	1974	February 4	1:00p	Jia Yin
1935	February 5	1:49a	Yi Hai	1975	February 4	6:59p	Yi Mao
1936	February 5	7:30a	Bing Zi	1976	February 5	12:40a	Bing Chen
1937	February 4	1:26p	Ding Chou	1977	February 4	6:34a	Ding Si
1938	February 4	7:15p	Wu Yin	1978	February 4	12:27p	Wu Wu
1939	February 5	1:11a	Ji Mao	1979	February 4	6:13p	Ji Wei
1940	February 5	7:08a	Geng Chen	1980	February 5	12:10a	Geng Shen
1941	February 4	12:50p	Xin Si	1981	February 4	5:56a	Xin You
1942	February 4	6:49p	Ren Wu	1982	February 4	11:46a	Ren Xu
1943	February 5	12:41a	Gui Wei	1983	February 4	5:40p	Gui Hai
1944	February 5	6:23a	Jia Shen	1984	February 4	11:19p	Jia Zi
1945	February 4	12:20p	Yi You	1985	February 4	5:12a	Yi Chou
1946	February 4	6:05p	Bing Xu	1986	February 4	11:09a	Bing Yin
1947	February 4	11:55p	Ding Hai	1987	February 4	4:52p	Ding Mao
1948	February 5	5:43a	Wu Zi	1988	February 4	10:43p	Wu Chen
1949	February 4	11:23a	Ji Chou	1989	February 4	4:27a	Ji Si
1950	February 4	5:21p	Geng Yin	1990	February 4	10:15a	Geng Wu
1951	February 4	11:14p	Xin Mao	1991	February 4	4:08p	Xin Wei
1952	February 5	4:54a	Ren Chen	1992	February 4	9:48p	Ren Shen
1953	February 4	10:46a	Gui Si	1993	February 4	3:38a	Gui You
1954	February 4	4:31p	Jia Wu	1994	February 4	9:31a	Jia Xu
1955	February 4	10:18p	Yi Wei	1995	February 4	3:14p	Yi Hai
1956	February 5	4:13a	Bing Shen	1996	February 4	9:08p	Bing Zi
1957	February 4	9:55a	Ding You	1997	February 4	3:04a	Ding Chou
1958	February 4	3:50p	Wu Xu	1998	February 4	8:53a	Wu Yin
1959	February 4	9:43p	Ji Hai	1999	February 4	2:42p	Ji Mao
1960	February 5	3:23a	Geng Zi	2000	February 4	8:32p	Geng Chen
1961	February 4	9:23a	Xin Chou	2001	February 4	2:20a	Xin Si
1962	February 4	3:18p	Ren Yin	2002	February 4	8:08a	Ren Wu
1963	February 4	9:08p	Gui Mao	2003	February 4	1:57p	Gui Wei

Table 4

YEAR	DATE	TIME	STEM / BRANCH	YEAR	DATE	TIME	STEM / BRANCH
2004	February 4	7:46p	Jia Shen	2014	February 4	6:21a	Jia Wu
2005	February 4	1:34a	Yi You	2015	February 4	12:09p	Yi Wei
2006	February 4	7:25a	Bing Xu	2016	February 4	6:00p	Bing Shen
2007	February 4	1:14p	Ding Hai	2017	February 4	11:49p	Ding You
2008	February 4	7:03p	Wu Zi	2018	February 4	5:38a	Wu Xu
2009	February 4	12:52a	Ji Chou	2019	February 4	11:28a	Ji Hai
2010	February 4	6:42a	Geng Yin	2020	February 4	5:18p	Geng Zi
2011	February 4	12:32p	Xin Mao	2021	February 4	11:08p	Xin Chou
2012	February 4	6:40p	Ren Chen	2022	February 4	4:58a	Ren Yin
2013	February 4	12:31a	Gui Si	2023	February 4	10:47a	Gui Mao

The year pillar.

The Month Pillar

To determine your month components, simply find your Western birth year in Table 5. Then locate your birth month. Continuing with our example, if you were born on July 1, 1961, at 7:45 P.M., find the row of months corresponding to 1961. Now follow your finger to the fifth Chinese solar month—Jia (stem) Wu (branch). Notice that Jia Wu begins on June 6 and ends on July 6 (July 7 marks the beginning of Yi Wei, the sixth solar month). The example's July 1 birth date falls in the fifth Chinese solar month. What do the times mean?

Corresponding to Beijing time (120°E), they indicate the exact time the month began. For example, Jia Wu began on June 6 at 6:46 A.M. If you were born on this date (or another date where the month changed) and do not live in northern China, you must compute the time of the beginning of the month from Beijing time to the time at your birth place to determine which solar month you belong to. For example, June 6 at 6:46 A.M. in Beijing is June 5 at 10:46 P.M. in London (0°) and June 5 at 2:46 P.M. in Los Angeles (120°W). These people would use Gui Si, the fourth solar month, as their birth month. Get the idea? Again, you only have to do the conversion if you were born on the first day of the solar month: February 4, March 6, April 5, May 6, 1961, for example).

Now, consulting Tables 1 (the Ten Heavenly Stems) and 2 (the Twelve Earthly Branches), determine the example's phases corresponding to her birth month, Jia Wu.

Table 5

1924 Jia Zi

1ST MONTH	2ND MONTH	3RD MONTH	4TH MONTH	5TH MONTH	6TH MONTH	7TH MONTH	8TH MONTH	9TH MONTH	10TH MONTH	11TH MONTH	12TH MONTH
Bing Yin 2/5 - 9:50a	Ding Mao 3/6 - 4:13a	Wu Chen 4/5 - 9:34a	Ji Si 5/6 - 3:26a	Geng Wu 6/6 - 8:02a	Xin Wei 7/7 - 6:30p	Ren Shen 8/8 - 4:13a	Gui You 9/8 - 6:46a	Jia Xu 10/8 - 9:53a	Yi Hai 11/8 - 12:30a	Bing Zi 12/7 - 4:54p	Ding Chou 1/6 - 3:54a

1925 Yi Chou

1ST MONTH	2ND MONTH	3RD MONTH	4TH MONTH	5TH MONTH	6TH MONTH	7TH MONTH	8TH MONTH	9TH MONTH	10TH MONTH	11TH MONTH	12TH MONTH
Wu Yin 2/4 - 3:37p	Ji Mao 3/6 - 10:00a	Geng Chen 4/5 - 3:23p	Xin Si 5/6 - 9:18a	Ren Wu 6/6 - 1:57p	Gui Wei 7/8 - 12:25a	Jia Shen 8/8 - 10:08a	Yi You 9/8 - 12:40p	Bing Xu 10/9 - 3:48p	Ding Hai 11/8 - 6:27a	Wu Zi 12/7 - 10:53p	Ji Chou 1/6 - 9:55a

1926 Bing Yin

1ST MONTH	2ND MONTH	3RD MONTH	4TH MONTH	5TH MONTH	6TH MONTH	7TH MONTH	8TH MONTH	9TH MONTH	10TH MONTH	11TH MONTH	12TH MONTH
Geng Yin 2/4 - 9:39p	Xin Mao 3/5 - 4:00p	Ren Chen 4/5 - 9:19p	Gui Si 5/6 - 3:09p	Jia Wu 6/6 - 7:42p	Yi Wei 7/8 - 6:06a	Bing Shen 8/8 - 3:45p	Ding You 9/8 - 6:16p	Wu Xu 10/9 - 9:25a	Ji Hai 11/8 - 12:08p	Geng Zi 12/8 - 4:39a	Xin Chou 1/6 - 3:45p

1927 Ding Mao

1ST MONTH	2ND MONTH	3RD MONTH	4TH MONTH	5TH MONTH	6TH MONTH	7TH MONTH	8TH MONTH	9TH MONTH	10TH MONTH	11TH MONTH	12TH MONTH
Ren Yin 2/5 - 3:31a	Gui Mao 3/6 - 9:51p	Jia Chen 4/6 - 3:07a	Yi Si 5/6 - 8:54p	Bing Wu 6/7 - 1:25a	Ding Wei 7/8 - 11:50a	Wu Shen 8/8 - 9:32p	Ji You 9/9 - 12:06a	Geng Xu 10/9 - 3:16p	Xin Hai 11/8 - 5:57p	Ren Zi 12/8 - 10:27a	Gui Chou 1/6 - 9:32p

1928 Wu Chen

1ST MONTH	2ND MONTH	3RD MONTH	4TH MONTH	5TH MONTH	6TH MONTH	7TH MONTH	8TH MONTH	9TH MONTH	10TH MONTH	11TH MONTH	12TH MONTH
Jia Yin 2/5 - 9:17a	Yi Mao 3/6 - 3:38a	Bing Chen 4/5 - 8:55a	Ding Si 5/6 - 2:44a	Wu Wu 6/6 - 7:18a	Ji Wei 7/7 - 5:45p	Geng Shen 8/8 - 3:28a	Xin You 9/8 - 6:02a	Ren Xu 10/8 - 9:11p	Gui Hai 11/7 - 11:50p	Jia Zi 12/7 - 4:18p	Yi Chou 1/6 - 3:23a

1929 Ji Si

1ST MONTH	2ND MONTH	3RD MONTH	4TH MONTH	5TH MONTH	6TH MONTH	7TH MONTH	8TH MONTH	9TH MONTH	10TH MONTH	11TH MONTH	12TH MONTH
Bing Yin 2/4 - 3:09p	Ding Mao 3/6 - 9:32a	Wu Chen 4/5 - 2:52p	Ji Si 5/6 - 8:41a	Geng Wu 6/6 - 1:11p	Xin Wei 7/7 - 11:32p	Ren Shen 8/8 - 9:09a	Gui You 9/8 - 11:40a	Jia Xu 10/9 - 2:48a	Yi Hai 11/8 - 5:28a	Bing Zi 12/7 - 9:57p	Ding Chou 1/6 - 9:03a

1930 Geng Wu

1ST MONTH	2ND MONTH	3RD MONTH	4TH MONTH	5TH MONTH	6TH MONTH	7TH MONTH	8TH MONTH	9TH MONTH	10TH MONTH	11TH MONTH	12TH MONTH
Wu Yin 2/4 - 8:52p	Ji Mao 3/6 - 3:17p	Geng Chen 4/5 - 8:38p	Xin Si 5/6 - 2:28p	Ren Wu 6/6 - 6:58p	Gui Wei 7/8 - 5:20a	Jia Shen 8/8 - 2:58p	Yi You 9/9 - 5:29p	Bing Xu 10/9 - 8:38p	Ding Hai 11/8 - 11:21a	Wu Zi 12/8 - 3:51a	Ji Chou 1/6 - 2:56p

1931 Xin Wei

1ST MONTH	2ND MONTH	3RD MONTH	4TH MONTH	5TH MONTH	6TH MONTH	7TH MONTH	8TH MONTH	9TH MONTH	10TH MONTH	11TH MONTH	12TH MONTH
Geng Yin 2/5 - 2:41a	Xin Mao 3/6 - 9:03p	Ren Chen 4/6 - 2:21a	Gui Si 5/6 - 8:10p	Jia Wu 6/7 - 12:42a	Yi Wei 7/8 - 11:06a	Bing Shen 8/8 - 8:45p	Ding You 9/8 - 11:18p	Wu Xu 10/9 - 2:27p	Ji Hai 11/8 - 5:10p	Geng Zu 12/8 - 9:41a	Xin Chou 1/6 - 8:46p

1932 Ren Shen

1ST MONTH	2ND MONTH	3RD MONTH	4TH MONTH	5TH MONTH	6TH MONTH	7TH MONTH	8TH MONTH	9TH MONTH	10TH MONTH	11TH MONTH	12TH MONTH
Ren Yin 2/5 - 8:30a	Gui Mao 3/6 - 2:50a	Jia Chen 4/5 - 8:07a	Yi Si 5/6 - 1:55a	Bing Wu 6/6 - 6:28a	Ding Wei 7/7 - 4:53p	Wu Shen 8/8 - 2:32a	Ji You 9/8 - 5:03a	Geng Xu 10/8 - 8:10p	Xin Hai 11/7 - 10:50p	Ren Zi 12/7 - 3:19p	Gui Chou 1/6 - 2:24a

1933 Gui You

1ST MONTH	2ND MONTH	3RD MONTH	4TH MONTH	5TH MONTH	6TH MONTH	7TH MONTH	8TH MONTH	9TH MONTH	10TH MONTH	11TH MONTH	12TH MONTH
Jia Yin 2/4 - 2:10p	Yi Mao 3/6 - 8:32a	Bing Chen 4/5 - 1:51p	Ding Si 5/6 - 7:42a	Wu Wu 6/6 - 12:18p	Ji Wei 7/7 - 10:45p	Geng Shen 8/8 - 8:26a	Xin You 9/8 - 10:58a	Ren Xu 10/9 - 2:08a	Gui Hai 11/8 - 4:44a	Jia Zi 12/7 - 9:12p	Yi Chou 1/6 - 8:17a

1934 Jia Xu

1ST MONTH	2ND MONTH	3RD MONTH	4TH MONTH	5TH MONTH	6TH MONTH	7TH MONTH	8TH MONTH	9TH MONTH	10TH MONTH	11TH MONTH	12TH MONTH
Bing Yin 2/4 - 8:04p	Ding Mao 3/6 - 2:27p	Wu Chen 4/5 - 7:44p	Ji Si 5/6 - 1:31p	Geng Wu 6/6 - 6:02p	Xin Wei 7/8 - 4:25a	Ren Shen 8/8 - 2:04p	Gui You 9/8 - 4:37p	Jia Xu 10/9 - 7:45a	Yi Hai 11/8 - 10:27a	Bing Zi 12/8 - 2:57a	Ding Chou 1/6 - 2:03p

1935 Yi Hai

1ST MONTH	2ND MONTH	3RD MONTH	4TH MONTH	5TH MONTH	6TH MONTH	7TH MONTH	8TH MONTH	9TH MONTH	10TH MONTH	11TH MONTH	12TH MONTH
Wu Yin 2/5 - 1:49a	Ji Mao 3/6 - 8:11p	Geng Chen 4/6 - 1:27a	Xin Si 5/6 - 7:12p	Ren Wu 6/6 - 11:42p	Gui Wei 7/8 - 10:06a	Jia Shen 8/8 - 7:48p	Yi You 9/8 - 10:25p	Bing Xu 10/9 - 1:36p	Ding Hai 11/8 - 4:18p	Wu Zi 12/8 - 8:45a	Ji Chou 1/6 - 7:47p

1936 Bing Zi

1ST MONTH	2ND MONTH	3RD MONTH	4TH MONTH	5TH MONTH	6TH MONTH	7TH MONTH	8TH MONTH	9TH MONTH	10TH MONTH	11TH MONTH	12TH MONTH
Geng Yin 2/5 - 7:30a	Xin Mao 3/6 - 1:50a	Ren Chen 4/5 - 7:07a	Gui Si 5/6 - 12:57a	Jia Wu 6/6 - 5:31a	Yi Wei 7/7 - 3:59p	Bing Shen 8/8 - 1:43a	Ding You 9/8 - 4:21a	Wu Xu 10/8 - 7:33a	Ji Hai 11/7 - 10:15p	Geng Zi 12/7 - 2:43p	Xin Chou 1/6 - 1:44a

1937 Ding Chou

1ST MONTH	2ND MONTH	3RD MONTH	4TH MONTH	5TH MONTH	6TH MONTH	7TH MONTH	8TH MONTH	9TH MONTH	10TH MONTH	11TH MONTH	12TH MONTH
Ren Yin 2/4 - 1:26p	Gui Mao 3/5 - 7:45a	Jia Chen 4/5 - 1:02p	Yi Si 5/6 - 6:51a	Bing Wu 6/6 - 11:23a	Ding Wei 7/7 - 9:46p	Wu Shen 8/8 - 7:26a	Ji You 9/8 - 10:00a	Geng Xu 10/9 - 1:11a	Xin Hai 11/8 - 3:46a	Ren Zi 12/7 - 8:27p	Gui Chou 1/6 - 7:32a

1938 Wu Yin

1ST MONTH	2ND MONTH	3RD MONTH	4TH MONTH	5TH MONTH	6TH MONTH	7TH MONTH	8TH MONTH	9TH MONTH	10TH MONTH	11TH MONTH	12TH MONTH
Jia Yin 2/4 - 7:15p	Yi Mao 3/6 - 1:34p	Bing Chen 4/5 - 6:49p	Ding Si 5/6 - 12:36p	Wu Wu 6/6 - 5:07p	Ji Wei 7/8 - 3:32a	Geng Shen 8/8 - 1:13p	Xin You 9/8 - 3:49p	Ren Xu 10/9 - 7:02a	Gui Hai 11/8 - 9:49a	Jia Zi 12/8 - 2:23a	Yi Chou 1/6 - 1:23p

1939 Ji Mao

1ST MONTH	2ND MONTH	3RD MONTH	4TH MONTH	5TH MONTH	6TH MONTH	7TH MONTH	8TH MONTH	9TH MONTH	10TH MONTH	11TH MONTH	12TH MONTH
Bing Yin 2/5 - 1:11a	Ding Mao 3/6 - 7:27p	Wu Chen 4/6 - 12:38a	Ji Si 5/6 - 6:21p	Geng Wu 6/6 - 10:52p	Xin Wei 7/8 - 9:19a	Ren Shen 8/8 - 7:04p	Gui You 9/8 - 9:42p	Jia Xu 10/9 - 12:57p	Yi Hai 11/8 - 3:40p	Bing Zi 12/8 - 8:18a	Ding Chou 1/6 - 7:24p

1940 Geng Chen

1ST MONTH	2ND MONTH	3RD MONTH	4TH MONTH	5TH MONTH	6TH MONTH	7TH MONTH	8TH MONTH	9TH MONTH	10TH MONTH	11TH MONTH	12TH MONTH
Wu Yin 2/5 - 7:08a	Ji Mao 3/6 - 1:24a	Geng Chen 4/5 - 6:35a	Xin Si 5/6 - 12:16a	Ren Wu 6/6 - 4:44a	Gui Wei 7/7 - 3:08p	Jia Shen 8/8 - 12:52a	Yi You 9/8 - 3:30a	Bing Xu 10/8 - 6:43p	Ding Hai 11/7 - 9:27p	Wu Zi 12/7 - 1:58p	Ji Chou 1/6 - 1:04a

1941 Xin Si

1ST MONTH	2ND MONTH	3RD MONTH	4TH MONTH	5TH MONTH	6TH MONTH	7TH MONTH	8TH MONTH	9TH MONTH	10TH MONTH	11TH MONTH	12TH MONTH
Geng Yin 2/4 - 12:50p	Xin Mao 3/6 - 7:10a	Ren Chen 4/5 - 12:25p	Gui Si 5/6 - 6:10a	Jia Wu 6/6 - 10:40a	Yi Wei 7/7 - 9:03p	Bing Shen 8/8 - 6:46a	Ding You 9/8 - 9:24a	Wu Xu 10/9 - 12:39a	Ji Hai 11/8 - 3:25a	Geng Zi 12/7 - 7:57p	Xin Chou 1/6 - 7:03a

1942 Ren Wu

1ST MONTH	2ND MONTH	3RD MONTH	4TH MONTH	5TH MONTH	6TH MONTH	7TH MONTH	8TH MONTH	9TH MONTH	10TH MONTH	11TH MONTH	12TH MONTH
Ren Yin 2/4 - 6:49p	Gui Mao 3/6 - 1:10p	Jia Chen 4/5 - 6:24p	Yi Si 5/6 - 12:07p	Bing Wu 6/6 - 4:37p	Ding Wei 7/8 - 2:52a	Wu Shen 8/8 - 12:31p	Ji You 9/8 - 3:07p	Geng Xu 10/9 - 6:22a	Xin Hai 11/8 - 9:12a	Ren Zi 12/8 - 1:47a	Gui Chou 1/6 - 12:55p

1943 Gui Wei

1ST MONTH	2ND MONTH	3RD MONTH	4TH MONTH	5TH MONTH	6TH MONTH	7TH MONTH	8TH MONTH	9TH MONTH	10TH MONTH	11TH MONTH	12TH MONTH
Jia Yin 2/5 - 12:41a	Yi Mao 3/6 - 6:59p	Bing Chen 4/6 - 12:12a	Ding Si 5/6 - 5:54p	Wu Wu 6/6 - 10:19p	Ji Wei 7/8 - 8:39a	Geng Shen 8/8 - 6:19p	Xin You 9/8 - 8:56p	Ren Xu 10/9 - 12:11p	Gui Hai 11/8 - 2:59p	Jia Zi 12/8 - 7:33a	Yi Chou 1/6 - 6:40p

1944 Jia Shen

1st MONTH	2nd MONTH	3rd MONTH	4th MONTH	5th MONTH	6th MONTH	7th MONTH	8th MONTH	9th MONTH	10th MONTH	11th MONTH	12th MONTH
Bing Yin 2/5 - 6:23a	Ding Mao 3/6 - 12:41a	Wu Chen 4/5 - 5:54a	Ji Si 5/5 - 11:40p	Geng Wu 6/6 - 4:11a	Xin Wei 7/7 - 2:37p	Ren Shen 8/8 - 12:19a	Gui You 9/8 - 2:56a	Jia Xu 10/8 - 6:09p	Yi Hai 11/7 - 8:55p	Bing Zi 12/7 - 1:28p	Ding Chou 1/6 - 12:35a

1945 Yi You

1st MONTH	2nd MONTH	3rd MONTH	4th MONTH	5th MONTH	6th MONTH	7th MONTH	8th MONTH	9th MONTH	10th MONTH	11th MONTH	12th MONTH
Wu Yin 2/4 - 12:20p	Ji Mao 3/6 - 6:38a	Geng Chen 4/5 - 11:52a	Xin Si 5/6 - 5:37a	Ren Wu 6/6 - 10:06a	Gui Wei 7/7 - 8:27p	Jia Shen 8/8 - 6:06a	Yi You 9/8 - 8:39a	Bing Xu 10/8 - 11:50p	Ding Hai 11/8 - 2:35a	Wu Zi 12/7 - 7:08p	Ji Chou 1/6 - 6:17a

1946 Bing Xu

1st MONTH	2nd MONTH	3rd MONTH	4th MONTH	5th MONTH	6th MONTH	7th MONTH	8th MONTH	9th MONTH	10th MONTH	11th MONTH	12th MONTH
Geng Yin 2/4 - 6:05p	Xin Mao 3/6 - 12:25p	Ren Chen 4/5 - 5:39p	Gui Si 5/6 - 11:22a	Jia Wu 6/6 - 3:49p	Yi Wei 7/8 - 2:11a	Bing Shen 8/8 - 11:52a	Ding You 9/8 - 2:28p	Wu Xu 10/9 - 5:42a	Ji Hai 11/8 - 8:28a	Geng Zi 12/8 - 1:01a	Xin Chou 1/6 - 12:11p

1947 Ding Hai

1st MONTH	2nd MONTH	3rd MONTH	4th MONTH	5th MONTH	6th MONTH	7th MONTH	8th MONTH	9th MONTH	10th MONTH	11th MONTH	12th MONTH
Ren Yin 2/4 - 11:55p	Gui Mao 3/6 - 6:12p	Jia Chen 4/5 - 11:23p	Yi Si 5/6 - 5:05p	Bing Wu 6/6 - 9:33p	Ding Wei 7/8 - 7:56a	Wu Shen 8/8 - 5:39p	Ji You 9/8 - 8:17p	Geng Xu 10/9 - 11:32a	Xin Hai 11/8 - 2:19p	Ren Zi 12/8 - 6:53a	Gui Chou 1/6 - 6:01p

1948 Wu Zi

1st MONTH	2nd MONTH	3rd MONTH	4th MONTH	5th MONTH	6th MONTH	7th MONTH	8th MONTH	9th MONTH	10th MONTH	11th MONTH	12th MONTH
Jia Yin 2/5 - 5:43a	Yi Mao 3/5 - 11:58p	Bing Chen 4/5 - 5:10a	Ding Si 5/5 - 10:53p	Wu Wu 6/6 - 3:21a	Ji Wei 7/7 - 1:44p	Geng Shen 8/7 - 11:27p	Xin You 9/8 - 2:06a	Ren Xu 10/8 - 5:21p	Gui Hai 11/7 - 8:07p	Jia Zi 12/7 - 12:38p	Yi Chou 1/5 - 11:42p

1949 Ji Chou

1st MONTH	2nd MONTH	3rd MONTH	4th MONTH	5th MONTH	6th MONTH	7th MONTH	8th MONTH	9th MONTH	10th MONTH	11th MONTH	12th MONTH
Jia Yin 2/4 - 11:23a	Ding Mao 3/6 - 5:40a	Wu Chen 4/5 - 10:52a	Ji Si 5/6 - 4:37a	Geng Wu 6/6 - 9:07a	Xin Wei 7/7 - 7:32p	Ren Shen 8/8 - 5:16a	Gui You 9/8 - 7:55a	Jia Xu 10/8 - 11:12p	Yi Hai 11/8 - 2:00a	Bing Zi 12/7 - 6:34p	Ding Chou 1/6 - 5:39a

1950 Geng Yin

1st MONTH	2nd MONTH	3rd MONTH	4th MONTH	5th MONTH	6th MONTH	7th MONTH	8th MONTH	9th MONTH	10th MONTH	11th MONTH	12th MONTH
Wu Yin 2/4 - 5:21p	Ji Mao 3/6 - 11:36a	Geng Chen 4/5 - 4:45p	Xin Si 5/6 - 10:25a	Ren Wu 6/6 - 2:52p	Gui Wei 7/8 - 1:14a	Jia Shen 8/8 - 10:56a	Yi You 9/8 - 1:34p	Bing Xu 10/9 - 4:52a	Ding Hai 11/8 - 7:44a	Wu Zi 12/8 - 12:22a	Ji Chou 1/6 - 11:31a

1951 Xin Mao

1st MONTH	2nd MONTH	3rd MONTH	4th MONTH	5th MONTH	6th MONTH	7th MONTH	8th MONTH	9th MONTH	10th MONTH	11th MONTH	12th MONTH
Geng Yin 2/4 - 11:14p	Xin Mao 3/6 - 5:27p	Ren Chen 4/5 - 10:33p	Gui Si 5/6 - 4:10p	Jia Wu 6/6 - 8:33p	Yi Wei 7/8 - 6:54a	Bing Shen 8/8 - 4:38p	Ding You 9/8 - 7:19p	Wu Xu 10/9 - 10:37a	Ji Hai 11/8 - 1:27p	Geng Zi 12/8 - 6:03a	Xin Chou 1/5 - 5:10p

1952 Ren Chen

1st MONTH	2nd MONTH	3rd MONTH	4th MONTH	5th MONTH	6th MONTH	7th MONTH	8th MONTH	9th MONTH	10th MONTH	11th MONTH	12th MONTH
Ren Yin 2/5 - 4:54a	Gui Mao 3/5 - 11:08p	Jia Chen 4/5 - 4:16a	Yi Si 5/5 - 9:54p	Bing Wu 6/6 - 2:21a	Ding Wei 7/7 - 12:45p	Wu Shen 8/7 - 10:32p	Ji You 9/8 - 1:14a	Geng Xu 10/8 - 4:33p	Xin Hai 11/7 - 7:22p	Ren Zi 12/7 - 11:56a	Gui Chou 1/5 - 11:03p

1953 Gui Si

1st MONTH	2nd MONTH	3rd MONTH	4th MONTH	5th MONTH	6th MONTH	7th MONTH	8th MONTH	9th MONTH	10th MONTH	11th MONTH	12th MONTH
Jia Yin 2/4 - 10:46a	Yi Mao 3/6 - 5:03a	Bing Chen 4/5 - 10:13a	Ding Si 5/6 - 3:53a	Wu Wu 6/6 - 8:17a	Ji Wei 7/7 - 6:36p	Geng Shen 8/8 - 4:15a	Xin You 9/8 - 6:54a	Ren Xu 10/8 - 10:11p	Gui Hai 11/8 - 1:02a	Jia Zi 12/7 - 5:38p	Yi Chou 1/6 - 4:46a

1954 Jia Wu

1st MONTH	2nd MONTH	3rd MONTH	4th MONTH	5th MONTH	6th MONTH	7th MONTH	8th MONTH	9th MONTH	10th MONTH	11th MONTH	12th MONTH
Bing Yin 2/4 - 4:31p	Ding Mao 3/6 - 10:49a	Wu Chen 4/5 - 4:00p	Ji Si 5/6 - 9:39a	Geng Wu 6/6 - 2:02p	Xin Wei 7/8 - 12:20a	Ren Shen 8/8 - 10:00a	Gui You 9/8 - 12:39p	Jia Xu 10/9 - 3:58a	Yi Hai 11/8 - 6:51a	Bing Zi 12/7 - 11:29p	Ding Chou 1/6 - 10:36a

1955 Yi Wei

1st MONTH	2nd MONTH	3rd MONTH	4th MONTH	5th MONTH	6th MONTH	7th MONTH	8th MONTH	9th MONTH	10th MONTH	11th MONTH	12th MONTH
Wu Yin 2/4 - 10:18p	Ji Mao 3/6 - 4:32p	Geng Chen 4/5 - 9:39p	Xin Si 5/6 - 3:18p	Ren Wu 6/6 - 7:44p	Gui Wei 7/8 - 6:07a	Jia Shen 8/8 - 3:50p	Yi You 9/8 - 6:32p	Bing Xu 10/9 - 9:53p	Ding Hai 11/8 - 12:46p	Wu Zi 12/8 - 5:23a	Ji Chou 1/6 - 4:31p

1956 Bing Shen

1st MONTH	2nd MONTH	3rd MONTH	4th MONTH	5th MONTH	6th MONTH	7th MONTH	8th MONTH	9th MONTH	10th MONTH	11th MONTH	12th MONTH
Geng Yin 2/5 4:13a	Xin Mao 3/5 10:25p	Ren Chen 4/5 3:32a	Gui Si 5/5 9:11p	Jia Wu 6/6 1:36a	Yi Wei 7/7 11:59a	Bing Shen 8/7 9:41a	Ding You 9/8 12:20a	Wu Xu 10/8 3:37p	Ji Hai 11/7 6:27p	Geng Zi 12/7 11:03a	Xin Chou 1/5 10:11p

1957 Ding You

1st MONTH	2nd MONTH	3rd MONTH	4th MONTH	5th MONTH	6th MONTH	7th MONTH	8th MONTH	9th MONTH	10th MONTH	11th MONTH	12th MONTH
Ren Yin 2/4 - 9:55a	Gui Mao 3/6 - 4:11a	Jia Chen 4/5 - 9:19a	Yi Si 5/6 - 2:59a	Bing Wu 6/6 - 7:25a	Ding Wei 7/7 - 5:49p	Wu Shen 8/8 - 3:33a	Ji You 9/8 - 6:13a	Geng Xu 10/8 - 9:31p	Xin Hai 11/8 - 12:21a	Ren Zi 12/7 - 4:57p	Gui Chou 1/6 - 4:05a

1958 Wu Xu

1st MONTH	2nd MONTH	3rd MONTH	4th MONTH	5th MONTH	6th MONTH	7th MONTH	8th MONTH	9th MONTH	10th MONTH	11th MONTH	12th MONTH
Jia Yin 2/4 - 3:50p	Yi Mao 3/6 - 10:06a	Bing Chen 4/5 - 3:13p	Ding Si 5/6 - 8:50a	Wu Wu 6/6 - 1:13p	Ji Wei 7/7 - 11:34p	Geng Shen 8/8 - 9:18a	Xin You 9/8 - noon	Ren Xu 10/9 - 3:20a	Gui Hai 11/8 - 6:13a	Jia Zi 12/7 - 10:50p	Yi Chou 1/6 - 9:59a

1959 Ji Hai

1st MONTH	2nd MONTH	3rd MONTH	4th MONTH	5th MONTH	6th MONTH	7th MONTH	8th MONTH	9th MONTH	10th MONTH	11th MONTH	12th MONTH
Bing Yin 2/4 - 9:43p	Ding Mao 3/6 - 3:57p	Wu Chen 4/5 - 9:04p	Ji Si 5/6 - 2:39p	Geng Wu 6/6 - 7:01p	Xin Wei 7/8 - 5:21a	Ren Shen 8/8 - 3:05p	Gui You 9/8 - 5:49p	Jia Xu 10/9 - 9:11a	Yi Hai 11/8 - 12:03p	Bing Zi 12/8 - 4:38a	Ding Chou 1/6 - 3:43p

1960 Geng Zi

1st MONTH	2nd MONTH	3rd MONTH	4th MONTH	5th MONTH	6th MONTH	7th MONTH	8th MONTH	9th MONTH	10th MONTH	11th MONTH	12th MONTH
Wu Yin 2/5 - 3:23a	Ji Mao 3/6 - 9:36p	Geng Chen 4/5 - 2:44a	Xin Si 5/5 - 8:23p	Ren Wu 6/6 - 12:49a	Gui Wei 7/7 - 11:13a	Jia Shen 8/7 - 9:00p	Yi You 9/7 - 11:46p	Bing Xu 10/8 - 3:09p	Ding Hai 11/7 - 6:02p	Wu Zi 12/7 - 10:38a	Ji Chou 1/5 - 9:43p

1961 Xin Chou

1st MONTH	2nd MONTH	3rd MONTH	4th MONTH	5th MONTH	6th MONTH	7th MONTH	8th MONTH	9th MONTH	10th MONTH	11th MONTH	12th MONTH
Geng Yin 2/4 - 9:23a	Xin Mao 3/6 - 3:35a	Ren Chen 4/5 - 8:42a	Gui Si 5/6 - 2:21a	Jia Wu 6/6 - 6:46a	Yi Wei 7/7 - 5:07p	Bing Shen 8/8 - 2:49a	Ding You 9/8 - 5:29a	Wu Xu 10/8 - 8:51p	Ji Hai 11/7 - 11:46p	Geng Zi 12/7 - 4:26p	Xin Chou 1/6 - 3:35a

1962 Ren Yin

1st MONTH	2nd MONTH	3rd MONTH	4th MONTH	5th MONTH	6th MONTH	7th MONTH	8th MONTH	9th MONTH	10th MONTH	11th MONTH	12th MONTH
Ren Yin 2/4 - 3:18p	Gui Mao 3/6 - 9:30a	Jia Chen 4/5 - 2:34p	Yi Si 5/6 - 8:10a	Bing Wu 6/6 - 12:31p	Ding Wei 7/7 - 10:51p	Wu Shen 8/8 - 8:34a	Ji You 9/8 - 11:16a	Geng Xu 10/9 - 2:38a	Xin Hai 11/8 - 5:35a	Ren Zi 12/7 - 10:17p	Gui Chou 1/6 - 9:27a

1963 Gui Mao

1st MONTH	2nd MONTH	3rd MONTH	4th MONTH	5th MONTH	6th MONTH	7th MONTH	8th MONTH	9th MONTH	10th MONTH	11th MONTH	12th MONTH
Jia Yin 2/4 - 9:08p	Yi Mao 3/6 - 3:17p	Bing Chen 4/5 - 8:19p	Ding Si 5/6 - 1:52p	Wu Wu 6/6 - 6:15p	Ji Wei 7/8 - 4:38a	Geng Shen 8/8 - 2:26p	Xin You 9/8 - 5:12p	Ren Xu 10/9 - 8:36a	Gui Hai 11/8 - 11:32a	Jia Zi 12/8 - 4:13a	Yi Chou 1/6 - 3:22p

1964 Jia Chen

1ST MONTH	2ND MONTH	3RD MONTH	4TH MONTH	5TH MONTH	6TH MONTH	7TH MONTH	8TH MONTH	9TH MONTH	10TH MONTH	11TH MONTH	12TH MONTH
Bing Yin 2/5 - 3:05a	Ding Mao 3/5 - 9:16p	Wu Chen 4/5 - 2:18a	Ji Si 5/5 - 7:51p	Geng Wu 6/6 - 12:12a	Xin Wei 7/7 - 10:32a	Ren Shen 8/7 - 8:16p	Gui You 9/7 - 11:00p	Jia Xu 10/8 - 2:22p	Yi Hai 11/7 - 5:15p	Bing Zi 12/7 - 9:53a	Ding Chou 1/5 - 9:02p

1965 Yi Si

1ST MONTH	2ND MONTH	3RD MONTH	4TH MONTH	5TH MONTH	6TH MONTH	7TH MONTH	8TH MONTH	9TH MONTH	10TH MONTH	11TH MONTH	12TH MONTH
Wu Yin 2/4 - 8:46a	Ji Mao 3/6 - 3:01a	Geng Chen 4/5 - 8:07a	Xin Si 5/6 - 1:42a	Ren Wu 6/6 - 6:02a	Gui Wei 7/7 - 4:22p	Jia Shen 8/8 - 2:05a	Yi You 9/8 - 4:48a	Bing Xu 10/8 - 8:11p	Ding Hai 11/7 - 11:07p	Wu Zi 12/7 - 3:46p	Ji Chou 1/6 - 2:55a

1966 Bing Wu

1ST MONTH	2ND MONTH	3RD MONTH	4TH MONTH	5TH MONTH	6TH MONTH	7TH MONTH	8TH MONTH	9TH MONTH	10TH MONTH	11TH MONTH	12TH MONTH
Geng Yin 2/4 - 2:38p	Xin Mao 3/6 - 8:51a	Ren Chen 4/5 - 1:57p	Gui Si 5/6 - 7:31a	Jia Wu 6/6 - 11:50a	Yi Wei 7/7 - 10:07p	Bing Shen 8/8 - 7:49a	Ding You 9/8 - 10:32a	Wu Xu 10/9 - 1:57a	Ji Hai 11/8 - 4:56a	Geng Zi 12/7 - 9:38p	Xin Chou 1/6 - 8:48a

1967 Ding Wei

1ST MONTH	2ND MONTH	3RD MONTH	4TH MONTH	5TH MONTH	6TH MONTH	7TH MONTH	8TH MONTH	9TH MONTH	10TH MONTH	11TH MONTH	12TH MONTH
Ren Yin 2/4 - 8:31p	Gui Mao 3/6 - 2:42p	Jia Chen 4/5 - 7:45p	Yi Si 5/6 - 1:18p	Bing Wu 6/6 - 5:36p	Ding Wei 7/8 - 3:54a	Wu Shen 8/8 - 1:35p	Ji You 9/8 - 4:18p	Geng Xu 10/9 - 7:42a	Xin Hai 11/8 - 10:38a	Ren Zi 12/8 - 3:18a	Gui Chou 1/6 - 2:26p

1968 Wu Shen

1ST MONTH	2ND MONTH	3RD MONTH	4TH MONTH	5TH MONTH	6TH MONTH	7TH MONTH	8TH MONTH	9TH MONTH	10TH MONTH	11TH MONTH	12TH MONTH
Jia Yin 2/5 - 2:08a	Yi Mao 3/6 - 8:18p	Bing Chen 4/5 - 1:21a	Ding Si 5/5 - 6:56p	Wu Wu 6/5 - 11:19p	Ji Wei 7/7 - 9:42a	Geng Shen 8/7 - 7:27p	Xin You 9/7 - 10:12p	Ren Xu 10/8 - 1:35p	Gui Hai 11/7 - 4:29p	Jia Zi 12/7 - 9:09a	Yi Chou 1/5 - 8:17p

1969 Ji You

1ST MONTH	2ND MONTH	3RD MONTH	4TH MONTH	5TH MONTH	6TH MONTH	7TH MONTH	8TH MONTH	9TH MONTH	10TH MONTH	11TH MONTH	12TH MONTH
Bing Yin 2/4 - 7:59a	Ding Mao 3/6 - 2:11a	Wu Chen 4/5 - 7:15a	Ji Si 5/6 - 12:50a	Geng Wu 6/6 - 5:12a	Xin Wei 7/7 - 3:32p	Ren Shen 8/8 - 1:14a	Gui You 9/8 - 3:56a	Jia Xu 10/8 - 7:17p	Yi Hai 11/7 - 10:12p	Bing Zi 12/7 - 2:51p	Ding Chou 1/6 - 1:59a

1970 Geng Xu

1ST MONTH	2ND MONTH	3RD MONTH	4TH MONTH	5TH MONTH	6TH MONTH	7TH MONTH	8TH MONTH	9TH MONTH	10TH MONTH	11TH MONTH	12TH MONTH
Wu Yin 2/4 - 1:46p	Ji Mao 3/6 - 7:51a	Geng Chen 4/5 - 12:54p	Xin Si 5/6 - 6:28a	Ren Wu 6/6 - 10:51a	Gui Wei 7/7 - 9:14p	Jia Shen 8/8 - 6:58a	Yi You 9/8 - 9:42a	Bing Xu 10/9 - 1:06a	Ding Hai 11/8 - 4:01a	Wu Zi 12/7 - 8:41p	Ji Chou 1/6 - 7:45a

1971 Xin Hai

1ST MONTH	2ND MONTH	3RD MONTH	4TH MONTH	5TH MONTH	6TH MONTH	7TH MONTH	8TH MONTH	9TH MONTH	10TH MONTH	11TH MONTH	12TH MONTH
Geng Yin 2/4 - 7:26p	Xin Mao 3/6 - 1:35p	Ren Chen 4/5 - 6:36p	Gui Si 5/6 - 12:08p	Jia Wu 6/6 - 4:29p	Yi Wei 7/8 - 2:51a	Bing Shen 8/8 - 12:40p	Ding You 9/8 - 5:30p	Wu Xu 10/9 - 6:59a	Ji Hai 11/8 - 9:57a	Geng Zi 12/8 - 2:36a	Xin Chou 1/6 - 1:43p

1972 Ren Zi

1ST MONTH	2ND MONTH	3RD MONTH	4TH MONTH	5TH MONTH	6TH MONTH	7TH MONTH	8TH MONTH	9TH MONTH	10TH MONTH	11TH MONTH	12TH MONTH
Ren Yin 2/5 - 1:20a	Gui Mao 3/5 - 7:28p	Jia Chen 4/5 - 12:29a	Yi Si 5/5 - 6:16p	Bing Wu 6/5 - 10:22p	Ding Wei 7/7 - 8:43a	Wu Shen 8/7 - 6:29p	Ji You 9/7 - 9:15p	Geng Xu 10/8 - 12:42p	Xin Hai 11/7 - 3:40p	Ren Zi 12/7 - 8:19a	Gui Chou 1/5 - 7:26p

1973 Gui Chou

1ST MONTH	2ND MONTH	3RD MONTH	4TH MONTH	5TH MONTH	6TH MONTH	7TH MONTH	8TH MONTH	9TH MONTH	10TH MONTH	11TH MONTH	12TH MONTH
Jia Yin 2/4 - 7:04a	Yi Mao 3/6 - 1:13a	Bing Chen 4/5 - 6:14a	Ding Si 5/5 - 11:47p	Wu Wu 6/6 - 4:07a	Ji Wei 7/7 - 2:28p	Geng Shen 8/8 - 12:13a	Xin You 9/8 - 3:00a	Ren Xu 10/8 - 6:27a	Gui Hai 11/7 - 9:28p	Jia Zi 12/7 - 2:11p	Yi Chou 1/6 - 1:20a

1974 Jia Yin

1st Month	2nd Month	3rd Month	4th Month	5th Month	6th Month	7th Month	8th Month	9th Month	10th Month	11th Month	12th Month
Bing Yin 2/4 - 1:00p	Ding Mao 3/6 - 7:07a	Wu Chen 4/5 - 12:05p	Ji Si 5/6 - 5:34a	Geng Wu 6/6 - 9:52a	Xin Wei 7/7 - 8:13p	Ren Shen 8/8 - 5:57a	Gui You 9/8 - 8:45a	Jia Xu 10/9 - 12:15a	Yi Hai 11/8 - 3:18a	Bing Zi 12/7 - 8:05p	Ding Chou 1/6 - 7:18a

1975 Yi Mao

1st Month	2nd Month	3rd Month	4th Month	5th Month	6th Month	7th Month	8th Month	9th Month	10th Month	11th Month	12th Month
Wu Yin 2/4 - 6:59p	Ji Mao 3/6 - 1:06p	Geng Chen 4/5 - 6:02p	Xin Si 5/6 - 11:27a	Ren Wu 6/6 - 3:42p	Gui Wei 7/7 - 2:00a	Jia Shen 8/8 - 11:45a	Yi You 9/8 - 2:33p	Bing Xu 10/9 - 6:02a	Ding Hai 11/8 - 9:03a	Wu Zi 12/8 - 1:46a	Ji Chou 1/6 - 12:58p

1976 Bing Chen

1st Month	2nd Month	3rd Month	4th Month	5th Month	6th Month	7th Month	8th Month	9th Month	10th Month	11th Month	12th Month
Geng Yin 2/5 - 12:40a	Xin Mao 3/5 - 6:48p	Ren Chen 4/4 - 11:47p	Gui Si 5/5 - 5:15p	Jia Wu 6/5 - 9:31p	Yi Wei 7/7 - 7:51a	Bing Shen 8/7 - 5:39p	Ding You 9/7 - 8:28p	Wu Xu 10/8 - 11:58a	Ji Hai 11/7 - 2:59p	Geng Zi 12/7 - 7:41a	Xin Chou 1/5 - 6:51p

1977 Ding Si

1st Month	2nd Month	3rd Month	4th Month	5th Month	6th Month	7th Month	8th Month	9th Month	10th Month	11th Month	12th Month
Ren Yin 2/4 - 6:34a	Gui Mao 3/6 - 12:44a	Jia Chen 4/5 - 5:46a	Yi Si 5/5 - 11:16p	Bing Wu 6/6 - 3:32a	Ding Wei 7/7 - 1:48p	Wu Shen 8/7 - 11:30p	Ji You 9/8 - 2:16a	Geng Xu 10/8 - 5:44p	Xin Hai 11/7 - 8:46p	Ren Zi 12/7 - 1:31p	Gui Chou 1/6 - 12:43a

1978 Wu Wu

1st Month	2nd Month	3rd Month	4th Month	5th Month	6th Month	7th Month	8th Month	9th Month	10th Month	11th Month	12th Month
Jia Yin 2/4 - 12:27p	Yi Mao 3/6 - 6:38a	Bing Chen 4/5 - 11:39a	Ding Si 5/6 - 5:09a	Wu Wu 6/6 - 9:23a	Ji Wei 7/7 - 7:37p	Geng Shen 8/8 - 5:18a	Xin You 9/8 - 8:03a	Ren Xu 10/8 - 11:31p	Gui Hai 11/8 - 2:34a	Jia Zi 12/7 - 7:20p	Yi Chou 1/6 - 6:32a

1979 Ji Wei

1st Month	2nd Month	3rd Month	4th Month	5th Month	6th Month	7th Month	8th Month	9th Month	10th Month	11th Month	12th Month
Bing Yin 2/4 - 6:13p	Ding Mao 3/6 - 12:20p	Wu Chen 4/5 - 5:18p	Ji Si 5/6 - 10:47a	Geng Wu 6/6 - 3:05p	Xin Wei 7/8 - 1:25a	Ren Shen 8/8 - 11:11a	Gui You 9/8 - 2:00p	Jia Xu 10/9 - 5:30a	Yi Hai 11/8 - 8:33a	Bing Zi 12/8 - 1:18a	Ding Chou 1/6 - 12:29p

1980 Geng Shen

1st Month	2nd Month	3rd Month	4th Month	5th Month	6th Month	7th Month	8th Month	9th Month	10th Month	11th Month	12th Month
Wu Yin 2/5 - 12:10a	Ji Mao 3/5 - 6:17p	Geng Chen 4/4 - 11:15p	Xin Si 5/5 - 4:45p	Ren Wu 6/5 - 9:04p	Gui Wei 7/7 - 7:24a	Jia Shen 8/7 - 5:09p	Yi You 9/7 - 7:54p	Bing Xu 10/8 - 11:19a	Ding Hai 11/7 - 2:18p	Wu Zi 12/7 - 7:02a	Ji Chou 1/5 - 6:13p

1981 Xin You

1st Month	2nd Month	3rd Month	4th Month	5th Month	6th Month	7th Month	8th Month	9th Month	10th Month	11th Month	12th Month
Geng Yin 2/4 - 5:56a	Xin Mao 3/6 - 12:05a	Ren Chen 4/5 - 5:05a	Gui Si 5/5 - 10:35p	Jia Wu 6/6 - 2:53a	Yi Wei 7/7 - 1:12p	Bing Shen 8/7 - 10:57p	Ding You 9/8 - 1:43a	Wu Xu 10/8 - 5:10p	Ji Hai 11/7 - 8:09p	Geng Zi 12/7 - 12:51p	Xin Chou 1/6 - 12:03a

1982 Ren Xu

1st Month	2nd Month	3rd Month	4th Month	5th Month	6th Month	7th Month	8th Month	9th Month	10th Month	11th Month	12th Month
Ren Yin 2/4 - 11:46a	Gui Mao 3/6 - 5:55a	Jia Chen 4/5 - 10:53a	Yi Si 5/6 - 4:20a	Bing Wu 6/6 - 8:36a	Ding Wei 7/7 - 6:55p	Wu Shen 8/8 - 4:42a	Ji You 9/8 - 7:32a	Geng Xu 10/8 - 11:02p	Xin Hai 11/8 - 2:04a	Ren Zi 12/7 - 6:48p	Gui Chou 1/6 - 5:59a

1983 Gui Hai

1st Month	2nd Month	3rd Month	4th Month	5th Month	6th Month	7th Month	8th Month	9th Month	10th Month	11th Month	12th Month
Jia Yin 2/4 - 5:40p	Yi Mao 3/6 - 11:47a	Bing Chen 4/5 - 4:45p	Ding Si 5/6 - 10:11a	Wu Wu 6/6 - 2:26p	Ji Wei 7/8 - 12:43a	Geng Shen 8/8 - 10:30a	Xin You 9/8 - 1:20p	Ren Xu 10/9 - 4:51a	Gui Hai 11/8 - 7:53a	Jia Zi 12/8 - 12:34a	Yi Chou 1/6 - 11:41a

1984 Jia Zi

1st Month	2nd Month	3rd Month	4th Month	5th Month	6th Month	7th Month	8th Month	9th Month	10th Month	11th Month	12th Month
Bing Yin 2/4 - 11:19a	Ding Mao 3/5 - 5:25p	Wu Chen 4/4 - 10:22p	Ji Si 5/5 - 3:51p	Geng Wu 6/5 - 8:09p	Xin Wei 7/7 - 6:29a	Ren Shen 8/7 - 4:18p	Gui You 9/7 - 7:10p	Jia Xu 10/8 - 10:43a	Yi Hai 11/7 - 1:45p	Bing Zi 12/7 - 6:28a	Ding Chou 1/5 - 5:35p

1985 Yi Chou

1st Month	2nd Month	3rd Month	4th Month	5th Month	6th Month	7th Month	8th Month	9th Month	10th Month	11th Month	12th Month
Wu Yin 2/4 - 5:12a	Ji Mao 3/5 - 11:16p	Geng Chen 4/5 - 4:14a	Xin Si 5/5 - 9:43p	Ren Wu 6/6 - 2:00a	Gui Wei 7/7 - 12:19p	Jia Shen 8/7 - 10:04p	Yi You 9/8 - 12:53a	Bing Xu 10/8 - 4:24p	Ding Hai 11/7 - 7:29p	Wu Zi 12/7 - 12:16p	Ji Chou 1/5 - 11:29p

1986 Bing Yin

1st Month	2nd Month	3rd Month	4th Month	5th Month	6th Month	7th Month	8th Month	9th Month	10th Month	11th Month	12th Month
Geng Yin 2/4 - 11:09a	Xin Mao 3/6 - 5:11a	Ren Chen 4/5 - 10:05a	Gui Si 5/6 - 3:30a	Jia Wu 6/6 - 7:44a	Yi Wei 7/7 - 6:00p	Bing Shen 8/8 - 3:52a	Ding You 9/8 - 6:34a	Wu Xu 10/8 - 10:08p	Jia Hai 11/8 - 1:12a	Geng Zi 12/7 - 6:02p	Xin Chou 1/6 - 5:13a

1987 Ding Mao

1st Month	2nd Month	3rd Month	4th Month	5th Month	6th Month	7th Month	8th Month	9th Month	10th Month	11th Month	12th Month
Ren Yin 2/4 - 4:52a	Gui Mao 3/6 - 10:55a	Jia Chen 4/5 - 3:44p	Yi Si 5/6 - 9:07a	Bing Wu 6/6 - 1:20p	Ding Wei 7/7 - 11:40p	Wu Shen 8/8 - 9:30a	Ji You 9/8 - 12:25p	Geng Xu 10/9 - 3:59a	Xin Hai 11/8 - 7:05a	Ren Zi 12/7 - 11:51p	Gui Chou 1/6 - 11:04a

1988 Wu Chen

1st Month	2nd Month	3rd Month	4th Month	5th Month	6th Month	7th Month	8th Month	9th Month	10th Month	11th Month	12th Month
Jia Yin 2/4 - 10:43a	Yi Mao 3/5 - 4:46p	Bing Chen 4/4 - 9:38p	Ding Si 5/5 - 3:02p	Wu Wu 6/5 - 7:13p	Ji Wei 7/7 - 5:33a	Geng Shen 8/7 - 3:19p	Xin You 9/7 - 6:11p	Ren Xu 10/8 - 9:44a	Gui Hai 11/7 - 12:48p	Jia Zi 12/7 - 5:34a	Yi Chou 1/5 - 4:45p

1989 Ji Si

1st Month	2nd Month	3rd Month	4th Month	5th Month	6th Month	7th Month	8th Month	9th Month	10th Month	11th Month	12th Month
Bing Yin 2/4 - 4:27a	Ding Mao 3/5 - 10:34p	Wu Chen 4/5 - 3:30a	Ji Si 5/5 - 8:54p	Geng Wu 6/6 - 1:05a	Xin Wei 7/7 - 11:20a	Ren Shen 8/7 - 9:05p	Gui You 9/7 - 11:54p	Jia Xu 10/8 - 3:28p	Yi Hai 11/7 - 6:34p	Bing Zi 12/7 - 11:21a	Ding Chou 1/5 - 10:34p

1990 Geng Wu

1st Month	2nd Month	3rd Month	4th Month	5th Month	6th Month	7th Month	8th Month	9th Month	10th Month	11th Month	12th Month
Wu Yin 2/4 - 10:15a	Ji Mao 3/6 - 4:21a	Geng Chen 4/5 - 9:14a	Xin Si 5/6 - 2:36a	Ren Wu 6/6 - 6:47a	Gui Wei 7/7 - 5:00p	Jia Shen 8/8 - 2:46a	Yi You 9/8 - 5:38a	Bing Xu 10/8 - 9:13p	Ding Hai 11/8 - 12:23a	Wu Zi 12/7 - 5:14p	Ji Chou 1/6 - 4:28a

1991 Xin Wei

1st Month	2nd Month	3rd Month	4th Month	5th Month	6th Month	7th Month	8th Month	9th Month	10th Month	11th Month	12th Month
Geng Yin 2/4 - 4:08p	Xin Mao 3/6 - 10:13a	Ren Chen 4/5 - 3:04p	Gui Si 5/6 - 8:27a	Jia Wu 6/6 - 12:37p	Yi Wei 7/7 - 10:52p	Bing Shen 8/8 - 8:36a	Ding You 9/8 - 11:27a	Wu Xu 10/9 - 3:01a	Ji Hai 11/8 - 6:08a	Geng Zi 12/7 - 10:56p	Xin Chou 1/6 - 10:09a

1992 Ren Shen

1st Month	2nd Month	3rd Month	4th Month	5th Month	6th Month	7th Month	8th Month	9th Month	10th Month	11th Month	12th Month
Ren Yin 2/4 - 9:48p	Gui Mao 3/5 - 3:52p	Jia Chen 4/4 - 8:45p	Yi Si 5/5 - 2:09p	Bing Wu 6/5 - 6:24p	Ding Wei 7/7 - 4:40a	Wu Shen 8/7 - 2:28p	Ji You 9/7 - 5:19p	Geng Xu 10/8 - 8:52a	Xin Hai 11/7 - 11:57a	Ren Zi 12/7 - 4:44a	Gui Chou 1/5 - 3:57p

1993 Gui You

1st Month	2nd Month	3rd Month	4th Month	5th Month	6th Month	7th Month	8th Month	9th Month	10th Month	11th Month	12th Month
Jia Yin 2/4 - 3:38a	Yi Mao 3/5 - 9:42p	Bing Chen 4/5 - 2:36a	Ding Si 5/5 - 8:02p	Wu Wu 6/6 - 12:15a	Ji Wei 7/7 - 10:31a	Geng Shen 8/7 - 8:17p	Xin You 9/7 - 11:07p	Ren Xu 10/8 - 2:41p	Gui Hai 11/7 - 5:46p	Jia Zi 12/7 - 10:33a	Yi Chou 1/5 - 9:46p

1994 Jia Xu

1st MONTH	2nd MONTH	3rd MONTH	4th MONTH	5th MONTH	6th MONTH	7th MONTH	8th MONTH	9th MONTH	10th MONTH	11th MONTH	12th MONTH
Bing Yin 2/4 - 9:31a	Ding Mao 3/6 - 3:37a	Wu Chen 4/5 - 8:31a	Ji Si 5/6 - 1:54a	Geng Wu 6/6 - 6:05a	Xin Wei 7/7 - 4:19p	Ren Shen 8/8 - 2:05a	Gui You 9/8 - 4:55a	Jia Xu 10/8 - 8:30p	Yi Hai 11/7 - 11:36p	Bing Zi 12/7 - 4:24p	Ding Chou 1/6 - 3:34a

1995 Yi Hai

1st MONTH	2nd MONTH	3rd MONTH	4th MONTH	5th MONTH	6th MONTH	7th MONTH	8th MONTH	9th MONTH	10th MONTH	11th MONTH	12th MONTH
Wu Yin 2/4 - 3:14p	Ji Mao 3/6 - 9:16a	Geng Chen 4/5 - 2:09p	Xin Si 5/6 - 7:31a	Ren Wu 6/6 - 11:43a	Gui Wei 7/7 - 10:02p	Jia Shen 8/8 - 7:53a	Yi You 9/8 - 10:49a	Bing Xu 10/9 - 2:27a	Ding Hai 11/8 - 5:35a	Wu Zi 12/7 - 10:22p	Ji Chou 1/6 - 9:31a

1996 Bing Zi

1st MONTH	2nd MONTH	3rd MONTH	4th MONTH	5th MONTH	6th MONTH	7th MONTH	8th MONTH	9th MONTH	10th MONTH	11th MONTH	12th MONTH
Geng Yin 2/4 - 9:08p	Xin Mao 3/5 - 3:10p	Ren Chen 4/4 - 8:03p	Gui Si 5/5 - 1:26p	Jia Wu 6/5 - 5:41p	Yi Wei 7/7 - 4:00a	Bing Shen 8/7 - 1:49p	Ding You 9/7 - 4:41p	Wu Xu 10/8 - 8:18a	Ji Hai 11/7 - 11:26a	Geng Zi 12/7 - 4:13a	Xin Chou 1/5 - 3:22p

1997 Ding Chou

1st MONTH	2nd MONTH	3rd MONTH	4th MONTH	5th MONTH	6th MONTH	7th MONTH	8th MONTH	9th MONTH	10th MONTH	11th MONTH	12th MONTH
Ren Yin 2/4 - 3:04a	Gui Mao 3/5 - 9:14p	Jia Chen 4/5 - 2:17a	Yi Si 5/5 - 7:51p	Bing Wu 6/6 - 12:13a	Ding Wei 7/7 - 10:36a	Wu Shen 8/7 - 8:19p	Ji You 9/7 - 11:03p	Geng Xu 10/8 - 2:27p	Xin Hai 11/7 - 5:22p	Ren Zi 12/7 - 10:02a	Gui Chou 1/5 - 9:11p

1998 Wu Yin

1st MONTH	2nd MONTH	3rd MONTH	4th MONTH	5th MONTH	6th MONTH	7th MONTH	8th MONTH	9th MONTH	10th MONTH	11th MONTH	12th MONTH
Jia Yin 2/4 - 8:53a	Yi Mao 3/6 - 3:03a	Bing Chen 4/5 - 8:06a	Ding Si 5/6 - 1:40a	Wu Wu 6/6 - 6:02a	Ji Wei 7/7 - 4:25p	Geng Shen 8/8 - 2:08a	Xin You 9/8 - 4:52a	Ren Xu 10/8 - 8:16p	Gui Hai 11/7 - 11:11p	Jia Zi 12/7 - 3:51p	Yi Chou 1/6 - 3:00a

1999 Ji Mao

1st MONTH	2nd MONTH	3rd MONTH	4th MONTH	5th MONTH	6th MONTH	7th MONTH	8th MONTH	9th MONTH	10th MONTH	11th MONTH	12th MONTH
Bing Yin 2/4 - 2:42p	Ding Mao 3/6 - 8:52a	Wu Chen 4/5 - 1:55p	Ji Si 5/6 - 7:29a	Geng Wu 6/6 - 11:51a	Xin Wei 7/7 - 10:14p	Ren Shen 8/8 - 7:57a	Gui You 9/8 - 10:41a	Jia Xu 10/9 - 2:05a	Yi Hai 11/8 - 5:01a	Bing Zi 12/7 - 9:14p	Ding Chou 1/6 - 8:50a

2000 Geng Chen

1st MONTH	2nd MONTH	3rd MONTH	4th MONTH	5th MONTH	6th MONTH	7th MONTH	8th MONTH	9th MONTH	10th MONTH	11th MONTH	12th MONTH
Wu Yin 2/4 - 8:32p	Ji Mao 3/6 - 2:42p	Geng Chen 4/4 - 7:45p	Xin Si 5/5 - 1:19p	Ren Wu 6/5 - 5:41p	Gui Wei 7/7 - 4:04a	Jia Shen 8/7 - 1:36p	Yi You 9/7 - 2:33p	Bing Xu 10/8 - 7:54a	Ding Hai 11/7 - 10:49a	Wu Zi 12/7 - 3:29a	Ji Chou 1/5 - 2:38p

2001 Xin Si

1st MONTH	2nd MONTH	3rd MONTH	4th MONTH	5th MONTH	6th MONTH	7th MONTH	8th MONTH	9th MONTH	10th MONTH	11th MONTH	12th MONTH
Geng Yin 2/4 - 2:20a	Xin Mao 3/5 - 8:30p	Ren Chen 4/5 - 1:33a	Gui Si 5/5 - 7:07p	Jia Wu 6/5 - 11:29p	Yi Wei 7/7 - 9:52a	Bing Shen 8/7 - 7:34p	Ding You 9/7 - 10:18p	Wu Xu 10/8 - 1:42p	Ji Hai 11/7 - 4:37p	Geng Zi 12/7 - 9:17a	Xin Chou 1/5 - 8:26p

2002 Ren Wu

1st MONTH	2nd MONTH	3rd MONTH	4th MONTH	5th MONTH	6th MONTH	7th MONTH	8th MONTH	9th MONTH	10th MONTH	11th MONTH	12th MONTH
Ren Yin 2/4 - 8:08a	Gui Mao 3/6 - 2:18a	Jia Chen 4/5 - 7:21a	Yi Si 5/6 - 12:55a	Bing Wu 6/6 - 5:17a	Ding Wei 7/7 - 3:40p	Wu Shen 8/8 - 1:23a	Ji You 9/8 - 4:07a	Geng Xu 10/8 - 7:31p	Xin Hai 11/7 - 10:26p	Ren Zi 12/7 - 3:06p	Gui Chou 1/6 - 2:15a

2003 Gui Wei

1st MONTH	2nd MONTH	3rd MONTH	4th MONTH	5th MONTH	6th MONTH	7th MONTH	8th MONTH	9th MONTH	10th MONTH	11th MONTH	12th MONTH
Jia Yin 2/4 - 1:57p	Yi Mao 3/6 - 8:07a	Bing Chen 4/5 - 1:10p	Ding Si 5/6 - 6:44a	Wu Wu 6/6 - 11:06a	Ji Wei 7/7 - 9:29p	Geng Shen 8/8 - 7:12a	Xin You 9/8 - 9:56a	Ren Xu 10/9 - 1:20a	Gui Hai 11/8 - 4:15a	Jia Zi 12/7 - 8:55a	Yi Chou 1/6 - 8:04a

2004 Jia Shen

1st Month	2nd Month	3rd Month	4th Month	5th Month	6th Month	7th Month	8th Month	9th Month	10th Month	11th Month	12th Month
Bing Yin 2/4 - 7:46p	Ding Mao 3/5 - 1:56p	Wu Chen 4/4 - 6:59p	Ji Si 5/5 - 12:33p	Geng Wu 6/5 - 4:55p	Xin Wei 7/7 - 3:18a	Ren Shen 8/7 - 12:59p	Gui You 9/7 - 3:44p	Jia Xu 10/8 - 7:08a	Yi Hai 11/7 - 10:03a	Bing Zi 12/7 - 2:43a	Ding Chou 1/5 - 1:52p

2005 Yi You

1st Month	2nd Month	3rd Month	4th Month	5th Month	6th Month	7th Month	8th Month	9th Month	10th Month	11th Month	12th Month
Wu Yin 2/4 - 1:34a	Ji Mao 3/5 - 7:45p	Geng Chen 4/5 12:48a	Xin Si 5/5 - 6:23p	Ren Wu 6/5 - 10:45p	Gui Wei 7/7 - 9:08a	Jia Shen 8/7 - 6:51p	Yi You 9/7 - 9:35p	Bing Xu 10/8 - 12:59p	Ding Hai 11/7 - 3:54p	Wu Zi 12/7 - 8:34a	Ji Chou 1/5 - 9:43p

2006 Bing Xu

1st Month	2nd Month	3rd Month	4th Month	5th Month	6th Month	7th Month	8th Month	9th Month	10th Month	11th Month	12th Month
Geng Yin 2/4 - 7:25a	Xin Mao 3/6 - 1:35a	Ren Chen 4/5 - 6:38a	Gui Si 5/6 - 12:12a	Jia Wu 6/6 4:34a	Yi Wei 7/7 - 2:57p	Bing Shen 8/8 - 12:40a	Ding You 9/8 - 3:24a	Wu Xu 10/8 - 6:48p	Ji Hai 11/7 - 9:43p	Geng Zi 12/7 - 2:23p	Xin Chou 1/6 - 1:32a

2007 Ding Hai

1st Month	2nd Month	3rd Month	4th Month	5th Month	6th Month	7th Month	8th Month	9th Month	10th Month	11th Month	12th Month
Ren Yin 2/4 - 1:14p	Gui Mao 3/6 - 7:24a	Jia Chen 4/5 - 12:27p	Yi Si 5/6 - 6:01a	Bing Wu 6/6 - 10:23a	Ding Wei 7/7 8:46p	Wu Shen 8/8 - 6:29a	Ji You 9/8 - 9:13a	Geng Xu 10/9 - 12:37a	Xin Hai 11/8 - 3:32a	Ren Zi 12/7 - 8:12p	Gui Chou 1/6 - 7:21a

2008 Wu Zi

1st Month	2nd Month	3rd Month	4th Month	5th Month	6th Month	7th Month	8th Month	9th Month	10th Month	11th Month	12th Month
Jia Yin 2/4 - 7:03p	Yi Mao 3/5 - 1:13p	Bing Chen 4/4 - 6:16p	Ding Si 5/5 - 11:50a	Wu Wu 6/5 - 4:12p	Ji Wei 7/7 - 2:35a	Geng Shen 8/7 - 12:18p	Xin You 9/7 - 3:02p	Ren Xu 10/8 - 6:26a	Gui Hai 11/7 - 9:21a	Jia Zi 12/7 - 2:01a	Yi Chou 1/5 - 1:10p

2009 Ji Chou

1st Month	2nd Month	3rd Month	4th Month	5th Month	6th Month	7th Month	8th Month	9th Month	10th Month	11th Month	12th Month
Bing Yin 2/4 - 12:52a	Ding Mao 3/5 - 7:02p	Wu Chen 4/5 - 12:05a	Ji Si 5/5 - 5:39p	Geng Wu 6/5 - 10:01p	Xin Wei 7/7 - 8:24a	Ren Shen 8/7 - 6:07p	Gui You 9/7 - 8:51p	Jia Xu 10/8 - 12:15p	Yi Hai 11/7 - 3:10p	Bing Zi 12/7 - 7:05a	Ding Chou 1/5 - 7:00p

2010 Geng Yin

1st Month	2nd Month	3rd Month	4th Month	5th Month	6th Month	7th Month	8th Month	9th Month	10th Month	11th Month	12th Month
Wu Yin 2/4 - 6:42a	Ji Mao 3/6 - 12:52a	Geng Chen 4/5 - 5:55a	Xin Si 5/5 - 11:29p	Ren Wu 6/6 - 3:51a	Gui Wei 7/7 - 2:14p	Jia Shen 8/7 - 11:57p	Yi You 9/8 - 2:41a	Bing Xu 10/8 - 6:05p	Ding Hai 11/7 - 9:01p	Wu Zi 12/7 - 1:41p	Ji Chou 1/6 - 12:50a

2011 Xin Mao

1st Month	2nd Month	3rd Month	4th Month	5th Month	6th Month	7th Month	8th Month	9th Month	10th Month	11th Month	12th Month
Geng Yin 2/4 - 12:32p	Xin Mao 3/6 - 6:43a	Ren Chen 4/5 - 11:46a	Gui Si 5/6 - 5:20a	Jia Wu 6/6 - 9:43a	Yi Wei 7/7 - 8:06p	Bing Shen 8/8 - 5:49a	Ding You 9/8 - 8:33a	Wu Xu 10/8 - 11:57p	Ji Hai 11/8 - 2:52a	Geng Zi 12/7 - 7:32p	Xin Chou 1/6 - 6:41a

2012 Ren Chen

1st Month	2nd Month	3rd Month	4th Month	5th Month	6th Month	7th Month	8th Month	9th Month	10th Month	11th Month	12th Month
Ren Yin 2/4 - 6:40p	Gui Mao 3/5 - 12:28p	Jia Chen 4/4 - 5:16p	Yi Si 5/5 - 10:40a	Bing Wu 6/5 - 2:50p	Ding Wei 7/7 - 1:21a	Wu Shen 8/7 - 11:26a	Ji You 9/7 - 2:44p	Geng Xu 10/8 - 6:42a	Xin Hai 11/7 - 9:56a	Ren Zi 12/7 - 2:32a	Gui Chou 1/5 - 1:16a

2013 Gui Si

1st Month	2nd Month	3rd Month	4th Month	5th Month	6th Month	7th Month	8th Month	9th Month	10th Month	11th Month	12th Month
Jia Yin 2/4 - 12:31a	Yi Mao 3/5 - 6:19p	Bing Chen 4/4 - 11:05p	Ding Si 5/5 - 4:28p	Wu Wu 6/5 - 8:44p	Ji Wei 7/7 - 7:09a	Geng Shen 8/7 - 5:14p	Xin You 9/7 - 8:33p	Ren Xu 10/8 - 12:31p	Gui Hai 11/7 - 3:45p	Jia Zi 12/7 - 8:21a	Yi Chou 1/5 - 8:07p

2014 Jia Wu

1ST MONTH	2ND MONTH	3RD MONTH	4TH MONTH	5TH MONTH	6TH MONTH	7TH MONTH	8TH MONTH	9TH MONTH	10TH MONTH	11TH MONTH	12TH MONTH
Bing Yin 2/4 - 6:21a	Ding Mao 3/6 - 12:07a	Wu Chen 4/5 - 4:54a	Ji Si 5/5 - 10:16p	Geng Wu 6/6 - 2:32a	Xin Wei 7/7 - 12:57p	Ren Shen 8/7 - 11:02p	Gui You 9/8 - 2:21a	Jia Xu 10/8 - 6:20p	Yi Hai 11/7 - 9:36p	Bing Zi 12/7 - 2:11p	Ding Chou 1/6 - 12:57a

2015 Yi Wei

1ST MONTH	2ND MONTH	3RD MONTH	4TH MONTH	5TH MONTH	6TH MONTH	7TH MONTH	8TH MONTH	9TH MONTH	10TH MONTH	11TH MONTH	12TH MONTH
Wu Yin 2/4 - 12:09p	Ji Mao 3/6 - 5:56a	Geng Chen 4/5 - 10:58a	Xin Si 5/6 - 4:11a	Ren Wu 6/6 - 8:20a	Gui Wei 7/7 - 6:30p	Jia Shen 8/8 - 4:51a	Yi You 9/8 - 8:10a	Bing Xu 10/9 - 12:09a	Ding Hai 11/8 - 3:25a	Wu Zi 12/7 - 8:01p	Ji Chou 1/6 - 6:47a

2016 Bing Shen

1ST MONTH	2ND MONTH	3RD MONTH	4TH MONTH	5TH MONTH	6TH MONTH	7TH MONTH	8TH MONTH	9TH MONTH	10TH MONTH	11TH MONTH	12TH MONTH
Geng Yin 2/4 - 6:00p	Xin Mao 3/5 - 11:46a	Ren Chen 4/4 - 4:32p	Gui Si 5/5 - 9:54a	Jia Wu 6/5 - 2:09p	Yi Wei 7/7 - 12:33a	Bing Shen 8/7 - 10:39a	Ding You 9/7 - 1:48p	Wu Xu 10/8 - 5:59a	Ji Hai 11/7 - 9:14a	Geng Zi 12/7 - 1:54a	Xin Chou 1/5 - 12:36p

2017 Ding You

1ST MONTH	2ND MONTH	3RD MONTH	4TH MONTH	5TH MONTH	6TH MONTH	7TH MONTH	8TH MONTH	9TH MONTH	10TH MONTH	11TH MONTH	12TH MONTH
Ren Yin 2/3 - 11:49p	Gui Mao 3/5 - 5:36p	Jia Chen 4/4 - 10:20p	Yi Si 5/5 - 3:42p	Bing Wu 6/5 - 7:57p	Ding Wei 7/7 - 6:21a	Wu Shen 8/7 - 4:27p	Ji You 9/7 - 7:46p	Geng Xu 10/8 - 11:47a	Xin Hai 11/7 - 3:03p	Ren Zi 12/7 - 7:40a	Gui Chou 1/5 - 6:26a

2018 Wu Xu

1ST MONTH	2ND MONTH	3RD MONTH	4TH MONTH	5TH MONTH	6TH MONTH	7TH MONTH	8TH MONTH	9TH MONTH	10TH MONTH	11TH MONTH	12TH MONTH
Jia Yin 2/4 - 5:38a	Yi Mao 3/5 - 11:25p	Bing Chen 4/5 - 4:20a	Ding Si 5/5 - 9:31p	Wu Wu 6/6 - 1:29a	Ji Wei 7/7 - 12:09p	Geng Shen 8/7 - 10:15p	Xin You 9/8 - 1:35a	Ren Xu 10/8 - 5:36p	Gui Hai 11/7 - 8:54p	Jia Zi 12/7 - 1:30p	Yi Chou 1/6 - 12:16a

2019 Ji Hai

1ST MONTH	2ND MONTH	3RD MONTH	4TH MONTH	5TH MONTH	6TH MONTH	7TH MONTH	8TH MONTH	9TH MONTH	10TH MONTH	11TH MONTH	12TH MONTH
Bing Yin 2/4 - 11:28a	Ding Mao 3/6 - 5:14a	Wu Chen 4/5 - 9:59a	Ji Si 5/6 - 3:28a	Geng Wu 6/6 - 7:33a	Xin Wei 7/7 - 5:57p	Ren Shen 8/8 - 4:03a	Gui You 9/8 - 7:24a	Jia Xu 10/8 - 11:25p	Yi Hai 11/8 - 2:42a	Bing Zi 12/7 - 7:20p	Ding Chou 1/6 - 6:06a

2020 Geng Zi

1ST MONTH	2ND MONTH	3RD MONTH	4TH MONTH	5TH MONTH	6TH MONTH	7TH MONTH	8TH MONTH	9TH MONTH	10TH MONTH	11TH MONTH	12TH MONTH
Wu Yin 2/4 - 5:18p	Ji Mao 3/5 - 11:03a	Geng Chen 4/4 - 3:48p	Xin Si 5/5 - 9:08a	Ren Wu 6/5 - 1:22p	Gui Wei 7/6 - 11:46p	Jia Shen 8/7 - 9:51a	Yi You 9/7 - 1:12p	Bing Xu 10/8 - 5:15a	Ding Hai 11/7 - 8:31a	Wu Zi 12/7 - 1:09a	Ji Chou 1/5 - 11:55a

2021 Xin Chou

1ST MONTH	2ND MONTH	3RD MONTH	4TH MONTH	5TH MONTH	6TH MONTH	7TH MONTH	8TH MONTH	9TH MONTH	10TH MONTH	11TH MONTH	12TH MONTH
Geng Yin 2/3 - 11:08p	Xin Mao 3/5 - 4:54p	Ren Chen 4/4 - 9:37p	Gui Si 5/5 - 2:57p	Jia Wu 6/5 - 7:09p	Yi Wei 7/7 - 5:33a	Bing Shen 8/7 - 3:40p	Ding You 9/7 - 7:01p	Wu Xu 10/8 - 11:04a	Ji Hai 11/7 - 2:21p	Geng Zi 12/7 - 7:00a	Xin Chou 1/5 - 5:46p

2022 Ren Yin

1ST MONTH	2ND MONTH	3RD MONTH	4TH MONTH	5TH MONTH	6TH MONTH	7TH MONTH	8TH MONTH	9TH MONTH	10TH MONTH	11TH MONTH	12TH MONTH
Ren Yin 2/4 - 4:58a	Gui Mao 3/5 - 10:42p	Jia Chen 4/5 - 3:22a	Yi Si 5/5 - 8:45p	Bing Wu 6/6 - 12:58a	Ding Wei 7/7 - 11:22a	Wu Shen 8/7 - 9:28p	Ji You 9/8 - 12:50a	Geng Xu 10/8 - 4:53p	Xin Hai 11/7 - 8:11p	Ren Zi 12/7 - 12:49p	Gui Chou 1/5 - 11:35p

2023 Gui Mao

1ST MONTH	2ND MONTH	3RD MONTH	4TH MONTH	5TH MONTH	6TH MONTH	7TH MONTH	8TH MONTH	9TH MONTH	10TH MONTH	11TH MONTH	12TH MONTH
Jia Yin 2/4 - 10:47a	Yi Mao 3/6 - 4:31a	Bing Chen 4/5 - 9:14a	Ding Si 5/6 - 2:33a	Wu Wu 6/6 - 6:46a	Ji Wei 7/7 - 6:10p	Geng Shen 8/8 - 3:16a	Xin You 9/8 - 6:38a	Ren Xu 10/8 - 10:41p	Gui Hai 11/8 - 2:00a	Jia Zi 12/7 - 6:38p	Yi Chou 1/6 - 5:25a

Thus, the example's life chart now looks like this:

	Hour	Day	Month	Year
	7:45p	1	July	1961
Stem			Jia	Xin
Branch			Wu	Chou
Stem Phase			Wood	Metal
Branch Phase			Fire	Earth

The Day Pillar

Determining your day pillar requires several steps and simple mathematics. You'll find Table 6 easier to read if you imagine it as one long chart. The *day number* begins with 0 and ends with 29 on the first chart, continuing with 30 and ending with 59 on the second chart. Following this idea, a month may begin on one chart and end on the other. For example, find January 1 on the first chart. If you skim down to the end of the column, you'll see that January 30 is the last entry. Now, move over to the first column on the second chart. The first entry commences with January 31. Continuing down the column, the last entry is March 1. March 2 is found on the second column in chart 1. Again, if you envision chart 2 taped to the bottom of chart 1, this seemingly complicated configuration becomes clear, the months flowing into each other. To avoid confusion, we suggest you take some time to practice reading this chart before proceeding.

◆ **Step One:** Find the day number in the following table corresponding to your birthday. Continuing with the example, you'll find July 1 on the first chart. This day's day number is 1.

Like converting meters to feet or centigrade to Fahrenheit, Table 6 is converting the Chinese solar calendar into the Western, or Gregorian, calendar. Counting January 1 as "0," a day number is the number of days into a year any specific day is. For example, February 10 is 40 days into the year. So, February 10's day number is 40. If the number of days into the year is greater than 60, 60 is subtracted from the total until the remainder is less than 60. For example, March 31 is 89 days into the year—89 − 60 = 29 day number. Say, August 10 is your birthday. August 10 is 221 days into the year. So, 221 − 60 − 60 − 60 = 41 day number.

Table 6

DAY #	DAY NUMBER CHART					
	DAY OF YEAR					
0	Jan1	Mar2	May1	Jun30	Aug29	Oct28	Dec27
1	2	3	2	Jul 1	30	29	28
2	3	4	3	2	31	30	29
3	4	5	4	3	Sep 1	31	30
4	5	6	5	4	2	Nov 1	31
5	6	7	6	5	3	2	
6	7	8	7	6	4	3	
7	8	9	8	7	5	4	
8	9	10	9	8	6	5	
9	10	11	10	9	7	6	
10	11	12	11	10	8	7	
11	12	13	12	11	9	8	
12	13	14	13	12	10	9	
13	14	15	14	13	11	10	
14	15	16	15	14	12	11	
15	16	17	16	15	13	12	
16	17	18	17	16	14	13	
17	18	19	18	17	15	14	
18	19	20	19	18	16	15	
19	20	21	20	19	17	16	
20	21	22	21	20	18	17	
21	22	23	22	21	19	18	
22	23	24	23	22	20	19	
23	24	25	24	23	21	20	
24	25	26	25	24	22	21	
25	26	27	26	25	23	22	
26	27	28	27	26	24	23	
27	28	29	28	27	25	24	
28	29	30	29	28	26	25	
29	30	31	30	29	27	26	

DAY #	DAY NUMBER CHART					
	DAY OF YEAR					
30	Jan31	Apr1	May 31	Jul 30	Sep28	Nov27
31	Feb 1	2	Jun1	31	29	28
32	2	3	2	Aug 1	30	29
33	3	4	3	2	Oct 1	30
34	4	5	4	3	2	Dec 1
35	5	6	5	4	3	2
36	6	7	6	5	4	3
37	7	8	7	6	5	4
38	8	9	8	7	6	5
39	9	10	9	8	7	6
40	10	11	10	9	8	7
41	11	12	11	10	9	8
42	12	13	12	11	10	9
43	13	14	13	12	11	10
44	14	15	14	13	12	11
45	15	16	15	14	13	12
46	16	17	16	15	14	13
47	17	18	17	16	15	14
48	18	19	18	17	16	15
49	19	20	19	18	17	16
50	20	21	20	19	18	17
51	21	22	21	20	19	18
52	22	23	22	21	20	19
53	23	24	23	22	21	20
54	24	25	24	23	22	21
55	25	26	25	24	23	22
56	26	27	26	25	24	23
57	27	28	27	26	25	24
58	28	29	28	27	26	25
59	Mar 1	30	29	28	27	26

The day pillar.

◆ **Step Two:** Find the number corresponding to your Western birth year from the Year Number Table 7. The example's birth year is 1961, a numeric value of 31.

◆ **Step Three:** Add the numbers from Steps One and Two together. Continuing with the example, 1 (Step One) + 31 (Step Two) = 32.

Year number chart.

Table 7

YEAR #	YEAR #	YEAR #	YEAR #
1924* 16	1949 28	1974 39	1999 50
1925 22	1950 33	1975 44	2000* 55
1926 27	1951 38	1976* 49	2001 1
1927 32	1952* 43	1977 55	2002 6
1928* 37	1953 49	1978 60	2003 11
1929 43	1954 54	1979 5	2004* 16
1930 48	1955 59	1980* 10	2005 22
1931 53	1956* 4	1981 16	2006 27
1932* 58	1957 10	1982 21	2007 32
1933 4	1958 15	1983 26	2008* 37
1934 9	1959 20	1984* 31	2009 43
1935 14	1960* 25	1985 37	2010 48
1936* 19	1961 31	1986 42	2011 53
1937 25	1962 36	1987 47	2012* 58
1938 30	1963 41	1988* 52	2013 4
1939 35	1964* 46	1989 58	2014 9
1940* 40	1965 52	1990 3	2015 14
1941 46	1966 57	1991 8	2016* 19
1942 51	1967 2	1992* 13	2017 25
1943 56	1968* 7	1993 19	2018 30
1944* 1	1969 13	1994 24	2019 35
1945 7	1970 18	1995 29	2020* 40
1946 12	1971 23	1996* 34	2021 46
1947 17	1972* 28	1997 40	2022 51
1948* 22	1973 34	1998 45	2023 56

* Leap Year

- **Step Four:** If the date occurs in a leap year (indicated by the asterisk after the year), add one to the sum. Otherwise, the sum remains the same. July 1 is after February 28 and it is not a leap year. If the example's birthday is March 20, 1960, she would add one to the sum because 1960 is a leap year and she was born after February 28.

- **Step Five:** If the sum is over 60, subtract 60 from it. If the sum is less than 60, use the sum. Thirty-two is less than 60 and becomes the resulting number. But let's take a person born on June 15, 1997. June 15 corresponds to 45 on the Day Pillar Table 6 (Step One). On the Year Number Table 7, 1997 corresponds to 40 (Step Two). Added together, 45 + 40 = 85 (Step Three). June 15 is after February 28 and is not a leap year. The sum remains the same (Step Four). Because the sum is over 60, you must subtract 60. Thus, 85 – 60 = 25.

◆ **Step Six:** The result in Step Five is the number of the day in question within the 60-day cycle. Continuing with the first example of the woman born on July 1, 1961, at 7:45 P.M., her resulting number is 32, which corresponds to Yi (Stem) Wei (Branch) on Table 8. Yi (wood) Wei (earth) is the example's day pillar.

Table 8

CYCLE OF SIXTY DAYS			
1	Jai Zi	31	Jia Wu
2	Yi Chou	32	Yi Wei
3	Bing Yin	33	Bing Shen
4	Ding Mao	34	Ding You
5	Wu Chen	35	Wu Xu
6	Ji Si	36	Ji Hai
7	Geng Wu	37	Geng Zi
8	Xin Wei	38	Xin Chou
9	Ren Shen	39	Ren Yin
10	Gui You	40	Gui Mao
11	Jia Xu	41	Jia Chen
12	Yi Hai	42	Yi Si
13	Bing Zi	43	Bing Wu
14	Ding Chou	44	Ding Wei
15	Wu Yin	45	Wu Shen
16	Ji Mao	46	Ji You
17	Geng Chen	47	Geng Xu
18	Xin Si	48	Xin Hai
19	Ren Wu	49	Ren Zi
20	Gui Wei	50	Gui Chou
21	Jia Shen	51	Jia Yin
22	Yi You	52	Yi Mao
23	Bing Xu	53	Bing Chen
24	Ding Hai	54	Ding Si
25	Wu Zi	55	Wu Wu
26	Ji Chou	56	Ji Wei
27	Geng Yin	57	Geng Shen
28	Xin Mao	58	Xin You
29	Ren Chen	59	Ren Xu
30	Gui Si	60	Gui Hai

The example's chart now looks like this:

	Hour	Day	Month	Year
	7:45p	**1**	**July**	**1961**
Stem		Yi	Jia	Xin
Branch		Wei	Wu	Chou
Stem Phase		Wood	Wood	Metal
Branch Phase		Earth	Fire	Earth

The Hour Pillar

To determine the components of your hour pillar, find the time of your birth in the Time column in Table 9. If you were born when Daylight Saving Time was in effect, you must subtract an hour from the time of your birth. If you're unsure if DST was in effect, one of the following books can help:

◆ *Doane's Worldwide Time Change Update*, by Doris Chase Doane (American Federation of Astrologers, Inc., 1991)

◆ *Time Changes in the USA*, also by Doris Chase Doane (American Federation of Astrologers, Inc., 1997)

Next, run your finger over one column to determine your branch component. To determine your stem component you must know your day stem, which you'll find at the top of Table 9. Then, run your finger down the column until it intersects with the Time line.

The hour pillar.

Table 9

		DAY STEM				
TIME	BRANCH	JIA or JI	YI or GENG	BING or XIN	DING or REN	WU or GUI
12p - 1a	Zi	Jia	Bing	Wu	Geng	Ren
1 - 3a	Chou	Yi	Ding	Ji	Xin	Gui
3 - 5a	Yin	Bing	Wu	Geng	Ren	Jia
5 - 7a	Mao	Ding	Ji	Xin	Gui	Yi
7 - 9a	Chen	Wu	Geng	Ren	Jia	Bing
9 - 11a	Si	Ji	Xin	Gui	Yi	Ding
11a - 1p	Wu	Geng	Ren	Jia	Bing	Wu
1 - 3p	Wei	Xin	Gui	Yi	Ding	Ji
3 - 5p	Shen	Ren	Jia	Bing	Wu	Geng
5 - 7p	You	Gui	Yi	Ding	Ji	Xin
7 - 9p	Xu	Jia	Bing	Wu	Geng	Ren
9 - 11p	Hai	Yi	Ding	Ji	Xin	Gui
11p - 12a	Zi	Bing	Wu	Geng	Ren	Jia

Correct for Daylight Savings Time, if necessary.

Concluding our example's life chart, she was born at 7:45 P.M. Adjusting for DST, her birth hour now becomes 6:45 P.M., which falls within the two-hour time block of 5 P.M. to 7 P.M. in the Time column. Her corresponding branch is You (metal). Our example's day stem is Yi. Run your finger down the Yi or Geng column until it intersects with the 5–7 P.M. time line. Yi is also her hour stem. Thus, her hour pillar is Yi (wood) You (metal).

Our example's completed life chart is as follows:

	Hour 6:45p*	**Day** 1	**Month** July	**Year** 1961
Stem	Yi	Yi	Jia	Xin
Branch	You	Wei	Wu	Chou
Stem Phase	Wood	Wood	Wood	Metal
Branch Phase	Metal	Earth	Fire	Earth

* Adjusted for Daylight Saving Time

If you haven't already entered your Four Pillars of Destiny information, please do so now in the following chart.

	Hour	**Day**	**Month**	**Year**
Stem				
Branch				
Stem Phase				
Branch Phase				

Your life chart.

Whew! You've completed your Four Pillars of Destiny life chart. Now what? This is where the fun begins. In Chapter 23, "The Four Pillars of Destiny, Part 2," and Chapter 24, "The Four Pillars of Destiny, Part 3," you'll learn how to determine your lucky colors, suitable careers, and environments. Based on what phases are favorable to you, you'll be able to ascertain if a 10-year period, a year, month, and even a day will be favorable, unfavorable, or somewhere in between. So, don't sign that important document just yet. Hold off making vacation plans and celebrations. Grasp fuller knowledge of your destiny by continuing to construct an understanding of your Four Pillars.

The Least You Need to Know

◆ The Chinese believe the first breath we take at birth determines our destiny.

◆ The Four Pillars of Destiny is a method of determining the qi you inhaled at birth.

◆ Each pillar is made up of a stem-branch component corresponding to a five-phase element.

Chapter 23

The Four Pillars of Destiny, Part 2

In This Chapter

- What is the Day-Master?
- Determining the timeliness of your Day-Master
- Determining a strong and a weak chart
- Determining your favorable and unfavorable phases
- Interpreting Princess Diana's chart

Now that you've assembled your chart, how do you interpret it? Before you can obtain insight, you must know how to acquire information and where to look. In this chapter, we'll continue with the Four Pillars method and its application with respect to the five phases. In so doing, we will zero in on the Day-Master and reveal how it offers a particularly personal assessment.

The All-Important Day-Master

Although The Four Pillars of Destiny dates to the Tang dynasty (618–907 C.E.), when astrologer Li Xuzhong developed it as a way to represent a person's birth data, the approach hasn't stayed constant. Over time, there have been many alterations. Perhaps the most significant ones involved focusing on the Day-Master as a means of illuminating a person's specific characteristics.

Wise Words

The **Day-Master,** or **Ziping Method,** developed by Song dynasty astrologer Xu Ziping, analyzes the five phases in your Four Pillars chart in relationship to how each phase affects the Day-Master (the day stem component of your Four Pillars chart).

Called the *Day-Master*, this method is also known as the *Ziping Method* after astrologer Xu Ziping and dates to the Song dynasty (960–1279 C.E.). The Day-Master helps you to identify which of the five phases you belong to. It can determine if you have a strong or a weak chart. Knowing the relative strength of your chart can lead you to a broader understanding of your relationship to the five phases, as you'll soon see.

The following illustration indicates where the Day-Master appears on your chart. The Day-Master is equivalent to the day stem phase component of your Four Pillars of Destiny chart.

The Day-Master.

	Hour	**Day**	**Month**	**Year**
Stem	Phase	Day-Master Phase	Phase	Phase
Branch	Phase	Phase	Phase	Phase

Now, refer to your life chart you just constructed in Chapter 22, "The Four Pillars of Destiny, Part 1," and pinpoint your Day-Master. You may want to paperclip that page, as you'll be referring to it throughout this chapter. Also, it's a good idea to have the tear-out card handy from the front of this book. We'll soon be analyzing the relationship between the phases and Day-Master.

The Timeliness of Your Day-Master

To determine the strength of your chart, you need to familiarize yourself with the timeliness of your Day-Master. Timeliness refers to the time of the year you were born—specifically, into which season you were born. Remember how the five phases correspond to the seasons? Here again, that information is important (see Chapter 6, "The Principle of the Five Phases," for a reminder). For the sake of clarity, let's reiterate. Wood corresponds to spring; fire to summer; metal to autumn; and water to winter. Earth is a special case, which we will deal with shortly.

Add to these phase/season relationships five possible conditions: *timely, weak, locked, dead,* and *ready*. These conditions refer to the phase's strength in the particular season into which you are born. For example, if your Day-Master is wood and you are born in spring, you are timely because wood is predominant in the spring. In summer, wood is weak. In later summer, wood is exceedingly weak but not yet dead. It is locked. Once autumn arrives, wood is *dead*. With winter, wood begins to repeat its cycle and is ready.

Wise Words

A phase is **timely** when it is in its season of predominance. A phase is **weak** when its energy has been depleted. A phase is **locked** when it is about to die. A phase is **dead** when it is completely controlled by another phase (in its own timely state). A phase is **ready** when it's about to begin the cycle again.

Each phase goes through a similar cycle, with its timely period corresponding to the season in which it is dominant. By the way, late summer is identified as an independent season because of the climate of China. Early to mid-summer is usually hot and dry and relates to the first two months of our Western summer. Late summer (the latter half of your Western summer) brings rain and dampness. The chart following lists the phases (except earth) and their timely conditions throughout the seasons.

Phase	Spring	Summer	Late Summer	Autumn	Winter
Wood	Timely	Weak	Locked	Dead	Ready
Fire	Ready	Timely	Weak	Locked	Dead
Metal	Locked	Dead	Ready	Timely	Weak
Water	Weak	Locked	Dead	Ready	Timely

Now, what of earth? As we mentioned, earth is a special case. It's a transitional phase, as you learned in Chapter 21, "Introducing the Twelve Animals of the Chinese Zodiac." Earth is timely in October, January, and April, or the final 18 days of autumn, winter, and spring. With summer, earth is not restricted to the final 18 days because of the inclusion of late summer as a separate season. Earth is timely (hence predominant) in late summer. Other than its periods of timeliness, earth is weak in autumn, locked in winter, dead in spring, and ready in summer.

If you haven't already determined if your Day-Master is timely, weak, locked, dead, or ready, do so now because this is the first step to interpreting your life chart you constructed in the previous chapter.

Day-Master Relations

Because this chapter is rather involved, let's review for a moment. In The Four Pillars of Destiny, there are eight components, one of which is the Day-Master. Each component is associated with a phase (fire, earth, metal, water, wood). To interpret a life chart, you examine how the Day-Master is affected by the other seven phases. How they relate to the Day-Master will lead you to the strength of your chart. The various relationships are categorized into five interpretive phases. They are …

Feng Facts

You can identify a chart's timeliness without knowing the specific birthday by referring to the phase in the month branch. For example, if the Day-Master is fire and the month branch is fire, the Day-Master is timely. Conversely, if the Day-Master is fire and the month branch is water, the Day-Master is dead. However, this method doesn't quite work for earth. In this case, you'll need to know the month branch animal sign, a factor illustrated in Chapter 21.

---

1. **Resource.** If a phase produces the Day-Master it is the resource phase. An example would be how wood (resource) produces fire (Day-Master). (You may want to review the five phases cycles in Chapter 6.) The resource phase is to the Day-Master as a mother is to her son. In human terms, resource corresponds to support from your parents and boss. An abundance of resource suggests you may be spoiled. A lack of resource means you tend to do things by yourself.

2. **Performance.** If a phase is produced by the Day-Master it is the performance phase. An example would be how earth (performance) is produced by fire (Day-Master). The performance phase is to the Day-Master as a son is to his mother. In human terms, performance corresponds to your talents, production, accomplishments, and achievements. A lot of performance means you are a very talented person. A lack of performance indicates you're a sure-footed worker.

3. **Power.** If a phase controls the Day-Master, it is the power phase. An example would be how water (power) controls fire (Day-Master). The power phase is to the Day-Master as a stern father is to his son or a strict teacher is to his pupil. In human terms, those who seek to control you also empower you to strengthen and succeed. An abundance of power suggests too many constraints. A lack of power could mean a lack of ambition and discipline.

Wise Words

The **resource** phase gives strength to, supports, and produces the Day-Master. The **performance** phase is produced by the Day-Master. The **power** phase controls, dominates, or empowers the Day-Master. The **wealth** phase challenges the Day-Master. The **parallel** phase is the same as the Day-Master.

4. *Wealth.* If a phase is controlled by the Day-Master, it is the wealth phase. An example would be how fire (wealth) is controlled by water (Day-Master). The wealth phase is to the Day-Master as a son is to his stern father. In human terms, the wealth phase indicates money, property, and success. An abundance of the phase suggests you exert a lot of energy to create and/or maintain your success and/or money and property. A lack of wealth indicates you must create opportunities yourself. It does not suggest you will not have money or a successful career.

5. *Parallel.* If a phase is simply the same phase as the Day-Master, it is the phase element. A parallel phase assists the Day-Master to make him strong. In human terms, parallel phases are your friends and competitors. An abundance of parallel may mean you have to compete for everything including money and love. A lack of this phase suggests loneliness and a lack of assistance from colleagues and friends.

Are you with us, so far? We know this stuff is complicated, but stick with it. In the end, it will be worth your while. Patience and perseverance prevail (say that 10 times fast).

Strong or Weak?

Now that you've determined the timeliness of your Day-Master and understand how each phase affects the Day-Master, you're ready to examine your chart as a whole. In this section, you'll learn if your chart is one of strength or weakness. But don't think the strength or weakness of your chart reflects you, the person. There are many powerful people who have weak charts, as you shall soon see.

It's also important to understand that analyzing a chart is no easy task. It takes experience, a keen eye, and a solid understanding of the subtleties of the five phase relationships. Apprentices under the tutelage of a master often study and train for years before going out on their own. In addition to what we present, there are many other factors that must be taken into consideration. For example, a phase in question could have hidden phases that influence the structure of the chart. Also, each phase corresponds to a familial relation, another factor that affects the reading. While there exist many other details that we won't go into, for our purposes, know that like analyzing Flying Star number combinations, there are often shades of gray. So, take it easy, and take your time. The two categories of charts follow.

The Strong Day-Master

A *strong Day-Master* is a chart that has lots of resources, lots of parallel, not much power, maybe some wealth, and not much performance. In other words, the person has a lot of support (resource), friends to assist him (parallel), good guidance (power), and some opportunity to succeed and make money (wealth), but little opportunity to show his talent (performance). Of course, he must be born in a timely season, or at least a season when the Day-Master isn't locked or dead. If he is untimely, this reduces the strength of the chart.

The following illustration shows an example of a strong Day-Master.

A strong Day-Master.

	Hour	**Day**	**Month**	**Year**
Stem	Wood	Metal	Water	Earth
Branch	Fire	Earth	Metal	Metal

First, we must determine the Day-Master's timeliness. What do you think? If you say it is timely, you are correct. The Day-Master metal is timely in a metal month. Now, let's look at why this is a strong chart. There are two resource (earth) phases nourishing the Day-Master and two parallel (metal) phases assisting compared to one wealth (wood), one power (fire), and one performance (water) phase, which deplete metal's strength.

Wise Words _____

A **strong Day-Master** means one with more resource and parallel phases than power, wealth, and performance phases. A person with a strong chart has many friends and many competitors. He derives much support from those around him who are more experienced, while getting few chances to demonstrate his own talents. Also, those with strong charts are susceptible to injuries received through the exhibition of their talents.

Those with strong Day-Masters include Al Gore, Mohammed Ali, Steve Forbes, Steffi Graf, and Monica Lewinsky.

The Weak Day-Master

What constitutes a *weak Day-Master?* Well, untimeliness is a factor. (However, if the Day-Master is timely, the chart may still be weak, but on the strong side of weak.) The presence of many power, performance, and wealth phases, and the lack of resource and parallel phases, are the other considerations. A person with a weak chart tends to be attracted to people who are talented and well disciplined. In fact, the weak chart person is often dominated and controlled, receiving little support from friends and those more experienced.

Here's an example of a weak Day-Master.

	Hour	Day	Month	Year
Stem	Water	Metal	Fire	Fire
Branch	Fire	Earth	Metal	Fire

A weak Day-Master.

In this illustration, the Day-Master is timely—metal born in a metal month. Yet, the chart is weak. Although the Day-Master is enhanced by one resource (earth) and assisted by one parallel (metal), it is surrounded by four power (fire) phases and one performance (water). Also, this chart lacks wealth (water), which would only serve to weaken it further. All factors considered, this chart is clearly weak.

Wise Words _____

A **weak Day-Master** is one with more power, performance, and wealth than resource and parallel. A person with a weak Day-Master is usually being challenged by power and authority, yet has enough intelligence to combat such confrontations. Also, he has much potential to use his talents to have spectacular achievements in favorable luck periods.

Those with weak Day-Masters include George W. Bush, Richard Nixon, Michael Jordan, Bill Clinton, and Marlene Dietrich.

What Are Your Favorable and Unfavorable Phases?

Before we get around to addressing this question directly, let's put forth a scenario. Let's say your Day-Master is wood. According to the relationship of the five phases, water (resource) produces wood while metal (power) controls wood. We accept as common sense that water is favorable and metal is unfavorable. But should we be so hasty? Obviously, water is essential to the growth and nourishment of a plant. Likewise, we need nourishment and support from our friends. But too much water can drown a plant, just as too many friends can sometimes overwhelm us. Similarly, we can chop down a tree with an ax, but we can prune it with shears to maximize its growth potential. So, again, what's favorable and what's unfavorable? How do we know which phase is best suited to meet our needs? The answer lies in the Four Pillars structure.

In Chinese philosophy, equilibrium is optimum. A phase that brings your Four Pillars to a state of equilibrium is your *favorable* phase. Sometimes, we may have more than one favorable phase. But, just as a phase can help you, a phase can potentially cause you harm, putting at risk your well-being. Such a phase (or phases) would be *unfavorable* to you.

A Strong Day-Master's Favorable and Unfavorable Phases

The following is a strong chart. The Day-Master is timely because metal (in the month branch) is born in autumn. Also, the Day-Master is enhanced by two resource (earth) phases and assisted by two parallel (metal) phases. It is controlled only by one power (fire)

Wise Words

A phase that brings balance to your chart is considered **favorable**. A phase that causes an imbalance is considered **unfavorable**.

phase and weakened by one performance (water) phase. There is only one wealth (wood) phase. To bring this chart to balance, more intelligence is needed. While weakening the Day-Master, water also enhances wealth (wood), whose maintenance is consistently draining energy from the Day-Master. The more chances to make money or to develop, the more energy drained from the Day-Master. Also, fire is considered favorable because it pushes the Day-Master to work harder toward greater accomplishments.

Water and fire are favorable for this strong chart. Earth and metal are unfavorable.

	Hour	**Day**	**Month**	**Year**
Stem	Earth	Metal	Metal	Earth
Branch	Water	Wood	Metal	Fire

So, what phases are unfavorable in this chart? Metal (parallel) and earth (resource). An abundance of metal brings more competitors, even enemies. Earth is considered unfavorable simply because it is suffocating the Day-Master.

Master Class

Favorable phases for a strong Day-Master are performance, power, and wealth. Unfavorable phases for a strong chart are resource and parallel. Wealth is also considered unfavorable if found in abundance.

A Weak Day-Master's Favorable and Unfavorable Phases

Although the Day-Master is timely, the following is a weak chart because the ratio of the performance (water)/power (fire)/wealth (wood) phases to the resource (earth)/parallel (metal) phases is unbalanced. The Day-Master must be strengthened. In this case, earth is favorable because it accomplishes three things. First, it will nourish the Day-Master. Second, earth will weaken the fire threatening the Day-Master. Finally, earth will control water. Also, metal is considered favorable to a lesser degree because inner strength is more effective than outside assistance.

	Hour	**Day**	**Month**	**Year**
Stem	Water	Metal	Fire	Fire
Branch	Wood	Earth	Metal	Fire

This Day-Master's unfavorable phases are fire, water, and wood because they weaken the Day-Master.

The Phases of Our Lives

So, where does all this lead? Knowing your favorable and unfavorable phases can help you in many ways. You'll know ...

- What colors enhance your health, wealth, and relationships, and what colors bring hardship and misfortune.
- What environments are best suited to you.
- What profession is suitable for you.

Master Class

Favorable phases for a weak Day-Master are resource and parallel. Unfavorable phases for a weak chart are power, performance, and wealth.

◆ With whom you are compatible.

◆ How to determine if a day, month, year, or 10-year period will be auspicious or inauspicious (something you'll learn more about in Chapter 24, "The Four Pillars of Destiny, Part 3").

Let's take an example. Say your favorable phase is fire, your unfavorable phase is water. Your lucky colors would then be red, purple, dark orange, and pink. Your unlucky colors are blue and black. So, following the five phase correlations, you're best suited to hot and dry environments. Fire industries like restaurants, fire fighting, and electrical engineering are suitable careers. In regard to compatibility, you'll have to find a spouse with plenty of fire in his or her Four Pillars.

The following table illustrates what kind of environments and careers correlate to each of the five phases.

Phase	Suitable Environment	Suitable Career
Wood	Luxuriant vegetated areas; high-rise buildings	Construction, carpentry, botany, stationary, publication, legal, textile, education
Fire	Desert; triangular structures	Electrical engineering, lighting, food industry, ammunition manufacturing
Earth	Mountainous; square structures	Real estate, agriculture, mining, sculpture, financial planner, secretary, consultant, accounting (any service-oriented position)
Metal	Behind bars (a joke); houses with domes or circular structures; houses with wrought-iron fences, aluminum window frames	Machinery, banking, jewelry, martial arts
Water	Living on or near any body of water; ranch houses	Naval, housekeeping, laundry, tourism, media, transportation, cruise industry

The list is exhaustive. An understanding of the five phases is the key to classifying career types. Now that you know your favorable and unfavorable phase, does your occupation fit your auspicious phases?

The Fate of Princess Diana

The example you used in the last chapter to assemble your chart was that of Princess Diana. Surprised? Let's examine her chart in terms of strengths and weaknesses.

Wood in summer is untimely. It's weak. There is no resource (water) to nourish Diana's Day-Master. Two power (metal) phases control, but empower her. There is one performance (fire) phase. Despite having two parallel (wood) phases that assist her, wood is considered neutral here. Diana's chart is weak. Water, her favorable phase, is the key to her survival. Metal is also favorable only if accompanied by water. Otherwise, metal is unfavorable. Earth (wealth), which controls water, is her unfavorable phase. Fire, which weakens her further, is also unfavorable. All total, Diana's chart is weak.

	Hour 6:45p*	Day 1	Month July	Year 1961
Stem	Wood	Wood	Wood	Metal
Branch	Metal	Earth	Fire	Earth

*Adjusted for Daylight Saving Time

Princess Diana's favorable phase is water, and metal if accompanied by water. Earth and fire are her unfavorable phases. Wood is neutral.

Below the Day-Master, the earthly branch is called the *Marriage Palace*. In Diana's Marriage Palace sits unfavorable earth. This means her marriage could not have been successful.

Wise Words _____

Your **Marriage Palace** corresponds to the phase beneath the Day-Master (the day branch). If its phase is favorable, your marriage, or prospects of getting married, will be successful. If the phase is unfavorable, then chances are slim your marriage can survive.

We'll continue to examine Princess Diana's chart in the next chapter.

The Least You Need to Know

♦ Your Day-Master is the key to interpreting your life chart.

♦ The timeliness of your Day-Master depends on the month in which you were born.

♦ The five phase relationships to the Day-Master determine if you have a strong or weak chart.

♦ Favorable phases bring a chart to balance, while unfavorable phases unbalance a chart.

♦ Favorable phases correspond to colors, the environment, suitable professions, and compatible people beneficial to your well-being; unfavorable phases are those colors, environments, professions, and people detrimental to your health, wealth, and relationships.

Chapter 24

The Four Pillars of Destiny, Part 3

In This Chapter

- ◆ What is luck?
- ◆ Calculating your 10-year luck periods
- ◆ Determining the auspiciousness of each 10-year luck period
- ◆ Determining the auspiciousness of each year
- ◆ More on the fate of Princess Diana

A farmer loses his horse. We say, "He's unlucky." The lost horse returns to the farm with a few wild horses. We say, "What a lucky guy!" The farmer's 18-year-old son rides one of the wild horses and is thrown, breaking his leg. We say, "He was unlucky." A war breaks out. The king summons all males from 18 to 30 years of age to join his ranks. Due to his disability, the crippled son of the farmer is exempt. We say, "Lucky boy!"

Sometimes we are lucky. At other times, we are unlucky. Is the path written in stone? No. It's written in our Four Pillars of Destiny. How do I determine my luck, you ask? Well, you'll need to know the stem and branch of your year and month pillars and your favorable and unfavorable phases. Also, you must have a good understanding of the five phase relationships. With this knowledge you can then learn what components of time are destined to bring favorable or unfavorable conditions.

The Axiom of Luck

We all know luck exists. It seems some people are just plain lucky. They win drawings, they win at gambling, they win sweepstakes. Seemingly, everything they touch "turns to gold." Some say they have "the luck of the Irish." You know the type. Then there are those who can't "get a break." They are "down on their luck;" "black clouds" follow them. We consider these unfortunate people unlucky.

We all know lucky and unlucky people. In fact, each of us has experienced good luck and bad luck throughout our lives. But can luck be proven? After all, it isn't something we can apply our five senses to. Luck can't be seen, touched, or smelled. You can't taste or feel luck. Yet, we agree it exists. Luck is a "fact" we accept without proof. In mathematics, a self-evident truth accepted on its intrinsic merit is called an *axiom*. For example, $1 + 1 = 2$ is an axiom. This equation does not have to be proven because it is accepted as truth.

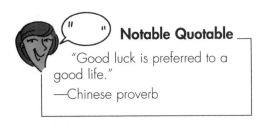

Notable Quotable

"Good luck is preferred to a good life."
—Chinese proverb

Wise Words

An **axiom** is a widely accepted fact based on its intrinsic merits. Because an axiom is a general truth, it does not have to be proven.

Okay, I buy this, you say. But can luck be *proven?* The Chinese believe luck is a function of time governed by the laws of nature. They believe luck is not random, but determinable. If luck were random, there would be no laws of nature. Physics would not exist. The universe would operate in a chaotic state. So, how do you determine luck? The Four Pillars of Destiny is only one method the Chinese use to measure the distribution of your luck. Let's see how.

Lucky Me

Webster's New Collegiate Dictionary defines luck as "a force that brings good fortune." The Chinese believe this "force" is actually qi. Specifically, the qi you inhaled at birth determines when your luck begins. From that point on, your luck is traditionally described in periods of 10 years. Does this mean that you'll have 10 years of fortune, followed by 10 years of misfortune? No. It means each fortunate period carries mostly favorable qi, while each unfortunate period carries mostly unfavorable qi.

First, though, you must determine when your first luck period begins. To determine this, you must know the stem and branch of your year pillar and its yin and yang polarity. (See the Cycle of Sixty Table 3 in Chapter 22, "The Four Pillars of Destiny, Part 1," for this information. All tables referred to in this chapter are to be found in Chapter 22.) For example, if your year pillar is Jia Zi (the first stem-branch combination), its polarity is yang. If your year pillar is Yi Chou (the second stem-branch combination), its polarity is yin. Based on the stem-branch polarity and your gender, you will fall into one of two categories and follow instructions accordingly: those for a yang male and yin female, or those for a yin male and yang female.

Yang Male or Yin Female, Please Step Forward

If you are a yang male or yin female, follow these simple steps to determine your 10-year luck periods. How do you know if you're a yang male or yin female? As just mentioned, simply consult the Cycle of Sixty Table 3 in Chapter 22. For example, if your year pillar is Jia Wu (number 31 in the cycle of 60), this stem-branch combination is yang. So if Jia Wu describes your year pillar and you are male, this would make you a yang male. You would then follow the instructions given below to determine your 10-year luck periods. However, if Jia Wu describes your year pillar and you are female, then you must follow the instructions pertaining to a yin male or yang female.

Step 1: Counting your birthday as "1," count *forward* to the *last day* of the Chinese solar month in which you were born. How many days is it? Let's use Princess Diana as an example. She is a yin female. The year 1961 is a Xin Chou year. Xin Chou's polarity is yin (see the Cycle of Sixty Table 3, number 38, in Chapter 22). Count forward until the last day of the solar month she was born into. So, referring to Table 5 (the Month Pillar charts), locate the fifth month of 1961 (Jia Wu). Notice the next solar month after her July 1 birthday begins on July 7 (Yi Wei). Counting July 1, six days remain in the fifth solar month (July 1, 2, 3, 4, 5, 6 = 6 days). July 7, the beginning of the sixth month, is *not* counted.

Step 2: Divide the number of days by three. If there is a remainder, round the answer up to the next whole number. The result is the age when your first 10-year luck period begins. If the result is "0," your luck begins at birth. Ten years old is the latest your luck period can begin.

But what of the years prior to when your luck begins? The auspiciousness—luck or fortune—of these years is determined by your month pillar, particularly the earthly branch phase. This component is called the *Parents Palace*. Until your first luck period begins, you are under the care of your

Wise Words

The **Parents Palace** is represented by the phase combination of your month pillar. You are governed by this combination until your luck period begins. This combination also represents your family background. If the combination is favorable to your Day-Master, your childhood more than likely was happy. If the combination is unfavorable to your Day-Master, you probably had an unhappy childhood.

parents as described by the phase in this palace and its relationship to your Day-Master (which we discussed in Chapter 23, "The Four Pillars of Destiny, Part 2").

Continuing with our Diana example, step 1's calculation yielded 6 days. So, 6 ÷ 3 = 2. Her luck begins at age 2.

Note: if there's no remainder (as in Diana's case), your luck changes every 10 years on your birthday. If the remainder is 1, drop the remainder. Your luck changes 120 days after your birthday and all subsequent birthdays every 10 years. If there's a remainder of 2, round this up to the next whole number (3). In this case, your first 10-year luck period begins 120 days before your third birthday and changes 120 days before your thirteenth, twenty-third, thirty-third birthday, and so forth. If the result is "0," your luck begins at birth.

Step 3: Based on the age your luck begins, each 10-year luck period begins 10 years after the previous one. It is customary to write these pillars from right to left. Thus, in Diana's case, her 10-year luck periods are as follows:

Princess Diana's 10-year luck periods.

Age	82-91	72-81	62-71	52-61	42-51	32-41	22-31	12-21	2-11

Using the empty chart we've provided on the following page, fill in this portion of your 10-year luck chart.

Step 4: The next question is, what stem and branch do you assign to each of these periods? You begin with your month pillar. Princess Diana's month pillar is Jia Wu. Next, find its position in the Cycle of Sixty Table 3 in Chapter 22. Jia Wu is number 31. You must now go to the *next* stem-branch combination in the cycle of 60. So, Yi Wei, number 32, represents Diana's first 10-year luck period. For each 10-year luck period that follows, move forward one position in the cycle of 60.

Feng Alert

For yang males and yin females only: To ensure an accurate calculation, count your birthday as "1" and count forward to the last day of the solar month you were born into. For example, if July 7 marks the beginning of the new month, July 6 is the last day counted.

Step 5: Finally, consulting the Ten Heavenly Stems Table 1 and the Twelve Earthly Branches Table 2 in Chapter 22, write down each stem-branch phase. Diana's finished chart reads as follows.

Now use the following blank chart to complete your own 10-year luck periods.

Age	82-91	72-81	62-71	52-61	42-51	32-41	22-31	12-21	2-11
Stem	Gui	Ren	Xin	Geng	Ji	Wu	Ding	Bing	Yi
Branch	Mao	Yin	Chou	Zi	Hai	Xu	You	Shen	Wei
Stem Phase	Water	Water	Metal	Metal	Earth	Earth	Fire	Fire	Wood
Branch Phase	Wood	Wood	Earth	Water	Water	Earth	Metal	Metal	Earth

Princess Diana's 10-year luck chart.

Age									
Stem									
Branch									
Stem Phase									
Branch Phase									

Your 10-year luck chart.

Yin Male or Yang Female, Please Step Forward

If you are a yin male or a yang female, follow these simple steps to determine your 10-year luck periods. (Again, you can determine your yin and yang polarity by consulting the Cycle of Sixty Table 3 in Chapter 22.)

Step 1: Counting your birthday as "1," count *backward* from the day of your birth to the *first day* of the Chinese solar month into which you were born. How many days is it? Let's take a yin male born July 26, 1975. (1975 is a Yi Mao year. According to the Cycle of Sixty Table 3, Yi Mao is Yin.) July 7 marks the solar month (Gui Wei) of his birth, the sixth month under 1975. From July 26 to July 7 there are 20 days.

Step 2: Divide the number of days by three. If there is no remainder, the result is the age when your first 10-year luck period begins. If the remainder is "1," drop the remainder. Your luck changes 120 days after your birthday and all subsequent birthdays every ten years. If the result is "0," your luck begins at birth. Ten years old is the latest your luck period can begin. The years prior to your first luck period are governed by your month pillar, or Parents Palace. Continuing with our example of a yin male, 20 days ÷ 3 = 6,

Feng Alert

For yin males and yang females only: To ensure an accurate calculation, count your birthday as "1" and count backward to the first day of the solar month you were born into. For example, if July 7 is the first day of the solar month, this is the last number counted.

remaining 2. Because there is a remainder of "2," he rounds the answer up to the next whole number. Thus, his first 10-year luck period begins 120 days before age 7. In subsequent luck periods, his luck changes 120 days before his seventeenth, twenty-seventh, and thirty-seventh birthday, and so forth.

Step 3: Based on the age your luck begins, each 10-year luck period begins 10 years after the previous one. The yin male example's 10-year luck period is calculated as follows:

Example's 10-year luck periods.

Age	87-96	77-86	67-76	57-66	47-56	37-46	27-36	17-26	7-16

Using the empty chart we've provided, fill in this portion of your 10-year luck chart.

Step 4: Determine what stem and branch to assign to each of these periods. You begin with your month pillar. The example's month pillar is Gui Wei (find its position in the Cycle of Sixty Table 3 in Chapter 22). Gui Wei is number 20. Now go to the *previous* stem-branch combination in the cycle of 60: Ren Wu, number 19, represents the example's first 10-year luck period. For each 10-year luck period that follows, move one position backward in the cycle of 60.

Step 5: Finally, consult the Ten Heavenly Stems Table 1 and the Twelve Earthly Branches Table 2 in Chapter 22 and write down each stem-branch phase. The example's chart reads as follows:

Example's 10-year luck chart.

Age	87-96	77-86	67-76	57-66	47-56	37-46	27-36	17-26	7-16
Stem	Jia	Yi	Bing	Ding	Wu	Ji	Geng	Xin	Ren
Branch	Xu	Hai	Zi	Chou	Yin	Mao	Chen	Si	Wu
Stem Phase	Wood	Wood	Fire	Fire	Earth	Earth	Metal	Metal	Water
Branch Phase	Earth	Water	Water	Earth	Wood	Wood	Earth	Fire	Fire

Now use the following blank chart to complete your own 10-year luck periods.

Your 10-year luck chart.

Age									
Stem									
Branch									
Stem Phase									
Branch Phase									

Wheel of Fortune

In a nutshell, if a 10-year luck period consists of your favorable phase(s), then that decade should prove fortunate. Is it really as simple as this? Let's break it down in terms of stems and branches. The earthly branch represents the foundation, stability; the heavenly stem, the prevailing qi for that 10-year period. It's important to note that while the stem's qi force acts quickly, the branch is more persistent. Stated another way, in the beginning of the 10-year cycle, luck is influenced mainly by the stem. The branch's influence is gradual. At the end of the cycle, the branch is more influential than the stem.

There are four possible combinations, all yielding an effect appropriate to the structure of your Four Pillars chart. They are …

1. **Favorable stem, favorable branch.** You are basically fortunate and influenced by favorable qi.

2. **Favorable stem, unfavorable branch.** You are generally unlucky, but there is favorable qi to change that from time to time.

3. **Unfavorable stem, favorable branch.** You are basically fortunate, but there is unfavorable qi to disturb you from time to time.

4. **Unfavorable stem, unfavorable branch.** You are basically unlucky; you are often subjected to the influence of unfavorable qi.

Before you set out to interpret your 10-year luck periods, let's fine-tune this general analysis. The nature of what will unfold depends on the kind of favorable/unfavorable stem-branch configuration for any given period. For example, let's take a resource/resource combination for a strong chart. This is an unfavorable/unfavorable combination, suggesting overindulgence and greed. Although things come easily to this person, he is probably spoiled rotten and would be unable to stand on his own two feet if forced to fend for himself. He's much more interested in taking than giving. Another unfavorable/unfavorable combination for a strong chart is parallel/parallel, suggesting a period of fierce competition. You'll most likely have to claw your way to the top. Unlike the first scenario, nothing will come easy in this 10-year period.

So you see, knowing the kind of qi is integral to how your free will can shape your destiny. If you knew in advance what the next 10-year luck period could bring, wouldn't you take precautions? Of course you would. Wouldn't you carry an umbrella in anticipation of an impending storm? If you calculate a strong resource/resource period for your son, wouldn't

Master Class

An unfavorable stem and unfavorable branch does not mean a 10-year sentence of disaster, misfortune, and illness without possibility of peace, comfort, and happiness. Just like yin and yang cannot exist without a hint of each other's opposing characteristic, so, too, can't misfortune exist without moments of fortune.

you take care not to spoil him, enabling him to be an independent adult? If you calculate you're in a strong parallel/parallel period, wouldn't you look extra hard for any and all available angles? Wouldn't knowing your possible destiny give you an edge? We hope it will. We hope you will use the Four Pillars to your advantage.

It Was a Very Good Year

Ten years is an awfully long time. A lot can happen. Marriage or divorce, promotion or unemployment, birth or death. It's difficult to be mindful of what a luck period brings. Can it be broken down into smaller increments? Sure! Not only can you analyze the auspiciousness of a 10-year period, you can also determine your luck on a yearly, monthly, daily, and even *hourly* basis. (Although we won't get into the minutia of calculating hourly luck, we'll help you determine your monthly and daily luck prospects in the next chapter.)

To determine your yearly luck, simply compare your favorable and unfavorable phases to the year's stem and branch in question. For example, 2002 is a Ren Wu (see the Year Pillar Table 4 in Chapter 22), or water/fire year. The year 2003 is a Gui Wei or water/earth year. In the space provided, indicate if the year's stem and branch are favorable or unfavorable for you by using a plus sign (+) for favorable, a minus sign (−) for unfavorable. Then write in each phase's relationship to your Day-Master (resource, parallel, performance, power, wealth).

	2002 2/4 - 2/3/03	
	Ren WATER	
	Wu FIRE	

	2003 2/4 - 2/3/04	
	Gui WATER	
	Wei EARTH	

Your Sixty Cycle's Destiny

While you're at it, why don't you determine the auspiciousness of each of the 60 stem-branch components? In the end, this exercise will prove much more fruitful than, say, watching *The Brady Bunch* reruns. In any case, you'll need to know this information to construct your own daily horoscope in the following chapter.

Simply indicate if the stem-branch phase is favorable or unfavorable for you, then write in each phase's relationship to your Day-Master.

Now you can better analyze each of the years inside a 10-year luck period. You'll notice a fortunate 10-year period is destined to carry mostly favorable yearly qi. Conversely, an unfortunate 10-year period will hold mostly unfavorable qi.

Master Class

Remember, a strong chart's favorable phases are performance, power, and wealth; its unfavorable phases are resource and parallel. A weak chart's favorable phases are resource and parallel; its unfavorable phases are performance, power, and wealth.

1 Jia WOOD ☐	2 Yi WOOD ☐	3 Bing FIRE ☐	4 Ding FIRE ☐
Zi WATER ☐	Chou EARTH ☐	Yin WOOD ☐	Mao WOOD ☐
5 Wu EARTH ☐	6 Ji EARTH ☐	7 Geng METAL ☐	8 Xin METAL ☐
Chen EARTH ☐	Si FIRE ☐	Wu FIRE ☐	Wei EARTH ☐
9 Ren WATER ☐	10 Gui WATER ☐	11 Jia WOOD ☐	12 Yi WOOD ☐
Shen METAL ☐	You METAL ☐	Xu EARTH ☐	Hai WATER ☐
13 Bing FIRE ☐	14 Ding FIRE ☐	15 Wu EARTH ☐	16 Ji EARTH ☐
Zi WATER ☐	Chou EARTH ☐	Yin WOOD ☐	Mao WOOD ☐
17 Geng METAL ☐	18 Xin METAL ☐	19 Ren WATER ☐	20 Gui WATER ☐
Chen EARTH ☐	Si FIRE ☐	Wu FIRE ☐	Wei EARTH ☐
21 Jia WOOD ☐	22 Yi WOOD ☐	23 Bing FIRE ☐	24 Ding FIRE ☐
Shen METAL ☐	You METAL ☐	Xu EARTH ☐	Hai WATER ☐
25 Wu EARTH ☐	26 Ji EARTH ☐	27 Gen METAL ☐	28 Xin METAL ☐
Zi WATER ☐	Chou EARTH ☐	Yin WOOD ☐	Mao WOOD ☐
29 Ren WATER ☐	30 Gui WATER ☐	31 Jia WOOD ☐	32 Yi WOOD ☐
Chen EARTH ☐	Si FIRE ☐	Wu FIRE ☐	Wei EARTH ☐
33 Bing FIRE ☐	34 Ding FIRE ☐	35 Wu EARTH ☐	36 Ji EARTH ☐
Shen METAL ☐	You METAL ☐	Xu EARTH ☐	Hai WATER ☐
37 Geng METAL ☐	38 Xin METAL ☐	39 Ren WATER ☐	40 Gui WATER ☐
Zi WATER ☐	Chou EARTH ☐	Yin WOOD ☐	Mao WOOD ☐
41 Jia WOOD ☐	42 Yi WOOD ☐	43 Bing FIRE ☐	44 Ding FIRE ☐
Chen EARTH ☐	Si FIRE ☐	Wu FIRE ☐	Wei EARTH ☐
45 Wu EARTH ☐	46 Ji EARTH ☐	47 Geng METAL ☐	48 Xin METAL ☐
Shen METAL ☐	You METAL ☐	Xu EARTH ☐	Hai WATER ☐
49 Ren WATER ☐	50 Gui WATER ☐	51 Jia WOOD ☐	52 Yi WOOD ☐
Zi WATER ☐	Chou EARTH ☐	Yin WOOD ☐	Mao WOOD ☐
53 Bing FIRE ☐	54 Ding FIRE ☐	55 Wu EARTH ☐	56 Ji EARTH ☐
Chen EARTH ☐	Si FIRE ☐	Wu FIRE ☐	Wei EARTH ☐
57 Geng METAL ☐	58 Xin METAL ☐	59 Ren WATER ☐	60 Gui WATER ☐
Shen METAL ☐	You METAL ☐	Xu EARTH ☐	Hai WATER ☐

The Cycle of 60 Favorability Chart.

The Fate of Princess Diana, Part 2

Let's reexamine Princess Diana's luck chart. In the last chapter, we determined her favorable phase is water (resource); metal (power) is favorable, too, but only if accompanied by water (otherwise metal is unfavorable). Her unfavorable phases are earth (wealth) and fire (performance). Wood (parallel) is considered neutral. With this in mind, let's analyze each of Diana's 10-year luck periods.

- **2-11: Wood and earth.** A neutral/unfavorable combination. Referring to her Four Pillars chart we constructed in Chapter 22, notice the month pillar, or Parents Palace, is represented by the earth phase. You have learned in this chapter an unfavorable phase in this position usually suggests an unhappy childhood. Also, earth represents the foundation of her first 10-year luck period, further depriving her of much-needed parental support through her formative years. Wood, the prevailing qi for this period, suggests competition from her siblings.

- **12-21: Fire and metal.** An unfavorable/favorable combination. Metal, her branch phase for this period, provides stability. Although beyond our scope here, there are traces of water hidden in her Shen (metal) branch. This small amount works wonders, particularly beginning in 1978. Her life becomes more enjoyable; there is more control. Diana was married in 1981. The prevailing qi, fire, is unfavorable as it slowly dries up the traces of water hidden in the branch. It shows she has the wisdom to overcome the control of her family. Nonetheless, this is draining her energy.

- **22-31: Fire and metal.** An unfavorable/unfavorable combination. The difference here is metal, the foundation for the 10-year period. It is not accompanied by water, making it an unfavorable phase. Although fire causes Diana to become more radiant and vibrant—the fairy-tale princess and world humanitarian—in reality, she is a humiliated wife. She is lonely and helpless as expressed by fire burning away wood (parallel).

- **32-41: Earth and earth.** An unfavorable/unfavorable combination. Without water to support her, the wealth (earth) phase is not favorable. Earth gives energy to the power (metal) phase only to irritate her further. The year 1995 is a turning point. Yi (wood) Hai (water) provided Diana with the resources and assistance to be courageous enough to tell the world she was an unfaithful and scorned wife. The next year, Bing (fire) Zi (water) provided her with wisdom and courage to negotiate her divorce. In 1997, Ding (fire) Chou (earth), Diana met her most unfavorable phases. Earth controlled her traces of water hidden in the year branch Chou. Fire burned and exhausted her wood, further enhancing the earth. Although earth represents wealth, it weakened her. At one time she was very emotionally and physically weak.

Princess Diana died on August 31, 1997. The year, month, and day pillars are respectively, Ding (fire) Chou (earth), Wu (earth) Shen (metal), and Yi (wood) Si (fire). The branches form a productive chain (fire-earth-metal) ending with the unfavorable power (metal) phase. Also, the stems form a productive chain (wood-fire-earth) ending in the unfavorable wealth (earth) phase. Her weak wood (Day-Master) is completely destroyed by metal. Does it mean she had to die? Well, not necessarily. There can be found worse days in the calendar. But, unfortunately, August 31 was a bad enough day for her.

Had Princess Diana survived this unfortunate decade, she would have gone into extensive periods of good luck. Her next 10-year period (age 42 to 51) would have been earth/water, or unfavorable/favorable. The foundation, water, would have nourished her weak Day-Master, giving her strength to manage her wealth, the unfavorable earth. Beginning at age 52, she would have entered a metal/water period, or favorable/favorable. Again, the foundation is most favorable. Metal is also favorable because it is accompanied by water. Since metal is power to wood, it suggests a happy marriage.

Could Diana have survived the accident if proper advice about her Four Pillars of Destiny were available to her? This is something we'll never know. In theory, if she had stuck to someone whose Four Pillars have a lot of water, it could have saved her. Unfortunately, this man was her former husband, the Prince of Wales! His Four Pillars contain a tremendous amount of water.

The Least You Need to Know

- The Chinese believe luck is a function of time and that it is determinable.
- When your 10-year luck period begins is determined by your gender and yin and yang polarity of your year pillar.
- If a period contains your favorable phases, the 10 years are likely to be fortunate. If a period contains your unfavorable phases, it will probably be an unfortunate decade.
- A more exacting analysis is to determine how the kind of qi will influence your well-being so that you can take proper precautions.
- Princess Diana's first three luck periods were unfortunate. Had she survived, great fortune awaited her.

25

The Four Pillars of Destiny, Part 4

In This Chapter

♦ More on how knowing your phases can benefit you

♦ Determining your lucky months

♦ Determining your lucky days

Let's face it, most of us like to check out our fate. Be it in the newspaper, *TV Guide*, or popular magazines, we can't wait to see what's in store for us. We're delighted when the general message brings good tidings. We're cautious when it's foreboding. We know the prediction is a generality, a one-size-fits-all statement. Nevertheless, we keep it in the back of our mind.

In this chapter, we teach you how to construct your daily horoscope. Though not the same as consulting a professional Chinese or Western astrologer, what you'll find here are specifics based on the strength of your chart and the con- figuration of your favorable and unfavorable phases.

What's in a Horoscope?

Let's say you're a salesperson. Although you conduct work mostly from your office, you call on clients and wine and dine them when you need to close a deal. If you had available a calendar describing your most auspicious, so-so, and unfavorable days, wouldn't you use this information to your advantage? Or say you're a police officer, teacher, or doctor. Wouldn't you want to know that you're in for a bad day, one bringing potentially unfavorable qi? Maybe nothing will happen, but you'll be on guard, ready to meet unexpected events. The point is, let qi work for you. How else can knowing your favorable and unfavorable phases help you? You'll know …

- When to sign important documents.
- The best days to travel.
- When to celebrate.
- An auspicious day to get married.
- The best days to invest, buy a lottery ticket, or gamble.
- When to stay home or take a day off.
- When to ask for a raise or a promotion.
- The most auspicious days to display your talent.
- The best days to ask for assistance, support, or advice.

There's no end to the benefits. Intrigued? In order to make sense of the rest of this chapter, you must already have completed the Cycle of 60 Favorability Chart in Chapter 24, "The Four Pillars of Destiny, Part 3." That done, let's move on.

That Was Then, This Is Now

Starting now, take stock of each day. Keep a diary. Compare what has unfolded each day, each month, and each year to what your favorable and unfavorable phases destine. Does a pattern emerge? Before long you'll have memorized what each of the 60 stem-branch combinations means to you. You'll consult your calendar regularly and plan your activities accordingly. We promise this method is a lot more accurate than calling a psychic hotline, or being inspired by any generalized material, including even the Chinese zodiac that we discussed in Chapter 21, "Introducing the Twelve Animals of the Chinese Zodiac."

For your convenience, we've categorized how a chart of strength and weakness will fare for each stem-branch combination. Use it as a reference, a starting point. Although we've described a generality, it's appropriate to the stem-branch combination for that of a strong and weak chart. Therefore, the prediction is much more specific than otherwise. Remember, a + indicates that the stem or branch in question is favorable to your Day-Master. A − indicates the stem or branch is unfavorable to your Day-Master.

Relationship to Day-Master	Strong Chart	Weak Chart
Resource/	Strong (–/–): You're spoiled rotten. The rug may be pulled from under you. Can you manage by yourself?	Weak (+/+): Use your resources. Call in favors. Ask and you shall receive. Support comes out of the woodwork.
Resource/ Performance	Strong (–/+): Goals are achieved, talents are exhibited. You get things done. Remember, flattery is like a drug. It may ruin you.	Weak (+/–): Although family and friends root for you, you'll have a difficult time meeting deadlines, accomplishing goals.
Resource/ Power	Strong (–/+): A double-edged sword. You'll be controlled and empowered by those surrounding you. Watch your back!	Weak (+/–): Allies seek to control you. While you need the support, remember, you hold the reins.
Resource/ Wealth	Strong (–/+): Opportunities to make money arise. Beware of competition. Look for new angles, fresh ideas. Think before you act.	Weak (+/–): Take it easy. You exert too much energy maintaining your success and wealth. Help is available.
Resource/ Parallel	Strong (–/–): Arguments. Potential lawsuits. Pick your battles. Don't say anything you'll regret. Take the day off.	Weak (+/+): Wow! You have more friends than you think. Party. Travel. Fundraise. Romance is likely.
Performance/ Performance	Strong (+/+): You'll get what you want. Let your talent shine. Books, lecture tours, publishing. Promotion likely.	Weak (–/–): You may be injured by your talent. Stay dormant. Play hooky. Don't do anything important.
Performance/ Resource	Strong (+/–): Although you'll have some opportunities to display your talent, you may be be undermined by those around you.	Weak (–/+): You'll get the advice and support you need. Keep the door open. Don't be taken advantage of.

continues

continued

Relationship to Day-Master	Strong Chart	Weak Chart
Performance/ Power	Strong (+/+): A surge of discipline drives you to achieve the impossible. You will get noticed. Celebrate!	Weak (–/–): You're overwhelmed. Stay home, rent a few movies, and don't answer the phone.
Performance/ Wealth	Strong (+/+): Now's the time to buy that big-ticket item you've had your eye on. Invest. You're appreciated and respected.	Weak (–/–): Although you're gifted, you tend to spin your wheels maintaining your gift. Hole up. Don't do anything important.
Performance/ Parallel	Strong (+/–): Don't ask for a raise just yet. Although your exceptional performance is noticed, competition lurks.	Weak (–/+): Use your talent to meet new people, make new friends. Romance? Maybe. Be mindful of injuries.
Power/ Power	Strong (+/+): No more procrastinating. You're driven to succeed. See your goals through. Tie up loose ends. Ask for a raise.	Weak (–/–): Litigation. Disagreements. Illness. Keep your mouth shut. Don't do anything important.
Power/ Resource	Strong (+/–): Don't let those around you steer you off track. Remember, work before pleasure.	Weak (–/+): You will get the help you need, but don't be compromised or controlled. You'll regret it.
Power/ Performance	Strong (+/+): An abundance of self-discipline propels you to higher levels, opening new doors to display your craft.	Weak (–/–): How can you get anything done if you're manipulated and suffocated? Stay home. Don't do anything important.
Power/ Wealth	Strong (+/+): You have the drive and ambition to create wealth. Promotion, new job likely. Invest. Buy a lottery ticket.	Weak (–/–): Don't pick a fight. You're spinning your wheels. Go to the beach. Walk the dog. Don't do anything important.

Relationship to Day-Master	Strong Chart	Weak Chart
Power/ Parallel	Strong (+/−): While you have the stamina to succeed, your colleagues stand in your way.	Weak (−/+): Don't be surprised if you get invited to an unexpected event. Set aside your inclination to decline and go.
Wealth/ Wealth	Strong (+/+): Invest. Buy a lottery ticket or raffle drawing. The cards are stacked in your favor. Deals abound.	Weak (−/−): The pressure and overtime are getting the best of you. You can't do it all. Don't make hasty decisions.
Wealth/ Resource	Strong (+/−): You have good ideas to generate income. Don't let your friends drag you down.	Weak (−/+): You have strong support. You may suffer from money loss. Don't overspend.
Wealth/ Performance	Strong (+/+): You have the wherewithal to use your talent to make money. Put some away for a rainy day.	Weak (−/−): Check your work. Be thorough. You may lose money because of hasty decisions. Stay dormant.
Wealth/ Power	Strong (+/+): New job, promotion, raise likely. You are happy. Celebrate. Travel. Invest.	Weak (−/−): You're exhausted. Stay home. Be extra cautious on the road. Travel not suggested.
Wealth/ Parallel	Strong (+/−): Your colleagues may take advantage of you. Don't be exploited. Money on the rise.	Weak (−/+): You can't see straight, you're working so hard. Delegate responsibility. Help is available.
Parallel/ Parallel	Strong (−/−): Your competitors have out-smarted you. You can't get a break. Don't do anything important.	Weak (+/+): Fund-raising. Charity donations. Colleagues are behind you. Celebrate. Travel. Make new connections.
Parallel/ Resource	Strong (−/−): Everybody is giving you a hard time. You are your own best friend. Stay home. Play hooky.	Weak (+/+): You have an army of supporters at your beck and call. Ask and you shall receive.

continues

continued

Relationship to Day-Master	Strong Chart	Weak Chart
Parallel/ Performance	Strong (–/+): Basically, you accomplish your goals. Nevertheless, you are met with opposition by your colleagues.	Weak (+/–): Good opportunities arise to make new connections and new friends. Romance is likely. Be a show-off.
Parallel/ Power	Strong (–/+): Don't take no for an answer. You must proceed to succeed despite what others might say.	Weak (+/–): Be cautious of accidents that may lead to lawsuits. Don't argue. Help is on the way.
Parallel/ Wealth	Strong (–/+): Money is on the rise. Buy a lottery ticket. Watch your back. You may be the subject of gossip.	Weak (+/–): You're admired by colleagues. Watch your investments. Money loss because of hasty decisions.

Now that you understand how each stem-branch combination can affect you, turn back to the Cycle of 60 Favorability Chart in Chapter 24. Become familiar with what Jia Zi or wood/water (the first in the cycle of 60) means to you. Maybe wood is your resource; water your parallel. If your chart is strong, this would be an unfavorable/unfavorable combination. If your chart is weak, it is a favorable/favorable combination. Maybe wood is your performance; water your parallel. This is a favorable/unfavorable combination for a chart of strength; an unfavorable/favorable combination for a weak chart. Get the idea?

Oh, What a Month!

So far, you've determined the auspiciousness of your 10-year period and what kind of qi the year may bring. Now, let's take it down a notch. To determine the auspiciousness of a particular month, simply refer to Table 5 (the Month Pillar charts) in Chapter 22. In the space provided in the following Solar Months chart (we've left this blank for you to fill in), first note the month in question on the top line. On the second and third lines, indicate the month's corresponding phases. In the boxes, use + or – to indicate a phase's favorability:

- ◆ If it's a +/+ month, put a + in the solar month box.
- ◆ If it's a –/– month, put a – in the box.
- ◆ If it's a +/– or a –/+ month, meaning an okay or average period, put a check mark in the box.

Feng Alert

You might think the best time to take a vacation is during a −/− month. Why put your job or business at risk during an inauspicious time? Actually, it's more beneficial to plan a vacation during a +/+ period. Lost luggage, stolen belongings, and unharmonious relations don't make for an enjoyable holiday.

Then indicate each phase's relationship to your Day-Master (resource, parallel, intelligence, power, wealth). As an example, here's how January 2003 correlates to one person's Four Pillars chart:

✓	1 / 6 - 2/3/02
Gui WATER	+ Wealth
Chou EARTH	− Resource

Now, it's your turn. Use the example's information as a model only!

Solar Months

Take a look at what you've just completed. How many favorable months will you be graced with? How many unfavorable months will you be subjected to? Remember, take notes. Got a raise? Met someone special? Jot it down. Then compare what's transpired to what was destined.

Around and Around We Go: Determining a New Sixty-Day Cycle

Assembling your daily horoscope is a snap. To find out the stem-branch combination marking the beginning of each month, you'll need to consult the Year Number Table 7 and the example's Cycle of Sixty Days, Table 8, from Chapter 22. For instance, take January 2003. According to the Year Number table, 2003 corresponds with the year number 11. Moving over to the example's Table 8, 11 corresponds with Jia Xu (or wood earth), the first day of January 2003. To determine the following days, simply refer to the Cycle of 60 Favorability Chart from Chapter 24. If January 1 is a Jia Xu day (number 11 in the cycle of 60), then January 2 is a Yi Hai, wood water, day (number 12 in the cycle of 60); January 3 is a Bing Zi, fire water, day (number 13 in the cycle of 60).

If January 1, 2003, equals number 11, how many days are there until the next cycle begins? The answer is 50: 11 + 50 = 61, or number one in the cycle of 60. Fifty days from January 1 is February 20. This satisfies the Day Pillar Table 6 (see Chapter 22). Day number 50 corresponds to February 20, April 21, June 20, August 19, October 18, and December 17. Learning this technique is a good way of staying on track. One error leads to a misjudging of the day, which may lead to misfortune. Who wants that?

Feng Alert _____

In a leap year, the dates corresponding to the day number in the Day Pillar Table 6 will be off by one. For example, the year 2004 is a leap year. January 1, 2004, is a Ji Mao or earth wood day—number 16 in the cycle of 60. Forty-five days remain until the next cycle begins. So, January 1 + 45 days = February 15, the first Jia Zi day of the year. Because of the leap year, the next cycle begins on April 15. Each new cycle follows on June 14, August 13, October 12, and December 11, a day earlier than what is indicated on the chart.

Day by Day

The question arises: Now that I've determined what kind of day January 1, 2003, is (Jia Xu), what day of the week does it begin on? Good question. Simply refer to the following table. First, find the year in question. Then, run your finger along the row to find the number 1, January. January corresponds with template number 3. Consulting the blank template charts 1 through 7, you'll see that template 3 begins on a Wednesday. For February and March 2003, you'd use template 6; for April use template 2; for May use template 4, for June use template 7; and so forth. Get the idea?

Table 1

TEMPLATE ► YEAR	1	2	3	4	5	6	7
2002	4, 7	1, 10	5	8	2, 3, 11	6	9, 12
2003	9, 12	4, 7	1, 10	5	8	2, 3, 11	6
2004	3, 11	6	9, 12	1, 4, 7	10	5	2, 8
2005	8	2, 3, 11	6	9, 12	4, 7	1, 10	5
2006	5	8	2, 3, 11	6	9	4, 7, 12	1, 10
2007	1, 10	5	8	2, 3, 11	6	9, 12	4, 7
2008	9, 12	1, 4, 7	10	5	2, 8	3, 11	6
2009	6	9, 12	4, 7	1, 10	5	8	2, 3, 11
2010	2, 3, 11	6	9, 12	4, 7	1, 10	5	8
2011	8	2, 3, 11	6	9, 12	4, 7	1, 10	5
2012	10	5	2, 8	3, 11	6	9, 12	1, 4, 7
2013	4, 7	1, 10	5	8	2, 3, 11	6	9, 12
2014	9, 12	4, 7	1, 10	5	8	2, 3, 11	6
2015	6	9, 12	4, 7	1, 10	5	8	2, 3, 11
2016	2, 8	3, 11	6	9, 12	1, 4, 7	10	5
2017	5	8	2, 3, 11	6	9, 12	4, 7	1, 10
2018	1, 10	5	8	2, 3, 11	6	9, 12	4, 7
2019	4, 7	1, 10	5	8	2, 3, 11	6	9, 12
2020	6	9, 12	1, 4, 7	10	5	2, 8	3, 11
2021	2, 3, 11	6	9	4, 7, 12	1, 10	5	8
2022	8	2, 3, 11	6	9, 12	4, 7	1, 10	5
2023	5	8	2, 3, 11	6	9, 12	4, 7	1, 10

To complete each day, refer to the Cycle of 60 Favorability Chart in Chapter 24. In each day box, indicate its auspiciousness. A +/+ gets a +, a –/– gets a –, a +/– or –/+ gets a check mark. To simplify the daily calendar, you may just want to indicate the cycle of 60 number and the corresponding stem-branch phases. For example, the January 1, 2003, box would look like this:

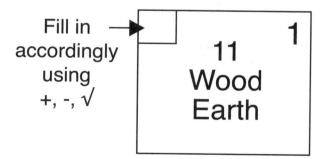

Template 1

MONDAY	TUESDAY	WEDNESDAY	THURSDAY	FRIDAY	SATURDAY	SUNDAY
1	2	3	4	5	6	7
8	9	10	11	12	13	14
15	16	17	18	19	20	21
22	23	24	25	26	27	28
29	30	31				

Template 2

MONDAY	TUESDAY	WEDNESDAY	THURSDAY	FRIDAY	SATURDAY	SUNDAY
	1	2	3	4	5	6
7	8	9	10	11	12	13
14	15	16	17	18	19	20
21	22	23	24	25	26	27
28	29	30	31			

Template 3

MONDAY	TUESDAY	WEDNESDAY	THURSDAY	FRIDAY	SATURDAY	SUNDAY
		1	2	3	4	5
6	7	8	9	10	11	12
13	14	15	16	17	18	19
20	21	22	23	24	25	26
27	28	29	30	31		

Template 4

MONDAY	TUESDAY	WEDNESDAY	THURSDAY	FRIDAY	SATURDAY	SUNDAY
			1	2	3	4
5	6	7	8	9	10	11
12	13	14	15	16	17	18
19	20	21	22	23	24	25
26	27	28	29	30	31	

Template 5

MONDAY	TUESDAY	WEDNESDAY	THURSDAY	FRIDAY	SATURDAY	SUNDAY
				1	2	3
4	5	6	7	8	9	10
11	12	13	14	15	16	17
18	19	20	21	22	23	24
25	26	27	28	29	30	31

Template 6

MONDAY	TUESDAY	WEDNESDAY	THURSDAY	FRIDAY	SATURDAY	SUNDAY
					1	2
3	4	5	6	7	8	9
10	11	12	13	14	15	16
17	18	19	20	21	22	23
24	25	26	27	28	29	30
31						

Template 7

MONDAY	TUESDAY	WEDNESDAY	THURSDAY	FRIDAY	SATURDAY	SUNDAY
						1
2	3	4	5	6	7	8
9	10	11	12	13	14	15
16	17	18	19	20	21	22
23	24	25	26	27	28	29
30	31					

Congratulations! You've made it through *The Complete Idiot's Guide to Feng Shui*. We sincerely hope you will apply your newfound knowledge to improve your well-being and share it with those important to you. Get others to experience these guides. Anyone can benefit from feng shui and Chinese astrology. Even if your loved ones are skeptical, conduct a reading for them. Let them see how simple adjustments can improve their health, wealth, and relationships. Win them over. Allow feng shui to demonstrate to them its power. Become a booster, a feng shui fellow. You only need to be a conduit. Allow feng shui to do the rest. Allow it to tantalize your family and friends with its alluring promises of universal harmony. They'll discover what you did: Feng shui works.

The Least You Need to Know

- Knowing your favorable and unfavorable phases can help you determine when to sign important documents, travel, celebrate, and stay home, among other things.
- A favorable month will have more favorable than unfavorable days, while an unfavorable month will have more unfavorable than favorable days.
- You can tailor a horoscope based on your chart's strength and phase favorabilities.
- There are a couple of ways to determine a day's stem-branch combination.

Appendix A

Glossary

After Heaven sequence   Called the Hou Tian in Chinese, this sequence of trigrams denotes motion, transformation, and the interaction of natural and human qi forces. This is the sequence used in feng shui.

annual star   A prevailing "star," or number, which ushers in yearly changes in the earth's qi field.

axiom   A widely accepted fact based on its intrinsic merits. Because an axiom is a general truth, it does not have to be proven.

azure dragon   A landform, building, trees, bushes, or fence located on the left side of your dwelling.

bagua   The eight trigrams of the *Yijing*.

Before Heaven sequence   Called the Xian Tian in Chinese, this is a sequence of trigrams representing an ideal reality where natural and human qi forces are in perfect balance.

black turtle   A landform, building, grove of trees, or fence supporting the back of your residence.

Book of Burial   Written in the fourth century C.E. by Guo Pu, this is the earliest extant text on the Form School of feng shui.

celestial equator   The circular path the constellations travel perpendicular to an imaginary line joining the celestial north pole to the earth's North pole. The Chinese use the celestial equator as a baseline to observe the times when stars will appear directly overhead.

Chinese zodiac   A popular system of astrology involving the relationships between 12 types of qi or signs expressed as animals: rat, ox, tiger, rabbit, dragon, snake, horse, sheep, monkey, rooster, dog, and pig.

Compass School   A term invented by Westerners, the Compass School holds that each of the eight (and 24 finer distinctions) cardinal directions has a different energy. It is a very computational method, relying on intellect rather than intuitive insights. In Chinese, Compass School is known as Liqi Pai (Patterns of Qi School).

Confucianism   Based on the sixth century B.C.E. teachings of Confucius, it is a complex system of ethics designed to cultivate social and moral principles. The philosophy was taught in Chinese schools from the beginning of the Han dynasty to the establishment of the People's Republic of China in 1949.

conscious mind   The waking state that gives us logic, reason, and willpower. The conscious mind represents 12 percent of our total mind power.

controlling cycle   A cycle of imbalance. Each phase controls its counterpart. Fire-metal-wood-earth-water represents the controlling cycle.

crimson bird   A footstool landform or body of water that faces your dwelling.

Cycle of Sixty   Represents all possible combinations (60) of the Ten Heavenly Stems and Twelve Earthly Branches. The year 2697 B.C.E. marked the first of the 60-year, or 60-stem-branch cycle.

Daoism   Concerned with the intuitive knowledge acquired by communing with nature and being at one with it (the Dao), the founding fathers of Daoism were a group of like-minded people who lived and taught from the fourth to the second century B.C.E.

Day-Master   The Day-Master is the day stem component of your chart. Also called the Ziping Method after astrologer Xu Ziping, the Four Pillars of Destiny analyzes how the five phases comprising your Four Pillars chart affect the Day-Master.

deductive reasoning   The method of reaching a conclusion by deducing general laws through observation.

Double Ruling Star at Facing   A dwelling that is considered Shuang Ling Xing Dou Xiang if both the ruling mountain and ruling water stars are located in the facing cell. In this case, it is easy for the occupants to make and retain money, but it is difficult for them to form stable relationships and maintain good health.

Double Ruling Star at Sitting   A dwelling that is considered Shuang Ling Xing Dou Zuo if both the ruling mountain and the ruling water stars are located in the sitting cell. In this case, it is easy for the occupants to form stable relationships and maintain good health, but it is difficult for them to make and retain money.

dragon's lair   In feng shui, all mountain ranges are called dragons. When the dragon meets the terrain, it is his lair (long xue). It is the place that attracts sheng qi and is considered the most auspicious site on which to build a home or bury the dead.

Eight House system   A method of determining the four lucky and unlucky directions for you and your home.

facing direction   Usually corresponds to the front side of a dwelling and is not necessarily where your front door is located.

favorable phase   A term used in a Four Pillars of Destiny analysis. It is the phase that brings balance to your chart.

feng shui   It literally means "wind water," the two natural forces that direct qi to a site. Figuratively, feng shui is the art and science of determining how your environment and your home affect you over periods of time.

Fibonacci sequence   A sequence of numbers named after a thirteenth-century mathematician, Leonardo of Pisa, also known as Fibonacci. Each number in the series is the sum of the two previous numbers.

fight or flight   A primitive and involuntary reaction triggered during moments of danger or anxiety. As man (and animals) evolved, some developed greater strength and aggressiveness (fight), while others developed agility, speed, and a sensitivity to the senses of smell, sight, and hearing (flight). Those who remained passive eventually became extinct.

five phases   Five physical elements in nature that represent the movement of qi. They are fire, earth, metal, water, and wood. The concept of the five phases is the backbone of Chinese medicine, acupuncture, and feng shui.

Flying Star   Xuankong Feixing in Chinese, it's a sophisticated and complex system of analyzing how time and space affect a building. The magnetic orientation of the dwelling, along with the year the home was built, are important factors that determine the innate character of the house.

Form School   Called Xingfa in Chinese, it's the first and oldest school of feng shui dating to the late Han era's publication of the *Classic of Burial* written by Qing Wuzi. Initially, its purpose was to orient tombs. The orientation of homes was later incorporated into the practice.

Fortunate Mountain Fortunate Water   A dwelling that is considered Wang Shan Wang Shui if the ruling mountain and water numbers are in their proper places. The ruling mountain star must be situated in the top, left position of the sitting cell. The ruling water star must be situated in the top, right position of the facing cell. This type of house is most favorable, bringing the highest possibility of fame, fortune, and good health.

Four Celestial Palaces   The Chinese macroconstellations called the crimson bird, azure dragon, black turtle, and white tiger represent the Four Celestial Palaces. Composed of seven constellations each, the macroconstellations comprise the 28 constellations of the Chinese zodiac.

Four Pillars of Destiny   Called Ziping Bazi in Chinese, it's a method of calculating and interpreting the five phases present at your birth. Each pillar represents a year, month, day, and hour expressed as a heavenly stem and an earthly branch. The Four Pillars of Destiny measures probabilities, not certainties, of your life's path.

Golden Ratio   Related to the Fibonacci sequence. By dividing each number in the series by the one that precedes it, the result produces a ratio that stabilizes at 1.61834. The Golden Ratio was understood by ancient builders such as the Egyptians, Greeks, and Mayans who believed everything in nature was determined by abstract universal laws that could be expressed mathematically.

Great Cycle   Called Da Yun in Chinese, it is made up of nine 20-year cycles. The nine cycles are divided into three 60-year periods called the Upper (Shang Yuan), Middle (Zhong Yuan), and Lower (Xia Yuan) Cycles. The year 1864 marks the beginning of the Great Cycle we're currently in. It ends February 4, 2044.

Hetu   Also called the River Map, it is a pattern of black (yang) and white (yin) dots purportedly found on a fantastic dragon-horse emerging from the Yellow River. The Hetu symbolizes the ideal world.

hexagram   A combination of two trigrams composes one hexagram. There are 64 total hexagrams.

house trigram   Determined by its sitting direction, which usually corresponds to the backside of a dwelling.

inductive reasoning   The method of reaching a conclusion by developing specific cases based on general laws.

kanyu   An art of divination; the precursor to feng shui. "Kan" means "way of the heaven" and "yu," "way of the earth." Together, kanyu translates, "Raise your head and study the sky. Lower your head and study the terrain."

known   A unit of communication that has been learned earlier in life. It can be positive or negative and will be accepted into the subconscious mind.

lunar month   The interval between the successive full moons. A lunar month lasts approximately 29½ days; each lunar year, 354 days.

luopan   A compass containing anywhere from 4 to 40 concentric information rings. A compass, be it a luopan or Western-style, is the tool of trade in feng shui.

Luoshu   Also known as the Luo River Writing, it is a pattern of black (yang) and white (yin) dots said to be found inscribed on a turtle's shell. The Luoshu correlates to the After Heaven sequence of trigrams.

Magic Square of Three   Related to the Luoshu. It is considered "magical" because three cells add up to fifteen along any diagonal, vertical, or horizontal line. The Magic Square is the numerological basis of feng shui.

Marriage Palace   A term relating to the Four Pillars of Destiny. It corresponds to your day-branch. If the phase is favorable, your marriage will be successful. If the phase is unfavorable, then chances are slim your marriage will survive.

mountain force   Associated with yin, it administers a person's health and relationships. Its qi enters a home through the walls, the building's mountainlike structures protecting the occupants. In classical feng shui terminology, the mountain star is synonymous with the sitting star and the stars on the top, left side of each cell.

parallel   One of five ways a phase relates to the Day-Master in a Four Pillars of Destiny analysis. The parallel phase is the same as the Day-Master.

Parents Palace   A term relating to the Four Pillars of Destiny. It is the phase combination of your month pillar representing your family background. If the combination is favorable to your Day-Master, your childhood more than likely was happy. If the combination is unfavorable, you probably had an unhappy childhood.

performance   One of five ways a phase relates to the Day-Master in a Four Pillars of Destiny analysis. The performance phase is produced by the Day-Master.

personal trigram   Determined by your birth year and gender.

poison arrow qi   Qi that is directed at you in a straight line. Also known as "killing breath," this qi is extremely inauspicious, carrying misfortune, illness, and even disaster.

power   One of five ways a phase relates to the Day-Master in a Four Pillars of Destiny analysis. The power phase dominates the Day-Master.

productive cycle   A cycle of balance and creation. Each phase produces or enhances the succeeding phase. Fire-earth-metal-water-wood represents the productive cycle.

qi   The underlying and unifying "substance" and "soul" of all things. Both physical and metaphysical, qi is the nourishing force at the heart, growth, and development of the heavens, earth, and humanity. It is also called "life's breath."

reductive cycle   A cycle that reduces the power of the dominating phase and restores the sequential balance of the phases in question. Fire-wood-water-metal-earth represents the reductive cycle. In feng shui, a reductive phase is used to remedy inauspicious qi.

resource   One of five ways a phase relates to the Day-Master in a Four Pillars of Destiny analysis. A resource phase produces the Day-Master.

Reversed Mountain and Water A dwelling that is considered Shang Shan Xia Shui if the mountain and water stars are improperly placed, reversed. Here, the ruling mountain star is improperly located in the facing cell. The ruling water star is improperly located in the sitting cell. A Reversed Mountain and Water star chart brings the probability of misfortune and illness for the 20-year period to which the ruling star corresponds.

sha qi Negative qi carrying inauspicious currents that can influence your well-being.

sheng qi Positive qi carrying auspicious currents that can influence your well-being.

sitting direction Usually corresponds to the backside of a dwelling. A sitting direction is determined by a compass reading.

solar year Time based on the revolution of the earth around the sun is a solar year.

strong Day-Master A Four Pillars of Destiny chart with more resource and parallel than power, wealth, and performance phases. A person with a strong chart has many friends and many competitors. He derives support from those around him, while getting few chances to demonstrate his own talents.

subconscious mind This is the area of the mind that receives and stores information. The subconscious mind represents 88 percent of our total mind power.

swastika A universal symbol generally accepted to be a solar emblem. It is derived from the Sanskrit *svastika*, meaning lucky, fortunate, well-being. The counterclockwise swastika formed within the Magic Square expresses future time.

synchronicity A concept developed by celebrated Swiss psychologist Carl Jung (1875–1961), it expresses the connection of acausal events within a limited time frame.

taiji A symbol illustrating the eternal interaction between yin and yang. The correct orientation is with its yang "head" positioned at the top-left side.

Ten Heavenly Stems Tian Gan in Chinese, they represent how the five phases alter with the passage of a year. The Chinese use the word "heaven" to mean "time." Hence, the Heavenly Stems record how qi changes with time.

totem An Algonquin word describing an animal or natural object with which a group feels a special attachment. Denoting group membership, the totem is worshipped by the members of the clan bearing its name.

trigram The eight trigrams are symbols representing transitional phases of all possible heavenly and human situations. Qian, Zhen, Kan, Gen, Kun, Xun, Li, and Dui represent the eight trigrams.

Twelve Earthly Branches Di Zhi in Chinese, they represent cycles of earth qi expressed by the year, month, day, and hour. A zodiacal animal is assigned to each branch.

Twenty-four mountains Directions of a luopan compass derived from the eight fundamental trigrams: Each trigram constitutes 45 degrees of the compass (8 trigrams × 45 degrees = 360 degrees). Each trigram is subdivided into three equal parts of 15 degrees each (3 parts × 15 degrees = 45 degrees). The total number of subdivided parts (3 parts × 8 trigrams) comprise the 24 mountains, each of which has a Chinese name.

unfavorable phase A term in a Four Pillars of Destiny analysis describing a phase that causes an imbalance in your chart.

unknown A unit of communication that is rejected by the critical area of the mind and will not enter the subconscious.

water force Associated with yang, it governs a person's wealth. Its qi enters a home through the windows and doors, the building's free-flowing waterlike edifices. The water star is synonymous with the facing star and the stars on the top, right side of each cell.

weak Day-Master A Four Pillars of Destiny chart with more power, performance, and wealth than resource and parallel. A person with a weak Day-Master is usually being challenged by power and authority, yet has enough intelligence to combat such confrontations.

wealth One of five ways a phase relates to the Day-Master in a Four Pillars of Destiny analysis. The wealth phase is dominated by the Day-Master.

white tiger A landform, building, trees, bushes, or fence located on the right side of your dwelling.

Wuji The beginning, the Great Void. Wuji is believed to be the fountainhead of creation and is expressed as a circle.

yang Represents the active principle in nature exhibited as light, heat, and dryness. On a human level, yang represents masculinity and the positive side of our emotions. Also, yang represents the realm of the living.

Yijing Also known as *The Book of Changes*. It is the first known attempt by the Chinese to formulate a system of knowledge around the interplay of yin and yang.

yin Represents the passive principle in nature exhibited as darkness, cold, and wetness. On a human level, yin symbolizes femininity and inertia. Also, yin represents the realm of the dead.

Zhouyi Also known as *The Changes of Zhou*, it is a divinatory system written by King Wen and his son the Duke of Zhou at the end of the second millennium B.C.E. In the Han dynasty (or before) commentaries were attached to the *Zhouyi* and renamed the *Yijing*.

Ziwei Doushu Purple Constellation Fate Computation, in English, it's a method of Chinese astrology that analyzes anywhere from 36 to 157 stars in accordance with your birth information. Ziwei Doushu uses the Chinese lunar calendar.

Appendix B

Common Questions and Practical Answers

Q: What exactly is feng shui?

A: Feng shui is the art and science of determining how the environment and your home affect you over periods of time. Feng shui can predict, prevent, and encourage events with great accuracy.

Q: Are there certain telltale factors that distinguish a classical-trained practitioner from one who uses modern techniques based on superstition and myth?

A: Yes. Simply, ask questions! First ask what kind of feng shui he or she practices. The answer should be classical or traditional Feng Shui. If the answer is Bagua School or Compass School, this could mean the consultant practices faux feng shui, where a home is divided into sections of wealth, health, family, career, etc. This method is too simplistic. Please see Chapter 1, "What Is Feng Shui?" for a review about authentic and faux schools of feng shui.

Q: I heard feng shui is a Daoist art. Is this true?

A: No. The philosophy of Daoism and the science of feng shui developed at the same time and share common roots. Although feng shui's origins are lost in history, the tradition actually predates Daoism, Buddhism, and Confucianism by several thousand years. As early as 6000 B.C.E., some sort of astronomical/astrological system was used to determine auspicious grave and dwelling sites.

Q: Do you need a compass to practice feng shui?

A: Yes. Just like a hair stylist needs a pair of scissors and a doctor needs a stethoscope, a feng shui practitioner needs a compass. But it doesn't have to be a Chinese luopan. A Western-style compass featuring two-degree gradations is sufficient. Without a compass, it's impossible to determine your home's trigram. Guesswork just won't do. Obtaining an accurate reading is the first step toward ensuring an accurate analysis. An incorrect assumption may cause harm to you and your family. For example, you wouldn't want your hair stylist to assume he or she has selected "Bombshell Blond"—your hair color. You would expect him or her to be certain. Furthermore, you would expect the stylist to have read and know the procedure thoroughly. Otherwise, your hair might fall out!

Q: Can feng shui really bring me health, wealth, and happiness?

A: Feng shui can only increase the probability of these things happening. For example, a Flying Star reading may indicate good fortune, but it's up to you to make it happen. Feng shui can only create an urge, increasing your motivation and likelihood of success. Feng shui is not a cure-all solution.

Q: Can you flush your wealth away if a toilet lid is left open?

A: Only if you empty your wallet into the bowl!

Q: Where's the best place to hang a mirror?

A: Historically, the use of mirrors to remedy qi has never been part of feng shui's tradition. The concept of mirrors as magical power devices that can stimulate, ward off, or absorb qi is a recent invention dating to the 1980s. This misconception is an excellent example of playing "telephone"—the childhood game where one kid whispers a sentence in the next kid's ear. At the end of the line, the sentence bears no resemblance to the original.

In ancient China, mirrors were made of bronze, polished on one side, with various cosmological designs on the other. These mirrors were similar to the precursor of the luopan compass, an ancient divination tool called the shipan, which was thought to reflect, or mirror, the perfect world before the demon Gong Gong battled Zhu Rong for the Empire. During the fight, the northwest mountain (one of eight separating heaven from earth) collapsed, causing the northwest to tilt upward, and the southeast, downward. As a model of the perfect world, the ancient cosmographs and bronze mirrors were thought to have magic power. Somehow, they have been mistakenly incorporated into feng shui.

Q: There are so many books and classes on feng shui. How do I know who's right?

A: It's up to you to search for the truth. Unfortunately, the ancient Chinese tradition of feng shui has been watered down and misrepresented. In large part, this is due to people not doing their homework. Our advice is to go directly to source material. Thumb through Joseph Needham's seven-volume work, *Science and Civilisation in China*. Check out scholarly material at the library or on the Internet. You do the homework. You decide fact from falsehood. Please see Appendix C, "Learn More About Feng Shui," for a credible list of reading material and websites of classical feng shui.

Q: When determining the construction year of a dwelling, how do you treat additions to a house?

A: The only reliable source is from Qing dynasty (1644–1911) feng shui master, Shen Zhu Reng's book, *Shen's Time and Space School* (*Shen Shi Xuan Kong Xue*). He says if the new and old parts are connected so that the qi can flow freely, and the main entrance is in the new part, then the whole house is considered new. Therefore, use the construction date affiliated with the addition. On the other hand, if the main entrance is in the old part of the house, then the whole house is considered old. In this case, use the original construction date of the house. If there is a door in the new addition, but the old entrance is retained and both doors are used, then the old part is old and the new part is new. Two Flying Star charts must be drawn.

Q: When determining the construction year of a dwelling, how do you treat a house whose roof was completely changed?

A: This is controversial. If the roof is removed and the inside of the dwelling is exposed for at least 24 hours, the house is considered new. Yet, some classical masters believe the roof must be exposed for one month, with a full moon shining on the floor. We'll go with the first scenario.

Learn More About Feng Shui

Books

A Brief History of Chinese Civilization, by Conrad Schirokauer. Harcourt Brace & Company, 1991.

The Cambridge History of Ancient China from the Origins of Civilization to 221 B.C.E., edited by Michael Loewe and Edward L. Shaughnessy. Cambridge University Press, 1999.

Chinese Astrology, by Derek Walters. The Aquarian Press, 1987.

The Chinese Astrology Workbook, by Derek Walters. The Aquarian Press, 1988.

Classical Five Elements Chinese Astrology Made Easy, by David Twicken. Writers Club Press, 2000.

The Complete Idiot's Guide to the I Ching, by Elizabeth Moran and Master Joseph Yu. Alpha Books, 2001.

Early China: Cosmos, Cosmograph, and the Inquiring Poet: New Answers to the Heaven Questions, by Stephen Field. The Annual Journal of the Society for the Study of Early China and the Institute of East Asian Studies, University of California, Berkeley, Volume 17, 1992.

Encounters with Qi: Exploring Chinese Medicine, by David Eisenberg, M.D., with Thomas Lee Wright. W.W. Norton and Company, 1985.

Fascinating Fibonacci: Mystery and Magic in Numbers, by Trudi Hammel Garland. Dale Seymour Publications, 1987.

Feng Shui: The Ancient Wisdom of Harmonious Living for Modern Times, by Eva Wong. Shambhala, 1996.

Feng Shui for Today, by Kwan Lau. Tangu Books, 1996.

The Feng Shui Handbook, by Master Lam Kam Chuen. Henry Holt, 1996.

Flying Star Feng Shui Made Easy, by David Twicken. Writers Club Press, 2000.

Fortune-tellers and Philosophers: Divination in Traditional Chinese Society, by Richard J. Smith. Westview Press, Inc. 1991.

Four Pillars and Oriental Medicine: Celestial Stems, Terrestrial Branches and Five Elements for Heaven, by David Twicken. Writers Club Press, 2000.

The Handbook of Chinese Horoscopes, by Theodora Lau. Harper & Row, 1979.

Heaven and Earth in Early Han Thought, by John S. Major. State University of New York Press, 1993.

The I Ching or Book of Changes, the Richard Wilhelm translation. Princeton University Press, 1950.

K.I.S.S. Guide to Feng Shui, by Stephen Skinner. Dorling Kindersley, 2001.

The Living Earth Manual of Feng-Shui, by Stephen Skinner. Arkana, 1982.

The Mystery of Numbers, by Annemarie Schimmel. Oxford University Press, 1993.

Number and Time, by Marie-Louise von Franze. Northwestern University Press, 1974.

Numerology, by Vincent Lopez. The New American Library, 1961.

Physics and Philosophy, by Werner Heisenberg. HarperCollins, 1962.

Professional Hypnotism Manual, by John G. Kappas, Ph.D. Panorama Publishing Company, 1999.

"Qi Through the Centuries and Around the World," by Dr. John Baker. *Qi: The Journal of Traditional Eastern Health and Fitness*, Vol. 1, No. 4, Winter, 1991.

The Religion of the Chinese People, by Marcel Granet. Oxford: Blackwell & Mott, 1975; originally published in French in 1922.

Science and Civilisation in China (6 volumes), by Joseph Needham. Cambridge University Press, 1956.

The Seven Mysteries of Life, by Guy Murchie. Houghton Mifflin Company, 1978.

A Short History of Chinese Philosophy, by Fung Yu-Lan. The Free Press, 1948.

Sources of Chinese Tradition, Volume 1, by William Theodore de Bary, Wing-Tsit Chan, and Burton Watson. Columbia University Press, 1960.

The Tao of Physics, by Fritjof Capra. Shambhala, 1991.

Tao the Ching, by Leo Tzu. Shambhala, 1989.

Magazines

Feng Shui for Modern Living, published by Feng Shui Media Group LLC. Published six times per year (February, April, June, August, October, and December). For more information call 1-800-310-7047 or visit their website: www.fengshui-magazine.com.

Qi: The Journal of Traditional Eastern Health and Fitness, published by Insight Graphics, Inc. Call 1-800-787-2600 for more information.

Websites

Val Biktashev and Elizabeth Moran

www.aafengshui.com

From the authors of *The Complete Idiot's Guide to Feng Shui* and *The Complete Idiot's Guide to the I Ching*, the comprehensive site seeks to educate the public about classical feng shui and the *Yijing*. Master Biktashev travels worldwide providing feng shui consultations. Elizabeth Moran travels extensively offering seminars and lectures about classical feng shui.

Cate Bramble

www.qi-whiz.com

An expansive site containing many thoroughly researched essays about feng shui and related applications. Cate is known for telling it like it is with a humorous touch! We especially recommend her articles debunking Black Sect feng shui.

Bill Clement

www.geocities.com/Athens/Delphi/9911

Feng Shui Information Resource has lots of pertinent information about classical feng shui. This excellent site features book reviews, book lists, articles, and a host of links to other traditional feng shui sites.

Raymond Lo

www.raymond-lo.com

Master Lo offers worldwide professional training courses in feng shui and The Four Pillars of Destiny, a method of Chinese astrology. Lo is the author of seven feng shui books in English and in Chinese.

John Mausolf

www.purefengshui.com

John is one of Australia's leading classical feng shui practitioners and teachers. His site boasts, "No gimmicks … just pure feng shui!" Check out his article debunking the Southern Hemisphere theory.

Eva Wong

www.shambala.com/fengshui

A unique and very informative site about feng shui. Look for her interesting article about feng shui's early masters.

Danny Van den Berghe's Flying Star and Four Pillars Software

www.fourpillars.net

Here, you'll find a software package for Flying Star feng shui and for The Four Pillars of Destiny. While the programs will create the charts, the software does not give an automated reading.

Joseph Yu

www.astro-fengshui.com

Master Yu offers online and worldwide in-class training courses in classical feng shui, Chinese astrology (The Four Pillars of Destiny and Zi Wei Dou Shu), and the *Yijing*. He is the co-author of the new edition of *The Complete Idiot's Guide to Feng Shui* and *The Complete Idiot's Guide to the I Ching*.

Feng Shui Fanzine

www.fengshui-fanzine.co.uk

A free online magazine dedicated to enlightening feng shui enthusiasts about the classical tradition.

Feng Shui Times

www.fengshuitimes.com

A terrific site with many informative articles written by well-known classical practitioners and masters.

Yahoo! Discussion Groups

Astro Feng Shui

Moderated by Master Joseph Yu, this list is open to the public. Discussion centers on classical feng shui. For more information and to subscribe, go to http://groups.yahoo.com/group/astrofengshui.

Basic Feng Shui

Moderated by Bill Clement, Elizabeth Moran, and Scott Ransom, the aim of this list is to provide a supportive atmosphere for people who are just beginning to study feng shui and who are not yet ready for elaborate technical discussions. For more information and to subscribe, go to http://groups.yahoo.com/group/basicfengshui.

Chinese Astrology

Moderated by Ray Langley, this discussion group focuses on Chinese astrology and classical feng shui. Although beginners are welcome, this list is mainly geared toward those with a solid foundation of the aforementioned traditions. Ray offers an extensive archive with many translations of Chinese texts. For more information and to subscribe, go to http://groups.yahoo.com/group/chineseastrology.

Chinese Feng Shui

Moderated by Wilson Chang, this group caters to the beginning, intermediate, and advanced student of classical feng shui. Interested participants are required to answer a brief questionnaire before membership is accepted. For more information and to subscribe, go to http://groups.yahoo.com/group/ChineseFS.

Fourpillars-Fengshui

Moderated by Peter Leung and Nina Wilson, this forum provides instruction and support for students interested in feng shui and The Four Pillars of Destiny. For more information and to subscribe, go to http://yahoo.com/group/fourpillars-fengshui.

I Ching Yijing

Moderated by Ray Langley, this group encourages discussion about the *Yijing*. For more information and to subscribe, go to http://groups.yahoo.com/group/IChing_YiJing.

Yijing I Ching

Moderated by Master Joseph Yu and Elizabeth Moran, this group was established to help the reader understand *The Complete Idiot's Guide to the I Ching*, written by the moderators. While you need not own the book to participate, it would be helpful. For more information and to subscribe, go to http://groups.yahoo.com/group/yijing_iching.

Feng Shui Products

Feng Shui Plus, Inc.

www.fengshuiplus.com

661-298-8670 (Southern California)

This site offers high-quality five phase remedies/enhancements. Assembled by interior designer and feng shui consultant Solange Mikucki, choose from a wide variety of affordable and stylish decorative items representing the fire, earth, metal, water, and wood phase elements.

To purchase Joseph Yu's luopan compass (as seen on the cover), please contact him at josephyu@astro-fengshui.com

Contact the Authors

American Healing Arts, Inc.
Val Biktashev and Elizabeth Moran
269 S. Beverly Drive, Suite 280
Beverly Hills, CA 90212
Phone: (323) 852-1381
Fax: (323) 852-1341
E-mail: GlobalFengShui@aol.com
Web address: www.aafengshui.com

Joseph Yu
Feng Shui Research Center
175 West Beaver Creek Road, Unit 5
Richmond Hill, Ontario L4B 3M1, Canada
Phone/Fax: (905) 881-8878
E-mail: josephyu@astro-fengshui.com
Web address: www.astro-fengshui.com

Chinese Periods and Dynasties

Chinese history is a fascinating discipline—rich, complex, and exhaustive. Remember, the Chinese have had flourishing civilizations for thousands of years. Looking at feng shui without even a rudimentary understanding of some historical basis is unwise. So much is inextricably woven into particular periods, events, and individuals. Throughout this book we have referred to individuals, dates, and dynasties. We hope this list will compare some of feng shui's evolutions with that of Chinese history. Please note, while it appears some dynasties may overlap, in fact, they do not. Only a thorough investigation of Chinese history can adequately account for this.

The dates reflecting China's legendary and prehistoric periods, and the dynastic dates of the Shang early Zhou, are speculative and subject to dispute.

Legendary Period	
Three Emperors	2852–2597 B.C.E.
Fuxi	2852–2737 B.C.E.
Shennong	2737–2697 B.C.E.
Huang Di (Yellow Emperor)	2697–2597 B.C.E.
Shao Hao	2597–2513 B.C.E.
Zhuan Xu	2513–2435 B.C.E.

continues

continued

Legendary Period

Five Rulers	2435–2197 B.C.E.
Di Ku	2435–2365 B.C.E.
Di Zhi	2365–2356 B.C.E.
Yao	2356–2255 B.C.E.
Shun	2255–2205 B.C.E.
Yu	2205–2197 B.C.E.

Prehistoric Period

Yangshao culture	c. 5000 B.C.E.
Longshan culture	c. 2500 B.C.E.
Xia dynasty	c. 2100–c. 1600 B.C.E.

Historical Period

Shang dynasty	c. 1600–1045 B.C.E.
Zhou dynasty	1045–221 B.C.E.
Western Zhou	1045–771 B.C.E.
Eastern Zhou	770–256 B.C.E.
Spring and Autumn Period	722–481 B.C.E.
Warring States Period	403–221 B.C.E.
Qin dynasty	221–206 B.C.E.
Han dynasty	206 B.C.E.–220 C.E.
Western Han	206 B.C.E.–24 C.E.
Eastern Han	25-220 C.E.
Three Kingdoms	220–280
Wei	220–265
Shu Han	221–263
Wu	222–280
Jin dynasty	265–420
Western Jin	265–316
Eastern Jin	317–420
Southern and Northern dynasties	420–589
Southern	420–589
Northern	386–581

Historical Period	
Sui dynasty	581–618
Tang dynasty	618–907
Five dynasties & Ten Kingdoms	907–960
Song dynasty	960–1279
Northern Song	960–1127
Southern Song	1127–1279
Liao dynasty (Khitan Tartars)	916–1125
Jin dynasty (Jurchen Tartars)	1115–1234
Yuan dynasty (Mongol)	1271–1368
Ming dynasty	1368–1644
Qing dynasty (Manchu)	1644–1911
Republic of China	1912–1949
People's Republic of China	1949–present

Learn More About Taking a Proper Compass Reading Using the 24 Mountains

Once you get the hang of it, taking an accurate compass reading and dividing your dwelling into eight equal sections is a snap. First, follow the directions below to determine the sitting and facing directions of your house:

1. Stand in front of your house or unit, the side corresponding to the facing side. Make sure your back is perfectly square with the house.

2. Holding your compass at waist level, rotate the compass dial until the red portion of the magnetic arrow aligns with north.

3. Read the compass grade at the index line (labeled the "bearing" line on the Silva Explorer Model 203). This is the facing direction. The grade magnetically opposite is the sitting direction.

4. Repeat steps 1, 2, and 3, taking a reading at two other locations parallel to the sitting side of your home as indicated by illustrations B and C.

In the following example (A) of an apartment unit, the compass grade at the index line reads 210°. If you're using Eight House methodology, according to the table in Chapter 11, "The Eight Houses, Part 2," your dwelling belongs to the Gen trigram (facing 202.5° to 247.5°). If you're using Flying Star, you must determine what kind of Gen house you have: Chou, Gen, or Yin. Referring to the table in Chapter 14, "The Flying Stars, Part 2," the dwelling belongs to the mountain Chou (202.5° to 217.5°). The unit sits NE1 and faces SW1.

A properly divided Gen dwelling ⊔ *NE1 and* ↑ *SW1 at 210°.*

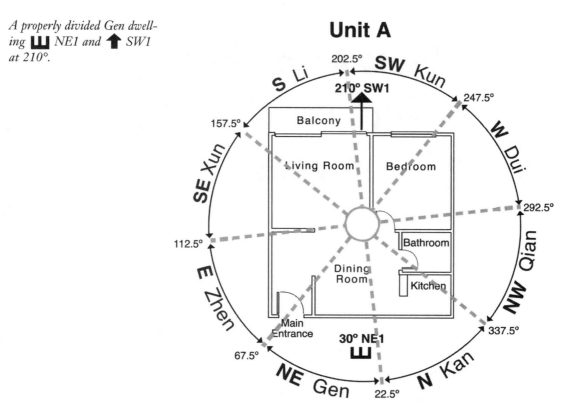

Now, follow these steps to divide your floor plan into eight equal sections corresponding to the eight fundamental directions (trigrams):

1. Note the facing degree on your floor plan (as illustrated).

2. With a pencil, mark the point where each of the eight directions begin and end (as illustrated). We suggest using a clear plastic 6-inch, 360° protractor with half-inch

gradations to help with this task. Found in any office supply store, we recommend the Mars College protractor. But be careful! Read the *inside* grades which ascend around the circular instrument. Before you proceed, it might be a good idea to compare the protractor with the figure of the simplified luopan compass in Chapter 14. (If you wish to purchase a luopan, please contact Joseph Yu at josephyu@astro-fengshui.com.)

3. Now, connect the dots to form eight equal sections.

Illustration B shows the same apartment sitting NE2 and facing SW2 at 225°.

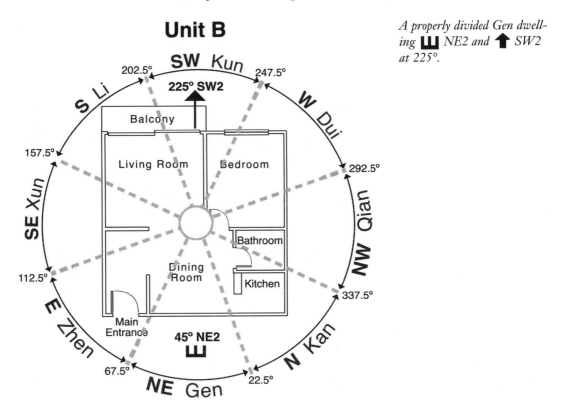

A properly divided Gen dwelling ⛰ NE2 and ⬆ SW2 at 225°.

Illustration C shows the same apartment sitting NE3 and facing SW3 at 240°.

A properly divided Gen dwelling ▥ *NE3 and* ⬆ *SW3 at 240°.*

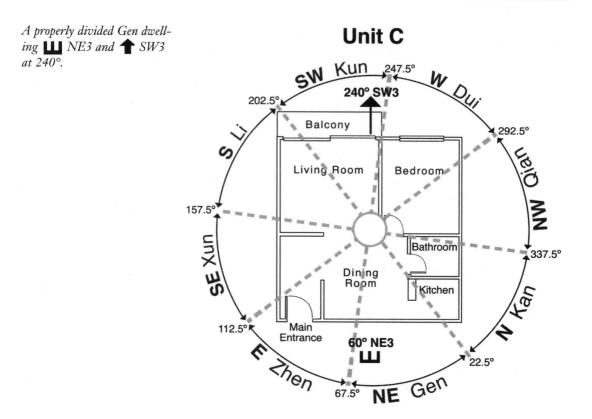

Taken together, you can see that depending on the facing degree, the sections are oriented somewhat differently for each of the three types of Gen dwellings (mountains Chou, Gen, and Yin).

Index

Numbers

10-year luck periods
    earthly branch, 325–326
        determining yearly luck, 326
        sixty cycle destiny, 326–327
    heavenly stem, 325–326
        determining yearly luck, 326
        sixty cycle destiny, 326–327
    yin and yang, 321–324
24 mountains
    compass readings, 367–370
    Flying Star, 165–167
        compass reading, 167
        luopan compass, 167–168

A

acupuncture, 47
After Heaven, eight trigrams, 81
analysis of Flying Star chart, 232–234
    home purchases, 253–255
analysis of chart, Day-Master, 311
    strong Day-Master, 311–312
    weak Day-Master, 312–313
ancient Chinese, Flying Stars, 154
    Hetu (River Map), 155–156
    Luoshu (Luo River Writing), 156–157
    Magic Square of Three, 157–160
annual stars, Flying Star, 235–236
    year 2002, 237–240
    year 2003, 240–242
Asian practitioners, 10–11
astrology
    China, 31-33
        predictions, 31-32

astronomy
    China, 31-33
axioms, 320
azure dragons
    Four Celestial Palaces, 88
    terrestrial configurations, 91

B

bagua. *See* trigrams; eight trigrams
balance remedies, 69–71
bed positions, 106–107
Before Heaven, eight trigrams, 81
benefits of Feng Shui, 13
Big Dipper, Eight Wandering Stars, 123
bigrams, 76
binary system, eight trigrams, 82–84
black turtle, terrestrial configurations, 91
Bohm, David
    hologram theory of universe, 23–24
    Yijing, 24
Bohr, Niels, quantum physics, 23
Book of Burial (Zhangshu), 90
The Book of Rituals, 161
books. *See* publications
buildings
    direction, 133–134
    five phases, 71

C

calculating The Four Pillars of Destiny, 287
    day pillar, 300–304
    hour pillar, 304–305
    month pillar, 289, 300
    year pillar, 287
Capra, Fritjof, *The Tao of Physics*, 42, 76

celestial equator, 89
central palaces, 225–226
chart of strength, Day-Master, 332–336
charts, Flying Star, 180–181
    facing star, 180–184
    sitting star, 180–184
    time star, 180
China
    astrology, 31-33
        predictions, 31-32
    astronomy, 31-33
    Greater Nature, 30
    inventions, 30
    Polo, Marco, 31
Chinese astrology versus Western astrology, 283
Chinese dynasties, 363–365
Chinese history
    historical periods, 364–365
    legendary periods, 363–364
    prehistoric period, 364
Chinese practitioners, 10
Chinese solar years, 169, 270–272
Chinese zodiac, 268
    Chinese solar years, 270–272
    compatibility among signs, 272–273
    incompatibility among signs, 273
    twelve animals, 274
        dogs, 278
        dragons, 276
        horses, 276–277
        monkeys, 277
        oxen, 275
        pigs, 278–279
        rabbits, 275
        rats, 274
        roosters, 278
        sheep, 277
        snakes, 276
        tigers, 275
    Twelve Earthly Branches, 268–269
    year branch, 274
chronomancy, 32

circles, home shapes, 103
Classic of Burial, 90
Compass School, 38-39
compasses
    24 mountains, 367–370
    Flying Star, 167
    home direction, 134–135
    luopan compass, 167–168
    taking an accurate reading, 367–370
compatibility
    among Chinese zodiac signs, 272–273
    Eight Wandering Stars, 125–127
    home purchase, 245–246
        comparisons, 251–252
        environmental factors, 248–251
        trigrams, 246–248
    home trigrams to personal trigrams, 132–133
    offices, 259–260
The Complete Idiot's Guide to the I Ching, 24, 42, 84, 169, 171
Confucianism
    philosophy, 33-34
        yin and yang, 34-35
Confucius, 33
conscious minds, 18–20
construction dates
    Great Cycle, 170
    home, 179–180
controlling cycles, five phases, 67
corner lots, terrestrial configurations, 94
crimson bird
    Four Celestial Palaces, 88
    terrestrial configurations, 90
cul-de-sacs, terrestrial configurations, 95
Cycle of 60 Favorability Chart, horoscopes, 327, 338–339
Cycle of Sixty, 285–286
Cycle of Sixty Days, horoscopes, 338
cyclic patterns, eight trigrams, 80–82

D

Da Zi Ran
  (Greater Nature), 30
Daode jing
  (*Tao Teh Ching*), 33
Daoism (Taoism), 33
  existence, yin and yang, 56–57
  Laozi (Lao Tzu), 33-34
  philosophy, 33-34
    nature, 34
    yin and yang, 34-35
  Wuji, 56
Darwin, Charles
  *On the Origin of the Species by Means of
    Natural Selection, or the Preservation of
    Favoured Races in the Struggle for Life*, 22
  evolutionary theory of universe, 22
day pillars, The Four Pillars of Destiny,
  300–304
Day-Master (Ziping Method), 308
  analysis of chart, 311
    strong Day-Master, 311–312
    weak Day-Master, 312–313
    chart of strength, 332–336
    The Four Pillars of Destiny, 307–308
      phase relationships, 310–311
      timeliness, 308–309
    Month Pillar charts, 336–337
    phases, equilibrium, 313–315
    strong, 314–315
    weak, 315
dead phases, 309
dead-end streets, terrestrial configurations,
  94
death cycle, numbers, 175
deductive reasoning, 21
desk locations, offices, 262–263
desk positions, 107–108
determining yearly luck, 326
diary, chart of strength, 332–336
Did Marco Polo Go to China?, 31

directions
  buildings, 133–134
  Eight House System, 114–115
    East Group, 114
    West Group, 114
  Eight Wandering Stars, 119–120
    personal trigrams, 120–123
  facing direction, 131
  home, 133–134
    compass, 134–135
  sitting direction, 131
Divisament dou Monde
  (*Description of the World*), 31
Doane's Worldwide Time Change Update, 304
dogs, Chinese zodiac, 278
Double Ruling Star at Facing, 220–221
Double Ruling Star at Sitting, 221–222
dragon's lair, Form School, 90
dragons, Chinese zodiac, 276
dynasties, Chinese, 363–365

E

earth, 64
earth qi, 45–46
earthly branches, 10-year luck periods,
  325–326
  determining yearly luck, 326
  sixty cycle destiny, 326–327
East Group, trigrams, 114, 123–125
Eastern culture, yin and yang, 62
ecliptic system, 89
Eight House System
  directions, 114–115
    East Group, 114
    West Group, 114
  home trigrams, 130–132
    facing direction, 131
    sitting direction, 131
  palaces, 142
    wandering stars, 147–148

personal trigrams, 115–116
  female, 117
  male, 116
  reference chart, 117–119
  qi, 145
  Wandering Stars, 142–143, 145
  Xing, Yi, 115
eight palaces. *See* palaces
eight trigrams, 75–77. *See also* trigrams
  bagua, 77–79
  cyclic pattern, 80–82
  mathematics, binary system, 82–84
Eight Wandering Stars, 119–120
  Big Dipper, 123
  compatibility, 125–127
  directions, 119
  East Group, 123–125
  Eight House, 142–145
  personal trigrams, 120–123
  West Group, 123–125
Einstein, Albert, theory of relativity, 23
elements of feng shui, 7–9, 36–37
enlightenment, universe, 21–22
environment, offices, 257–258
  desk location, 262–263
  remedies, 263–264
environmental factors, home purchase,
  248–251
equilibrium, phases, 313–314
  strong Day-Master, 314–315
  weak Day-Master, 315
equipment, 11
evaluating office environments, 258–259
  compatibility, 259–260
existence, 56
  Daoism, yin and yang, 56–57
  taiji, 59–60
  yang, 58–59
  yin, 57–58

F

facing direction, home trigrams, 131
facing stars, Flying Star, 180–184
*Fascinating Fibonaccis: Mystery and Magic in
  Numbers*, 26
faux feng shui, 5–7
  mind, 20
  Western schools, 6, 20
favorable phases, 314–316, 332–336
  Princess Diana, 317
females, personal trigrams, 117
feminine yin, 57–58
feng shui
  elements, 7–9, 36–37
  misconceptions, 5–7
  questions and answers, 353–355
  yin and yang, 62
feng shui IQ test, 4–5
Fibonacci Sequence, Golden Ratio, 25–26
fire, 64
five phases, 63–64
  buildings, mirrors, 71
  controlling cycle, 67
  productive cycle, 66–67
  qi, 148–150
  quiz, 72–73
  remedies, 69–71
  seasons, 64–66
  weakening cycle, 67–69
flat terrain, home location, 100
floor plans
  Flying Star, 184–185
  home, 136–138
    non-square, 138–140
  phases, wandering star, 145–147
flying annual stars, 237
Flying Star (Xuankong Feixing), 154
  24 mountains, 165–167
    compass reading, 167
    luopan compass, 167–168
  analysis of chart, 232–234

ancient Chinese, 154
    Hetu (River Map), 155–156
    Luoshu (Luo River Writing), 156–157
    Magic Square of Three, 157–160
annual star, 235–236
    year 2002, 237–240
    year 2003, 240–242
annual star chart, 236
chart, 180–181
    facing star, 180–184
    sitting star, 180–184
    time star, 180
floor plan, 184–185
flying annual star, 237
home position, 185
home purchase, analysis of chart, 253–255
mountain star, 216, 224–225
numbers, 177
    calculating home construction date,
      179–180
    time star, 178–179
offices, 260–262
Purple-White Flying Palace (Zibai
  Feigong), 183
ruling star
    Double Ruling Star at Facing, 220–221
    Double Ruling Star at Sitting, 221–222
    Fortunate Mountain Fortunate Water,
      217–218
    Reversed Mountain and Water,
      218–220
star combinations, 226–231
time star, 225
water star, 216, 223–224
yin and yang, 215–216
Form School, 37-38
  dragon's lair (long xue), 90
  totems, 89
Fortunate Mountain Fortunate Water,
  ruling star, 217–218
Four Celestial Palaces
  terrestrial configurations, 90–91
    azure dragon, 91
    black turtle, 91
    buildings, 92–93

crimson bird, 90
    landforms, 92
    rivers, 93–95
    roadways, 93–95
    white tiger, 90
  totems, 88
    azure dragon, 88
    celestial equator, 89
    crimson bird, 88
    ecliptic system, 89
    mysterious black turtle, 88
    white tiger, 88
The Four Pillars of Destiny, 282–283
  10-year luck periods, 325–326
    determining yearly luck, 326
    sixty cycle destiny, 326–327
  calculating, 287
    day pillar, 300–304
    hour pillar, 304–305
    month pillar, 289, 300
    year pillar, 287
  Day-Master, 307–308
    phase relationships, 310–311
    timeliness, 308–309
  horoscope, 332
  luck, 320
  stem-branch combinations, 338
free will, 282
furniture arrangements, 109
Fuxi, *Shangshu (Classic of History)*, 155

G

Garland, Trudi Hammel, *Fascinating
  Fibonaccis: Mystery and Magic in Numbers*, 26
Giles, Herbert Allen, 14
Golden Ratio, Fibonacci Sequence, 25–26
Great Cycle (Da Yun), 169
  time, 169
  construction date, 170
Greater Nature, China, 30
Greeks, concept of universe, 21
Guanzi, 90
guest bedroom/office, homes, 252

H

The Handbook of Chinese Horoscopes, 279
Hanyu Pinyin Wenzi, 15
harmony, world vision, 27
health risks, home location, 98
heaven qi, 44–45
    "Full-Moon Madness," 45
heavenly stems, 10-year luck periods,
    325–326
    determining yearly luck, 326
    sixty cycle destiny, 326–327
Heisenberg, Werner, quantum physics, 23
Hetu (River Map), 155–156
hilltops, home location, 99
historical periods, Chinese history, 363–365
holistic theories, universe, 23–24
    Bohm, David, 23–24
    Newberg, Andrew, 24
    quantum physics, 23
    Sheldrake, Rupert, 24
    theory of relativity, 23
home entrances, 104–105
home locations
    health risks, 98
    land, 98–99
        lots, 101–102
        terrain, 99–100
home positions, Flying Star, 185
home purchases
    compatibility, 245–246
        comparisons, 251–252
        environmental factors, 248–251
        trigrams, 246–248
    Flying Star, analysis of chart, 253–255
home shapes, 102–104
    circle, 103
    rectangle, 103
    square, 103
    triangle, 102–103
    wavy, 103

homes
    direction, 133–134
        compass, 134–135
    Eight House System, 114–115
    floor plan, 136–138
        non-square, 138–140
    trigrams, 130–132, 136
        compatibility to personal trigrams,
            132–133
        facing direction, 131
        sitting direction, 131
horoscopes
    Cycle of 60 Favorability Chart, 327,
        338–339
    Cycle of Sixty Days, 338
    Four Pillars of Destiny, 332
    Year number table, 302, 338
horses, Chinese zodiac, 276–277
hour pillars, The Four Pillars of Destiny,
    304–305
houses. *See* homes
human qi, 46–47

I

I Ching (Book of Changes), 159
inclines, home location, 100
incompatibility among Chinese zodiac signs,
    273
inductive reasoning, 21
inherent characteristics of numbers, 172–173
    death cycle, 175
    life cycle wheel, 174
    rulers, 173
inventions, China, 30
inverted trapezoid lots, home location, 102

J–K–L

Jin Shu (history of Jin dynasty), 268
Jung, Carl, synchronicity, 171

Kant, Immanuel, empirical and rational study of universe, 21–22
kanyu (way of heaven and earth), 37
knowns, subconscious, 19

land, home location, 98–99
    lots, 101–102
    terrain, 99–100
landforms, terrestrial configurations, 92
Laozi (Lao Tzu), Daoism, 33-34
legendary periods, Chinese history, 363–364
Leibnitz, Gottfried Wilhelm von, mathematics, 83
life cycle wheels, numbers, 174
Liqi Pai, (Patterns of Qi School), 38
locked phases, 309
lots, home location, 101–102
    inverted trapezoid lot, 102
    rectangular lot, 101
    square lot, 101
    trapezoid lot, 101
    triangular lot, 102
    yards, 101
luck
    The Four Pillars of Destiny, 320
    Parents Palace, 321
    yin and yang, 320–321
        10-year luck periods, 321–324
luopan compass, Flying Star, 167–168
Luoshu (Luo River Writing), 156–157

M

Magic Square of Three, 157–160
main entrances, homes, 251
males, personal trigrams, 116
Marriage Palace, 317
masculine yang, 58–59
master bedrooms, homes, 252
mathematics, 24–25
    eight trigrams, binary system, 82–84
    Fibonacci Sequence, Golden Ratio, 25–26

Leibnitz, Gottfried Wilhelm von, 83
    patterns, 26
meandering paths, terrestrial configurations, 95
metals, 64
Millennium, world vision, 27
minds, 18
    conscious, 18–20
    faux feng shui, 20
    subconscious, 18–20
        knowns, 19
        unknowns, 19
mirrors, five phases, 71
monkeys, Chinese zodiac, 277
month pillars, The Four Pillars of Destiny, 289, 300
Month Pillar charts, Day-Master, 336–337
mountain forces, yin and yang, 216
mountain stars, Flying Star, 216, 224–225
mysterious black turtles, Four Celestial Palaces, 88
Mystery of Numbers, 172

N

nature, Daoism, 34
Needham, Joseph, *Science and Civilization in China*, 160
Neolithic Chinese, 37
Newberg, Andrew, mystical union with God, 24
Newton, Sir Isaac, model of universe, 21
Nine Imperial Palaces, 160–162
    number nine, 161–162
    Science and Civilization in China, 160
number nine, Nine Imperial Palaces, 161–162
numbers
    Flying Star, 177
        calculating home construction date, 179–180
        time star, 178–179

inherent characteristics, 172–173
    death cycle, 175
    life cycle wheel, 174
    rulers, 173
probability, 170
    synchronicity, 171–172
numerological divination, *Yijing*, 36

O

offices
    environment, 257–258
        desk location, 262–263
        remedies, 263–264
    evaluating environment, 258–259
        compatibility, 259–260
    Flying Star, 260–262
On the Origin of the Species by Means of Natural Selection, or the Preservation of Favoured Races in the Struggle for Life, 22
oneiromancy, 32
orientation, taiji, 60
oxen, Chinese zodiac, 275

P

palaces
    central, 225–226
    Eight House, 142
    Marriage Palace, 317
    Parents Palace, 321
    wandering stars, 147–148
parallel phase relationships, 311
Parents Palace, 321
patio entrances, homes, 252
patterns, mathematics, 26
performances, phase relationships, 310
personal trigrams, 115–116
    Eight Wandering Stars, 120–123
    female, 117
    home trigram compatibility, 132–133
    male, 116
    reference chart, 117–119

phase relationships, The Four Pillars of Destiny, 310–311
    parallel, 311
    performance, 310
    power, 310
    resource, 310
    wealth, 311
phases
    Day-Master, equilibrium, 313–315
    dead, 309
    favorable, 314–316, 332–336
        Princess Diana, 317
    five qi, 148–150
    locked, 309
    ready, 309
    timely, 309
    unfavorable, 314–316, 332–336
        Princess Diana, 317
    wandering star, 145–147
    weak, 309
philosophy
    Confucianism, 33-34
        yin and yang, 34-35
    Daoism, 33-34
        nature, 34
        yin and yang, 34-35
physiognomy, 32
pigs, Chinese zodiac, 278–279
Pinyin system of romanization, 14–15
Planck, Max, quantum physics, 23
plastromancy, 32
poison arrow qi, 50
Polo, Marco
    China, 31
    Divisament dou Monde (Description of the World), 31
power
    phase relationships, 310
    qi, 47–48
        poison arrow qi, 50
        sha qi, 49–50
        sheng qi, 49

practitioners, 9, 11
  Asian, 10–11
  benefits, 13
  Chinese, 10
  supplies, 11–13
predictions, astrology, 31-32
prehistoric periods, Chinese history, 364
Princess Diana
  luck chart, 328–329
  phases, 317
probability numbers, 170
  synchronicity, 171–172
productive cycles, five phases, 66–67
Pu, Guo, *Zangshu (Book of Burial)*, 37, 90
publications
  Book of Burial, 90
  The Book of Rituals, 161
  Classic of Burial, 90
  The Complete Idiot's Guide to the I Ching,
    24, 42, 84, 169, 171
  Daode jing, *(Tao Teh Ching)*, 33
  Did Marco Polo Go to China?, 31
  Divisament dou Monde
    (Description of the World), 31
  Doane's Worldwide Time Change Update,
    304
  Fascinating Fibonaccis: Mystery and Magic in
    Numbers, 26
  Guanzi, 90
  The Handbook of Chinese Horoscopes, 279
  I Ching (Book of Changes), 159
  Jin Shu (history of Jin dynasty), 268
  Luoshu (Luo River Writing), 156
  Mystery of Numbers, 172
  On the Origin of the Species by Means of
    Natural Selection, or the Preservation of
    Favoured Races in the Struggle for Life, 22
  Science and Civilization in China, 160, 355
  Shangshu (Classic of History), 155
  The Tao of Physics, 42, 76
  Ten Wings, 42
  Time Changes in the USA, 304
  Yijing (The Book of Changes), 24, 32, 35-36,
    169

Zangjing (Classic of Burial), 37
Zangshu (Book of Burial), 37
Zhuangzi
    (Chuang Tzu), 34
Purple Constellation Fate Computation
  (Ziwei Doshu), 281
Purple-White Flying Palace (Zibai Feigong),
  183

Q

qi (life breath), 5, 42–43
  Eight House, 145
  Eight Wandering Stars, 119–120
  Eight House System, 114–115
  five phases, 148–150
  other cultures, 43
  perpetual movement, 43
  power, 47–48
    poison arrow qi, 50
    sha qi, 49–50
    sheng qi, 49
  three forces, 43–44
    earth qi, 45–46
    heaven qi, 44–45
    human qi, 46–47
  yin and yang, eight trigrams, 75–77
quantum physics, universe, 23

R

rabbits, Chinese zodiac, 275
rats, Chinese zodiac, 274
ready phases, 309
rectangles, home shapes, 103
rectangular lots, home location, 101
reference charts, personal trigrams, 117–119
remedies, five phases, 69–71
resources, phase relationships, 310
Reversed Mountain and Water, 218–220
rivers, terrestrial configurations, 93–95

roadways, terrestrial configurations, 93–95
   corner lot, 94
   cul-de-sac, 95
   dead-end street, 94
   meandering path, 95
   sharp bend, 95
   straight road, 94
   T-junction, 94
   U-shape, 95
   Y-junction, 95
rooms, 106
   bed position, 106–107
   desk position, 107–108
   furniture arrangement, 109
roosters, Chinese zodiac, 278
rulers, numbers, 173
ruling stars
   Double Ruling Star at Facing, 220–221
   Double Ruling Star at Sitting, 221–222
   Fortunate Mountain Fortunate Water, 217–218
   Reversed Mountain and Water, 218–220

S

scapulimancy, 32
Schimmel, Annemarie, *Mystery of Numbers*, 172
schools
   Compass School, 38-39
   Form School, 37-38
Science and Civilization in China, 160, 355
seasons, five phases, 64–66
September 11 attacks, synchronicity, 171–172
sha qi, 49–50
   sight sha, 49
   smell sha, 50
   sound sha, 50
   taste sha, 50
   touch sha, 50
Shangshu (Classic of History), 155
sharp bends, terrestrial configurations, 95

sheep, Chinese zodiac, 277
Sheldrake, Rupert, morphic field theory of universe, 24
sheng qi, 49
   sight sheng, 49
   smell sheng, 49
   sound sheng, 49
   taste sheng, 49
   touch sheng, 49
sight sha, 49
sight sheng, 49
sitting directions, home trigrams, 131
sitting stars, Flying Star, 180–184
sixty cycle destiny, 10-year luck periods, 326–327
sloping hills, home location, 100
smell sha, 50
smell sheng, 49
snakes, Chinese zodiac, 276
sortilege, 32
sound sha, 50
sound sheng, 49
square lots, home location, 101
squares, home shapes, 103
star combinations, Flying Star, 226–231
stem-branch combinations, 338
straight roads, terrestrial configurations, 94
strong Day-Master, 314–315
   analysis of chart, 311–312
subconscious minds, 18–20
supplies, 11–13
swastika, 160
synchronicity
   Jung, Carl, 171
   probability, 171
   September 11 attacks, 171–172

T

T-junctions, terrestrial configurations, 94
taiji
   existence, 59–60
   orientation, 60

The Tao of Physics, 42, 76
taste sha, 50
taste sheng, 49
Ten Heavenly Stems, 283–284
Ten Wings, 42
terrains, home location, 99–100
    flat terrain, 100
    hilltop, 99
    sloping hill, 100
    steep incline, 100
terrestrial configurations
    azure dragon, 91
    black turtle, 91
    crimson bird, 90
    Four Celestial Palaces, 90–91
        buildings, 92–93
        landforms, 92
        rivers, 93–95
        roadways, 93–95
    white tiger, 90
theory of relativity universe, 23
three forces of qi, 43–44
    earth qi, 45–46
    heaven qi, 44–45
    human qi, 46–47
tigers, Chinese zodiac, 275
time, 169, 283
    Cycle of Sixty, 285–286
    Great Cycle, 169
        construction date, 170
    Ten Heavenly Stems, 283–284
    Twelve Earthly Branches, 284–285
    Yijing, 169
Time and Space Flying Stars (Xuankong
  Feixing), 183
Time Changes in the USA, 304
time stars, Flying Star, 178–180, 225
timeliness, Day-Master, 308–309
timely phases, 309
totems, 88
    Form School, 89
    Four Celestial Palaces, 88
        azure dragon, 88
        celestial equator, 89

        crimson bird, 88
        ecliptic system, 89
        mysterious black turtle, 88
        white tiger, 88
touch sha, 50
touch sheng, 49
trapezoid lots, home location, 101
triangles, home shapes, 102–103
triangular lots, home location, 102
trigrams, 82. *See also* eight trigrams
    bagua, 77-79
    cyclic pattern, 80–82
    East Group, 114, 123–125
    eight, 75–77
    Eight House System, 114–115
    home, 136
    home purchase, 246–248
    home trigrams, 130–132
        facing direction, 131
        sitting direction, 131
    mathematics, binary system, 82–84
    personal trigrams, 115–116
        Eight Wandering Stars, 120–123
        female, 117
        male, 116
        reference chart, 117–119
    West Group, 114, 123–125
    yin and yang, 35
twelve animals, Chinese zodiac, 268–269,
  274
    dogs, 278
    dragons, 276
    horses, 276–277
    monkeys, 277
    oxen, 275
    pigs, 278–279
    rabbits, 275
    rats, 274
    roosters, 278
    sheep, 277
    snakes, 276
    tigers, 275
Twelve Earthly Branches, 284–285

U–V

U-shapes, terrestrial configurations, 95
unfavorable phases, 314–316, 332–336
    Princess Diana, 317
universe, 20–23
    Darwin, Charles, 22
    enlightenment, 21–22
    Greeks, 21
        deductive reasoning, 21
        inductive reasoning, 21
    holistic theories, 23–24
        Bohm, David, 23–24
        Newberg, Andrew, 24
        quantum physics, 23
        Sheldrake, Rupert, 24
        theory of relativity, 23
    Kant, Immanuel, 21–22
    Newton, Sir Isaac, 21
unknowns, subconscious, 19

W

Wade, Sir Francis, 14
Wade-Giles system of transliteration, 14–15
wandering stars. *See also* Eight Wandering
    Stars
    palaces, 147–148
    phases, 145–147
water, 64
water forces, yin and yang, 216
water star, Flying Star, 216, 223–224
wavy shapes, home shapes, 103
weak Day-Master, 315
    analysis of chart, 312–313
weak phases, 309
weakening cycles, five phases, 67–69
wealth, phase relationships, 311
Wen, King
    Yijing (The Book of Changes), 32, 35
        numerological divination, 36
        origins, 35-36

West Group trigrams, 114, 123–125
Western astrology versus Chinese astrology,
    283
Western culture, yin and yang, 61
Western schools, faux feng shui, 6, 20
white tigers
    Four Celestial Palaces, 88
    terrestrial configurations, 90
Wilhelm, Richard, *I Ching (Book of Changes)*,
    159
wood, 64
Wood, Frances, *Did Marco Polo Go to China?*,
    31
world imbalance, yin and yang, 61
    Eastern culture, 62
    Western culture, 61
world vision, Millennium, 27
wu zhong liu xing zhi qi, 65
Wuji, Daoism, 56
wuxing, 65

X–Y–Z

Xing, Yi, Eight House System, 115
Xingfa (Form School), 38

Y-junctions, terrestrial configurations, 95
Yan, Zou, 56
yang
    eight trigrams, 76
    existence, 58–59
    masculine, 58–59
yards, 101. *See also* lots
year 2002, annual star, 237–240
year 2003, annual star, 240–242
year branches, Chinese zodiac, 274
year number tables, horoscopes, 338
year pillar, The Four Pillars of Destiny, 287
Yigua (Changing Trigrams), 114
Yijing, 24, 169
    time, 169

Yijing (*The Book of Changes*), 32, 35
   numerological divination, 36
   origins, 35-36
yin
   eight trigrams, 76
   existence, 57–58
   feminine, 57–58
yin and yang, 55–56
   Confucianism, 34-35
   Daoism, 34-35, 56–57
   eight trigrams, 75–77
   feng shui, 62
   Flying Star, 215–216
   luck, 320–321
      10-year luck periods, 321–324
   mountain force, 216
   opposites, 34
   trigrams, 35
   water force, 216
   world imbalance, 61
      Eastern culture, 62
      Western culture, 61
Yunsong, Yang, 10

Zangjing (*Classic of Burial*), 37
Zangshu (*Book of Burial*), 37
Zhenglang, Zhang, 83
Zhong, Guan, *Guanzi*, 90
Ziping Method (Day-Master), 308
Zhuangzi, (*Chuang Tzu*), 34

A Little Knowledge Goes a Long Way ...

Check Out These
Best-Selling
COMPLETE IDIOT'S GUIDES®

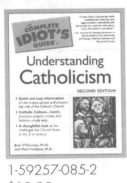

Understanding Catholicism
SECOND EDITION

1-59257-085-2
$18.95

Learning Spanish
THIRD EDITION

0-02-864451-4
$18.95

The Bible
SECOND EDITION

0-02-864382-8
$18.95

Grammar and Style
SECOND EDITION

1-59257-115-8
$16.95

Playing the Guitar
SECOND EDITION

0-02-864244-9
$21.95 w/CD

Personal Finance in Your 20s & 30s
SECOND EDITION

0-02-864374-7
$19.95

The Perfect Resume
THIRD EDITION

0-02-864440-9
$14.95

Buying and Selling a Home
FOURTH EDITION

1-59257-120-4
$18.95

Windows XP

0-02-864232-5
$19.95

More than *400 titles* in *30 different categories*
Available at booksellers everywhere

ALPHA